The Dismantling of the Good Neighbor Policy

The Dismantling
of the Good Neighbor Policy

by Bryce Wood

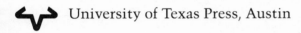 University of Texas Press, Austin

First Edition, 1985

Requests for permission to reproduce material from this work
should be sent to Permissions, University of Texas Press,
Box 7819, Austin, Texas 78713.

Library of Congress Cataloging in Publication Data
Wood, Bryce, 1909–
    The dismantling of the good neighbor policy.
    Bibliography: p.
    Includes index.
    1. Latin America—Foreign relations—United States.
2. United States—Foreign relations—Latin America.
I. Title.
F1418.W682   1985   327.7308   84-20950
ISBN 0-292-71547-1

Contents

Acknowledgments

It is a pleasure to recognize those who have helped in the preparation of this book. I wish to thank the staffs of the National Archives, and especially Sally Marks, for many courtesies; the Public Record Office, and in particular T. R. Padfield, for the cheerful provision of documents; and the Library of Congress for its efficient searches for missing materials. At the Library, the late William E. Carter, Dolores Moyano Martin, and Everette E. Larson made my stay as a visiting scholar rewarding. At the Brookings Institution, with the isolation and library assistance that are its mark, Alice Neff and Laura Walker, her successor, were most helpful in obtaining interlibrary loans, and Joseph Grunwald and Neil H. Cullen were responsible for my appointment as a research scholar.

I also wish to thank the officers of the Eisenhower, Roosevelt, and Truman libraries for their hospitality and careful attention to my requests for information.

To a group of retired foreign service officers my debt is incalculable. They listened to my questions and provided answers of the greatest value, as is evident from the text. To Philip W. Bonsal, Willard L. Beaulac, John C. Dreier, Edward A. Jamison, William L. Krieg, R. Richard Rubottom, Jr., and Robert F. Woodward, my deepest thanks. Dr. Jamison read my drafts with care and offered pungent criticisms, some of which I accepted. Messrs. Beaulac and Woodward generously permitted direct quotation from their letters to me.

My wife and former colleague, Kay Key Wood, proposed that the term "dismantling" be used in the title, and there it is. Her encouragement throughout the writing is greatly valued.

Introduction

The Good Neighbor policy was a policy; it was not simply rhetoric, as were the Good Partner and other so-called policies that followed it. It was policy in that it was "principled action, demonstrating in promise and behavior over a period of time such evidence of continuity that assumptions of stability may with confidence be based upon it" (Wood 1961: 356).[1] It was "principled action" because the United States not only renounced intervention and interference in domestic politics, but it actually did not intervene or interfere. (This marked a radical change from the 1920s, when intervention and interference were normal features of inter-American relations.) It rested upon the anticipation of reciprocity from Latin American countries—the expectation that favorable responses would be forthcoming to initiatives from Washington on matters of mutual concern. Further, the State Department anticipated that Latin American states would exercise restraint on such issues as their treatment of foreign business enterprises. Finally, in the six meetings of foreign ministers held between 1933 and 1942, the idea was accepted that consultation among all American states was the way in which important questions should be settled, at first by unanimous vote of the parties involved, and after 1948 by two thirds.

Nonintervention and noninterference were negative features of nonaction in the Good Neighbor policy, but they were necessary abstentions for the United States if there were to be a society of twenty-one juridically, but not militarily, equal nations. All parties counted on economic assistance, consultation procedures, and other cooperative activities to provide the substantive basis for what turned out to be the remarkable effort toward international collaboration on which the American republics had embarked. The policy was carried out effectively from 1933 to 1943 by word and by action, so that both Latin and North Americans came to count upon it. The understandings reached were codified, as far as possible, at the Rio de Janeiro

Conference in 1947 and the Bogotá Conference in 1948, in the form of the Inter-American Treaty of Reciprocal Assistance and the Charter of the Organization of American States (OAS).

The intimate connection between the Good Neighbor policy and these two treaties is not always fully recognized. Once the principle of regionalism had been made formal in Article 51 of the United Nations Charter, the governments of Latin America were amenable to the idea of a regional organization, since their experience with the Good Neighbor policy inclined them toward confidence in the United States' maintenance of that policy. They were willing to accept the conditions of a military alliance, a political relationship based on obligations of nonintervention, and consultation with decisions made by less than unanimous vote. In this sense, the two treaties, and the OAS itself, were logical conclusions to and extensions of the Good Neighbor policy.

The OAS was a bold experiment by a voluntary association of sovereign states of unequal strength and varied interests. It proved to be unworkable, and its dismantling has accompanied that of the Good Neighbor policy itself, attesting to the intimacy of their relationship.

The Good Neighbor policy was dismantled in 1954 with the overthrow of the government of Pres. Jacobo Arbenz of Guatemala. Dismantling started during World War II in Argentine–United States relations. The methods used were based on U.S. perceptions of security in the minds of persons in positions of responsibility in Washington.

It is not the purpose of this study to provide a general account of the relations between the United States and Latin America during World War II and after. Its purpose is to describe the temptations laid before the leaders of one powerful state by some of its twenty occasionally recalcitrant neighbors, and the ways of reacting that it found. Restraint was difficult when it could readily use power in the form of providing arms or granting favors—or withholding both. Restraint was demanded by policy that had been converted into treaties; at the same time, it was challenged by the policies of far weaker states that seemed to threaten the war effort or political stability in the hemisphere. These were challenges to the security of the United States itself, as viewed in Washington, and were therefore of national importance.

To begin with, some definitions are in order. By renouncing intervention, the United States agreed in public and by treaty not to send armed forces to any Latin American country, unless requested to do so. By giving up interference in domestic affairs, U.S. officials decided among themselves not to offer advice, exert economic pres-

sures, or make shows of force to affect or influence local political issues. A high point of noninterference was reached in the autumn of
1935 when Willard L. Beaulac, assistant chief, Division of Latin
American Affairs, assured a visiting Nicaraguan politician who regretted Beaulac's hesitation to give any advice on the situation in
Nicaragua that "there was no hesitation at all on my part; that I was
determined not to give him advice" (ibid.: 144). The solution of the
Mexican and Venezuelan oil disputes with the United States, which
were negotiated by equals and not determined by arbitral tribunals,
were good examples of "the mild-mannered methods" of the Good
Neighbor policy.[2] As early as the end of 1938, these methods were
noted as being of importance to Great Britain, "for it means that our
own vested interests will have to develop a new technique of rather
expensive cooperation with the countries in which they are operating, instead of relying upon our diplomatic artillery—which is largely
condemned to firing blank ammunition."[3]

These were nonactions, concessions, exercises in restraint, on the
part of the great power. They were, however, manifest before the outbreak of World War II, and they were faithfully observed by the
Department of State. They therefore provided a solid base for the
growth of wartime collaboration among the American republics.
They were, however, no more than the base, an essential base that
had to be maintained, it is true, but new structures of policy had to
be built upon it to meet the demands of war.

New names were needed for the new policies—multilateralism,
continental solidarity, mutuality of interests, and the evocation of
reciprocity. Multilateralism was emphasized at the inter-American
conferences of Lima (1938), and the foreign ministers' meetings in
Panama City (1939), Havana (1940), and Rio de Janeiro (1942). This
meant that decisions regarding the hemisphere would be taken together, after consultation, and emphasis was given to unanimity in
the decisions reached. The term "Monroe Doctrine" fell into dis-
favor, and "continental solidarity" took its place. Six months before
his resignation, undersecretary of state Sumner Welles defined "the
proper concept of the Good Neighbor policy" as "one of mutuality of
interests based upon the self-respect and sovereignty of each of the
twenty-one American republics" (ibid.: 314).[4]

Washington found it necessary to evoke reciprocity because Latin
American governments did not respond quickly enough to the requirements of the wartime situation as viewed in Washington; hence
the acceptance of negotiation of the oil dispute with Mexico in 1941
as the price of the use of Mexican air bases for planes going to Pan-

ama; hence, also the employment of the Export-Import Bank as the source of loans to most of the Latin American countries as early as the Panama Meeting of Consultation in 1939.

The final element in this complex of policy ideas and actions was personality. Roosevelt was admired for his changes in domestic policy as well as for being the founder of the Good Neighbor policy; Cordell Hull, as secretary of state, was favorably known for taking the initiative in calling on Latin American diplomats at the Montevideo Conference in 1933, for his trade agreements, and for his attendance throughout subsequent meetings. Sumner Welles, although austere in manner, was always generous of his time, willing to listen to ambassadors, and ready to respond to the economic needs of countries adjusting to the conflict; Latin Americans respected him and had confidence in his promises and his judgment. That these three men were in charge of hemispheric policy for a full decade beginning in 1933 was of great importance.

It was with this baggage of policy that the Americas faced World War II. As a British official put it, "The Good Neighbour Policy of forbearance, if it has done something to diminish the previous fear of 'Yankee imperialism,' has encouraged an unwelcome independence of behaviour."[5] This was an accurate statement of the dilemma facing the Good Neighbor—how much independence would be permitted?

This view of the Good Neighbor policy moved away from absolute notions of nonintervention. The principle of nonintervention was firmly set in resolutions, but if it were only "forbearance," how firm was it?

Diplomats of this period did not differentiate between nonintervention and noninterference; both were regarded as prohibited by the Good Neighbor policy. There was a vague zone between them that was not covered either by treaty or by Hull's instruction of 30 April 1936 against interference on the grounds that it might lead to intervention. Noting that Central American governments in the past had often sought the "advice" of the United States, Hull said that the United States had frequently yielded to the requests: "It has usually developed, however, that such advice rapidly came to be considered as intervention and, in fact, sometimes terminated in actual intervention. The result in a majority of cases was that, at the best, doubtful assistance was rendered to the governments, and the relations of the United States with those governments, and with other Latin American governments, were actually prejudiced" (ibid.: 148–149).

This vague zone was that of foreign policy, as distinct from that of domestic affairs. In the 1930s the United States did not interfere in the foreign relations of other American states. It did, but only in collaboration with other American powers, endeavor to bring about peace in the wars in the Chaco, Leticia, and the Marañón, but no one regarded this as interference. With the coming of World War II, however, the Department of State regarded a minimum of continental solidarity in foreign policy as of great importance and viewed deviations from the standard harshly. It was in this connection that the policy of the Argentine government was the occasion for the first breaches in the policy of the Good Neighbor.

One of the reasons for my interest in this policy is the cacaphony of voices raised to proclaim its termination. For example, "One of the conclusions that can be drawn from this study is that the good-neighbor policy . . . continued in effect only from 1930 to approximately 1940, when the United States, confronted with diplomatic and eventually military thrusts from the Axis powers, began once more to assert a dominant role in the Western hemisphere" (Dozer 1972: viii). Or: "Roosevelt's death marked the end of Good Neighbor diplomacy" (Gellman 1979: 209). The Ecuadoran ambassador, Galo Plaza, said on the occasion of Spruille Braden's publication of the "Blue Book" in February 1946, "Whatever the outcome of the Argentine elections, Roosevelt's Good Neighbour policy and the work of the Pan American Union [are] now a dead letter."[6] Henry Morgenthau, formerly secretary of the treasury, commented in 1946 that "in the past year the heritage of good will which accrued to us in Latin America through President Roosevelt's Good Neighbor policy has been largely dissipated" (*PM* [9 May 1946]). Nelson A. Rockefeller in 1952, an election year, stated that the Truman administration had "underestimated the underlying importance to us of this traditional relationship from all points of view—spiritual, psychological, political, economic and strategic; . . . [and] lost much of the idealism and sympathy and the spirit of common purpose symbolized by the Good Neighbor policy" (*New York Times* [23 April]).

Finally, this selected list should mention the remark by Stephen Schlesinger: ". . . The CIA-sponsored takeover by Col. Castillo Armas [in Guatemala, 1954], though it accomplished its purposes, had immense long-range costs for the United States. In the minds of Latins, it tore FDR's 'Good Neighbor Policy' to tatters and unequivocally reinstated the 'right' of U.S. intervention throughout the hemisphere" (*The Nation* [28 October 1978], p. 439).

These differences in viewpoint have their sources in definitions of the Good Neighbor policy. From naïve opinions on the termination, such as that of the renewal of U.S. assertion of "a dominant role" in the hemisphere, to the equation of Roosevelt's death with the end of the policy, to more sophisticated explanations, the judgment of this book is that the noninterference aspect of the Good Neighbor policy underwent serious modifications in the 1943–1944 period; was restored in the spring of 1945; was again subject to perturbations from 1945 to 1947; was rehabilitated from 1947 to 1953; and was finally and fatally attacked thereafter, beginning with the intervention and interference in Guatemala in 1954.

There were, of course, friendly relationships maintained after 1954, and the United States continued economic assistance. The OAS voted to support the United States in the missile crisis, and it played a role in the U.S. occupation of the Dominican Republic in 1965. The Alliance for Progress followed the attempt to intervene in Cuba at the Bay of Pigs. However, the threat of U.S. intervention and interference has, since 1954, influenced the actions of politicians and leaders throughout the hemisphere, as it did not do when the Good Neighbor policy was observed.

Acronyms

ARA	American Republics Affairs, a division of Department of State
CIA	Central Intelligence Agency
CIAA	Office of the Coordinator of Inter-American Affairs
CPD	Emergency Advisory Committee for Political Defense
DS	Department of State
DSB	Department of State *Bulletin*, a weekly
FO	Foreign Office of Great Britain. All British records cited are from FO 371, designation of the political file
FRUS	*Foreign Relations of the United States*, a series of annual volumes; the most recently published on the Western Hemisphere is for 1952–1954
FSO	Foreign Service Officer of the United States
IAPC	Inter-American Peace Committee, an agency of the OAS
MNR	*Movimiento Nacional Revolucionario*, National Revolutionary Movement, Bolivian political party
NA	National Archives of the United States, comparable to the PRO
NSC	National Security Council
OAS	Organization of American States
PRO	Public Record Office, London, comparable to the NA

The Dismantling of the Good Neighbor Policy

1. Setting the Stage

The Meeting of Consultation and the Castillo Government

In the month after Pearl Harbor, the American states met in Rio de Janeiro to give effect to their declared principle that aggression against one state was aggression against all. "This was a life-and-death struggle, the result of which could only mean freedom and advancement for Latin America or domination and probably occupation by the Axis" (Hull 1948: 2: 1145). Beyond the many agreements on cooperation, the most important resolution concerned breaking diplomatic relations with the Axis powers.

Washington recognized that Argentina was unlikely to cut off relations with the Axis, and Hull and Welles agreed that the breaking of the principle of continental solidarity was preferable to acceptance of a compromise formula permitting Argentina to refrain from a diplomatic rupture. However, in Rio de Janeiro Welles finally accepted a text in which the American republics only recommended to each other that they break relations. When Hull heard this on a radio broadcast, he telephoned Welles in Rio and "spoke to him more sharply than I had ever spoken to anyone in the Department. I said I considered this a change in our policy, made without consulting me, and the equivalent of a surrender to Argentina" (ibid.: 1149).[1] Roosevelt was then brought on the line and said he would accept "the judgment of the man on the spot" (Welles 1951: 117). Hull said that he was "frankly very angry that Welles had acted as he had" and added that "we were to pay heavily in the future for this failure at Rio." In a telegram to Roosevelt Welles said that "it seemed to me, therefore, in the highest interest of our own country, that I should make every effort to preserve unity and yet at the same time *achieve the objectives upon which you and I agreed*" (*FRUS* 5 [1942]: 36–39; emphasis mine).[2]

Adolf A. Berle, assistant secretary of state, tells of receiving a call from an "almost heartbroken" Hull, "a thoroughly angry man," before Hull called Welles. Hull said he thought "Sumner had been undermining him; that he had gone over his head to the White House; that he had worked up the Rio Conference without getting authority either from the President or from Secretary Hull, each thinking that he had arranged it with the other. He intimated that a lot of things were going to change. [Laurence] Duggan [chief, Division of American Republics Affairs] and I tackled the job of trying to salvage the situation for we both agreed that the revised resolution was disastrous." However, Berle, the next morning, thought that Roosevelt's suggestion that "the best thing to do was to let well enough alone and make what we could out of it . . . was good judgment." Berle also describes himself as "heart-broken because Sumner is one of my best friends, and I could not take any view except that, in accepting the pretty miserable compromise, he had given away a strong position, and lost a large amount of the tremendous force of American unity and of United States leadership, and probably compromised (though I think not irretrievably) our whole position. We shall have to take back the territory bit by bit" (diary, 24 January 1942, box 213: 7–8).

Welles had, through real consultation, achieved a unanimously accepted recommendation and maintained the unity of the American states. These were not inconsequential achievements, despite Hull's opposition, and it is probable that the worst effect of Welles's action was the serious deterioration in his relationship with Hull, which culminated in Welles's resignation, accepted on 25 September 1943.

The relationship had never been a happy one. Welles had been named undersecretary by Roosevelt, when R. Walton Moore had been Hull's candidate for the post. Because of early and intimate contacts, Welles frequently went over Hull's head to the president, with the latter's, but without Hull's, permission, as he apparently had done on the resolution on breaking relations with the Axis. The situation was recognized in the Department of State as being a difficult one. "Welles, with Roosevelt's support, usurped many of the Secretary's functions, and Hull did not attend any of the summit meetings. The situation was destructive of morale for many of us in the department, and we were most unhappy about it" (Bohlen 1974: 129).[3] In the summer of 1943, Hull said that Roosevelt "decided on his own" that Welles could no longer hold his position, and Welles resigned. Hull placed his main emphasis on Welles's "disloyalty to me," but pointed out also a number of policy issues on which their views were dissimilar (Hull 1948: 2: 1229–1230).[4]

For a year and a half after the Rio Conference, however, Welles was undersecretary, and he stated that, until January 1944, with the forced resignation of Pres. Pedro P. Ramírez of Argentina, "the policy of the United States had been governed by the same principles as those which had been scrupulously observed from the time the Good Neighbor Policy was first proclaimed." At the same time, United States policy was "suddenly transformed" unilaterally and without consultation, to deny recognition to the new government of Pres. Edelmiro J. Farrell and to demand similar action by Latin American governments (Welles 1947: 125–126). Welles's explanation for the change in policy would probably have been couched in terms of Hull's "Anti-Argentine bias," which had, by the beginning of 1942, become "almost psychopathic" (Pratt 1964: 2: 713).

Hull's anti-Argentine bias apparently originated in 1936 at the Buenos Aires Conference, when foreign minister Carlos Saavedra Lamas of Argentina successfully opposed Hull's resolution on peace proposals, ostensibly because it would interfere with rules of the League of Nations. Sharp words were exchanged and Saavedra "did not extend the usual courtesy of seeing me off" (Hull 1948: 1: 499). At the Lima (1938) and Havana (1940) conferences, Hull had successfully appealed to Pres. Roberto M. Ortiz of Argentina, over the heads of Argentine delegates, to secure resolutions desired by the U.S. government, since it was the "unfortunate policy" of Argentine politicians "to remain aloof from any movements of leadership in the hemisphere unless they themselves were furnishing the chief leadership and policies" (ibid.: 609).[5]

However, by the time of the Rio Conference in 1942, Ramón Castillo had become the acting president of Argentina, as Ortiz had been forced to relinquish his powers because of illness (he resigned in June 1942). Castillo proved unbending in his refusal to break off relations with the Axis. As seen from London, Argentina was "pursuing a considered policy of non-entanglement, with a slight bias to the enemy; and they are not likely to be deflected from such a policy by direct pressure (which neither we nor State Department advocate) or by the sort of appeasement which commends itself to Mr. Sumner Welles. Nothing but a change of government can bring about an improvement, and even then the improvement might not be so very great."[6]

If Welles's policy was "appeasement," it was also the policy of Berle, who said that "threatening or turning the screw on the Argentine Government" would be "contrary to the good neighbour policy and had proved abortive and harmful in the past. Practice of the United States Government was to make the logic of the situation clear and inevitable and then to sit back and watch it play."[7] The British view was that they could be well satisfied with the result of the Rio Conference: "It is better to have secured unanimity than a more heroic policy with the Argentine completely dissociated from it."[8] Finally, "Apart from the fact that for the first time in history twenty-one American republics have voted unanimously on the principle of solidarity in self defense, the United States of America, our allies [sic], can now proceed with the business of winning the war without so much anxiety of trouble arising on their southern flank . . . from our point of view the Conference can have none but good results."[9]

In the United States the Department of State took the view that the conference had been successful. Welles thought that Chile might break off relations as early as March 1942, and that Argentina could not then long withstand the combination of its isolation and its inability to obtain lend-lease materials.[10] At the same time, he reported to Norman Armour, U.S. ambassador in Buenos Aires, that he "would be amazed at the bitterness of the feeling which has been engendered in important circles here" toward the government of Argentina.[11]

The bitterness in Washington was caused in part by the efforts of Argentina to organize a bloc of countries, including Bolivia, Chile, Paraguay, Peru, and Uruguay, in support of its position against breaking off diplomatic relations. Foreign minister Enrique Ruiz Guiñazú was reported to be "feverishly lobbying them for the formation of southern neutral bloc," although his efforts "failed completely."[12] From the notion of a bloc, which for the time being included only Chile, Argentina moved toward the formation of a group of states that would accept Argentine leadership in foreign affairs and toward the instigation of coups-d'état such as that in Bolivia in December 1943, which precipitated the sudden transformation in Hull's policy just mentioned.

However, in the months immediately following the Rio Conference the Department of State took a position against the efforts of the Treasury Department and the Board of Economic Warfare to freeze Argentine assets. A memorandum dated 14 May 1942 and intended for Roosevelt defended Argentina's "active collaboration" in "some aspects of our war effort" while admitting that it had not severed diplomatic relations with the Axis. It further stated that Argentine public opinion was becoming "more and more insistent upon a more effective collaboration by Argentina with the democracies." Beating Argentina "over the head with an economic club" would make the American republics "wonder whether we had repudiated our present policy and returned to the days of the Big Stick" (*FRUS* 5 [1942]: 471f). The argument won Roosevelt's support: " 'It just won't do,' he told Treasury Secretary Henry Morgenthau, 'It would kill our whole Good Neighbor Policy'" (Blum 1967: 197).[13]

Roosevelt's view of the importance of the Good Neighbor policy was echoed in England:

Mr. Hull and Mr. Roosevelt have built up, in the minds of the Latin American peoples, a new faith in the United States. The Good Neighbour policy has gone far to liquidate the legacy of suspicion left by a quarter of a century of interventionist diplomacy; and it is a vital interest of the United States that it should not be compelled to deviate at any point from the broad lines of the new policy or to appear to jeopardize the economic or political independence of any Latin American State at the risk of arousing again the suspicions of all.[14]

Within a week after Pearl Harbor, the Foreign Office began to talk about making a frank expression of displeasure with the way in which Argentina was facing the war. It decided, however, to talk with the State Department first, since "Mr. Welles is a champion turner of the other cheek as far as Latin America is concerned and I cannot see him countenancing any plain talk, however camouflaged, by us."[15] While awaiting word from Lord Halifax about his talks at the State Department, Perowne noted that what the British wanted was "*complete* cooperation, but I doubt whether that will prove possible of attainment, as, apart from the war, the community of interest is perhaps insufficient, and the Good Neighbour Policy a great obstacle."[16] The Foreign Office's attitude was summed up in a telegram to Washington:

In our view, the Good Neighbour Policy, which has so greatly improved the prospects of co-operation between the United States and the smaller Central American Republics, is unlikely to produce similar effects when applied to the relations between the United States and a country such as the Argentine. We do not believe that to indulge the Argentine Government by pursuing the Good Neighbour Policy to a logical conclusion will serve any more than threat of direct pressure, to deflect that Government for an instant from their chosen policy.[17]

Earlier in December, but after Pearl Harbor, the Foreign Office had "approached the Americans with offers of collaboration, and even with suggestions for minor forms of pressure (to be exercised by us) upon the Argentines, with a view to inducing in them a better frame of mind at the then forthcoming Conference. Our offers were politely declined, as were also our suggestions, though it is true that at

Rio the U.S. Under-Secretary for Commerce did hint that we might take some action in connexion with shipping."[18] However, "Up to only the other day, the State Department, in the interests of the Good Neighbour Policy and of Pan-American defence, were busy 'appeasing' the Argentine." By mid-April, however, "appeasement, as might have been expected, not succeeding, the State Department has now begun to 'turn the heat' on the Argentines in various ways (e.g., low priority for military supplies), and wants us to help in getting the Argentines off the fence on which they are at present seated."[19]

The Department of State, however, was slow in putting pressure on Argentina, apart from refusing military supplies, an action that Welles had forecast at Rio de Janeiro. Duggan thought that Anglo-American policy should be in harmony and ought to be "directed towards securing the maximum possible economic contribution from the Argentine to the war effort, rather than to scoring diplomatic successes such as the severance of relations between the Argentine and the Axis countries." In his view "sanctions had to be applied either totally or not at all if they were to achieve the object desired and not merely create irritation."[20]

Welles was against sanctions:

> The bedrock upon which this new epoch of inter-American understanding is founded is the recognition in fact, as well as in word, that every one of the 21 American republics is the sovereign equal of the others. That implies that interference by any one of them in the internal affairs of the others is inconceivable. . . . If the Government of the United States ever again undertakes within the New World a policy which constitutes interference, direct or indirect, in the domestic political concerns of our neighbors, the day when that policy is undertaken marks the end of all friendship and understanding between the American peoples. (*DSB* [21 February, 1942]: 167)

It is significant that Welles here used the word *interference*. He and others often appeared to use "intervention" and "interference" as though there were no difference between them, despite the fact that in terms of the Good Neighbor policy itself, the two were carefully distinguished (Wood: 1961: chap. 4). Intervention is one form of interference, involving invasion by troops, or supply of arms, or training, or transportation of military forces. Interference refers to a broad range of actions, which may be no more than advice on a domestic political situation or nonrecognition and the application of economic sanctions. The policy of nonintervention was, from 1936 to 1954, regarded as admitting of no exceptions. The policy of noninterference was only fairly strictly adhered to by U.S. diplomats between 1936 and 1944.

It is important to note that these negative policies of inaction, adopted by the United States, were intra-American in effect; that is, they applied to a hemisphere that in 1936 was not menaced from without. Nonintervention was a commitment applicable to all American states, but noninterference was a self-denying ordinance that applied only to the United States, and presumably it was not applicable, until the provisions of the OAS Charter of 1948, to the Latin American countries.

In these early days of 1942, the Department of State saw no need for accepting British help with Latin American affairs. Sumner Welles met the British ambassador to Brazil, Sir Noel Charles, only incidentally on one occasion at the Rio Conference, and this was resented in both Rio and London. Wayne Taylor, assistant secretary of commerce, told Charles that there was no reason to ask Welles for suggestions as to what Britain might do, since both Welles and Duggan "were really fundamentally opposed to asking us to help the U.S. in any American problem."[21]

Chile's Breaking Off Relations with the Axis

The new policies, however, had no effect on changing Argentina's determination to refrain from breaking off relations with the Axis. The situation with respect to Chile was different, since it had not been so uncompromisingly opposed to such action (see Francis 1977: chaps. 1, 4). The United States actually sent certain armaments to Chile early in 1942 for the protection of coastal areas and promised that planes would be supplied if relations with the Axis were severed. Claude G. Bowers, "while avoiding threats, which were considered inconsistent with the 'good neighbour' policy and also likely to produce an unfavourable rather than a favourable reaction," had suggested to Pres. Juan Antonio Ríos that Chile could not expect favors from the United States as great as those extended to countries that had committed themselves.[22]

In the summer of 1942 an elaborate bargaining dance was carried on by the two governments. In mid-June Ríos asked Bowers for a loan or credits in the value of $100 million. In response, Bowers read a telegram from Welles, "which, while disclaiming any intention of linking economic with political questions, made it clear that a rupture was desired."[23] Welles in a talk with the Chilean ambassador, Rodolfo Michels, said he thought it was highly important that Chile sever relations with the Axis before the visit Ríos planned to Washington, the first by a Chilean president to the United States (*FRUS* 6 [1942]: 32–34).

Responding to a telegram from Bowers about loans to be received by Chile, which Chilean ministers said "may seem like bargaining, but that they assume some agreements will be made by us, and apparently they ask only an agreement in principle before action," Hull said that "the logic of the commitments of the American Republics regarding inter-American solidarity and collaboration in the face of attack by non-American powers required the severance of diplomatic relations between the American Republics and the aggressor powers. This is not a subject for bargaining. . . . We are prepared to render such assistance within the limits of existing circumstances to Chile should it sever diplomatic relations. We cannot discuss this assistance until after we know what Chile's policy is to be."[24]

Bowers told Sir Charles Orde, the British ambassador in Santiago, that, on instructions from Washington, he had conveyed the view that "there could be no question of bargaining for a rupture of relations with the Axis Powers."[25] Orde's view was that "the right moment having been missed at the outset, and impulsive action avoided, the critical and cautious side of the Chilean character is uppermost, and unless some incident occurs to change the scene or unless the United States Government decide that the stake at issue justified the virtual abandonment of the good neighbour policy and the exercise of severe pressure, the prospects of a satisfactory change of policy now seem somewhat remote."[26]

Throughout 1942 the prospects remained remote, and on October 8 Welles made a speech in which he noted that two American states still gave bases to the Axis for "hostile activities" by enemy agents:

As a result of the reports on Allied Ship movements sent by these agents . . . ships have been sunk without warning while plying between the American republics, and as a result many nationals of these countries have lost their lives within the waters of the Western Hemisphere. But I cannot believe that these 2 republics will continue long to permit their brothers and neighbors of the Americas, engaged as they are in a life-and-death struggle to preserve the liberties and the integrity of the New World, to be stabbed in the back by Axis emissaries operating in the territory and under the free institutions of these 2 republics of the Western Hemisphere. (*DSB* [10 October 1942]: 810)

As a result of the speech, Ríos called off his scheduled trip to Washington, and the Argentine government sent a stiff memorandum (dated 10 October) to the Department of State expressing its "extreme displeasure" at Welles's statements and asking for particulars (*FRUS* 5 [1942[: 210–211). Welles responded with a memorandum on November 4 that referred to a memorandum delivered to the Argentine government on November 3, detailing evidence of German military espionage in that country. This memorandum named Germans in Argentina engaged in espionage who provided information via clandestine radios and other means. "The work done by these agents has been extremely accurate and especially harmful to the Allied powers as well as to the neutral American Republics. Millions of dollars worth of ships, merchandise, petroleum, munitions and foodstuffs have been sent to the bottom of the sea due to the efforts of these agents" (ibid.: 218–224). Welles also told Amb. Felipe Espil on November 4 that "there was no use of mincing words with regard to the position of the present Argentine Government. It was constantly giving lip service to the principles of the Good Neighbor Policy and to the ideal of inter-Amerian solidarity, and yet, at the same time, it was not only permitting a desperately serious situation of the kind now complained of to continue, but it had also, to all intents and purposes, refrained from any practical implementation of the definite commitments which the Argentine Government made at the Rio de Janeiro conference" (ibid.: 233–234).

Espil hoped that the memorandum would not be made public, but Welles gave no commitment, and it was made public when transmitted by the Emergency Advisory Committee for Political Defense (CPD) in its first annual report. This committee was set up at the Rio Conference in 1942. Its members were Argentina, Brazil, Chile, Mexico, Uruguay, Venezuela, and the United States, and its purpose was to study and coordinate measures by the various states to combat subversion. It was chaired by Alberto Guani of Uruguay, the U.S. member was Carl B. Spaeth, and it met in Montevideo. It is of interest as one of the first efforts at multilateral cooperation in the hemisphere. The CPD developed plans against subversion, and each country used them as it saw fit. It could only recommend courses of action, but its recommendations were taken seriously because of the community of interest among American states to protect themselves from Axis subversion. Its most controversial decisions were those to publish the U.S. notes of 30 June 1942 to Chile, and of 3 November 1942, to Argentina, which was "at variance with accepted diplomatic practice" (Samponaro 1979: 35).[27] The CPD also proposed, in the case of the Bolivian revolution of December 1943, that the American states should consult before according recognition to this and other regimes for the war's duration.

Welles, by means of his speech of 8 October, was certainly putting strong pressure on both Argentina and Chile. He had told Amb. Michels on 16 October that it was no doubt the intention of Pres. Ríos to break off relations with the Axis, "but that of course the Ambassador would remember that upon very many occasions in the past this Government had been advised to the same effect and that, nevertheless, regrettably enough, no action had been taken" (*FRUS* 5 [1942]: 214–215). Believing that the Chilean people were not being told by their government about the extent of Axis espionage, Welles added pressure by asking the CPD to make public on November 4 a memorandum on the Chilean situation like that on Argentina. (The Chilean member of the CPD voted against publication but was overridden.)

Shortly before the Welles speech, it was thought in the British Foreign Office that, whereas a rupture of Axis relations by Chile was "in the nature of things, inevitable," the Chileans had not reached any conclusions about the timing and manner in which it would be "(1) most dignified; (2) most profitable; (3) most appropriate. . . . The Chileans are still watching the Solomon Islands and an unfavourable turn there would almost certainly delay a decision to break off relations. They would also require a fairly dramatic insult to the national pride."[28]

The British reaction to the speech by Welles was that it was a "gaffe" that might have been avoided by private diplomacy. However, Welles "may have made up his mind that the situation in both countries was hopeless and sought to have appealed over the heads of the governments to the peoples concerned."[29] In Brazil, Maurício Nabuco, the secretary general of the Brazilian Foreign Office, said that "in any case Chile as well as Argentina deserved what they got." Sir Noel Charles, the British ambassador, said that there were also "many Brazilians who consider that Mr. Welles' speech is a further indication of his in-comprehension of Latin-American mentality."[30]

Philip W. Bonsal, Duggan's deputy, was reported as saying that the Department of State would not budge from its position, "which they felt was completely justified and which he [Bonsal[said the Chilean Government knew was justified. . . . Furthermore the Chileans had for some time been playing fast and loose with the United States Government and the United States Government was thoroughly sick of this."[31] After talking with Welles, the British ambassador, Lord Halifax, reported that the department

[has] for the time being at all events decided to adopt the policy of "cold shoulder" without indulging in pinpricks over minor matters. The State Department's policy in fact seems to be to adopt an increasingly tough attitude towards the Argentine with a view to convincing them that their present policy does not pay and that if it is continued they cannot expect to be treated on the same basis as other Latin countries. At the same time State Department will, in carrying out this policy, avoid taking steps which could be represented or regarded by the Argentine as having been taken purely out of pique.[32]

In Chile there was "much anti-American feelings among the public, but responsible Chileans seem as much concerned as angry."[33] One immediate result was the resignation of the Chilean foreign minister, Ernesto Barros Jarpa; a second was that the Chilean government arrested some Nazi agents. Pres. Roosevelt renewed his invitation to Ríos to visit the United States. It was accepted, and R. A. Gallop, Perowne's assistant, wrote that "it looks as though Mr. Sumner Welles' outburst has done even less short term damage than we had supposed."[34]

Early in November, it was thought in the Foreign Office that

Chile is undoubtedly moving towards a breach, impelled principally by U.S. economic pressure and by the war situation, especially in the Pacific. She would like it to appear that a rupture, when it comes, is of her own volition, but Mr. Sumner Welles seems determined not to allow her even this little luxury. He probably argues that without these touches of the spur the Chilean horse could never be got over the jump. It certainly is a reluctant jumper, but it is difficult not to feel that the spurs have been overdone and that their effect on U.S.-Chilean relations will still be felt when the rupture with the Axis has long been a matter of history.[35]

The Chileans had got left behind by not acting sooner, and each passing day made the break more difficult, especially since the Axis was careful not to provide any incident on which a break might have been based. "The only advantages which their breaking of relations would now present would be the further isolation of Argentina, the removal of a not perhaps very dangerous focus of intrigue at Santiago, and the saving of Mr. Welles' Pan American face—something which Mr. Welles himself doesn't seem very interested in at the moment."[36]

Perhaps the specificity of the information given by Welles on December 12 to Amb. Raúl Morales Beltrami was the last flick of the spurs in inducing Chile's decision. Welles gave the ambassador two documents prepared by the Department of the Navy. The first gave information transmitted by Station PYL in Chile to Germany about U.S. ship movements. The second listed the ships sunk following transmittal of information: The *Santa Rita, Berganger, Mikoyan, Maldanger, Ogontz.*

As an illustration of the above, in the case of the Ogontz, which was a vessel of 5037 gross tons, 390 feet in length, and of U.S. registry, this ship arrived at Iquique, Chile, on May 2, 1942, and departed on May 5 with a cargo of nitrates. It transited the Panama Canal and departed for Mobile, to arrive there on May 22, but on May 19 it was sunk in approximately latitude 23° 30' north and 86° 37' west, eleven days after information was transmitted by station PYL, giving the location, description, destination, and cargo of the vessel.[37]

It is of considerable interest that no comparable, specific statement was made for ships sunk by Axis action leaving Argentina, and that the Foreign Office was never able to extract from the Admiralty any statement of ships sunk by German submarines as a result of clandestine wireless from Argentina.[38]

Finally, on 20 January 1943, Chile broke off relations with the Axis. The president's speech gave "no adequate reason for abandoning at long last the role which Chile had played for the past year. . . . So ends a rather inglorious chapter in Chilean history which would have been closed earlier if the President had been a man of stronger character."[39] In this despatch, Orde gave due credit to Welles, whose speech, "which caused the visit to be cancelled, provided the turning-point by leading to the fall of Señor Barros and a fuller realisation that different policy was necessary. Only then was a beginning made in educating public opinion." And in an FO Minute on this despatch, Gallop noted that "this is not the first, fine careless rupture which it would have been a year ago, nor is it the very belated attempt to curry favour with the United Nations, which it might have been 9 months hence." (The president finally did go to the United States in October 1945, where he slept at the White House and was given all other usual honors.)

Within a month negotiations for the transfer of airplanes to Chile had been completed. At the beginning of March, Gen. Oscar Escudero, commander of the Chilean Army, and described as "unquestionably democratic in outlook and our friend" (*FRUS* 5 [1942]: 816), arrived in the United States to discuss various aspects of military cooperation. On March 2 an agreement was signed for a loan of fifty million dollars for the purchase of arms and ammunition, with easy repayment terms.

Chile was in the fold, and Welles could feel satisfied with his tactics. He would not have regarded this as interference in Chilean domestic affairs: he had made no demands for changes in the Chilean government, but had merely pointed out to the Chilean people some of the disadvantages to inter-American solidarity and the war effort of the United Nations that were implicit in Chile's foreign policy. He had exerted pressure, but would have claimed that it was of a neighborly type and related only to Chile's international policy in wartime. The way was now clear to focus U.S. displeasure on Argentina as the single obstacle to the greatly desired unity of the hemisphere.[40]

2. Relations with Argentina to 4 June 1943

Argentina was of course a very different problem from Chile. Chile had, after Pearl Harbor, a keen fear of Japanese naval incursions, and it was not until this fear was dissipated that it broke off relations with the Axis. Further, the Chileans were far more dependent upon the U.S. market than were the Argentines, and emigration to Chile was not marked by the rush of Italians that had poured into Buenos Aires since the 1890s. Argentina, the most European of the South American countries, had a higher per capita income than any and had wrested primacy in South America from Brazil after 1900. Its trade was mainly with Europe, notably Britain, in beef, wheat, linseed, and leather, and that trade made the country prosperous during World War II. Some Argentines, especially in the military, had dreams of restoring the dominance exerted in the Southern Cone by the Viceroyalty of Río de la Plata at the end of the Spanish empire. Argentina had resisted the growth of hemisphere solidarity that the Good Neighbor policy had stimulated and was equally disinclined, much to the surprise and dismay of the British government, to show any signs of gratitude (other than carrying on commerce with Britain during the war) for the large part British investment played in its development.

The proclaimed lists, or "blacklists," of firms with which U.S. companies were requested to have no business transactions were initiated in 1941, and the system was further developed in 1942 and later.

Ever since its inception the other American Republics have been strenuously opposed to the list. . . . It was urged at first that the maintenance of the list was inconsistent with our Good Neighbor policy. Later, after most of the other American Republics had broken off diplomatic relations with the Axis and many of them had declared war, their opposition was predicated on the theory that the maintenance of the list was an affront to the sovereignty of countries which were our allies. We have been able to counteract this opposition in part by justifying the list as an emergency measure designed to prevent United States goods from falling into the hands of inimical persons in the other American Republics during the war.[1]

In March, after it was clear that Argentina would not implement the Rio de Janeiro obligations, and after Chile's breach of Axis ties, Welles had sent to Norman Armour a memorandum setting forth the rationale for the issuance of the "Proclaimed List of Certain Blocked Nationals" (*FRUS* 5 [1943]: 312–325).[2] The statement noted that the proclaimed list and its controls "operate solely as regulations applicable to persons subject to the jurisdiction and laws of the United States," so that there could be "no question of infringing the rights of Argentine citizens or the laws and constitution of the Argentine Republic." Further, to bring the proclaimed list within the scope of the Good Neighbor policy, Welles's memorandum pointed out that certain persons served as "cloaks" for pro-Axis firms; with regard to them, "while this Government, pursuant to its fixed policy of nonintervention in the internal affairs of other countries and out of respect for the sovereignty of other nations, scrupulously respects the right of such persons to deal with whomever they choose," the U.S. government would "exercise its sovereign rights and responsibilities in determining whether under existing conditions it can permit its citizens to trade with persons and firms abroad who, for their own reasons, choose to traffic with and thereby assist our enemies in their avowed purpose of destroying this nation and the democratic principles on which it stands."

The application of the proclaimed list, in the sense of the actual determination of the individuals and companies to be listed, gave rise to dissatisfaction in Britain. As early as May 1942, the U.S. ambassador in Brazil, Jefferson Caffery, had agreed to deletions from the list without consulting his British colleague, Sir Noel Charles. "The question is really one of the protection of British interests and influence in Latin America against American aggression," wrote the minister of economic warfare.[3] "The Americans make no secret of the fact that their object is not merely to thwart the enemy's war activities in Latin America but to stamp out his influence there for good. His firms are to be put right out of business and there can be no doubt that the dream is that they should be entirely supplanted by

Americans. Unless we play our hand skillfully, we shall be supplanted, too." However, "Mr. Caffery is in his satrapy and will countenance no opinion or influence but his own."[4]

Gallop's view was that "it is of course true that the United States is showing an increasing tendency to regard Brazil as a special preserve and to improve their economic position there at our expense. Of this we have many indications such as Mr. Sumner Welles' comparison of the United States position in Brazil with ours in Egypt, and the remark of Mr. Warren Pierson of the Export and Import Bank to the effect that 'you can have Argentina while we will have Brazil.'"[5]

Of the American ambassadors, Caffery was more frequently remarked upon than any other. He was reported to have said that "the British were thoroughly detested in Brazil and that the President had no use for us—'what have the British ever done for Brazil?'"[6] His Irish extraction and his conversion to Catholicism were noted, as was the fact that his two chief aides in Rio de Janeiro were Irish-Americans. On the other hand, Maurice Butler pointed out that, despite Caffery's "malignant attitude" toward Britain,[7] it was difficult to believe that he was "wholly noxious." There was the unfortunate fact that "our authorities in Trinidad offended Mrs. Caffery, and American Irish Roman Catholics as a class are our enemies." Still, Caffery had been given the "job of ensuring U.S. predominance in Brazil and he intends to see it through regardless of treading on the toes of others."[8] Halifax spoke to Welles about a "lack of cooperation" between Caffery and Charles, and subsequently Charles reported a "marked change in cordiality in the conduct of business and in personal relations."[9]

Bitterness over U.S. policy with regard to the proclaimed list was ameliorated somewhat by a report from Washington that the Department of State's "feeling about excluding British interests from Latin America is less strong than it was before," and that U.S. officials were beginning to admit that British support might be helpful in the cases of Argentina and Chile.[10] This impression was strengthened by an instruction to U.S. missions in Latin America that urged upon them "the necessity of the closest cooperation with their British colleagues," since "relations between the American and British communities in the other American Republics are still characterized by mutual suspicion and bitter rivalry, a situation which, unfortunately, has existed to a greater or less degree for many years."[11]

In Venezuela, Amb. Donald Gainer reported that, although in general relations between the British and U.S. "colonies" were satisfactory, he could not entirely escape the feeling that behind all the good cooperation which undoubtedly exists, there is a feeling on the American side that European countries are really intruders both politically, territorially, commercially and strategically in this hemisphere. . . . There are a very few Americans who are unfriendly towards the British but they have no influence even among their own people and I regret also to say that there are certain members of the British Community whose blimpish complacency and refusal to see any good points in foreigners of any nationality must be as obnoxious to Americans as it is to me. These persons are chiefly to be found among the ladies of the British Colony.[12]

An indication of the attitude of Pres. Castillo is provided by the following quotation from a talk with an Argentine citizen:

I am not going to permit the sovereignty of the country to be impaired. And now I will ask you something: do you believe that Brazil is an independent country? All the north is occupied by North American forces and a Brazilian cannot penetrate into the occupied zone. The chief of the naval forces is a North American and so is the chief of the air and land forces. Is Brazil a sovereign country? If the North Americans should wish to occupy a part of our territory to establish bases, every officer without distinction of rank would beg leave to resign from the Army and the Navy. . . . I am a friend of the United States as we all are, but these people are not diplomats and we cannot yield to force without impairing our own dignity.[13]

Castillo was correct in pointing to the degree of integration of the U.S. and Brazilian armed forces; this was part of the price of Brazil's receiving substantial military aid from the United States, but it was also evidence of Brazil's wholehearted support for the cause of the Allied forces. Brazil had declared war on the Axis after the sinking of vessels and the loss of Brazilian soldiers. The British commercial counselor, R. L. Nosworthy, allowed some of his prejudice to show in reporting that the Brazilian government, "starting with Vargas, is purely American-minded and Aranha is one of the worst, but of course a good deal of what they say and do must be set down to cupboard love. . . . But in their negotiations with the Americans they can be tough and they must often drive the American delegations to distraction, hacking their shins between mouthfuls of jam. . . . The most serious thing we have to face is the determination of the

Americans (that is to say, not the State Department nor the Embassy here) to tie up the country with contracts for post-war."[14]

The Argentines made fun of the Brazilians, calling their country Brasil—Estados Unidos instead of Estados Unidos do Brasil, and it was reported that among the armed forces and in the bureaucracy, there were some "who contend that the Argentine neutrality policy is not because the Government favours the Axis but because they dislike and distrust the U.S.A. so much. There is a real fear of North American domination, and no amount of 'Good Neighbour' policy seems to dispel the idea."[15]

The position of the Department of State in the spring of 1943 was well characterized by Perowne:

> The intrigues of the enemy Embassies in Buenos Aires constitute a direct menace to the security of the Americas for which the United States is responsible. It may well be fatal, moreover, for the realization of the Pan-American ideal, for which President Roosevelt's Administration has so zealously striven, if one Power is shown to be able successfully to stand out in a matter of this kind which concerns the welfare of all. It is particularly unsatisfactory from the State Department point of view that this Power should be one which had always shown itself recalcitrant to American leadership in the Western Hemisphere. It is also aggravating that owing to the nature of her economy Argentina should be able to appear to continue to profit by her ill-doing, while the more virtuous Powers which have broken off relations with Germany, but are not so fortunately situated economically, are losing trade and prospects as a consequence of the war. Finally, on the moral plane, Argentina by persisting in remaining neutral is showing herself a traitor to the sacred cause of Pan-Americanism.[16]

On the other hand, Argentina had in no important respect "caused us serious direct damage in the prosecution of the war." When the question of the completeness of the Argentine radio decree was under discussion "the Admiralty were unable to provide us with any proof that a message from one of the Axis Embassies in Buenos Aires had led to an attack on, far less to the sinking, of a British vessel." Although the British officially "deplored" Argentine policy, there was no real occasion for them to worry about it; "while maintaining our attitude of sorrowful regret at the Argentine obstinacy," the North Americans should be allowed to take the lead in measures "designed to bring Argentina to heel."[17] To the extent that the North

Americans were moved by "thwarted rage," as distinct from "enlightened self-interest,"[18] the British should be all the more studious in avoiding any connection with "vindictive pressure" on the part of the United States.[19]

On 4 June 1943, the Castillo government was ousted by an army rebellion headed, briefly, by Gen. Arturo Rawson, and then by Gen. Pedro P. Ramírez. It was Armour's view that "one, if not the prime motive, in the movement was to put the Armed Forces in a position to obtain war material and they know that to accomplish this a condition precedent is the severance of relations with the Axis" (*FRUS* 5 [1943]: 369–370).[20]

Amb. Sir David Kelly noted the alienation of sectors of the Argentine public caused by the generals' revolution: "Many influential and respectable Argentine civilians, however experienced, did not hesitate to express to foreign friends, their humiliation at the purely military character both of the revolution and of the Governments which emerged from it, which placed Argentina, to their mind, on the level of a 'nigger republic.'"[21]

The Department of State had at first hoped "that this coup might mean a move not only in the direction of continental solidarity but also towards liberalising the administration of domestic affairs. Both these hopes were shattered when the constitution of the first government was revealed. . . . All attempts to create a united front amongst the other Republics appear to have been abortive. From the beginning the State Department hoped that by withholding recognition they could force the new government into more positive declarations concerning its future foreign policy." However, the affair turned into "a scramble to see who would recognise the first," and Duggan admitted that

> it was a bitter blow that this movement should have been led by
> Brazil of all countries and was at the instance of Dr. [Oswaldo]
> Aranha [minister of foreign affairs] . . . who is so often held up as
> an intimate confidant of Mr. Welles and the greatest exponent of
> collaboration with the United States in the Southern hemi-
> sphere. . . . These events have provided the first real revolt on the
> part of the other American republics from United States tutelage
> since Argentina's recalcitrance at the Rio conference. It is pos-
> sible that it will have given the State Department pause to think,
> and to wonder how much of the edifice of Pan Americanism they
> have laboured so long, with such earnest good will and patience
> and with such expenditure of treasure to build, is substance and
> how much is shadow.[22]

Aranha himself explained his action to Amb. Charles by saying that he was

> well-pleased with his "coup de maitre" in being first in the field to recognise new Argentine Government because, by so doing he thinks he has: (1) been able to prove to his critics in Brazil that he is a true Latin American; and (2) been able to obtain Argentine sympathy; and (3) their possible co-operation in "continental" politics; (4) made a gesture with view to obtaining sympathy of other Latin American States who suspect that Brazil and particularly Dr. Oswaldo Aranha is the tool of United States "forward" policy in South America; (5) been able to prove to the United States that Brazil remains chief link between them and South America since he knows how to manipulate these wayward Latins and make them appreciate the beauties of Pan-Americanism under United States-Brazilian guidance; (6) thus materially assisted in consolidating Brazil's leadership of South America.[23]

The complexity of Aranha's motivations indicate the inadequate simplicity of Duggan's interpretation of the rapid recognition by Brazil. The United States fell into line by recognizing the Ramírez regime on June 11.

3. Relations with the Ramírez Administration

At the end of June, Welles summarized U.S. policy in a thoughtful review of the Argentine situation. He began by noting that "over a decade ago the President announced his policy of the Good Neighbor. Our strict adherence to this policy, demonstrated time after time, convinced the people of the other American republics of the sincerity of our intentions." Welles said that if Argentina now expected to secure military supplies, it would have to break off relations of all types with the Axis powers and "engage wholeheartedly in activities designed to defend the hemisphere." However, "although a break of relations by Argentina at this time would not constitute the significant contribution to the war effort of action taken immediately after the Rio de Janeiro meeting, nevertheless it would be important in completing the solidarity of the American Republics. With the preparations for the postwar already in full swing it is obviously becoming of increasing importance to Argentina herself to be a party to these deliberations."

Then in a concluding paragraph, Welles said,

> One basic point which I think you must emphasize in any conversation you have is that the determination of its foreign policy is a matter for the sole determination and decision of the Argentine Government. In such determination this Government has not interfered, does not interfere, and will not interfere. But if the Argentine Government modified its existing foreign policy so as to comply with the obligations and recommendations entered into at the Conference at Rio de Janeiro and in other existing inter-American agreements so that it joins wholeheartedly, practically, and effectively in the defense of the Western Hemisphere, this Government will of course be prepared to discuss the measures of cooperation which in the judgment of the United States

could be offered to the Argentine Government in the general interest of the security of the New World and of the United Nations war effort. (*FRUS* 5 [1943]: 419–424)[1]

Again, it is of interest that Welles here used the term "interfere," rather than "intervene." It is also of interest that he was avoiding placing Argentina in the position of a bargainer. The Argentines knew what had happened when Chile finally severed relations with the Axis and they could expect equal treatment, or better. There is nothing in this letter that reveals a loss of patience; the tone is measured and calm, almost that of a diplomatic note to Argentina, rather than the "Dear Norman" letter that it was.

Although Armour reported that Ramírez had said that "he could give his guarantee that the break would take place not later than August 15,"[2] it appeared that the government could not make up its mind. At first it claimed that a "large section, especially of provincial opinion . . . is not prepared for this action."[3] Later, however, Kelly reported that "the President's difficulty lies not at all with the general public but with important section of Army officers. He is trying to gain over as many as he can of these."[4]

Faced by this frustrating situation, Merwin L. Bohan, economic adviser to the U.S. embassy, recommended, as had Armour earlier, that "the Argentines . . . 'should be left to stew in their own juice'; that instead of running after them and seeking their cooperation for the carrying out of the resolutions of the Rio and Washington conferences, the United States Government should abandon all the conversations that have been in progress to that end and should pursue a policy of 'friendly reserve,' but at the same time should not inflate the Argentine's view of their own importance."[5] Bonsal had earlier proposed a comparable line: "I do not believe that it is possible to secure political action from Argentina through a direct threat of economic reprisals in the absence of such action. Either the Argentines would think we were bluffing and would do nothing or the action taken would be accompanied by widespread resentment which would poison Argentine relations with us for many years."[6]

Meanwhile, there were hopes, which gradually faded, of an Argentine break. Early in June the department sent Armour a list of fourteen "specific steps of a positive nature," beginning with the breaking off of Axis relations, that Argentina could take (*FRUS* 5 [1943]: 417–418).[7] Giving the Argentine government every chance, Armour recommended that "our Government should do everything possible to ease the way, even though it might appear that we are departing from a policy already decided upon." He admitted that other American states might protest, especially Brazil, which had cooperated with the United States when it was dangerous to do so. However, he felt "that the Department will agree that the future of inter-American solidarity and cooperation is really involved: that if this war were to come to its victorious conclusion without Argentina having come in wholeheartedly on the side of the democracies, continental cooperation in the future would be more difficult" (ibid.: 436).[8]

On July 27, as it began to look more and more improbable that Argentina would break off relations on August 15, as Ramírez had promised, Hull called Armour to Washington. He noted that Armour's estimate of the "type of regime that seems to be evolving internally holds forth diminishing hopes for a constructive orientation in its foreign policy. We therefore believe it opportune to re-examine the relationships between the two countries as well as those between Argentina and the other American republics and the rest of the world" (ibid.: 443).[9]

On the occasion of Armour's recall, the Argentine foreign minister sent a letter to Hull that blasted all the hopes formerly entertained by Armour and the Department of State that Argentina was ready to rejoin the American family of nations. The letter from Adm. Segundo R. Storni reviewed Argentina's contribution to the United Nations war effort, particularly through its continued supply of meat and wheat. The new government could not bring about a change in foreign policy (the break in Axis relations) "because our country was not ready for it." Further, "The war having reached its present stage, when defeat is inexorably drawing closer to the countries of the Axis, this unexpected rupture [of relations] would furthermore put Argentine chivalry to a hard test." The letter stated that "it is not just to maintain the attitude of suspicion assumed towards a country such as ours," and that Pres. Roosevelt should make a "gesture of genuine friendship toward our people; such a gesture might be the urgent provision of airplanes, spare parts, armaments and machinery to restore Argentina to the position of equilibrium to which it is entitled with respect to other South American countries" (ibid.: 447–451).[10]

The department's reply, drafted by Bonsal and described as "a model of crudeness" (Conil Paz and Ferrari 1966: 111), was damaging to Argentina's position. The two were published, and a storm of comment, nearly all of it critical of Argentina, raged in the hemisphere's press. Hull recalled Argentina's commitments made at the Rio Conference, which furnished "a convincing expression of the reason why the situation of neutrality which Your Excellency states the Argentine Republic has had to observe up to now has not been understood." With regard to arms supplies, "I must point out emphatically that questions of military and naval equilibrium as between American republics are surely inconsistent with the inter-American doctrine of the peaceful settlement of international disputes to which so many practical contributions have been made by Argentine statesmen. . . . Since Argentina, both by its words and its actions, has indicated clearly that the Argentine armed forces will not under present conditions be used in a manner designed to forward the cause of security of the New World, and, thereby, the vital war interests of the United States," a lend-lease agreement with Argentina was impossible. Hull expressed "deep regret" at Argentina's course since the Rio Conference: "Thus the failure of the Argentine Government to comply with its inter-American commitments has not only resulted in the non-participation of Argentina in the defense of the continent in a most critical period, it is also depriving Argentina of participation in the studies, discussions, meetings and arrangements designed to solve the post-war problems mentioned above" (*FRUS* 5 [1943]: 454–460).[11]

Storni was dismissed as soon as the letters were published on September 7. Following Armour's return to Buenos Aires in October, he reported that Ramírez had complained that the exchange "had not created a favorable atmosphere inviting cooperation by his Government. He was emphatic on the lack of understanding and comprehension in the United States of Argentina's position. I told him very frankly why I felt neither the Government nor the people of the United States sympathized with or could pretend to understand the course followed by his Government. The interview lacked entirely the cordial tone which marked my talk with him last July" (ibid.: 463).[12]

Bonsal asked whether the Foreign Office would not issue a statement associating itself with Hull's letter to Storni. "The Argentine Government committed a consummate betise, the U.S. Government gave them the only possible reply and now suggest that we should give them public support. . . . It is surely no matter for surprise that Mr. Hull should have castigated this kind of nonsense and I do not see that we can quarrel with the Americans for publishing the correspondence."[13] After some hesitation, Anthony Eden, minister for foreign affairs, issued a statement claiming that the British government

remain disappointed at the determination of successive Argentine governments to maintain neutrality during a struggle which so patently threatens the principles which animated the founders

of the Western Republics. It has, moreover, never been understood in Great Britain why Argentina, alone of the Western Republics, has failed to give effect to the recommendation of the
Rio Conference regarding the severance of diplomatic relations
with the Axis powers, with the result that Axis nationals are still
free to conspire on Argentine soil against the interests and security of the United Nations.[14]

It was thought at this time that the State Department "realised at
last that the policy of alternate bullying and cajoling has been a failure. . . . In other words, we feel that from now on Argentina may
well be treated with hardboiled realism, with few of the refine-
ments of the New Deal and the Good Neighbour. The departure of
Welles may accelerate this," but the economic agencies of the U.S.
government would probably take the lead in exerting pressure on
Argentina.[15]

The Treasury returned to its ideas of freezing Argentine assets on
learning that Armour had made the same proposal on October 20
and argued that "the Embassy believes that blocking would be interpreted in Argentina as directed against the Government and not
against the people and would be generally understood" (ibid.: 493).[16]
Edward R. Stettinius, Jr., the successor to Sumner Welles, cabled
Hull, who was in Moscow, that the department opposed the blocking
of funds, which was intended both by the Treasury and Armour as a
method of "upsetting . . . the present Argentine Government rather
than an economic warfare purpose." In the department's view, the
proposal would strengthen the Ramírez regime, because of "the su-
persensitivity of Argentines to any suggestion of outside pressure."
Hull agreed, and on October 25 Roosevelt asked that the suggestion
be tabled, but that it be reviewed every week or two (ibid.: 495,
496).[17] A consideration that affected the department's view was that,
fundamentally, freezing "would, however, be considered both in Argentina and, more importantly, in the other American republics as
an abandonment by us of the non-intervention policy upon which,
the inter-American system, with all its positive benefits, rests."[18]

The glaring duality in the policy of the State Department was
brought out clearly by Bohan in a talk with the commercial counselor of the British embassy in Buenos Aires. Bohan said he would
"raise the issue of the inconsistency of continuing to treat Argentina
both as an essential source of supplies for the United Nations and as
a Nazi hot-bed and nursery garden for German post-war interests. It
was ridiculous that he should have to beg for linseed one day and be
as objectionable as possible the next day." Perowne said that Bohan

"hits the nail on the head," and the Americans "ought to make up their minds how they mean to deal with the situation thus presented." He thought the British would "have to help them over this or try to." To Sir David Scott, however, the "overriding consideration" was that "any serious interruption in our supplies from Argentina would gravely hamper our war effort." The "hot bed" danger would depend on the completeness of the Allies' victory over Germany. "Besides, the wheel will surely have turned in Argentina before any noxious seeds come up after the war."[19]

To the Foreign Office, according to Gallop, the dilemma was easy to solve: "If the State Department could reconcile themselves to the fact that . . . there is nothing practical they can do to bring about the fall of the present Government, and that any distinction drawn between the Government and the Argentine people is purely academic, there would now appear little difference between the attitude of the State Department and ours." But Perowne was worried about public opinion in the United States, "to which the Administration is at all times sensitive. . . . For how can we bring it home to the United States public that Argentine supplies are *essential* to the war effort without at the same time proving to the Argentines that (as they assume) they are 'on velvet' where we are concerned?" It was unavoidable that Britain "*must* stand with the U.S. over Argentine matters, and convince the Argentine and the world that we are united."[20]

Toward the end of 1943, Halifax made a general assessment of the Good Neighbor policy:

It is difficult to say whether there ever was any widespread illusion on their [State Department's] part about the attitude of the neighbouring republics towards this country. It may well be that certain government agencies such as the office of the CIAA were bemused by their own propaganda and thought that they had produced that degree of Pan-American brotherly love which they were so lavishly attempting to buy. While there are no people on earth more well-intentioned than Americans, there are also none more surprised when their good intentions are not always appreciated and understood by others. Equally are they prone to resentment when disillusionment comes.

Halifax did not expect that there would be a return "to the bad old days of Marine landing parties and occupation. Certain lessons have been learned and this, I think, is one of them." Gallop thought that this despatch showed clearly "why the U.S. Govt. are now less reluctant than they were in the heyday of Mr. Sumner Welles' 'Good

Neighbour' policy (and of the threat to the Straits of Dakar) to take a tougher line with 'the little brown brothers' and why we may expect them to be influenced in this sense by their public opinion."

In Scott's view, the United States was "only now getting out of the 'pioneer,' 'bash straight ahead' mentality, *vis-à-vis* foreign countries. They are beginning to learn that impatience and emotion are bad counsellors if you want harmonious foreign relations [and] that independent sovereign states must be treated as such." However, "the process is slow, and their inherent emotionalism, intolerance of outside advice and lack of coordination in their Governmental machine will make it slower. . . . But their main teacher must be bitter experience in wch. unfortunately we are liable to be involved."[21]

Along the same line, it was Perowne's view that "we should be grateful to the Good Neighbour policy, which has been of great help as regards the war, though some of the activities it has involved have caused alarm and despondency among H.M. representatives and British residents and interests in Latin America, by reason of the consequences it might be expected to have for our local commercial, etc. prospects." In this review of the Good Neighbor policy, stimulated by the report of Sen. Hugh A. Butler (R.-Nebraska) published in the *Reader's Digest* (December 1943), Perowne maintained this balanced view:

> In spite of the façade of brotherhood, the U.S. are fundamentally feared and disliked by the Latin Americans, and just at present this dislike seems to be keenly felt. Conversely, despite the production of huge bibliographies of Latin American music and so forth, the U.S. at heart despises, and probably rather dislikes, the dagoes to the South, and there is evidence of distinct impatience at Washington at the waywardness of the "lesser breeds of men without the law." But we do not stand to gain, either now or after the war, by a state of affairs in which the U.S. would be at loggerheads with any, or all, of its western hemisphere neighbours. We must therefore hope that what is best in the Good Neighbour principle will survive to stabilize conditions in both sub-continents.

Scott's comment on this Minute was: "I agree, but until the Americans have gained greater political wisdom in external affairs and have learned to substitute for the G.N. policy something wch. corresponds more with the day to day needs of international relations, we are bound to have ups and downs in U.S.-L.A. relations."[22]

These comments went to the heart of the question of the utility of the Good Neighbor policy as one that was feasible for a great power. Perowne's reference was, presumably, to the U.S. policy in Mexico, where the United States' weak defense of the oil companies gave the British no ammunition for a stronger position than that adopted in Washington. Scott raised the issue of the policy's suitability for "the day to day needs" of interstate relations, thus questioning the relevance of bringing in ideas about the "inter-American system" and "continental solidarity" as they affected policy. This criticism of North American thinking was found throughout British commentaries (I shall discuss it later).

A revolution occurred in Bolivia at this time that changed the course of policy. The Department of State attributed the revolution "entirely to backing and inspiration from the Argentine," and Hull told Halifax that there was reason to believe that the coup had been "brought off with help of Germans largely from Argentina."[23] "Uruguay was nervous and the United States Government were sending a battleship there."[24]

The Foreign Office recognized the validity of Hull's fears that the Bolivian revolution "was engineered from the Argentine" and the justification for Washington's concern that there might be a spread of the trouble "and the eventual creation in Latin-America of a pro-totalitarian bloc of countries with a definite anti-U.S. bias." Butler recommended that Britain might consider taking an "extraordinary step" to convince Hull that his anxieties were being taken seriously in London. Hull, however, was proposing "sanctions," which to the British meant limiting the export of Argentine meat, which would "delay victory in Europe. . . . For when Germany is utterly crushed, totalitarianism in the pro-Axis form will surely fizzle out in the Argentine, and the sooner Germany is crushed, the sooner will the U.S. Government be freed of their worst headaches in Latin-America. The main fire will be out and the satellite ones will die too."[25]

Hull was not alone in seeing Argentine plots in South America. The Chilean government was reported as fearing that the Bolivian revolution might presage "similar moves fomented by Germans in Argentina, in Chile, Peru and Brazil"; and the secretary general of the Ministry of Foreign Affairs in Brazil was in accord with Chile that the Bolivian coup was the work of German Argentines.[26] Finally, the Argentines were trying to attract Uruguay to their orbit, as part of two policies: "to separate Uruguay from her present close association with Brazil, and similarly to separate Brazil from the United States, at the same time advocating the formation of a strong Latin American *bloc vis-à-vis* the United States, so as to remove any danger of a local 'front' against Argentina herself made up of Brazil,

Bolivia and Paraguay." Perowne wrote that it was "quite clear that the Argentine Govt. wish to build up a South American *bloc* in opposition to the United States," although he did not believe that Argentina was "working in the *German* interest, except where that interest may happen to coincide with their own."[27]

On January 3 Hull had raised the question of Britain's talking "tough to Argentina" and proposed the issue of a joint examination by the United States and Britain. The British, however, were wary, in part because, as Halifax put it, "one can never feel quite sure of the precise degree of definition that his [Hull's] apparent assent carries." Perowne was not sure that "sitting down" with the North Americans would be useful, since the result might be either a decision to do nothing "or a rift in the Anglo-U.S. lute." Scott agreed: "There are regions of folly into which we cannot reasonably be expected, however loyal, to follow the U.S. Govt." Hull presumably wanted to talk about stopping the purchase of Argentine meat and other supplies, and to this the British were adamantly opposed.[28]

Argentina was showing "a tendency characteristic of European rather than of Latin American dictatorships to intrigue with like-minded elements in neighboring countries with a view to the installation of regimes friendly to it and to the Germans who are encouraging these tendencies with an eye to the post-war period. They have already been successful in Bolivia and it is as yet too early to say that the infection will not spread to Paraguay, Chile, Peru, Ecuador, and even possibly to Brazil." This caused perturbation in the United States, since it threatened it "with an aggressive nationalist, specifically anti-US, authoritarian South America which they would regard as a menace to their security."[29]

Kelly talked with Armour about a joint statement on Argentina, and Kelly asked "how the proposed drastic intervention in the internal affairs of the leading Spanish speaking Republic could be reconciled with 'the good neighbour policy.'" Armour responded that "this was precisely why it was essential that His Majesty's Government should share on a 50-50 basis (i.e. share the unpopularity)."[30] John J. McCloy, then assistant secretary of the army, in response to a Morgenthau tirade against Argentina, said that "halfway measures were useless and unless the United States was prepared to send a battle fleet to the Plate, which would have disastrous consequences . . . the wisest policy was to wait until the war was finished when the Argentine [group of code letters omitted] presented a comparatively easy problem to solve." Gallop felt that this exchange clearly illustrated "the complete failure of the U.S. Govt. to *coordinate* their Argentine policy, which lies at the root of all our difficulties."[31]

In a talk with Halifax, Hull said he was recommending to Roosevelt that the department should issue a statement on Argentina, recall Armour, freeze all Argentine funds, and embargo all trade with Argentina of "a pro-Axis kind." Hull was afraid Argentina would start a movement, as in its aid to the Bolivian revolutionaries, "which would spread all through South America" and constitute "a real danger to the war effort." In his view, "time was of essence." Both the United States and Britain should "show their teeth since the Argentines were saying that neither Government would ever do anything."[32] The FO said it hoped Hull would wait before recalling Armour, "until views of Combined Boards as to effect of any action on war effort have been ascertained."[33]

Prime Minister Winston Churchill, in a message to Eden, said that "it would seem to be very serious" if Kelly were not recalled along with Armour. "Considering all they have done and are doing it would be most imprudent and short-sighted for us to let a definite divergence be seen between our policies in respect of this shameful and caitiff neutral, and might let loose a flood of ill-will. We ought to prove ourselves a loyal ally."[34]

The views of the Foreign Office at this juncture were expressed in a telegram to Halifax:

> Mr. Hull's approach appears to be essentially emotional and to be based on insufficiently co-ordinated examination of question where the true interest of United States Government lie[s]. In particular, he fails to distinguish between danger which Argentine Government constitutes during and after the war. . . .
>
> Action must either be (1) direct intervention to replace Argentine Government, or (2) indirect intervention through sanctions effective enough to bring about revolution as a result of economic collapse. (1) is incompatible with the good-neighbour policy and Atlantic Charter. (2) would only be politic if it did not injure the war effort. Otherwise it must postpone the day of victory in Europe and in consequence the day when pro-German influences in Argentina will lose most of their power to do harm. Incidentally we see no likelihood of our being able to apply sanctions to this effect or indeed to an extent likely to achieve more peaceable elimination of Government or a change in their policy.[35]

If both alternatives mentioned in this telegram were to be rejected as criteria for "action," then in the view of the foreign office no action whatever should be taken and, specifically, public statements by

Hull should cease. Duggan, in effect, joined with the British by asking Hull directly: "Are we trying to brand Argentina as a renegade for not having complied with the Rio resolutions? Are we trying to make life uncomfortable for Argentina so that she will not meddle in other people's business? Are we trying to bring about a climate in Argentina conducive to revolution? Or are we just generally sore at Argentina and want to do something? What results are looked for from a statement excoriating Argentina?" His own view was that "the way to the heart of the Argentines is through their stomach . . . the people are apathetic to questions of foreign policy and, alas, even to the type of government they want to live under." If the United Nations were willing to undertake sacrifices, then "it is suggested that a meeting of Foreign Ministers be convened." It might also help if the United States were to approve a few economic development projects in other Latin countries.[36]

This view was strongly buttressed by Bonsal, who wrote on the same day: "We should not issue any broad indictment of Argentina nor should we place in effect economic sanctions unless we have full assurance of complete British and Brazilian cooperation and unless we believe the objective to be obtained, namely, the overthrow of the present allegedly hostile Argentine Government, is worth the hostility during the next generation of most of the Argentine people."[37]

Undeterred by these views from his principal advisers on Latin American policy, Hull in mid-January gave Halifax a memorandum entitled "Connections of the New Bolivian Regime with Elements Hostile to Continental Defense." In it details (including the names of involved Argentines) were given of Argentine assistance to Bolivian revolutionaries after a visit by Víctor Paz Estenssoro to Buenos Aires.[38] The message would be given publicity in Washington within a week.

On seeing the memorandum, Armour raised a question: "Is not the real basis for an indictment of the Argentine Government that they are a totalitarian government attempting to extend their system of government to other American Republics and that they have actually succeeded in the case of Bolivia?" Armour was concerned that "a statement alone even coupled with general freezing would not result in rallying the opposition forces to concerted action against the government. Coupled with action along lines suggested, however, it might have the desired effect although here again this would largely depend on the extent to which Argentine economy was effectively hurt" (*FRUS* 7 [1944]: 230–231).[39] Here Armour was touching on the question of a split in Argentina between the government and the people on the question of neutrality policy, a split that the British commentators denied existed and called "academic," but one on which U.S. policy heavily depended.

In the meantime Halifax had gone over Hull's head and talked to Roosevelt, saying "with suitable apologies, that I thought Mr. Hull was perhaps rather over-anxious about it and that I should have thought myself our wise course would have been to be a bit reserved to the Argentine now but make sure of getting all we wanted from them and then if we wished to put them on the mat after the war, we could no doubt do it without too much difficulty."[40]

Hull, however, was not to be put off and proposed to make a statement in the following form:

> This Government has been aware that subversive groups hostile to the Allied cause have been plotting disturbances against the American Governments co-operating in defence of the hemisphere against Axis aggression. Argentina, the one American Republic which maintains friendly relations with the Axis Powers, serves as the principal base from which these subversive activities [group undec. are directed (?)]. The attitude of the Argentine Government in permitting these activities and in accepting the applause of pro-Axis elements cannot be reconciled with any friendliness to the Allied cause.
>
> On December 20th 1943 the Bolivian Government was overthrown by treachery and force under circumstances linking this action with the subversive groups above mentioned.

Therefore, since this movement toward the substitution of other governments with Axis support "would have been a serious menace to the effective prosecution of the war by the Allies and to the safety of the hemisphere," the United States, following consultation with other American governments, would not recognize that of Bolivia.[41]

Hull's determination to act in this fashion caused a flurry of activity in London. The Foreign Office was worried primarily about possible interruption in the flow of supplies from Argentina caused by the action of the United States. The British were dependent upon Argentina for the following percentages of imports into Britain alone: "Wheat 14%, Linseed 70%, Carcass meat 40%, Canned meat 29%, Hides 35%. The meat ration could not be cut, and it was doubtful if the U.S.A. could replace supplies from Argentina. . . . It would be false to suggest that the U.K. would suffer more than the U.S. from interruption in Argentine supplies; the resultant deficiencies would affect all the United Nations."[42]

Halifax reported that "if the U.S. proved determined to make a statement, we should have to consider whether disadvantages of a statement on our side, presumably not followed by any action, were greater than disadvantages of getting badly out of step with the U.S. Administration."[43] The Foreign Office had requested a statement from the Combined Boards on the effects of a loss of Argentine supplies, and Hull was urged not to act on his proposed "sanctions," including freezing and Armour's recall, until the Combined Boards had acted.

We could not afford to run any risk over sanctions and it was obvious that nothing but prolonged and most stringent sanctions could produce what Mr. Hull wanted, i.e. overthrow of present Argentine Government and German influences in Argentina. While sympathizing with Mr. Hull, we did not agree with him as to the degree of danger constituted to the war effort by the continued existence of the present Argentine Government. If Mr. Hull was determined upon some action, then a statement by each of us would be the least harmful step, which we should prefer to withdrawal of Ambassadors.[44]

Reports from the chiefs of staff in London and by the Combined Boards in Washington emphasized that "a cessation of Argentine food exports would have an extremely serious effect on the war effort."[45] Hull, in talking with Halifax, said that it would be very difficult to change his proposed statement: "The various governments concerned had been notified. The President had agreed to it as part of a triple procedure of freezing, recall of the Ambassador, and the issue of the statement. Unless the President changed his mind he did not see how alteration was possible." The United States "simply could not sit still and watch the whole structure of solidarity built up over ten years sapped and mined away. It would take a generation to rebuild it." Hull did not rate seriously the risk to supplies as a result of what the United States proposed to do.[46]

Churchill wrote to Roosevelt at this point, saying,

I beg you to look into the formidable consequences which would follow our losing their [Argentina's] hides, meat and other supplies. We get from them one-third of our meat supply. If this is cut out, how are we to feed ourselves plus the American Army for OVERLORD? . . . An immediate cessation of Argentine supplies, our Chiefs of Staff consider, will disrupt military operations on the scale planned for this year. I cannot cut the British ration lower than it is now. . . . I must inject my solemn warning of the gravity of the situation which will follow if the Argentine supplies are interrupted. To recall our Ambassadors means only that the field is left open for the Germans. These rascals know the hold they have over us for the time being and have calculated very carefully.[47]

At this time of Anglo-American crisis, a curious thing happened. The Argentine government "discovered" that an Argentine consul, Osmar Hellmuth, who had been taken by the British at Trinidad on 29 October 1943, "had been proved to be an enemy agent" and that an investigation would be made to "put an end to all activity contrary to the nation's international policy."[48] On the following day, 22 January, Hull said that the Argentines "had obviously got wind of conversations in progress between H.M.G. and the U.S.A." Duggan commented that Hellmuth's "confession might warrant publishing as it contained a clear implication of the direct complicity of members of the Argentine Government including President Ramírez" in an attempt to secure German armaments.[49]

No direct evidence as to the reasons for the Argentine action can be deduced from the documentation available in Washington or London. The evidence from Hellmuth was damning enough—when had the British communicated it to Buenos Aires? The Argentines may have been sitting on the report for some time, being fairly certain that the British would not publish it. On the other hand, the British may have been saving it for use on just such an occasion as this, in order, by irrefutable proof of espionage, to bring about a break with the Axis states. In this way, London would have been able to avoid having to join with the United States in what it felt would be a futile effort to bring pressure on Argentina, with a real risk of interfering with the smooth supply of agricultural products for British civilians and United Nations forces that were preparing for the invasion of Europe in June 1944. The Argentines probably heard from one of the American states consulted by the United States that full freezing of Argentine funds was being contemplated.[50]

From a subsequent review of the situation, however, there appeared to be good reason to suppose that the Foreign Office had chosen well the timing of release to Argentina of the news of Hellmuth's arrest and of some of the information gained from his interrogation. "On the announcement of his arrest in January" [the arrest was on 29 October 1943], Argentina

not only hastened to disavow Hellmuth, but now, for the first time, publicly admitted the existence (which it had hitherto de-

nied but which was well-known to everyone else) of Axis espionage organisations. The rupture, General Gilbert [Argentina's
foreign minister] declared, was due to the violation of Argentine
neutrality; it was the result, said President Ramírez, of the un-
masking of Axis spy organisations by the Federal Police.

It would be childish to suppose that this official explanation
was the true explanation. Having decided to give in to the Allies,
wrote the *Christian Science Monitor* (27 Jan.) the Argentine
Government preferred to surrender to a European ally, not to the
United States. . . . The Government was uncertain whether or
not sanctions would be imposed, and it was apprehensive also of
a public exposure by the United States of its connivance at Axis
espionage and at the Bolivian *coup d'état*. Nor, perhaps was
President Ramírez entirely unmoved by the arrival at Montevideo of United States warships, whose commander, Vice-
Admiral Ingram, remarked that it was the job of an armed force
in war-time "to support our friends and bring discomfort to our
enemies"[51]

Hull at this time was sufficiently concerned to make inquiry as to
the possibility of the use of force against Argentina. "In reply to the
question of the Department of State relative to the recognition of the
present Argentine Government, it is the view of the United States
Chiefs of Staff that no action should be taken which might require
the use of force, as the means for such action are not now available."[52] That such an inquiry could have been made indicates at the
very least that Hull was leaving no stone unturned to find ways to
bring pressure to bear on Argentina. This letter, signed by Adm.
Leahy, and the British refusal to consider shutting off imports of
Argentine meat, prevented the department from going as far as
some officials would apparently have been willing to go in exerting
pressure.

On January 24 the Argentine foreign minister, Alberto Gilbert,
told Armour that his government, as a result of the Hellmuth case,
had decided to break off relations with the Axis in the next few days.
However, this would be done only on condition that the United
States take no action "which might give rise to interpretation that
Argentine Government's action was taken under pressure." Armour
said that the Department of State would on that day (24 January)
make an announcement that would involve Argentina in the Bolivian revolution. Gilbert replied, "Surely there is time to stop this in
view of what I have just told you" (ibid.: 231–232).[53] Armour made
no promise but he informed Washington immediately, and on the

same day, Hull saw Roosevelt, who agreed that it would be desirable to delete any reference to Argentina from the statement of nonrecognition of the new Bolivian regime. Armour told Gilbert of this, at which "he seemed greatly relieved." Armour added that the break in relations would be insufficient unless "accompanied by stern action against Argentine nationalists and others, who have been collaborating with Axis and carrying on subversive activities aimed at governments of neighboring countries." Gilbert said that the United States had been "right and they [Argentina] were wrong in our [U.S.] insistence that Nazi espionage was going on here and they intended 'chivalrously' to admit this in presentation of the case" (ibid.: 232–234).[54]

The Argentine public, however, believed that "Argentina broke relations as result of pressure from abroad. Naturally the United States is the unanimous choice among those who hold that theory. Very many also believe that the credit should be shared by Great Britain. The exact nature of the pressure varies with the individual theory but all agree it must have been immensely powerful" (ibid.: 246).[55] Later, Col. Juan Domingo Perón was said to have gained access to a U.S. despatch "showing that the British were not prepared to join us [the United States] in economic sanctions against Argentina because of their dependence on this country for supplies, particularly meat. Perón is reported to have used this material effectively against Gilbert in the recent blowup, as evidence that he had been bluffed by the United States into breaking relations with Axis" (ibid.: 250–251).[56]

Another factor in the equation was a visit at about this time of U.S. warships to Montevideo. Although the visit was not mentioned in the Buenos Aires press, "this did not mean that the Argentine Government had not been influenced by the potential threat these ships represented."[57] The ships were the cruiser *Memphis*, and the destroyer *Somers*; they were under the command of Vice-Adm. Jonas H. Ingram. Shortly after his arrival on 18 January, "Admiral Ingram brought from Brazil three Mariner bombers which spent several days here, making occasional flights over the city and surrounding country."[58]

The Ingram mission originated in a suggestion from Uruguayan ambassador Juan Carlos Blanco to Bonsal that "Montevideo is very vulnerable to attack from Buenos Aires and that a successful assault on the Uruguayan Capital could under present conditions be carried out by a very small 'commando' group" (ibid.: 1591).[59]

Within a week, Ingram had been ordered to Montevideo, "the expressed purpose of the visit being an expression of solidarity with and friendship toward the present Government of Uruguay" (ibid.).[60]

"It is obvious that visit is widely interpreted as a timely indication of our support of Uruguay which will not be lost on Argentina" (ibid.: 1592).[61]

The building of an air base at Laguna del Sauce, sixty miles east of Montevideo, commenced shortly afterward, and lend-lease arms were supplied to Uruguay later in 1944. In July the Uruguayan minister of defense, Gen. Alfredo B. Campos, said he was concerned "over bellicose atmosphere in Argentina. He recognized that for Argentina to start war would be suicidal adventure but he considers Argentine military regime irresponsible and capable of anything. He views with concern concentration of forces by both Argentina and Brazil along common border and also recent creation by Argentina of two new divisions in provinces fronting on Uruguay River" (ibid.: 1600–1601).[62]

Vice Adm. Ingram describes his political activities when in Montevideo in letters to Adm. Ernest J. King, which, for their directness and possible effect in Argentina, deserve quotation:

> The State Department may consider me a diplomat but I know better—I am just a plain warrior—but honest. This gives me a big edge with these South Americans.
>
> We hit the "jackpot" because we arrived at a time when things hung in the balance. It could have turned either way, but spunky little Uruguay responded like the thorough-bred she is.
>
> Briefly, the situation was that all factions in Uruguay were fighting each other, and at the same time were both being influenced and pushed around by Argentina. . . . Along with it all they have a fear of Argentina. . . . Within four days [15 to 22 January] we had the Uruguayan outfit united, all for the U.S.A. and defiant of our enemies. In fact, they even led the U.S.A. in refusing to accept the Bolivian outfit.
>
> At the same time I was hard at work on the Argentine. I have two or three good friends over there. My neck was out like a giraffe, but I did let the boys from the Pampas in on three secrets:
>
> a. I was their friend; we did not need their help in the war; that the coordinated Brazilian and U.S.A. forces in the South Atlantic were capable of handling every situation; but that the Americans would expect full cooperation from the Argentines to promote Hemisphere Solidarity.
>
> b. I told them that it was surely in the cards that the nations who won the war were going to write the peace and that the

terms of this peace would have a great influence on the destiny
of all nations. Furthermore, that Nazi leaders were going to be
dragged out wherever they might be lurking and duly punished.

c. Last, but not least, that if the Argentines should try any
aggressive action against Brazil, I knew enough about the new
armaments of Brazil to know that it would be suicide for the Argentines. Also that Buenos Aires would be laid to waste just like
Hamburg in broad daylight in short order.

All of this had its effect. Contrary to the State Department's
people, I have steadily held out that Argentina would swing into
line. But the upper crust have no love for the U.S.A.

British influence is not for the "good neighbor" policy. The
British stake in the Argentine is great, and the British are their
best customers. For this reason it is apparent that British pressure
should be more effective if they would apply it. To date, however,
they would just as soon leave the U.S.A. behind the eight ball. . . .

I don't know how much credit the State Department will throw
our way. All Ambassadors have been both exceedingly friendly
and cooperative, but they are also pretty cagey. This I know. We
put the old steel into Uruguay and they know it. The Argentine
flop-over was due to many things. We contributed our part. They
have much housecleaning yet to do and may even revolt before it
is over. All of these Latin countries have political troubles that
would require hours to even attempt to explain.[63]

Ingram concluded that the mission "was an unqualified success
from every angle" and suggested that it might be necessary to send
some units of his force to Montevideo periodically, "if the situation
warrants and will permit." His views were reported to Perón and may
have been influential in warning Argentina that Uruguay was no
place to try anything like the aid given to the Bolivian rebels.[64]

In a talk with Charles in Rio de Janeiro, Ingram said that the
"United States Government have virtually guaranteed armed support to President Vargas to keep his Government in power during period of war. If this is correct United States may have promised support to Brazil and Uruguay in event of Argentine aggression!" Charles
added that Ingram had said that "he had thrown his weight about in
Montevideo where he had been sent to make a show of force. He had
gone beyond his instructions and had as much as implied that he
could easily destroy Buenos Aires with the 200 planes which he had
at his disposal. He does not claim that he caused the change in mind
of the Argentine Government but he thinks he may have given the
final push."[65]

The United States held out against recognition of the Bolivian regime until 23 June 1944. In a talk with Fernando Iturralde Chinel, the special representative of the Bolivian junta, Duggan said that "Bolivia must best know what elements in the revolutionary junta were undesirable and it was up to Bolivia to work out its own situation and not up to the United States to tell Bolivia what to do. . . . We would not assume the undignified and dangerous position of meddling into Bolivia's local politics (ibid.: 446).[66] Armour was instructed to tell Gilbert that the United States "has scrupulously refrained from interfering in the internal policies of other countries. This Government, therefore, will refrain from giving any specific indication as to the changes necessary in the Bolivian Junta in order to secure our recognition" (ibid.: 447).[67]

Another element in the crisis of January 1944 was the fear of other Latin American countries that "Argentina may have plans to encourage similar revolutions elsewhere." If the United States did not take steps to help these countries, theorized Hull, "the Good Neighbor Policy and our war effort might be seriously jeopardized." Efforts should be made immediately to provide Brazil with "additional arms and equipment" (ibid.: 567, 568).[68] Roosevelt shared Hull's views and favored action that would cause the Argentine "plot" to be "nipped in the bud." Aid should go to Brazil "so as to give Brazil an effective fighting force near the Argentine border such as 2 or 3 divisions of motorized regiments" (ibid.: 568).[69] As a result, arms shipments to Brazil were increased. "The curious and somewhat sinister aspect of these proposed arms deliveries to Brazil is that they are being sent for reasons of S. American politics, and *not* to equip the Brazilian Expeditionary Force."[70]

At about this time, Gallop produced a memorandum containing a section entitled "Disillusionment with the Good Neighbour Policy":

> The resignation of Mr. Sumner Welles, the chief architect of the good neighbour policy, coincided with a growing disillusionment with that doctrine in both the northern and southern hemispheres. The Latin American countries, which are a byeword [sic] for touchiness and ingratitude, and which had always taken a somewhat sceptical view of the motives underlying United States concern for Pan-Americanism, were inclined to feel that the "sacrifices" had been inadequately requited. Moreover, American largesse in the form of loans from Export-Import Bank, &c, had been somewhat uneven in its incidence and indiscriminate in its distribution. Coupled with the shortage of commodities, they had contributed to inflation, and by augmenting the

perquisites of office, had increased the dissatisfaction of politicians excluded from power.

Somewhat similar feelings prevailed, if for different reasons in the United States. They received their most extreme expression in the exaggerated charges brought by Senator Butler before Congress in November that the Administration had squandered six hundred million dollars in the pursuit of the good neighbour policy without any corresponding benefit. The Senator's charges were rebutted without great difficulty, and the good neighbour policy was publicly vindicated, but the feeling remained in the official as well as public mind that indiscriminate largesse to Latin America must be retrenched, and if there were no signs as yet of a return to the "big stick" and "dollar diplomacy," there was undoubtedly less disinclination to "talk tough" to the exasperating Argentines. Sight should not be lost of this general reorientation in considering the most recent developments.[71]

Similarly, a Canadian diplomat commented that the United States needed

the tolerance and long-range patience of Britain, the subtle flattery of Germans, the soft-religious and cultural approaches of Spain. The United States technique of neighbourliness is wrong, and is defeating its own aims. . . . The principal lesson for Canada to learn from all this is that a normal calm respect and sympathy is more effective than either an aggressive protestation of good neighbourliness, or a carping criticism or coercion. . . . The United States having been more critical and impatient, has only succeeded in making itself unpopular, had promoted nationalistic xenophobia and has gained no corresponding benefits.[72]

Aranha told Charles that he had "used restraining influence" on Hull with respect to demands on Argentina, but he said also that "Brazil had no desire to fall out with her next door neighbours and he hoped that he could serve in kindly liaison or advisory capacity to smooth over difficulties."[73] In a talk with Valtim Boucas, a Brazilian who asserted that the Department of State wished to put a halt to the "tremendous expenditures being made in Brazil," Campbell, the British minister in Washington, said, "We get certain indications here that the honeymoon of Pan-Americanism may be drawing to a close, leaving behind the problems of day-to-day matrimony. In the meantime, however, the ardently wooed bride seems to have been so spoilt by the lavish gifts of courtship that she has come to expect them as a matter of course, and is apt to sulk when they are no longer forthcoming. For his part, the new bridegroom may think her a bit *exigeante!*"[74]

Meanwhile, in Argentina the Ramírez government was tottering. It appeared that Gilbert, in agreement with Ramírez, informed the GOU (Gobierno, Orden, Unión), the inner group of the army colonels, of the decision to break off relations with the Axis. The colonels would have none of this, however, and forced the resignation of Gilbert and others on 14 February. Personal factors were also involved, since Gilbert had opposed the colonels' "constant interventions."[75]

Very soon after the break in Axis relations, the Argentine government began pressing the United States and Britain for various concessions, for example, permission for powder factory materials from Germany to leave Gibraltar: and membership in the United Nations Relief and Rehabilitation Agency for Argentina. However, these requests were not granted, for the two governments were by no means satisfied that Argentina's breaking off relations was in itself sufficient to justify confidence in its new attitude. The State Department said that the United States was pleased with the severance of relations, but "failure of the Argentine Government thus far to take other effective and thorough measures to supplement the break in relations has heightened speculation as to the real intent of that Government. . . . If no further energetic action is forthcoming, the break of relations can only be considered a subterfuge." Armour was asked to present these criticisms to the foreign minister, but he was also to indicate certain possible actions by the United States, such as provision of spare parts for the Argentine navy, the release of some critical materials, and a review of Argentine needs for petroleum (ibid.: 249–251).[76]

At this time, however, Duggan said that Hull's opinions

had changed very much as a consequence of the recent developments in that country. . . .

While deploring the setting-up of a Fascist dictatorship in this hemisphere, in view of the important supply considerations involved, Mr. Hull now seemed to be of the opinion that the Argentine should be left to stew in their own juice for the moment, provided they made no attempt to set up similar regimes in neighbouring countries. . . .

The impression gained in these conversations was that the findings of the Combined Boards have created a profound effect on Mr. Hull and the subordinate members of the State Department and may prevent future irresponsible or impetuous suggestion regarding sanctions.

Perowne judged here that the department was "showing a welcome disposition to wish to march in step with us and with all the Latin American states in regard to it. Meanwhile this telegram shows that our efforts in the previous crisis have by no means been in vain and that we may, in fact, congratulate ourselves on what they seem to have achieved in bringing the State Department up against realities and away from seeing everything in terms of newspaper headlines."[77]

4. Failure of Nonrecognition

Hull's euphoric attitude did not last very long, for on 24 February Ramírez was forced to resign, to be succeeded by Gen. Edelmiro J. Farrell, with Juan Perón as minister of war. The Department of State, after assuring itself that Ramírez had not resigned voluntarily but had been ousted by a coup d'état, issued a statement on March 4 declaring that "groups not in sympathy with the declared Argentine policy of joining the defense of the Hemisphere" were behind Ramírez's "resignation." The Department of State thereupon instructed Amb. Armour "to refrain from entering into official relations with the new regime pending developments. This is the present status of our relations with the existing Argentine regime" (*FRUS* 7 [1944]: 259–260).[1]

On 26 February the department had proposed consultation on recognition in accordance with the resolution of the Montevideo Emergency Advisory Committee for Political Defense (CPD), which had been applied in Bolivia's case in December. The Argentines had also sent out notes requesting recognition of the Farrell regime, and Chile's foreign minister, Joaquín Fernández, instructed his ambassador in Buenos Aires, Conrado Ríos Gallardo, to establish relations immediately. Ríos Gallardo "took great pleasure in directing a kick at the United States by stating when he delivered a reply to the Argentine note that this was his happiest visit to the Argentine Foreign Office in five years of service in Argentina."[2] The author of this memorandum, J. Kenly Bacon, concluded that "this action by Chile gives us cause of meditation. Is our system of inter-American solidarity built upon a foundation of sand? Or is it solid rock?"

Bonsal indicated lack of agreement in the State Department on how to treat Argentina in a memorandum to Duggan on March 4. He suggested that he thought it a mistake for the department to state that it was ordering Armour to refrain from entering official relations with the new Argentine government: "This statement gives the impression that the U.S. would not recognize the Farrell regime, and so freezes our position. Further, it emphasizes the fact that Chile and the United States have already taken different positions." Armour was being prevented from "forcefully setting forth the bases of our policy, [and] we have pretty well boxed ourselves in and . . . we must now look forward rather to good luck than to good management to get us out of a position which in my mind is wholly unsatisfactory. I do not wish to be interpreted as advocating 'appeasement' in the case of Argentina. . . . We and the other United Nations need Argentina and she needs us. Only Germany is the gainer from any real rift between us."[3]

The degree to which the situation had changed in two weeks was shown by Stettinius's remark that "if the United States Government were willing to cut the meat ration of the civilian population here by 15% they could supply meat that we [the British] were at present getting from the Argentine." On learning of this, Bonsal, who had "been consistently helpful . . . expressed some surprise [at Stettinius's remarks] . . . and has said that he will advise against any threat of action which we cannot effectively take."[4] In Rio, P. M. Broadmead, Charles's successor as ambassador, inquired whether Brazil would issue a statement comparable to those given out by Britain and the United States. The response was in the negative, because, "in dealing with Argentina, Brazil had to remember that she was a neighbour rather than a 'good neighbour.'"[5]

In a talk with Sen. Eduardo Cruz-Coke of Chile, Bonsal reminded him that "the public here is very insistent on action against Argentina and that it felt it should know the Government's feelings towards Argentina." The senator, however emphasized "that we should let the other American republics take the lead while we worked quietly with economic pressure."[6] An indication of the intensity of popular feeling was given by Halifax in saying that Col. [Frank] Knox, secretary of the navy, "talked to me somewhat wildly about having a showdown with Argentina, whose fleet was useless, etc. Asked by [William J.] Donovan and Admiral [Chester] Nimitz on what grounds war could be declared he replied 'Axis agents, espionage, etc.' The above should be regarded as personal and probably does not amount to much beyond showing that anti-Argentine agitation may have high backing."[7]

The fact that Ramírez was forced from office gave rise to the view that the policy of Farrell and Perón would likely put greater pressure on Argentina's weaker neighbors to form an anti–North American bloc. The Department of State therefore cabled to Montevideo that "it may be desirable for an American cruiser to pay another visit to

Montevideo at this time," and Amb. William Dawson replied that it "would be very desirable, convenient and acceptable."[8] However, when it was learned that Adm. Ingram would lead a squadron of the *Memphis*, a cruiser, four destroyers, and a seaplane tender, Armour said it would be interpreted in Buenos Aires "as pressure on Argentina. This was certainly interpretation given Ingram's visit prior to Argentina's breaking relations."[9] Dawson then expressed similar reservations and said that Ingram had informed him that

> length of visit will depend on circumstances. Naval Attaché is informed that a seaplane tender will arrive on March 10 indicating approaching visit of seaplanes. This is quite different from the visit of a cruiser with an officer of less rank which I had anticipated. I feel that before proceeding with plans the advisability and opportuneness of visit should be carefully weighed in light of developments of last two days and possible coming developments as respects recognition or non-recognition of Argentine regime. The proposed visit would undoubtedly be interpreted as a display of force designed to exert pressure in manner which the Uruguayan Government might find inopportune or embarrassing depending on or even irrespective of whether it recognized Argentine regime, refuses recognition or is undecided.[10]

Dawson was authorized to get acceptance of the visit from Pres. Juan José Amézaga and to say that "the movement of the vessels in question was planned prior to recent developments and that it was designed as a routine operational visit."[11] He reported that Amézaga saw no objection to Ingram's visit and added that "the Admiral and his vessels will be very welcome."[12] However, Aranha insisted that Caffery "inform the Department that he believes firmly that it would be a mistake for Admiral Ingram to visit Montevideo at this time. I [Caffery] said that I believed we were trying to bolster up Uruguay. 'That is definitely not the way to do it,' he replied. 'Your people will make a mistake if they send Admiral Ingram to Uruguay at this juncture.'"[13]

On being informed of this, Armour reiterated that he wished "to be on record that in my opinion the visit of our ships at this time to Montevideo would produce an unfortunate impression here in that it would undoubtedly be interpreted by our friends as well as by our enemies as pressure." He added that friendly Argentines considered that the United States was "trying to force Farrell to declare war on Axis. Absurd as this belief may seem, presence of our vessels in Uruguay at this critical moment, could only add weight to this type of enemy's propaganda."[14] Pres. Roosevelt, however, did "not want the visit called off or the number of ships diminished," despite Aranha's comments. He asked that Ingram be instructed "to stay in Montevideo only two days and to give out as the reason for his trip the need to take on fuel and other supplies."[15]

In talking with Capt. Oswald S. Colclough of the Navy Department, Bonsal apparently raised the question of changing Ingram's orders although he was at sea, bound for Montevideo. Colclough reported to Stettinius that there were technical reasons militating against breaking radio silence and that "the Navy here would be somewhat reluctant to interfere with Admiral Ingram's dispositions as to the composition of his forces." Colclough also said that the seaplane tender was "a very small auxiliary vessel and in no sense a 'carrier,' to use the expression employed by one or two of those at the meeting this morning." Bonsal added, "Under the circumstances, I recommend that we permit this to go forward as planned, I feel that we are now definitely committed and that any change would be disadvantageous."[16]

Stettinius accepted this recommendation and added that "the President does not wish the visit to be cancelled at this time nor does he wish any reduction made in the number of vessels accompanying the Admiral. These instructions are being conveyed to Admiral Ingram."[17] On the same evening, however, the president changed his mind, and messages were hastily sent to Ingram, who turned back, and to Amb. Dawson, stating that the visit had been "postponed," and that the visit of the seaplane tender "was left to Ingram's discretion."[18] Ingram made no subsequent visit. This form of military pressure was thus (only barely) cancelled, although it was apparently regarded as being within the limits of the Good Neighbor policy.

Bonsal expressed dissatisfaction with Hull's policy and thought that the department's line had been "unrealistic" since the Bolivian revolution of 20 December 1943. "It seems to me that a clear-cut recognition of this fact at the top level in the Department is essential if we are to work ourselves out of the situation in which we now find ourselves." He accompanied this thinly veiled criticism of Hull with a summary of his own position: "Non-recognition and economic pressure (including the threat of it) are wholly unsuitable tools with which to combat nationalism, non-cooperation and Axis espionage activities in the other American Republics. Not only do they fail to secure the immediate results but they produce situations which are destroying the confidence and good-will which we have built up in South America during the past decade."[19]

Amb. Orde explained Chile's recognition of the Farrell government by saying that Chile did not "consider that the good-neighbour policy involves adherence to the American point of view on every occasion"; rather, Chile considered "that within continental unity each country keeps its own personality and policy. Chile has not noticed the fulfillment (by the United States) of the real necessities of a policy of solidarity and as she does not see any chance of the fulfillment of the promises which have been made to her she does not wish to assume the responsibility of following a policy which would set against her a neighbour who is economically so strong."[20]

On the broader character of the Good Neighor policy, Orde pointed out that "the recognition of Farrell's régime by Chile, Bolivia, Paraguay and now apparently Uruguay, has formed just that *bloc* of outcasts from pan-Americanism which Mr. Sumner Welles foresaw." Talks with American officials and journalists indicated that they realized that pan-Americanism was not workable at that time and that these persons were "much more inclined to accept a United Nations policy in which the individual countries of South America would figure rather as members of the United Nations than as the members of any American union sponsored and led by the United States." Orde concluded that "the good-neighbour policy was never understood by South America," as several Chileans had recently remarked. It was regarded as an expression of the over-generosity of a rich Uncle Sam and it was not realised that it was essential that other American countries should be also good neighbours to one another." A FO Minute by Gallop on this despatch accurately summarizes the feature of the Good Neighbor policy: "Chile acted as much from pique and a desire to assert her independence of the U.S. as from pure expediency. We can agree with the criticisms of both U.S. policy towards Latin America and the Latin American failure to realize that a Good Neighbour policy must carry two-way traffic if it is to survive."

Indicating his sensitivity to charges of "intervention" against the United States, Hull told Juan Carlos Blanco, the Uruguayan ambassador, that

No government known to be sympathetic to the Axis which has come into power by forcing out a preceding government likewise known to have Axis sympathies has the remotest right to invoke the doctrine of intervention to protect a seething mass of German intrigue and plotting within its boundaries, and to some extent within the government. It is a travesty on the doctrine of intervention for any government or group of military officials who are the real power behind it to deny all their sister nations the right of self-defense by attempting to shield behind the doctrine of intervention a notorious state of pro-Axis activities within their boundaries.[21]

In accordance with Hull's view on intervention, Col. H. B. Blake-Tyler, attached to the British embassy, noted that a conflict was arising in Washington about "what is intended by the 'Good Neighbour' policy and non-intervention." In Welles's view, and that of South American diplomats, "the hands of the United States are tied in the face of anything that may happen inside Latin American countries." However, Blake-Tyler commented,

> The notion which the State Department is trying to push now with the help of their friend, Dr. Guani, is that all the Latin American nations ought to consider it their joint concern when a threat to the peace or stability of the hemisphere presents itself by reason of the regime in power in any of these countries. This of course is the wedge of returning to intervention which is gaining ground in the State Department, largely through the exasperation which they have experienced in the recent dealings with some of their more recalcitrant and unreasonable good neighbours. There is too another complication about which they are becoming increasingly sensitive. If they intervene to uphold a status quo they are open to accusations of upholding a reactionary regime which is exploiting the country, viz. Peru and Guatemala. If they do not intervene, the alternative may be a form of dangerous National Socialism, i.e. Argentina. It is of this last that they seem to be the most apprehensive at the moment, hence their support of Dr. Guani's Committee [CPD], in the hope that somebody else will share the burden of being governess. They have, moreover, precedents for intervention of a sort. For instance, all the principal Latin American countries tried to stop the Chaco War. More recently they have been trying to settle the boundary dispute between Peru and Ecuador.

Thus, according to Blake-Tyler, the CPD would be used by the United States to the maximum "to enforce their ideas of a form of collective security in this hemisphere." For the moment, nonrecognition, as in Bolivia and Argentina, was the chosen weapon, since "it satisfied the American impulse to do something with the least possible harmful consequences." "None of the above," he concluded, will be news, "but it is interesting to watch the gropings for a foreign policy here. We must never forget the 'holier than thou' which is a part of the Americans' creed to the outside world and which earns for them such cordial dislike!"

Gallop said, with respect to these comments, that "the degree in which it is possible or desirable to intervene in the internal affairs of another country is a question of which we are likely to hear more in the future, especially in view of the American 'impulse to do something with the least possible harmful consequences' in cases where we, faced with the impossibility of doing anything really useful, would prefer to do nothing."

Great Britain and the United States in the face of "a totalitarian system of government gradually strengthening its hold" on Argentina, had been powerless to prevent the process, "except by sacrificing our principles of non-intervention." Argentina's weakness alone had prevented it from becoming a real menace to its neighbors. However, Scott, in his FO Minute, did not agree that intervention would have "prevented the process," and he feared that Argentina had been "helped by the kind of half intervention which has been practiced by the U.S. and has given them the worst of both worlds." He noted that Hull had recently said that "nations were entitled to freedom from outside interference so long as they respected the rights of others." This meant to Scott that there was no difference between the British view and that of Hull: "For both of us risk of disturbance of the peace is the justification for intervention. But in the application of the principle there may be divergencies of opinion and there is no doubt that in the case of Argentina Mr. Hull's interpretation of the principle has been affected by feelings of personal pique and spite and a regard for popular feeling in the U.S. He has thus allowed his judgment to be swayed by factors which should have no—or little place in the formulation of foreign policy."[22]

The State Department's indecision about policy was manifest in the next several days. On April 3 Armour was asked to talk with Kelly about ways to open the road toward recognition. Three requests were to be made of the Argentine government: (1) that it take effective measures to foil Axis activities; (2) that it appoint new members of the cabinet who "would inspire confidence for collaboration for hemisphere security"; and (3) that it fix "a date for general elections" (ibid.: 265–266).[23] Armour's response was that point (3) "would be dangerous for either of us to bring up unless Perón himself raises it since it might well be resented as interference in their internal affairs."[24] It was thought in Washington that concrete proof of Argentine action along the foregoing lines would enable Hull to face a hostile and skeptical press. One argument Hull used was "that 'capitulation' of Bolivia (whose recognition seems to be *imminent*) confirmed efficacy of his [Hull's] policy towards '*recalcitrants*.'" Gallop commented that "we are now clearer as to what the State Department are really aiming at. Their desiderata are clearly inspired more by Mr. Hull's mood rather than by Mr. Duggan's judgement." However, in his opinion, points (2) and (3) could not "be put forward as conditions or demands without incurring the charge of intervention in Argentine internal affairs."[25]

It was these demands, involving political interference in Argentina, that became the theme of U.S. policy from April to November 1944, when Hull resigned as secretary of state.[26] With Armour instructed to avoid talks with Argentine officials, Hull was content for a time to await developments. It was reported that his "opinion has hardened."

> The difficulty is that Hull is under constant pressure from the
> press and elsewhere not to give any semblance of appeasement or
> compromise with evil for the sake of expediency. This coupled
> with the fact that the United States are feeling their gigantic eco-
> nomic strength and are in a cocky mood, makes them more than
> unusually difficult to deal with where Neutrals are concerned or
> where they feel there is active opposition to them such as in
> both Bolivia and Argentina. The Administration is being accused
> constantly of having no foreign policy. In order to prove that he
> has one Hull may sometimes be tempted to take action (or in
> this case inaction) where he would not if saner counsel or less
> regard for domestic politics prevailed.[27]

In view of Armour's statement that relations with the Argentine were deteriorating, Hull gave approval for Armour to arrange a talk between Kelly and Farrell along the lines of Hull's three points. The talk was, however, not productive. When Farrell asked if he should get rid of minister of interior Perlinger, "Kelly hesitated replying but on Farrell's insistence said, 'Yes, if you wish to inspire confidence.' Farrell then said that he could not do this; that Ministers could not be appointed and dismissed under foreign dictation." Farrell expressed concern about getting supplies from the United States: "In fact if conditions continued as they were they would have to go back to ox-cart stage and this would not be his fault." In general the impression Kelly obtained was that Farrell thought that the United States did not intend to recognize his government, that it had it "in for him personally and merely trying to delay matters by raising obstacles."[28]

This interview began an intensive Department of State examination of policy toward Argentina. The study commenced with a May 3 memorandum, "The Argentine Alternatives," by Walter N. Walmsley, Jr., the department's Brazil desk man, which strongly upheld the Good Neighbor policy. The memorandum began,

> The objective should be to derive the maximum benefit to the war effort from Argentina with a minimum adverse effect on the inter-American system.
> One of the main troubles seems to have been that we have overstressed the importance of Argentine measures morally abhorrent to us, but realistically of minimum effect on the war effort but of maximum effect in weakening inter-Americanism. Similarly, out of a combination of irritation and frustration, we have with full moral justification lashed out publicly at Argentina and adopted measures of minimum practical effect but of considerable usefulness in bolstering the popularity of the extremists.[29]

A policy of "maximum sanctions" should be discarded "for fear of seriously jeopardizing the large field of possible cooperation and because all of the accumulated benefits of the Good Neighbor policy would be lost. It would be unthinkable for any one American country to arrogate to itself the right to apply unilaterally sanctions against another American country." No one, either, would suggest "appeasing" the Argentine, so that it became necessary to examine "what formula and method are available for recognition which could not be interpreted by Argentina as intervention yet would obtain the maximum available under present conditions of benefit to prosecution of the war." First, action should be taken secretly. Second, emphasis should be upon fulfilling the war requirements of the United States; "instead of reaching for the moon we accept such cooperation as is available without real prejudice to the war effort." On May 12, the issue involved was raised sharply by assistant secretary of state, Dean Acheson:

> The issue as I see it is whether our objective should be to reach a Modus Vivendi with the present Argentine Government or whether it is to attempt to bring about the replacement of that Government.
> Mr. Duggan's telegram [based on Walmsley's memorandum] proceeds on the theory that in the economic field we can and must have the cooperation of the Argentine Government; that these matters are more important to us than the political matters

upon which disagreement exists; that an attempt should be made to present a settlement of the political issues which the Argentine Government can accept and that if this can be done we should recognize the Argentine Government. The settlement would involve the Argentine Government taking voluntarily certain steps calculated to reduce Nazi activities in Argentina and to bring Argentina within the frame work of the Rio and Washington resolutions. . . .

The contrary view is that the present Argentine Government is fundamentally hostile to our political policy; that it is deeply totalitarian and Fascist in organization and conduct; that this constitutes a source of danger both to this Government's external policy and, should we recognize it, to this Government's standing at home and that our long-run interests are better served by attempting to bring about the replacement of the Government rather than by attempting to achieve a Modus Vivendi with it. . . .

It is probably true that a policy of non-recognition without more will not be productive of results and may result in a disintegration of the non-recognition front. Therefore, a policy which was directed toward the replacement of the Argentine Government would involve some new and public step such as freezing which would indicate that this Government is not prepared to collaborate with the present Argentine regime.

Such noncollaboration would include suspension of coal and oil exports to Argentina and continued refusal to permit Argentina to participate in international and inter-American conferences. "It is probably true that at the present time these steps in themselves would not cause sufficient economic pressure upon Argentina to overthrow the Government, but if they were consistently applied and increased as opportunity offered and if at the same time the war took a decided turn in favor of the United Nations, there is a reasonable probability that the Argentine Government and people would be convinced that Argentina could not expect, under the present regime, to play any part in the arrangements following Axis defeat." The issue presented by Duggan was "a fundamental one," which should be settled before going ahead with either policy.[30]

The next few days involved intense discussions within the department and with Armour. Duggan's draft telegram was not sent, but on May 17 it appeared that those advocating nonrecognition had won the debate. A telegram was sent to Rio de Janeiro and other capitals, signed by Hull and approved at a meeting at which Adolf A. Berle, Jr., Breckinridge Long, Dean Acheson, Green H. Hackworth, Eric C.

Wendelin, and Joseph F. McGurk were present, all of whose agreement with Hull could be counted upon. It is significant that Duggan and Walmsley were not present, a fact that indicated the defeat of their point of view.[31]

The telegram stated that developments since February had strengthened "the conviction that the elimination of Ramírez and his principal collaborators represented a reaction against the severance of relations with the Axis and the adoption of a systematic policy aimed at liquidation of democratic institutions within Argentina and the undermining of inter-American solidarity and cooperation in the United Nations war effort." Listing a number of failures by the Farrell regime to act against the Axis, the telegram continued,

> In its relations with the other American Republics the present Argentine regime has sought to present the existing situation as a conflict between Argentina and the United States, with the former in the role of valiant defender of national sovereignty and independence. The fact on the contrary is that the continued interference of the Argentine regime in the internal affairs of other American countries constitutes a grave threat to continental unity. . . .
>
> The present policy of the Argentine regime appears to be to ask all of the benefits of the American family of nations but at the same time to assist the Axis enemies of the American nations wherever advantageous. It is inconceivable to the United States, millions of whose men are now offering their lives in a crucial and titanic battle for the safety of the Hemisphere and of civilization, that the Argentine regime should be recognized unless by its acts it demonstrates a complete and basic change in policy and definite and sincere commitment to the United Nations cause. . . .
>
> It is the firm opinion of this Government that under the conditions described there should be no thought of recognizing the present regime in Argentina and thus strengthening it and encouraging it in its present course.[32]

In authorizing Armour to talk with foreign minister Orlando Lorenzo Peluffo, Hull emphasized the considerations in this telegram. In his report on the talk Armour noted that Peluffo said that the government "intended to fully implement the break but they must do it in their own way and with no evidence of foreign pressure." Once recognition was accorded "they would do everything we wished, in fully and loyally implementing the break in relations, and cooperating wholeheartedly in continental security measures." According to Armour, Peluffo could not understand the U.S. position on nonrecognition: "Frankly, many of his colleagues in the Government felt that our real aim had been to attempt to overthrow the Government by giving comfort and assistance to those opposed to it." Armour's response was that the United States had no desire "to interfere in their internal affairs. . . . The idea that we were trying to overthrow their Government was of course ridiculous. All that we desired were acts to convince us that his Government was determined to orient its foreign policy in the direction of collaboration with the other American republics in continental defense and security." The U.S. public would not understand a change in policy "without clear evidence in the form of acts. . . . The point at issue, it seemed to me, was evident: he maintained that recognition must come first, and that the acts would follow, while our point of view was that these acts, or certain of them, should be taken prior to a change in our position." The acts in question were internment of Axis diplomats, control of the main Nazi business firms, and liquidation of pro-Axis propaganda media, among others.[33]

Armour agreed to meet again, this time with Perón, Peluffo, and others, on June 3. At his second talk, however, the same deadlock occurred: "They could not appear to act under pressure, while on our side as I had explained we could not even if we wished justify recognition without certain acts having previously been taken. At this Peluffo interposed to suggest we leave matters to 'our great ally Providence' to decide" (ibid.: 276–277).[34]

In a later telegram, not printed in *Foreign Relations of the United States*, Armour stated that he had replied to a suggestion that it was the United States' real aim to "bring about downfall of Farrell regime," that the United States in signing the Buenos Aires protocol on nonintervention in 1936 "merely confirmed policy we were already following and that we made it a point scrupulously to observe our commitments. When I added no pressure had been brought to bear to secure the break in relations, Perón remarked this was not story told by [foreign minister] Gilbert who had justified decision on threat presented by presence Admiral Ingram and our ships in Montevideo and possibility of bombers to follow. To protect Gilbert, I shifted conversation to other matters."[35]

Gallop thought that the United States was making two mistakes in dealing with Argentina: "(1) they are endeavouring to alter the composition of the Argentine Government, instead of making the best of an admittedly bad business. The cards they hold are sufficient for the second course, not for the first. (2) They are using the recognition weapon as a test not of the legality of the regime, its only proper function, but of the political desirability of its members."[36] A third mistake, pointed out by Kelly in connection with the elaborate arrangements Argentina made to send the body of the Brazilian ambassador, José de Paula Rodrigues Alves, to Rio de Janeiro on an Argentine warship, was "the essential illogicality of maintaining ambassadors indefinitely in a country with whose Government they have no relations."[37] Halifax, looking back, said that "those in the State Department thus defeated have therefore returned to their tents; leaving the field to the 'tough boys', in the confident belief that these will fail."[38]

However, Halifax reported Duggan as preparing a memorandum formally presenting his views on "a more conciliatory policy." "Again in strictest confidence Duggan urged that I [Halifax] should take an early opportunity of speaking personally and frankly to Mr. Hull; who is evidently not amenable to pressure by his own Department unless it coincides with his own views." [Marginal comment: "Why not?: What else is Ambassador for? A.E. (Anthony Eden)."] Halifax was authorized to approach Hull and indicate a concern about "the Argentine deadlock." To eject the government "by force is clearly out of the question. So are economic sanctions which would have to be 100% to do the trick, might not succeed even then and are in any case completely ruled out by renewed conclusions of Combined Boards and Combined Chiefs of Staff."[39]

At this critical moment, Perón made a speech to Argentine army officers in which he said that war was an inevitable social phenomenon, that the only way to secure peace was to prepare for war, and that preparation for war must be total. The Department of State seized on the speech, which sounded like some of Hitler's speeches before 1939, as evidence that Argentina was planning attacks on its neighbors. British comment was calmer, however, and Scott wrote, "I confess that the speech does not disturb me much, for I cannot believe that the Argentine people are of a temper to put its precepts into action and I should say that they had considerable resources of passive obstructionism in them." R. Henderson commented that "whether or not the text of this lecture has been mutilated in the State Department for the personal benefit of Mr. Hull, it is little wonder that he has reacted violently to it." Gallop noted that "Colonel Perón's principal complaint against the State Department was that they had twisted his references to the economic development and expansion of Argentina into professions of territorial expansion. There is nothing in the speech to justify this last interpretation. The speech, however, is quite bad enough as it stands."[40]

By June 20, Hull had made up his mind. According to Spaeth, "the whole question had been precipitated in Hull's mind by the receipt of two despatches from Armour." These had indicated that different Latin American countries were following different policies toward Argentina, and that Perón and Peluffo had said that they would not implement the break in relations until after their government was recognized. Hull thought, therefore,

> that it was useless to try to come to terms with a Government in which the control lay in the hands of those who wished to institute a full blown Fascist dictatorship. As a consequence he had consulted the President who was in complete agreement. He had made it clear to subordinate officials such as Duggan and Spaeth that his decision was irrevocable. The hole in the corner diplomacy of seeing individual members of the Government on the side had been both fruitless and undignified, and he was determined to put an end to it.[41]

On June 22, Armour was instructed to leave Buenos Aires, and Hull sent a circular telegram to U.S. diplomats in the American republics except Argentina, Bolivia, and Chile setting forth the U.S. position. After reviewing the obligations of the American nations, the telegram noted that following 1942 the Argentine government had followed "a separate and divergent course. By persisting in that course the government of Argentina has not only given aid and comfort to the declared enemies of all of the other Republics, but has seriously undermined the entire structure of Hemisphere solidarity. This is the fundamental issue on which the entire question of recognition of the Farrell government rests." Argentina had thus "jeopardized the security of the Hemisphere and destroyed the unity of the Americas at a crucial moment of their history." The ordinary rules for recognition of a regime in time of peace do not apply in war, and "any pretense that . . . collective action by the family of American nations constitutes intervention is without foundation and disregards completely the basis upon which all of the non-recognizing governments have predicated their action, to wit: the common defense and security of the continent" (ibid.: 315, 320).[42]

Armour did not return to Buenos Aires, and recognition was withheld until April 1945. Hull requested of Halifax that Kelly be withdrawn from Buenos Aires, since the Argentines were "(1) out to break South American solidarity which was very important both now and after the war and (2) holding on to their German connexions and sympathies." Hull also said that "political cut-throats (a clear reference to Sumner Welles' efforts to discredit his policy) would not (repeat not) deter" him.[43]

An insight into attitudes within the State Department at this critical time is provided by a telegram from Halifax:

> Duggan who as you know has all along championed modera-
> tion, told the Counsellor [Hadow] privately and in strictest confi-
> dence that he was greatly perturbed as to whither Mr. Hull's pol-
> icy towards Argentina would lead the United States.
>
> Mr. Hull's hatred of Argentina was becoming an obsession; he
> would listen to no advice from his Department contrary to his
> preconceived views; and had just lectured representatives of Latin
> America in Washington individually about Argentina in a man-
> ner highly distasteful to Latin sensibilities.
>
> Duggan felt he could no longer loyally implement a policy that
> *harked* back incessantly upon hemisphere security, in which
> Latin America no longer took interest and which was not in line
> with the President's good neighbour policy.
>
> He himself had tried therefore to substitute a more realist and
> *forward* looking solution of the Argentine problem, based upon
> the common economic interests of this hemisphere after the
> war. But he had failed and was shortly resigning rather than be a
> party to Mr. Hull's "frantic bull-dozing" and ineffectual pin-
> pricking.
>
> Duggan is of course a Sumner Welles man and has suffered of
> late for attacks his mentor has made upon Mr. Hull's policy. . . .
> But second in charge of his department Bonsal is also leaving for
> Spain and head of Brazilian Department Walmsley another fear-
> less moderate who opposed "toughness" is being sent to Por-
> tugal. Latin American Division is therefore now staffed by juniors
> with neither power nor influence to curb Mr. Hull.
>
> This was evidently Duggan's motive for saying with evident
> conviction that "Great Britain alone could now render United
> States a valuable service by refusing to be rushed into a critical
> decision."
>
> On the other hand this conversation reveals Duggan's fear that
> Mr. Hull has taken the bit between his teeth and will not be
> denied; though Duggan took manifest comfort in the fact that
> Mr. Hull had not ranted or been violent with me, as proof that he
> may think twice before going ahead without us.

In an FO Minute Scott wrote that "it would be salutary if someone in our Embassy were to explode to Mr. Hull and tell him that in not consulting us beforehand he has treated us quite monstruously [*sic*], that his policy is imbecile; that British interests in the Argentine are infinitely more important than American ones and that we decline to follow him in any measures which, in our view, might be liable to hamper the war effort or prejudice our interests. That would be the way to clear the air and let him see that other people besides himself can feel strongly about questions—and perhaps make him watch his step." In a comment on this Sir Alexander Cadogan, the permanent undersecretary, said: "That would be a great relief. Though I don't know how it would work with Mr. Hull in his present mood. Anyhow, I hope we shall refuse to be rushed, and that Sir D. Scott's point may at the appropriate moment be put forth firmly to Mr. Hull, though perhaps not explosively."[44]

Eden's disinclination to recall Kelly was overcome by Roosevelt's direct appeal to Churchill to the effect that the "collective effect" of the action of the American republics "will be seriously prejudiced if Kelly stays on in Buenos Aires." Churchill replied on July 1 that Kelly was being recalled, although he said that "I do not myself see where this policy is leading to nor what we expect to get out of the Argentines by this method. I only hope it will not adversely affect our vital interests and our war effort. I hope you will not mind my saying, as is my duty, that we ourselves were placed in an invidious position by this American decision, to which we are now asked to conform, being taken without consultation with us. We were faced with a fait accompli."[45]

The appeal in Hull's telegram of June 22, in addition to his talks with Latin American ambassadors in Washington, brought about a nearly unanimous withdrawal of ambassadors, although chargés and the U.S. air mission remained in Buenos Aires. "It is quite clear that whatever the Latin American Governments say, Mr. Hull intends to go his own way. He wants them to be a bunch of 'Yes-men.'"[46]

Hull's next-to-last "no-man" in the Department of State was Laurence Duggan, who left a memorandum dated June 24 and entitled "Argentina," apparently as a matter of record to express his views, rather than as an instrument intended to influence the policy set forth in Hull's telegram of two days earlier. This memorandum is only partially reproduced in *Foreign Relations of the United States*, and certain elements not printed there justify reproduction here. Duggan suggested "that in considering hemisphere-security problems greater weight has been given to the Fascist trappings of the present regime than to the cold realities of Argentina's danger to the war effort." Argentina was experiencing "a severe case of *nation-*

alism," which meant a widely felt sense of failure to "realize its special destiny in South America."

> Argentine reasoning runs this way: The United States and Argentina are the two most progressive and developed countries among the American Republics. Each in his own area should assume leadership. But the United States is not satisfied with ruling the roost in North America. It wants to boss the whole show. Brazil is the United States stooge in South America. The Good-Neighbor Policy and continental solidarity are nothing but crafty policies of the United States for the exercise of hegemony over the entire continent. We Argentines must oppose this because it is cutting in on our sphere of influence. (Part 2)

This sense of frustration had "led to a fantastic sensitivity to any suggestion of United States pressure—a sensitivity particularly acute among the military." Ramírez and Gilbert were thrown out not because of objections to the break in relations with the Axis "but simply because the colonels believed that Ramírez and Gilbert had bowed to United States pressure."

Continuing, Duggan said that there was a strong trend toward democracy in Argentine life, but the military regime was currently "holding its own by waving the banner of outside interference with Argentine sovereignty—in other words, nonrecognition. . . . The termination of nonrecognition would mark the turning point in the fortunes of the present military clique." There would not be an immediate shift in power, but there would be a gradual return to democratic institutions. However, a development in the direction of fascism was possible, especially since Perón's recent speeches had "the ring of those of Mussolini." However, Duggan doubted that this line would be chosen "unless our own attitudes make it inevitable."

Latin American governments were expressing doubts as to the wisdom of U.S. policy toward Argentina for several reasons. First none of them believed that Argentina represented the alleged menace to the war effort: "In that, they [the Latin American governments] may have shown more sense than we." Further, "They think we fail to distinguish between matters of proper concern to us because of hemisphere-security considerations and those we just do not like about the regime itself" (part 3). Again, "They think that we do not know how to deal with Argentines. They think the best course would have been to have left Argentina strictly alone after the Rio conference instead of prodding and pricking her"; and "they think they detect in all the talk about economic sanctions a return by Uncle Sam to the Big Stick" (part 4).

Duggan took the view that "our relationships with the other American republics are in an extremely *precarious* condition because of the Argentine situation. . . . *We are in danger of losing the high favor we have enjoyed at a time when we need it more than ever*" (end of part 4: original emphasis).

Duggan then noted the background of the policy of the past decade: "The other American republics came to see that Uncle Sam was not going to bash them over the head when he became annoyed or when he wanted something they were not prepared to give. They respected our restraint when we were provoked by those who sought to take advantage of the Good-Neighbor Policy" (part 5).

> Much of the present restlessness arises from our failure to take any steps—even to make a gesture towards seeking the views of the other countries regarding postwar political problems. As a consequence, they are deeply hurt. They interpret our continuous talk of responsibility by the four major powers as an indication that we don't care what they think. Unless *immediate* steps are taken, this feeling will deepen into a real distrust, which in turn may be capitalized upon by some other great power." (Part 6)

The impasse with Argentina could be solved "by holding *immediately* a meeting of Foreign Ministers," to deal with the Argentine question but also to improve the chances of success of the United States postwar plans. "The convocation of such a meeting is the type of bold, imaginative step necessary to break the Argentine impasse. It would definitely appeal to all the other governments. Its chances of successfully solving the Argentine problem are believed infinitely greater than any other course yet suggested" (part 7).[47]

Comparing the Duggan and Hull communications, one is immediately struck by the fact that Duggan referred time and again to "the Good Neighbor policy" (four times) and to "the Good Neighbors" (three times). Duggan stated, for example, "A decade of the Good-Neighbor Policy has produced remarkable confidence by the other American republics in the United States. Indeed, our history has no parallel for the present situation." In contrast, in the whole of the Hull message, there is not a single mention of the Good Neighbor policy, although "intervention," the "security of the hemisphere," and "the unity of the Americas" are referred to. It appears that Hull and his associates did not wish to mention the Good Neighbor policy in order to avoid giving any opportunity to critics of the message to argue that, in refusing to recognize Argentina or to accept any mediation by other American republics such as was suggested by Paraguay, or to convoke a meeting of foreign ministers, the United States might be effectively accused of violating that policy's principles.

This was a time of reassessing the policy of the Good Neighbor both within and without the State Department. Welles in his newspaper columns continued to urge the recognition of the Arentine regime, and Hadow wrote to Gallop that there should have been a meeting of the American states just after the Bolivian revolution. The United States had not maintained the political unity of the Americas; it had not consulted the American states on the shape of a future peace; and it had failed to reach understandings with them on economic arrangements. The State Department's policy "has been generally static or retrograde. What is equally damaging, it has demonstrated a lack of any comprehension of, or allowance for, the psychology and susceptibilities of our neighbours." Without a "return to the practice of the enlightened principles of the 'good-neighbour policy' as it was originally carried out, the deterioration in inter-American relations which has already set in cannot be arrested."[48]

Hadow expressed regret at Duggan's leaving: "But we must, I fear, count Duggan out soon, as he feels he has shot his bolt and does not like what he fears will happen owing to the apparent impossibility of moving Hull from his pre-conceived plan for dealing with Argentina by masterly inactivity. Duggan will be a great loss to the cause of sensible long-distance planning and moderation."[49] Similar views were expressed about Bonsal, who had reported from Santiago on May 19 that the Argentine regime was becoming stronger, rather than weaker, and that nonrecognition had "not strengthened the democratic elements in Argentina. . . . There is reason to believe that if we had had relations with Argentina since March 4, we could have achieved a certain amount of progress in the direction of securing the adoption of anti-Axis measures." According to him, "Unless we feel that the situation warrants the adoption of economic sanctions, we should immediately devote ourselves to the finding of a face saving formula in which all of the Republics which have followed our line in this matter can cooperate. . . . No one can be more concerned than I am at the present dominance of undemocratic and anti-democratic elements in Argentina. I am convinced, however, that nonrecognition is no more a corrective or even a helpful influence in this case than it would be if applied to the case of other Republics where democracy is currently in abeyance."[50]

The expression of such views, however, could make no progress against Hull's state of mind. According to the secretary of state, "There were those who had been advocating the recognition of Argentina, but . . . such a doctrine was 1000% [*sic*] false, especially when it was preached to the Allied nations which have been betrayed by Argentina." Hull here referred to "the two horrible steps" taken by Argentina: "the desertion of the Allied cause and the lending of important support to the Axis powers and, secondly, the infliction through desertion, of the deadliest blow against the whole Pan American policy of unity and joint resistance against the Axis forces."[51] Hull's views no doubt intensified upon hearing of the following remark Armour made in talking with the Chilean foreign minister: "In the celebration of the holiday on June 4 the stage settings, such as the throne with the condor above it and banners, reminded one exactly of the old Nazi days in Nürnberg or Mussolini and the Fascist party in Rome."[52]

In London, following Kelly's withdrawal, Eden wrote that "the trouble is that so far as we can tell, Mr. Hull would only regard the situation as 'cleared up' if the Argentines surrendered unconditionally and no Argentine Government which showed signs of doing this could survive a moment. . . . I am afraid that Mr. Hull may now attempt to take too exacting a line, thus making further concessions by the Argentines impossible. There is also a danger of the American press saying things which will make it difficult for the Argentine Government to adopt a reasonable attitude without loss of face."[53]

Hadow in one of his frequent accounts of the situation inside the Department of State, accounts that are not matched by any of the documentation from the department itself, describes it as one in which

nerves are on edge on both sides; and, with Hull in a sustained and cold fury against the Argentine Government which both Stettinius and Berle back up in their talks to us, I am uneasy at the possibility of sudden action, with its usual corollary of a request that HMG shall forthwith follow suit. From Duggan— more frank than the others since he is defeated and leaving—I learnt only yesterday that HULL's attitude is now to "hang Argentina on a high moral hook"; try to rope the Latin American nations into first Coventry and then Sanctions undefined; and trust to luck that "something will turn up" that will give him a chance of "knocking out this gang." That is apparently what HULL outlined at the Departmental conference this week.

Hadow concluded by saying that Hull "remains tough and determined; and he is a confirmed Kentucky Feudist!" (Hull was actually
born in Tennessee, although not far from the Kentucky border.)[54]

At this time, John M. Cabot, chief of the Division of Caribbean
and Central American Affairs, talked with Blake-Tyler "rather gloom-
ily of the future of the 'Good Neighbour policy'":

> He said that at its inception the "Good Neighbour" policy had
> degenerated into a race between various American Government
> Agencies (and particularly the Rockefeller Office [CIAA]) to see
> which could spend the most money to acquire the maximum
> amount of good-will in the various countries in this hemisphere.
> This rake's progress had been slowed down now for about a year
> and at the present time was going on at a more reasonable and
> reasoned rate. The result had been the creation of a resentment
> which in some cases amounted to more than the temporary pur-
> chased good-will. But the boot was now on the other leg. Ameri-
> cans were disgusted with the ingratitude which Latin American
> countries were showing and it would only take one more situa-
> tion like that existing in Argentina today, in Cabot's opinion, to
> bring about a severe reversal of opinion here. The result might
> well be a positive antagonism towards Latin America rather than
> a courting of her friendship.
> Cabot said that many people in the Department had been
> pointing out these dangers for some time but the avalanche of
> expenditures and the confusion of rival agencies had been such
> that the policy had to run its inevitable course. . . .
> Cabot thought that the future "Good Neighbour" policy would
> be what we have reported in the past as being likely, namely, a
> sensible and balanced outlook, where it was realised that there
> were great common interests between this country and her
> neighbours and that it was to this country's advantage that her
> neighbours should be both prosperous and peaceful. He did not
> look for a revival of "dollar diplomacy" nor of intervention in
> any other form. Indeed he thought that unless a condition ex-
> isted which was definitely dangerous and inimical to this coun-
> try, such as those which persist in Argentina, the United States
> would view with complete detachment the evolutions and revo-
> lutions which were bound to take place as Latin America emerged
> from the chrysalis of colonial states run for the benefit of very
> few to social conditions more comparable with the rest of the
> world.[55]

Uruguay, in response to Hull's memorandum of June 22, was concerned about an Argentine response, perhaps a reprisal, and on July 12, was given assurance of military assistance:

> Caffery reports that Vargas and Aranha are in agreement with our statement of the need for assurances of military support to Uruguay in event of Argentine aggression. You [U.S. ambassador William Dawson] are accordingly authorized to inform the President and the Foreign Minister in strict confidence that in the event of attack we are prepared to extend the necessary military and naval assistance. You may, in your discretion, also state that we have consulted the Brazilian Government and have been assured of its cooperation. We are likewise prepared to extend all necessary economic assistance in the event of Argentine reprisals and you may so inform the President and Foreign Minister.[56]

On his way to London, Kelly called on Hull and said that the Farrell regime should be presented "with specific conditions, strict compliance with which might be calculated to bring recognition." Hull, however, replied that Farrell and his government "must know what was expected of them." Kelly wondered whether the United States meant that it would not "recognize the present Argentine regime under any circumstances." Could the United States hold the Latin Americans in such a case, particularly since there did not appear to be in Argentina "any opposition sufficiently strong to throw out the present regime." Hull refused to predict whether he could hold the Latin American states, but said the issue was an "immediate threat to the whole continental unity and the prosecution of the war today." He was not asking Britain to do anything "that might jeopardize their sources of supply in Argentina"; rather, it should

> approach this whole question from the larger aspect and base their position on these larger principles rather than on whether or not the Argentine Government had, or would be willing, to comply with this or that point. The fact was that the line-up of the Argentine Government as at present constituted and the whole atmosphere down there was definitely bad, was a menace to the Allied cause, and he felt the only way to handle it and perhaps to bring them to their senses would be for all the nations to continue in their present policy of non-recognition.[57]

Gallop thought this was a discouraging interview, which revealed the sterility of the department's Argentine policy. "Mr. Hull is pursuing his vendetta with Argentina with the unreasoning zest of a Kentucky mountaineer. He seems to be incapable of articulated thought or of relating his objectives to the means at his disposal. Like Hitler, he prefers talking to listening and nothing that Sir D. Kelly said seems to have 'registered' with him." Eden commented: "Mr. Hull at his most purblind, and he was able to get away with too much."[58]

The next day, Hull apologized to Campbell for "a 'stump oration'" in Kelly's presence:

> The issue was that Argentina was a deserter. The war was what he was thinking of, and it was essential that Argentina should not be allowed by her intrigues, etc., to break up the solid position the United States Government had tried to build in this hemisphere behind themselves and us. . . . The policy of appeasement advocated by Welles and others would at once be taken by the other Latin American countries as a sign that the United States Government and we were not in earnest over the principles at stake and as the signal for starting to disintegrate hemisphere solidarity. We must stick to our principle in spite of the campaign of pole-cats [marginal comment: "i.e., Sumner Welles."], since the Latin American countries might otherwise assume that what the latter advocated was the real policy of the United States Government and His Majesty's Government and act accordingly. In fact it was because they were on the point of doing so that he had taken the rapid decision to withdraw the United States Ambassador without delay.

Hull added that "internal policy was not the affair of the United States, and he would not intervene, but the Argentine Government knew well enough what character evidence of change of heart would have to assume." Gallop commented that Hull had "realized how completely he failed to make out to Sir D. Kelly any sort of case for his Argentine policy in relation to the war effort, and has set out to correct this by his most unconvincing argument. As regards desiderata it is clear that he would only be satisfied by a change of regime but is unwilling to admit this intervention in Argentine internal affairs."[59]

The tension in the department over Argentina was described in another of Hadow's personal, "inside" accounts that concentrated on personalities:

> As for SPAETH he is under such high emotional strain that frankly it is difficult to "talk Turkey" with him on an unemo-

tional basis. He seems to feel so deeply that Argentina is a "traitor" that counter-arguments are met with doubts of one's moral integrity and references to British "counting-house mentality" which, did I not know him for the good fellow he is, would I fear provoke reactions highly undesirable from one who is not always given to smooth-talking! Yet I know that he will not desert his ideals; and he went the length the other day of standing out against HULL about the desirability of publishing yesterday's Sermon. . . .

The result was an insulting reference to his being as bad as other Appeasers; and Spaeth now has his tail between his legs as well as trying to speak with His Master's Voice

In a talk between Hadow and Duggan, who made a "valedictory statement" to Hadow and was "the best friend and the stoutest little fighter for common-sense that I have had to deal with since I came up," Duggan had been thinking of "his last contribution . . . to 'those who have treated me fairly, listened to the American point of view with patience and been prepared to DISCUSS matters from a long-term standpoint of mutual interest.'" He felt that the British would have to pursue discussion with Hull immediately, with firmness, and at a level that would "force Hull to listen to the other side of the case. Hull, he added (as we know) listens to None of his subordinate officials, to no one who does not agree with him on Argentina and only to Press-views of the iniquity and danger of Argentina. He has now adopted a 'High Moral Level' as his best platform for keeping Latin America from 'horse-trading' with Argentina; and refuses either to lay down a Policy, to look before he leaps, or to temper his outbursts with 'sane thinking about tomorrow.'" Duggan said that Hull's arguments in conference were invariably on the order of the following:

a) Latin American countries and Governments can and must be kept in line by forceful persuasion such as the declarations which they are first given and then said to agree with; since they dare not say they disagree.

b) BRITAIN will never, in the last analysis, take a line divergent from that of United States of America over Argentina because of repercussions on other problems over which Britain needs American help for her vital needs.

Therefore, he argues, it is safe to go ahead; and provided he is given the "proofs" of Argentine iniquity at the proper time he can be counted upon not to recant or draw back.

This, said Hadow, may be said to be "an ex parte statement by one who was originally a WELLES man and who is being sent out into the wilderness as such. But I do not think so; and I judge DUGGAN—with his close contact with every Latin American Embassy in this capital and a very long connection despite his 35 years, with Latin America—to be the shrewdest *thinker* about this problem, from a long-term standard, that I have met in the State Department."[60]

Hull, immediately following his statement of July 26, made efforts to obtain supportive statements from Latin American governments and repudiated the idea of a "mediation" by any Latin American government in the United States–Argentine difference (ibid.: 335). Spaeth reported to Hull that "all of the American governments have approved our statement of the basic issues as well as of the supporting facts. We have no reason to believe that any of the governments which have withdrawn their chiefs of mission will authorize their return to Buenos Aires for some time to come." Eleven countries, including Brazil, Peru, Colombia and the Caribbean states "issued public statements in support of our stand," but others were for various reasons reluctant to do so.[61] One reason may have been fear of Argentine action against them. For example, the Argentines quickly indicated their resentment of the Brazilian statement by curtailing shipment of meat to Rio de Janeiro.

In Britain Churchill joined the other heads of state issuing statements on Argentina by saying in the House of Commons on August 2,

> We all feel deep regret and also anxiety as friends of Argentina that in this testing time for nations she has not seen fit to declare herself wholeheartedly, unmistakably and with no reserve or qualification upon the side of freedom and has chosen to dally with the evil, and not only with the evil but with the losing side. I trust that my remarks will be noted, because this is a very serious war. It is not like some small wars in the past where all could be forgotten and forgiven. Nations must be judged by the part they play. Not only belligerents but neutrals will find that their position in the world cannot remain entirely unaffected by the part they have chosen to play in the crisis of the war. (Ibid.: 337–338)[62]

In the meantime, the department continued to endeavor to find support for its policy of nonrecognition of Argentina. Hull asked that Rockefeller's office "continue to hammer the Argentine theme. . . . The idea is that he [Hull] does not want the campaign to die down. We must keep beating the drums."[63]

In mid-August, Halifax recounted a talk with Hull and Cadogan:

> [Hull] regarded the question with all its possibilities for the
> present and the future as almost the greatest question after the
> war with which the United States had to deal. . . . He hoped that
> if the United States and we continue our joint policy of cold-
> shouldering Argentina this would in time, though he did not
> know how, effect a change for the better with a different and bet-
> ter Government. If however, these hopes were denied, he still
> would not bargain for recognition against practical desiderata be-
> cause he would feel that in bargaining he was weakening moral
> principles on which as a rock we could stand. He somehow felt
> that we did not adequately appreciate the gravity of the issues
> involved or the danger of compromising with Satan.

Halifax reported that Hull was occasionally inconsistent but on the
whole stated his position with "moderation and with deep conviction. He claimed that United States opinion was overwhelmingly behind him. Sumner Welles' criticism had fallen flat."[64]

Somewhat along the lines of Duggan's "swan song," Bonsal, shortly
before he left Washington to become public affairs officer in Madrid,
wrote a lengthy memorandum to Armour. From the point of view
"of the relative success of human endeavors," said Bonsal, "continental solidarity must be said substantially to have achieved the
maximum expected of it by its most ardent informed supporters" in
the period since the Rio de Janeiro Conference. However, if the impression "gets abroad in the countries to the south of us—and I believe that it is growing—that we are disposed to crack the whip and
use our strength to get the neighbors in line against their convic-
tions, much of what has been achieved since 1933 will have been destroyed." He noted that in July the department had "issued a very
strong blast at Argentina." He presumed that "we informed the other
Governments of what we planned to do and that we obtained in most
cases their acquiescence. But that is not consultation in the true
inter-American sense." As he and Duggan had proposed in April
1944, he still believed a meeting of foreign ministers was essential to
patch up relations with Argentina:

> Recrimination will produce nothing. If Argentina is a danger to
> her neighbors and hence to the peace and security of the conti-
> nent, if the present Argentine domestic regime is a poisonous
> form of fascism likely to infect the continent and to furnish a
> refuge for the remnants of old world systems of aggression and

world conquest, then surely the matter is one for the consideration of the entire continent. . . .

A continental system held together by the infallibility of the
Department of State on all matters of common interest and by
the economic and political power of the United States is neither
possible nor desirable. The restoration of a truly consultative system at as early a date as possible seems imperative.[65]

This memorandum was written at far too late a date to influence
Hull, but it served to ease Bonsal's conscience and to provide, if only
for the files, a statement of the views that he had been steadily expressing for over a year. His emphasis on the "restoration of a truly
consultative system" is worthy of special note.

A British evaluation of the situation was given at this time in a
thoughtful letter to Gallop from Evelyn Schuckburgh, the chargé in
Buenos Aires. He said that Farrell and associates were "seriously per-
turbed and bewildered" as a result of Hull's memorandum of July 26,
for they had finally realized that "they are up against a very tough
proposition in Mr. Hull . . . none of the other American republics
were going to break away openly, [and] when he has his team well in
hand Hull is capable of extreme actions." Amb. Escobar, on returning from Washington, informed the government that Hull was "absolutely adamant," and that Aranha said that "Brazil was absolutely
firm behind the State Department and prepared to back them to any
extent. This news so greatly impressed Perón and Peluffo that they
arranged for Escobar to go to Campo de Mayo and tell the same story
to the '*leones*' [i.e., highly nationalist army officers]." Escobar did so,
giving rise to great debates among the colonels and junior officers of
the army. Schuckburgh had been urging "gestures of appeasement"
toward the United States, but Argentine officials had always replied
that they must go slow: "We risk our lives if we make any suggestion
that can be interpreted as surrender to the United States." A difficult
situation in Argentina affected foreign policy:

This revolutionary government is very much less sure of its
ground, less united, and less certain as to which elements in the
country it principally relies upon for support, than is generally
supposed. The description of Colonel Perón as "the strong man
of Argentina" is, like most "Time" and "Life" clichés, a dangerous misrepresentation of the facts. He may be the most ambitious and colourful and perhaps the most intelligent of the
revolution leaders but he is very far indeed from being able to
impose his will and can only survive by skillful cavassing for

support inside and outside the army and by a very elastic attitude towards questions of principle. The general opinion at present is that it is most doubtful whether 50% of the army are behind Perón. I would not say that there is any leader in the Argentine at present who can count on the *personal* loyalty of any considerable proportion of the army, in the sense that they would obey his orders regardless of his policy. Every major and every captain has his own views on internal and foreign policy, and the Government has to carry a majority of soldiers with it in almost every step it takes.

Schuckburgh said Farrell and Perón had been "trying to persuade the Campo de Mayo extremists that it is a political necessity, disagreeable perhaps but ineluctable, to make concessions to the United States." However, "no Argentine Government could sell the nation's 'dignity' in return for a recognition to which they consider themselves juridically entitled." "A grudging admission from Washington that they have taken 'an isolated step in the right direction' (as in the case of the exchange of diplomats) would be scarcely less damaging to them than a gloating assertion that 'at last they have seen that Mr. Hull was right all along.'" The chargé thought it would be necessary to "wrap it in some warm and encouraging cover"; the type of cover he had in mind would be "invitations to Argentina to take part in international conferences, or to take a share in international schemes of rehabilitation or relief, especially in Europe. A meeting of American Ministers for Foreign Affairs, with Argentina present, might not be a bad start off, though not in the form suggested by Sumner Welles, with the Argentine Minister for Foreign Affairs in the dock!" This proposal indicates how close the British were at this time to the approach Duggan and Bonsal suggested.[66]

In a press conference on September 7 Hull for the first time publicly used the term "Fascist" as descriptive of the Argentine regime. In his statement of July 25, his strongest term had been "extremist, pro-Axis elements" as descriptive of those who overthrew Gen. Ramírez. Henceforth, Buenos Aires was to be regarded as a "potential source of infection for the rest of the Americas."[67]

The Hull charges of "fascism" suggested in Argentina that the United States had changed its ground, since its "emphasis is no longer on Argentina's interference with war effort but rather on long-term, continental considerations." "When the Argentine Government finally reach the conclusion that they are being asked for unconditional surrender their actions might become more openly hostile towards Pan-American system than at present."[68] In London the view was that Hull's description of the colonels as "fascist . . . does not fit them,"[69] and in Washington, Hadow wrote that Hull was "afraid not so much of 'Fascism' in Latin America as of the PER-SONAL REBUFF he will suffer (with Sumner Welles and others gloating on the side-lines) if he cannot HUMILIATE Argentina."[70]

The "single, basic point" on which Hull stood, "together, as I [Hull] believe, with most of the other American governments,"

is that the present lawless, fascist regime in Argentina is a real menace and danger to this hemisphere and that therefore all the American nations can well afford to say so and to act in concert accordingly. It is to my mind the very height of absurdity to try to coax back into the family of American republics an unprin-cipled government that has adopted fascism and made its coun-try its abiding place, on the theory that by so doing we shall restore purity and decency and integrity to the very doctrines of unity which this fascist regime has done its best to destroy. Un-less we keep pure and undefiled those doctrines and policies of our hemispheric unity and solidarity and the sound principles underlying the great cooperative organization built up during the years before Pearl Harbor, the whole idea of hemispheric coopera-tion will become undermined and discredited and will soon be abandoned by respectable nations. As I have said, and repeat, the danger is manifest and unless we guard against it it will in all probability spread up the continent. (Ibid.: 352–353)[71]

To Halifax Hull showed memoranda indicating "that the British could aid us to the extent necessary without endangering their meat situation." Roosevelt's earlier assurance to Churchill about meat really meant that the British could cooperate fully with the United States "without in the least endangering the meat situation" and that they were in a strong position in a "buyer's market" in securing Argentine meat. "However, it seems that the British officials were far more fearful about the risk" than were the Americans, who based their views on a careful look at the circumstances. Hull reiterated his views on the "Fascist lawless government" in Argentina and said that if the British attitude caused the failure of U.S. policy, the United States would have to state publicly "the full facts as it finds them for the reason that the whole future of Pan Americanism is measurably at stake" (ibid.: 351–352).[72]

In a report of this talk, Halifax said that "Cassandra was very gloomy." He had pointed out to Hull that the hard fact remained that we must get our people fed and they had had 4½ years on short commons. . . . If, as a result of our action, which was by implication in his view beastly tender to Argentines, his Argentine policy failed, public opinion in the United States and South America would certainly wish to know why. Inevitable result would be to show diverse policy between United States Government and ourselves which would be generally damaging; particularly to us, so he appears to think, though he did not say so, rather than to United States Government whose record would be very clean.

Halifax added that there was nothing in the minds of the British government except "the imperative necessity to secure our meat supply," and "the danger on which I had frequently spoken to him [Hull] of defeating our own and his broad purpose in Argentina by continued publicity." Halifax concluded by saying that Hull had spoken "with much emphasis and conviction but our exchanges were quite friendly, though, as always, conducted against a background of baffled virtue and somewhat injured innocence." Hull's frame of mind was described by Butler, who said that the threat of publicity suggested "that Mr. Hull is getting v. anxious as to success of his policy."[73]

This was almost Hull's last effort against Argentina, for he resigned as secretary of state less than two months later. At the end of September, however, he convinced Roosevelt to issue a statement by saying that the president's name had been used in Washington, London, and Argentina "in ways calculated to confuse and injure our foreign policy interests, and during a pivotal period." Hull quoted the head of the United Press as saying that "if the British do not let us down he has little or no doubt that the group of desperados in charge of the Argentine government could be cleaned out within a short time. Up until my last communication with you [Hull], the British were not really beginning to do their best in the matter." Roosevelt referred to the "extraordinary paradox of the growth of Nazi-Fascist influence and the increasing application of Nazi-Fascist methods in a country of this hemisphere, at the very time that those forces of oppression and aggression are drawing ever closer to the hour of final defeat and judgment in Europe and elsewhere in the world." He added that the Argentine government had "repudiated solemn inter-American obligations on the basis of which the nations of this hemisphere developed a system of defense to meet the challenge of Axis aggression." He said he was making this public statement because various sources in the United States and elsewhere were "fabricating and circulating the vicious rumor that our counsels are divided on the course of our policy toward Argentina" (ibid.: 356–357).[74] The president made no reference to the Good Neighbor policy.

Besides forbidding U.S. ships to call at Argentine ports for the purpose of carrying any Argentine exports, the United States in September began prohibiting exports to Argentina, except those regarded as necessary to maintain public health and safety. The United States itself took this action, but it would request that the British and other supplying countries "adopt similar restrictions" (ibid.: 420–422).[75]

This "September program" immediately ran into difficulties. The British objected and refused to accept the export prohibitions. The Brazilian ambassador in Washington told Halifax he would say to Hull that "Brazil had, against its better judgment, loyally followed the United States policy against Argentina; but was getting increasingly restive at United States failure to consult anyone over a problem which was endangering the position of the Brazilian Government because of repercussions upon Brazilian economy."[76]

Questions about the U.S. policy were also raised in the business community. The Department of State warned against making investments in Argentina, since U.S. policy was not related only to the war: "*If that 'fascist' government survives the war, our opposition to it will remain*. We can give no assurances for the future of American investments there."[77] Hull stated that as long as the "military-Fascist group" was "in control of *any* Argentine Government, the Government of the United States will refuse to accredit an ambassador to Buenos Aires and will do everything possible to prevent such government from gaining strength through commercial intercourse with the United States" (ibid.: 361–363).[78] This statement, in addition to Roosevelt's declaration of September 29, had made it clear "to most of the republics that there will have to be a change of government in Argentina before recognition can be considered," and therefore proposals for a mediation between the United States and Argentina, which were rife in the summer of 1944, had been abandoned.[79]

At the end of October, Perowne wrote that "something like a crisis" existed with the United States because of "the state of mind of Mr. Hull, who has persuaded himself that the existing Argentine Government presents a real menace to the security of the United States and to the peace of the Western Hemisphere." Since ambassadors had been withdrawn from Argentina in July, Hull had "continued his implacable vendetta against the Farrell Government" and, more recently, he had, through several notes, made requests for British cooperation in putting pressure on Argentina by making only month-to-month meat purchases, and in other ways.[80]

Two sets of circumstances at this time were responsible for a change and ultimately for the breaking of the impasse with Argentina. The first was Argentina's request for a meeting of foreign ministers to consider its nonrecognition. This request (of October 28) came as a surprise to the Department of State. It was thought to have been the result of suggestions for a meeting of consultation that had been made by Sumner Welles in his recent newspaper columns and, as hinted by the British, of Brazilian advice to the Argentine government. Proposals for a meeting had also been made for the purpose of coordinating planning for the peace by the American republics, especially with regard to the meeting of the great powers at the Dumbarton Oaks Conference. Indications that a favorable view would be taken of the Argentine request were evident in a letter from Rockefeller, soon to be named assistant secretary of state, to Stettinius:

> If we are to preserve the future peace and security of the world, a solution other than force must be found for the type of problem presented by Argentina's present regime. Regardless of whether her present action is sincere, it affords us the opportunity of meeting a major security problem through the process of consultation and joint action in accordance with the principles of the Good Neighbor Policy and the proposals of the Dumbarton Oaks Conference.
>
> If we do not accept this challenge, we will have endangered the very principles upon which the solidarity of this Hemisphere is based.[81]

The second set was Hull's resignation, a week after Roosevelt had been elected for a fourth term, his replacement by Stettinius, and the appointment of Nelson A. Rockefeller as assistant secretary of state for the American republics. Ill health forced Hull's resignation, and he left office before his Argentine policy could be brought to a conclusion. He says in his memoirs: "I believe that, if Britain and the United States had brought common economic, diplomatic, and moral pressure to bear upon the Argentine Government, with the backing of most of the American Republics, we could have induced that Government to cease being an active friend of our active enemies. There was no other way to do it" (1948: 2: 1419).

Breckenridge Long gives a melancholy account of Hull's state of mind just before his resignation:

> The conversation then ranged around the past intrigues against him—Wallace's activities, Welles' White House connections and

activities—the manner in which Hull had been embarrassed—
policy decided without his knowledge from time to time—Morgenthau being taken to Quebec the last time. . . .

It was a sombre conversation. . . . He was tired of intrigue. He
was tired of being by-passed. He was tired of being relied upon
in public and ignored in private. He was tired of fighting battles
which were not appreciated. He was tired of making speeches and
holding press interviews—tired of talking and tired of service. But
he would not take any public step before election. . . . All the elements have been there and little by little the accumulation has
piled up resentment—something of smoldering anger—and the
end of a long career is near at hand—ending not in satisfaction,
as it should, but in bitterness. (Israel 1966: 387–388)

5. Recognition of the Farrell Government

The Changing of the Guard

With new men came new policies. Stettinius, who had a good record as lend-lease administrator, was no expert on foreign relations and was especially at sea when confronted by Latin American issues. His first inclination was to follow Hull's policies, but he was forced by constraints beyond his control to modify them. Rockefeller, who had never been a follower of Hull's policies, found ways to get around them. He confounded his colleagues and ended up by recognizing an Argentine regime that they had said the United States would never recognize. Rockefeller apparently operated orally, leaving little in the way of memoranda of conversation or notes on the theory of policy. At any rate, the period between December 1944 and August 1945 (when he served in the department) is largely barren of documentary evidence as to what he was doing.

Stettinius's early efforts to "out-Hull Hull," as Armour put it privately to Hadow,[1] were evident in a 21 November memorandum to Roosevelt. In this document he made anew the case against "military-fascist" Argentina and asserted that U.S. measures taken during the past five months had "caused a steady deterioration in the position of the Farrell regime." Consequently, that government had taken measures to create "a paper record of compliance" with the agreements of the Rio Conference of 1942; however, it had not taken any action against the "powerful group of Nazi financial and industrial houses" in Argentina. "The Argentine move for a meeting [of the OAS] was a bold and desperate stratagem to obtain recognition. The Farrell government was 'on the ropes' and the move for a Meeting of Ministers was designed to give it a 'breather' and open the way for at least a 'draw.'"

In these circumstances, the department favored holding a conference to consider postwar problems, but it was "unalterably opposed to any attempt to negotiate a 'formula' with the Argentine regime with a view to recognizing it." Still, the department did not wish to oppose a session to discuss the Argentine problem and indicated that it was willing to agree that such a session be held into which it would go "'loaded for bear' with the purpose of obtaining a final, irrevocable condemnation of the present Argentine regime." Stettinius closed the memorandum by saying that, "unless there is a real turnover in Buenos Aires, the Department will do everything possible to maintain the 'quarantine' to the full extent in political relations, and to the maximum extent consistent with the war effort in economic relations." Efforts would continue with the British, since "our most competent observers maintain that if such support were forthcoming and sharply brought home to the Colonels, we could liquidate the problem in no time at all."[2]

This was all vintage Hull, but it soon became musty. As early as December 7, an Associated Press story quoted an anonymous department official as saying that a "softening" in policy toward Argentina was foreseen, "which could not have been made previously without loss of face for Mr. Hull, [but] could be made now that Mr. Stettinius has succeeded him." Rockefeller was said to favor such a change in policy.[3] More important, the whole question of policy toward Argentina was raised by John E. Lockwood, who had come to the department from the CIAA when Rockefeller was appointed assistant secretary of state. In Lockwood's view, the United States should seek two objectives: (1) "to accomplish any results which will facilitate the prosecution of the war. . . ." and (2) "to do everything possible towards the development in Argentina of a democratic regime responsive to the will of the Argentine people, friendly to the United Nations and to inter-American cooperation." Since the United States could not "intervene in the internal affairs of Argentina," the only realistic approach was "to endeavor to obtain as much as we can in the direction of democratic developments in Argentina, plus the maximum of Hemisphere cooperation." Lockwood frankly recognized the difficulties presented by public opinion:

> One of the major dilemmas with regard to Argentina is that the American people have for the most part acquired an impression with regard to Argentina that her injury to the war effort is greater than it probably is, and they underestimate entirely her contribution to the war effort. In addition, they probably believe that Democracy in Argentina is much more practicably obtainable as the result of any action which we can take than it in fact is. As a result, we are in the dilemma that the American people are apt to think that we are resorting to appeasement unless we

take steps which are beyond the realms of the practical and which are apt not only not to achieve our goal but to make the situation worse. This is particularly the case with the liberal and leftist elements. It is much less the case among the conservatives.[4]

Despite the freshness of his views, Lockwood was clearly unaware at this time of the negotiations to have the Argentine question considered at the end of the Mexico City Conference, scheduled for February 1945. Further, he was completely out of touch with other members of the department who were still writing memoranda on Argentina that would serve as the shotgun "loaded for bear" at that planned confrontation.[5]

The department was following two lines of approach to the Argentine situation—the old one of Hull, and the new one of Rockefeller. The division became apparent early in January 1945, when Stettinius gave Roosevelt a memorandum outlining a policy toward Argentina that would involve the "establishment of an interim government as provided for by the constitution," declare war on the Axis, dissolve Axis organizations and jail Axis individuals, terminate the state of siege, call elections, and secure guarantees that Argentine officials would cooperate fully in taking measures against the Axis.[6] Spaeth and Wendelin stated that they had not initialed the memorandum because the Division of River Plate Affairs had not been "informed of the purpose" of it and because it constituted "a departure from the policy hitherto pursued by the Department." Hull, they pointed out, had refused to state conditions for recognition and, "although the Department may now wish to change this approach, we believe that there is a need for careful consideration of the reasons for and against the change." Further, "The proposal that one of the conditions be a termination of the state of siege and prompt action to call elections . . . represents a radical departure from our policy of non-intervention."[7]

To the extent that Stettinius's memorandum might have been the work of Rockefeller, it is not impossible that it was influenced by the latter's knowledge of Perowne's views. The latter on December 8 made a general review of the Argentine–British–United States triangle. He noted that the British had accepted various U.S. initiatives on condition that Argentine exports to the United Kingdom remain "at the level required for the prosecution of the war." He regretted that the publication of Hull's letter to Storni, about which the British were not consulted, rallied "to the side of the extremists many people of moderate and pro–United Nations sentiments, who felt that the dignity of the nation had been intolerably affronted by the terms of the letter (however justified by the facts they might be) and by the fact of its publication." The British had withdrawn their ambassador from Buenos Aires, "but there have also been a number of occasions when we were not consulted; and when public action was taken by you which was bound to affect our position and interests."

Of greater importance to Perowne, however, was the department's interpretation of the Argentine political situation. Britain was not aware of

a threat from a country 7,000 miles away from the shores of Great Britain or the United States, with a largely agricultural population, two-sevenths that of ours and less than one-tenth of yours, whose nationals are, in the main, unwarlike, which is not highly industrialized, whose army is insignificant, and which, without air force or navy to speak of, has little prospect of obtaining either on a serious scale. . . . In our considered view, this Government is nationalistic, and totalitarian-minded; and it is composed largely of men inexperienced in national or international affairs, who have picked up bad ideas ready-made, without properly understanding them, or have been influenced by people with German connexions and interests. But we have never regarded them as specifically pro-German, or as working intentionally in the Axis interests. . . . They have, in our view, only become deliberately pro-German and pro-Axis as a body if they felt that the way in which they were being treated left them no other alternative. We believe too that the power to infect neighbouring countries, anyway since the Bolivian episode, has sensibly diminished—for one thing, owing to the Axis Powers' collapse in Europe—and that it is unlikely to revive, unless indeed the Argentines are enabled to exploit Spanish-American pride on a continental scale.

Finally, Perowne noted that the United States objective was

to stamp out nazism in Argentina, and certainly we would like to get rid of nazism everywhere, but we have never been fully convinced that the means you propose are in fact suitable to achieve this end. . . . In this order of ideas, we should fear that certain kinds of pressure might reinforce the tendencies you are determined to extirpate, not only in Argentina, but throughout the whole of Latin America. Our alleged indifference conceals very

real anxiety on this point. As we see it, we have nothing to gain
from hostility to your country in Latin America; we have had
occasion only to rejoice at the success of the good-neighbour
policy.

As an appendix, Perowne listed a number of personnel changes in
and other activities of the Farrell administration that indicated that
the Campo de Mayo and the Club del Plata had much less influence
than formerly, as the result of pressures from the United Nations and
"the turn of war news against the Campo de Mayo."[8]

That Rockefeller's advent meant a change in policy was made clear
by Hadow, who wrote that he was "evidently and justifiably nervous
lest the 'old hands' such as SPAETH (who is to go in 3 or 4 weeks
[Rockefeller] told me) should 'slip out a copy' to such as Drew Pearson, or 'het up' STETTINIUS before Rockefeller can feel his way and
gradually get going." Hadow foretold "considerably better relations
over ARGENTINA: which problem Rockefeller intends to solve 'on a
business-man's basis' if given the opportunity to do so by 'the theo-
rists and sore-thumbs' as he bluntly called them! For this, he also
said, he MUST have our aid; for otherwise the problem was 'incapable of solution.'"[9]

The Chapultepec Conference

The arrangements with Mexico for the convening of a conference are
adequately covered in *Foreign Relations of the United States* and
need not be recounted here, except to note that the United States
successfully insisted that the Argentine case be considered, if at all,
only at the end of the meeting and that Argentina not be permitted
to particpate in the meeting itself. The department prepared an elaborate set of memoranda for use in making its case against Argentina,
along the lines of the November 21 Stettinius memorandum to
Roosevelt.[10] In view of the known desires of Mexican foreign minister Ezequiel Padilla that the Argentine problem be considered, it was
evidently expected that the memoranda would be utilized, but they
were not. Among the papers is the (unusual) "Memorandum for General [George V.] Strong," a member of the delegation to Mexico City.
The memo is entitled "The Argentine Problem," but the author is
unknown. From the point of view and the style, however, it was almost certainly prepared in the War Department, not in the Department of State. This memorandum stated that, when the United
States announced its nonrecognition of Argentina in July, "that attitude could have been called a policy, but it has proved too weak to

cause a change of government in Buenos Aires and too antagonistic to permit the Argentine to re-enter the community of American Republics. Thus, the ever growing proportions of the schism in the ranks of hemispheric solidarity is now seriously endangering our whole Latin American position and, even more important, jeopardizing our vast plans for the global organization of peace and security and international trade and commerce." This memorandum contrasts sharply with those prepared in the Department of State and could have served as a guide to the line followed by Rockefeller, and then Stettinius, as the conference unfolded.

Three principal tenets had directed Argentine policy: (1) extreme nationalism; (2) "determination to assume and maintain a position of leadership in South America, even at the cost of open competition with the United States; . . . and (3) an orientation toward Europe and unwillingness to take any action in concert with the other American states which could be interpreted as clearly antagonistic to any of the European nations. . . . The very fact that there was, until recently, the mere possibility of a German victory made her determined not to displease the potential controller of her economic life." "Can Argentina be justly charged with active collaboration with the Axis to the detriment of our war effort? Or, does a more objective appraisal of the long detailed history of her policy not show that she has adhered to a program of neutrality in consonance with her historic policy, colored on the one hand by her public's sympathy with the Allied cause, and on the other, with her long standing feeling of rivalry with the United States?"

Noting that "continental solidarity is a splendid phrase" and that "the Administration in Washington was still under the impression that powerful states could be impressed by a ringing denunciation voiced by a Pan American Conference . . . the Argentines understood that words alone would be wasted and that the Germans were fully aware of the hollow nature of the so-called Pan American solidarity." There had been "a continuity in Argentine policy which our own [i.e., U.S.] has lacked." Argentina knew that its most intimate relations were with Europe and it objected to a Pan American grouping because it would

> strengthen the dominant position of the United States over all of Latin America. . . . Because of her close economic ties with Europe and a sense of racial superiority over her neighbours, less white in composition, she objects almost as strongly to the political collaboration of the South American states. In so far as she envisages at all any supernational organization including the

states of the southern continent, it is not in terms of an organization based on the democratic principles of the equality of the member states, but in terms of a hegemony with herself as leader.

The memorandum concluded with a recommendation that Argentina be enabled to reenter the international community:

> Whatever may have been the irritations of the past few years and however justified our annoyance with Argentina, our policy today must serve the interests of the International Organization.
>
> There is much ground for construing the recent note of Argentina as a sincere effort to remedy the situation. Just as, at the end of the last war, she agreed to sell wheat to the Allies and sought to gain a seat at the Peace Conference, so, today, she would move into the zone of the victors. Nevertheless, her active antagonism to the cause of international collaboration at this point might splinter the Oaks of Dumbarton. Her support for the International Organization is therefore desirable and some concessions should be made to gain it.
>
> Thus, while maintaining an ever watchful attitude and continuing wariness of Argentine professions of unselfishness, our own best interests, those of the Western Hemisphere, and the cause of world peace, alike dictate that we should not further contribute to discord. We must, in the hope of demonstrating amity among the Good Neighbors, take all measures consistent with the dignity of the United States, to assist Argentina to regain a proper position in the "stable and authentic order in the American community."[11]

Stettinius, who had accompanied Roosevelt to the Yalta conference and stopped to talk with Vargas in Rio de Janeiro on his way to Mexico City, found "the Argentine situation boiling. The Argentines seem prepared to desert the Axis and join the good neighbors. They have considerable support in their maneuvering but so far we have been able to hold the line. However, I am convinced that we should take decisive action promptly in order to maintain the initiative." He had just reviewed "with the FBI our accounts against Argentina," and he was "now confident that, while a year ago there was substance relative to Axis relationships, of recent date it has been more of an emotional feeling on the part of the American people and within our own government, rather than any substantial evidence that there is actual aid to the enemy. Rear Admiral [Harold C.] Train, who is with me here as Naval Advisor on the Argentine, supports this view." Since Perón would "remain in the Argentine whether we like it or not and elections are forecast within six months in which he will probably be elected president in keeping with the Vargas pattern," Stettinius suggested the following formula to the president:

> The Argentine Government immediately to declare war on Germany and Japan; to announce simultaneously its desire for the formation of an Inter-American Committee on which there would be an Argentine representative as well as a representative of the United States to intensify practical measures of continental defense, including control of subversive activities; Argentina to give public notice of troop dispersions now concentrated adjacent to the Brazilian and Chilean borders to allay the suspicions of their neighbors; Argentina to subscribe to all of the resolutions at the Mexico City Conference. . . .
> After Argentina has met with all these conditions in the final act of the conference the head of each delegation of the American Republics would announce publicly that his government has resumed normal relations with the Argentine Government.[12]

Roosevelt approved this suggestion, but Stettinius cabled again on March 6 that Argentina had rejected the plan proposed on February 22. In view of this,

> There is complete unanimity among all American Republic delegations here that only course now is to pass resolution at end of conference saying that the absence of representation of Argentine people at this conference is deplored but necessary because circumstances regarding Argentine participation in war have not changed and expressing the hope that in the interest of continental unity the Argentine nation may find it possible after this conference adjourns to adhere to and implement the Act of Chapultepec and other acts of this conference as well as qualify for membership in the United Nations. . . . This resolution will be adopted at final plenary session.[13]

Roosevelt approved this "message on the Argentine question," and this became the final form of the action of the conference.[14]

Specifically, the resolution adopted at the conference hoped that Argentina might "put itself in a position to express its conformity with and adherence to the principles and declarations resulting from the Conference of Mexico" and expressed confidence that Argentina

would "cooperate with the other American Nations, identifying itself with the common policy these nations are pursuing, and orient-
ing its own policy so that it may achieve its incorporation into the
United Nations as a signatory to the Joint Declaration entered into
by them."[15]

The *Report* of the U.S. Delegation states that Padilla sent a copy of
the resolution to the Argentine government. Then:

> On March 27 the Government of Argentina announced that it
> accepted the invitation of the Mexico City Conference and would
> adhere to the Final Act. At the same time Argentina declared a
> state of war against the Axis countries and announced that it
> would immediately initiate measures to prevent any activities in-
> terfering with the war effort of the United Nations, or threaten-
> ing the peace and good-will, welfare, and security of the American
> nations. . . . On April 9 it was announced that the other twenty
> American republics, after consultation, had unanimously decided
> to resume diplomatic relations with Argentina. (*Report*, p. 38)

This formal statement of what happened was far from telling the
whole story—a fascinating tale of deviousness that can be only partially understood, since documentation is nearly entirely lacking in
the archives of the Department of State, only some of the relevant
materials are at present available in London, and since it is evident
that efforts have been made to shroud the details in secrecy.

From Mexico City Hadow reported that Perón appeared unwilling
to declare war on Germany:

> The Latin American heads of delegations who discussed the Ar-
> gentine problem with Rockefeller in secret session succeeded in
> persuading him that an "Anglo-Saxon" U.S. Government must
> not continue to give the lead if the necessary solution were to be
> effected in the face of Argentine touchiness and pride. For all the
> above unguents and mollifying recipes, the hard fact remains that
> Argentina has been put to the acid test of declaring war and satis-
> fying those whom she considers her inferiors with regard to her
> moral integrity and house-cleaning. The pill is a bitter one to
> swallow and I am not optimistic of the outcome of all this typi-
> cally Latin American verbiage and manoeuvering [*sic*].[16]

However, R. H. S. Allen noted that "the rather discouraging state of
affairs reported on here has been considerably improved by Mr.
Rockefeller's direct approach to the Argentine Counsellor in Wash-

ington on March 11 . . . and can, we may hope, largely be discounted by this time."[17] Commenting on the Mexico City resolutions, Nevile Montagu Butler wrote that "the outstanding point is that whereas Mr. Cordell Hull was entirely opposed to any dealings with Colonel Perón and his 'Fascist' Government, this enterprising and possibly dangerous Colonel seems to have got away with it. . . . Actually the line taken by the Conference fits in very much with what we have recommended for months past."[18]

Bypassing the Department of State

In February Rockefeller had sent a personal emissary, former Costa Rican ambassador to the United States Rafael Oreamuno to see Perón and try to persuade him to relinquish power to the president of the Supreme Court of Argentina, who would then declare war on the Axis and supervise national elections. During the Chapultepec Conference, however, Rockefeller heard that Perón had refused. The Oreamuno visit indicated that Rockefeller did not trust Edward Reed, the chargé in Buenos Aires, to deal effectively with Perón. Rockefeller, further, did not want any word of this proposal to get to others in the Department of State; with his personal access to Roosevelt, and Stettinius's inattention to Latin America, Rockefeller felt free to indulge in personal diplomacy (Gellman 1979: 200, 207).[19]

On March 11, in his "direct approach" to the Argentine counselor in Washington, Rockefeller made a number of suggestions about what Argentina should do to secure recognition, including declaring war on the Axis. At the same time, he asked the British government to authorize its chargé d'affaires in Buenos Aires, Sir Andrew Noble, to have an interview with Perón to deliver the same suggestions on behalf of the governments of the United States and the United Kingdom. The documentation here is incomplete, but significant. Noble had cabled that members of the Radical party in Argentina were unhappy about Perón's good prospects for achieving recognition: "Their complaint that this could saddle Argentina indefinitely with an unwanted dictatorship reflects their desire that Foreign Powers should remove Perón, an achievement of which the opposition is incapable." On this telegram there is an FO Minute by Perowne: "Perhaps Sir A. Noble will be able to throw more light on Col. Perón's mentality and intentions after the interview we have authorized him to have with the Vice President."[20] As later evidence will prove, the request came from Rockefeller, almost certainly through Hadow, although there is a gap here in the British records, and nothing whatever about this extraordinary *démarche* in the U.S. documents.

On March 14, at a meeting in Blair House, Washington, called "at the insistence of [Pedro Leão] Velloso," Brazil's foreign minister, Rockefeller and Amb. Avra M. Warren met with the heads of a dozen Latin American missions to answer the Argentine government's request for information as to what would·be necessary to gain recognition, since the terms of Resolution 59 did not expressly state the requirements. At the meeting it was decided that recognition would be granted if Argentina declared war on the Axis powers, "expressed conformity with the principles and declarations of the Final Act and complied with such principles and declarations," and signed the Final Act of the Chapultepec Conference. Further, the United States would request that Argentina be invited to sign the Joint Declaration of the United Nations. (*FRUS* 9 [1945]: 373–374).[21] This document, which dropped Rockefeller's condition of February that governing authority in Argentina be given to the Supreme Court, was taken by Rockefeller to Roosevelt, who initialed it on March 16. This was the basis for Noble's talk with Perón.

It is not entirely clear whether the new text was Rockefeller's own, or whether it had been worked out at the meeting with Velloso and others, as no record has been found. It is of interest, however, that the document emerged from a type of consultation—miniconsultation—that Hull had rejected and Spruille Braden, as assistant secretary of state, was to reject. This document emphasized that consultation was a necessary element of the Good Neighbor policy (the rejection of this method was to be a characteristic of the policy of the Eisenhower administration in the case of Guatemala).[22]

Rockefeller's action was strongly criticized later by Charles E. Bohlen, then special assistant to the secretary of state for liaison with the White House. According to Bohlen,

[Roosevelt's] powers of concentration were slipping . . . he was forced to rely more than he would have normally on the good faith and judgment of his advisers. Some persons took advantage of his condition, I am sorry to say. For example, an officer of the American government—I was told it was Nelson A. Rockefeller, then Assistant Secretary of State—put before Roosevelt a memorandum authorizing an invitation to Argentina to be a founding member of the United Nations. This is a nearly forgotten matter now, but it was a direct breach of our agreement at Yalta that only those nations that declared war on Germany could be initial members. Argentina did not qualify. Roosevelt signed the memo without fully realizing its content. (1973: 206–207)

Rockefeller acted swiftly to bring about the recognition of Argentina, through one of the most remarkable maneuvers in the history of U.S. diplomacy, and one that is unique, so far as is known, in inter-American affairs. Sir Andrew Noble talked with Perón, alone, on 20 March 1945:

> In order to avoid any danger of leakage the meeting had been arranged through an intermediary. We proceeded by a devious route to the Vice-President's flat which is in an inconspicuous block in a side street. Marching past the plain-clothes guards who were hanging round the entrance, we went up to the flat, the door of which was opened to us by Colonel Perón's notorious mistress. A few minutes later Colonel Perón, who had been making a political speech, arrived and the others retired to another room. We then had a conversation in Italian, which Colonel Perón speaks fluently, lasting for about an hour and a half.

Noble pointed out that the Argentine government "had a very bad press abroad; they were universally regarded as a pack of dictators who favoured nazism and fascism." At the moment, however, things were taking a turn for the better: "There had been some changes in America, and perhaps a growing realisation that Argentina, whose economic co-operation was essential not only in the western hemisphere but also in the world as a whole, could not be isolated indefinitely. Colonel Perón remarked that 'it is the stomach that is speaking, the world needed Argentina's foodstuffs.'"[23] Noble did not say to Perón that he was "speaking on official instructions or with the sanction of the United States authorities"; he did say to the Foreign Office that he spoke "on lines of Mr. Rockefeller's conversation with Argentine Chargé d'Affaires (Washington telegram No. 1623), except that I added that I thought it would help if the Argentine Government announced a date for holding of an election. As regards 'clamping down upon particular Axis interests,' I suggested that it might not be a bad idea to expel Fritz Mandl, whose presence in Argentina gave rise to much unfavourable propaganda."[24]

The envoy pointed out to Perón that "it was necessary for Argentina to act and to act quickly because there could be no certainty that the favourable situation would last for long." If he [Noble] were running the Argentine government he would (1) accept the Chapultepec Declaration; (2) declare war on the Axis powers; (3) "look around for some striking action to demonstrate that Argentina was doing things and not merely talking," for example, expel Fritz Mandl;

and (4) "it might help if the Argentine Government could announce the date for the holding of elections."

Perón said he thought the first two of these suggestions might be met. "He had to take account of the views of the army, but he did not expect any opposition from them; they would do what they were told"; and civilian nationalists "were not capable of much more than shouting in the streets." He remained vague on Mandl and on a date for elections, nor did he raise the question of recognition, or of an invitation to San Francisco. "I deduce that the reports that he had received from Washington and London (see Washington telegram No. 1623 and your telegram No. 2505 to Washington) had left him with the impression that recognition would follow more or less automatically and that the only difficulty as regards San Francisco would be the question of the resumption of relations with Russia."[25] On this point Noble said that, "speaking entirely personally, I thought that action on lines he had suggested should lead to a settlement of the 'Argentine question.' He remarked at one point that it was necessary to save 'face' all around. So far as Argentina is concerned this is certainly true, as the people here are unbelievably sensitive to any suggestion that they are acting under outside pressure. Some tact may therefore still be necessary in handling the final stages of this question."[26] Noble's impression was that "Perón had decided to accept the Chapultepec declaration and to declare war on the Axis; I hope I have succeeded in riding him off a declaration of war on Japan alone, if he ever seriously contemplated this. But he may not find it quite as easy as he made out to bring into line others whose consent is in practice necessary." It was rumored that no decision was likely for about ten days, since Perón was to take a trip to Bahía Blanca, but the trip was canceled, presumably in response to Noble's requests for rapid action.[27]

Commenting on Noble's telegrams, Henderson minuted, "While Sir A. Noble seems to have handled Colonel Perón excellently, and to have used a degree of firmness most appropriate to the occasion and the man, the interview has not got us a great deal further; but the fault is certainly not Sir A. Noble's." Allen agreed with Henderson that Perón wanted "above all to be accepted as president of Argentina," and that he would not get anywhere so long as the impasse with the United States persisted. "But he has some comprehensible grounds for caution since Argentine leaders are liable to be suddenly eliminated, politically, if not physically, when they appear to obey the dictates of the Northern Colossus." Perowne thought that "we have done what we can" and suggested that "we might approve Sir A. Noble's language and make sure that Mr. Hadow informs Mr. Rockefeller."[28] Hadow did inform Rockefeller, probably orally, for I have found no record.

In full recognition of the extraordinary character of this diplomatic exchange, Perowne noted that Noble's despatch of March 22 should be printed, "but as the *fact* of the interview is unknown to the United States Embassy Buenos Aires, we shd. be careful abt. the distribution. It shd. therefore be printed in a series that the Americans do not see, and conceivably with a warning attached, so that H.M. Missions who have not seen the telegrams may not blurt the whole thing out to their U.S. colleagues!"[29] In comparable efforts to shield themselves, Rockefeller and perhaps Stettinius left no trace in the Department of State archives, nor, apparently, in their personal papers, that they made use of a British diplomat to get their message to Perón, thus entirely bypassing the embassy of the United States, as well as the Department of State.[30]

It may be noted in this connection that Kelly later reported that Perón wanted to explore with Noble "the means of reconciliation with the U.S., as he did with the Counsellor early last year." Kelly was dubious about such exploration. In March 1945, the British "were then in the closest possible understanding as regards Argentine policy with Mr. Stettinius and Mr. Nelson Rockefeller, and it was in express, though secret, agreement with the latter that Sir A. Noble spoke to Colonel Perón about the need of Argentina to go to war with the Axis, etc. This she eventually did, thus gaining recognition and eventual admission to U.N.O. (although this, Sir A. Noble was careful not to promise)." The situation was entirely different now, as opposed to the situation in March 1945, in view of Braden's policies. Further, Perón already had "(as we know, but cannot admit) his own contacts with the U.S. Embassy at B.A. Moreover, exploration of this kind of topic might commit us insensibly to some form of 'intervention' in Argentine politics, which it has been our great success to have avoided up to date." Noble should "refuse to be drawn, and firmly refer Colonel Perón to the U.S. Embassy."[31]

Following a week of frantic activity, Perón prevailed, and on March 27 Argentina accepted the first two of Noble's suggestions (set forth in the meeting of March 14 in Blair House); Mandl was imprisoned and his properties seized the following week. Recognition by all the American republics and Britain followed on April 9; Kelly returned immediately, Spruille Braden was named as ambassador to succeed Armour and arrived in late May.

Perón's task was not an easy one. "The Government and the Army groups controlling policy continue to debate the agonizing question of what to do to achieve Argentina's full reincorporation into the

American family of nations and yet not in the doing be forced into acts that might cast such discredit upon them as to endanger their position." The economic situation, arising from shortages in many fields, was serious; but on the other hand, the government "must avoid any action that might too greatly humble Argentine pride."[32] Berle reported that on the night of March 26, a meeting was held at the Campo de Mayo to organize a revolution. "Perón went to the barracks and personally talked to a group of them after which the opposition subsided."[33]

The closest hint of what went on that I have found in the American documentation is an exchange of letters in which Hadow informed Rockefeller that, "according to a message sent privately by Perón to Noble," Argentina had decided to accept the terms offered. Hadow favored recognition of Argentina and congratulated Rockefeller "on the manner in which you have brought a difficult and delicate problem to this successful conclusion." Rockefeller replied that, "now that our friends to the South actually have taken the final plunge," he wanted to thank Hadow for his help and to say that "the cooperation of your government has meant a great deal to the Department. . . . You have rendered a very real service to both our countries."[34]

Halifax desired to "place on record the genuine tribute paid by Rockefeller to Noble and Shuckburgh for their part in the last minute offensive which, Rockefeller generously recognized, had turned the tide in our favour just before very awkward negotiations might have swept us back almost to the starting point."[35] Noble thought that Rockefeller had been "wise to climb down though his wisdom perhaps boils down to no more than the acceptance of the inevitable. And I wish I could believe that it is the last we shall hear of 'non-recognition'; it has done nothing but harm in Manchuria, Abyssinia and here. . . . If Rockefeller can educate the American public to the idea that recognition does not imply approval and that unpleasant facts do not become any nicer because you shut your eyes to them, he will have done us all a service."[36]

Hadow, in one of his illuminating letters, threw some light on Rockefeller's motives. He sympathized with Noble in having to conceal his doings from chargé Reed:

> Unfortunately, the latter [Reed], and I believe even more either [Edward P.] Maffitt or Sheldon Thomas [FSOs] (I cannot be certain which), have managed to convince Rockefeller and also I believe Stettinius of their "disloyalty" to the policy which Stettinius and

Rockefeller initiated as soon as they took over Latin American
affairs in the State Department.

In this "conspiracy" both Wendelin, late of Buenos Aires and
now in the Latin American Section of the State Department, and
Berle—whom Stettinius had ousted and sent, very much against
his will, to Rio—were also believed to be involved. In short, it
became a fight between the old non-recognition "tough boys" and
those under Rockefeller who saw the need of ending this impossible situation on terms.

Such was Rockefeller's distrust of his own people that he paid
us the signal compliment of trusting us more than Americans
and so used you [Noble] as his Chosen Instrument.

But, throughout, Rockefeller has been insistent upon not letting Reed have anything of what was going on. His main reason, I
fancy, is his fear that if once Berle gets proofs of what Rockefeller
has done and how he has done it he will have no hesitation in
trying to blow both Rockefeller and Stettinius sky high in re-
venge for the "kick upstairs" delivered to him (Berle) while he
was at Mexico.

Noble, in replying said that he would not claim that his "interview with Perón was decisive; probably the most that could be said
would be that it strengthened his hand in following a policy that he
had already decided on. The two points on which it probably helped
most were in getting the Argentine Government to realise the need
for quick action and in riding them off the idea of a declaration of
war on Japan alone." He asked Hadow to ask whether Rockefeller
would at some later time give Reed "some account of what happened,
explaining that the State Department were so anxious to prevent any
premature leakage that they insisted that knowledge of what was happening was confined to the absolute minimum number of people."[37]

Apparently Rockefeller did not tell Reed anything. Rockefeller
was afraid not only of Berle, however, for he undoubtedly wanted to
get Argentine acceptance of his version of the formula of the meeting of March 14 without anyone in the United States knowing what
it was. In this regard, he presumably had taken to heart Lockwood's
"dilemma" that the people of the United States thought Argentina
had harmed the war effort more than it had, and that it would be easy
for the United States to secure democracy there; therefore the U.S.
public was "apt to think that we are resorting to appeasement unless
we take steps which are beyond the realms of the practical."

As previously indicated, Argentina was to have "expressed conformity with the principles and declarations of the Final Act and *complied with such principles and declarations*" before recognition would be accorded. The Argentine note of acceptance of the terms set by the meeting of March 14 stated that "there shall be taken immediately all emergency measures incident to the state of belligerency, as well as those that may be necessary to prevent and repress activities that may endanger the war effort of the United Nations or threaten the peace, welfare or security of the American nations" (ibid.: 371–372).[38] Finally, in its circular note of April 4, the Department of State listed nine steps Argentina had then taken "*in compliance with* the principles and declarations of the Final Act of the Mexico City Conference." These included among others the declaration of war and adherence to the Final Act of Mexico City, blocking of Axis funds, and the taking over of assets of Axis firms. "In the Department's opinion, the evidence given above indicates that Argentina *is taking appropriate steps to fulfill the terms of the Mexico City resolution as interpreted at the meeting held by Foreign Minister Velloso in Blair House.* The Department, therefore, feels that as matters are proceeding in a satisfactory manner, recognition should be extended" (ibid.: 374–375).[39] This completed the formal requirements: Argentina was duly recognized on April 9 by all American states and Great Britain and was subsequently elected, over Russian objections, as an original member of the United Nations.

In substance, the Department of State claimed that the Argentine settlement was in accord with tradition. "Relations with the other American republics are guided by the Good Neighbor Policy. . . . Politically, one of the major aims of the Good Neighbor Policy is the establishment and maintenance of a system of inter-American cooperation. . . . The policy of the United States is to encourage the adoption and implementation by Argentina of policies which will lead to its support of the war effort and cooperation with other members of the Inter-American system."[40]

6. Failure to Oust Perón

Perón is Elected

Whether the list of actions by Argentina indicated that it had "complied with" the resolutions of Chapultepec was subsequently to be debated. Braden was to deplore the Rockefeller-engineered incorporation of Argentina into the United Nations, but it was Hull who was its severest critic: "To me, the hasty recognition of the Farrell regime through the establishment of diplomatic relations, and the admission of that regime to an organization of the very United Nations for whose defeat it had hoped and worked—*compliance with the requirements of the other Republics being still unproved*—was the most colossal injury done to the Pan American movement in all its history" (Hull 1948: 2: 1408; emphasis mine).

As early as the beginning of June 1945, Halifax reported that attacks were being made on the Department of State and Avra Warren "for having so hastily assumed that the Argentine Government had undergone a change of heart."[1] Perowne wrote that "the fact of course is that the S.D. [State Department] did *not* believe in a change of heart in the A.G. [Argentine Government] but had come to understand that a continuation of non-recognition was breaking up Pan Americanism, and endangering Anglo-U.S. cooperation and the rehabilitation of Europe. They therefore resolved on 'recognition' but the needs of saving their faces . . . entailed the necessity for certain action on the part of the A.G. wh. cd. be *represented* as involving a change of heart. To do them justice I don't think they harped much on this story; but the Hull policy made the pretence necessary."

Warren, who had headed a mission to Buenos Aires that included a general and an admiral (which caused the raising of Brazilian eyebrows), was reported as saying that he had found there a real public and official intention in Argentina to carry out the Mexico City resolutions (*New York Times* [21 April 1945]).

Argentina was again in a position to be treated as a good neighbor by all American states, but two developments threatened this status almost immediately after it had regained it. In the first place, Argentina's policy changed. As Wendelin put it:

> It seems quite apparent that Perón and company are playing a double game: on the one hand they will take such action as they may be forced to take in the international field (i.e., "cooperation" with the United States, establishment of relations with Soviet Russia, detention of Nazi agents, "intervention and liquidation" of Nazi firms and other organizations in Argentina, etc.); on the other hand far from moving in the direction of a restoration of constitutional government, the holding of free elections, the lifting of the state of siege, the restoration of freedom of the press, of speech, and of public assembly, and other measures which would *implement the resolutions of Mexico City within Argentina*, the government is already moving within two weeks after its recognition by the United States and the other American republics, to liquidate all opposition and to consolidate its dictatorial control over the country. It is obvious that they are taking at full face value our public declarations to the effect that we are not interested in the internal affairs of Argentina.[2]

To use an expression from the British documents, Wendelin was one of the "tough boys" who had supported Hull's policy, and he was probably quite unhappy that the department was now saying publicly that it was not concerned about internal Argentine politics. However, those politics would probably not have been of great concern to Rockefeller and Stettinius, had not a new man, Spruille Braden, been appointed ambassador in Buenos Aires, and had he not brought with him a new theory of foreign policy, antagonistic to the principles of the Good Neighbor policy.

Braden had been ambassador in Bogotá and Havana, and in the spring of 1945 he sent to the department a despatch, "Policy Re Dictatorships and Disreputable Governments," which was a revision of an earlier memorandum sent in January. Dated April 5, the memorandum was sent by acting secretary Joseph C. Grew on 28 May 1945 to all missions except that in Havana, as "a most interesting discussion of a problem which deserves careful consideration."[3] Braden put the issue in the following prejudicial form: "How does the Good Neighbor Policy bear upon our relations with dictatorships and disreputable governments? Or to put it another way: Can we retain untarnished and unblemished our resolute self respect and the respect of others for us while maintaining at the same time friendly, cooperative relations with such governments? The answer in considerable measure is obvious; we cannot, excepting under special circumstances and within certain limitations." He favored policies of "aloof formality" that excluded loans or military cooperation with such governments.

The ambassadors' responses to Grew's inquiry concerning the memorandum were mixed. Beaulac (Paraguay) doubted that "coolness" had much effect on governments and asked, "What wise man or wise group of men is going to decide which governments are reputable and which are disreputable?"[4] Robert F. Woodward (Guatemala) thought that Braden's suggestions "for wielding an influence in domestic affairs" might well be beyond the power of an ambassador, "unless we frankly abandon the principle of non-intervention."[5] John C. White (Peru) asked how, if the United States refused to supply military equipment, it could "prevent a dictator from obtaining it from Europe or some other place?" Agreeing with Beaulac, he thought it preferable to place "emphasis on upholding individual rights rather than through any prescribed system of government."[6]

Others were in accord with Braden; still others, notably in Argentina and Brazil, did not respond in any way. It is unlikely that Braden saw these responses while ambassador in Buenos Aires, since a report on the matter was not prepared until October 1945.[7] In any case, neither his policy in Buenos Aires nor in Washington until June 1947 indicated that he had been influenced by his critics.

In the spring of 1945 Noble expressed an appreciation of the Argentine political situation:

> The people here are fundamentally materialists; and to a nation of materialists neutrality was not a bad policy; it left Argentina free to shape her policy to suit the course of the war, and meanwhile it did not prevent her from doing profitable business with any country able to send ships to her ports. The main political disadvantage was that the policy was unpopular with the United States, but to the average Argentine this was almost a source of pleasure.
>
> Since the withdrawal of the Ambassadors, foreign affairs have held the limelight and the Government have often been able to rally support by exploiting the one feeling common to almost all Argentines, namely, dislike of the United States and intense resentment at any sign of coercion from Washington. Unless the State Department again play into his hands, Colonel Perón will no longer be able to use this weapon.
>
> The mass of the Argentine people still retain the mentality of

the immigrant, and of the immigrant from a politically backward country, who is shy of mixing himself up in political questions and concerned almost exclusively with making his fortune in the country in which he has settled.[8]

Braden and Perón had a pleasant conversation on June 1, but on July 11, Braden cabled that he thought Britain and the United States together should restrict economic assistance and cut off military aid and that both should follow the recommendations in his despatch no. 9103. This policy should be followed "until such time as Nazi militaristic control of this country has been replaced by a constitutional and cooperating democracy. For us to fail to pursue this course would be to betray our guiding principles" (*FRUS* 9 [1945]: 391–393).[9] With this telegram, Braden played into Perón's hands, as Noble had feared, and "swung back to the old line," as Kelly had predicted even earlier.[10] Braden's continued speeches against the Farrell regime gave rise to questions, even on the part of persons hostile to the government, as to "whether Argentina is to be governed from the Casa Rosada or from the United States Embassy." Kelly said further that he would "be inclined to give a pause to public statements on Argentine affairs. . . . I feel, however, that he [Braden] gets a thrill from each successive sensation produced by his 'open diplomacy.'"[11] Allen noted on this despatch, "Mr. Braden has a tough, bullying temperament and has set himself the task of unseating the Farrell-Perón govt. whatever the consequences"; and Perowne commented, "Mr. Braden's last post was Cuba and he is accustomed to viceregal prerogatives."

The uncertainties of U.S. policy were "primarily due to the violent public criticism aroused in Liberal and Left Wing quarters by their handling of the motion of admission of Argentina to membership of the San Francisco Conference and perhaps to the sense of guilt which this outburst widely engendered."[12] It was Perowne's view that

the "fascism" of Colonel Perón is only a pretext for the present policies of Mr. Braden and his supporters in the State Department; their real aim is to humiliate the one Latin American country which has dared to brave their lightning. If Argentina can effectively be cowed and brought to patent submission, State Department control over the Western Hemisphere (so the State Department imperialists no doubt think) will be established beyond a peradventure. This will contribute at one and the same time to mitigate the possible dangers of Russian and European influence in Latin America, and remove Argentina from what is considered to be our orbit. I think we must wait a few more days before trying to make up our minds what we shd. do.[13]

Five days later Perowne cabled John Balfour of the embassy in Washington to express inquietude "at the attitude and activities of Braden," because he feared that "repetition of last year's unsatisfactory position and atmosphere of uncertainty and strife which Ambassador seems determined to create in Buenos Aires is necessarily inimical to achievement of our short and long range objectives where Argentina is concerned, to say nothing of possible ultimate harm to Anglo–United States relations as well."[14]

In Buenos Aires, John M. Cabot, counselor of embassy, wrote,

It was clear to me that Braden was getting up to his neck in internal Argentine politics, and was enjoying it like the fighter he was. Nelson Rockefeller had also become concerned, because his policy of establishing better relations with Argentina was coming apart at the seams. After receiving a letter on the subject from John Lockwood, Rockefeller's assistant, I expressed my concern to Braden, forcefully pointing out the dangers of getting involved in the country's internal affairs. I was the more impelled to do this because I had been brought up on the doctrine of nonintervention and I could recall various episodes in which intervention had ended disastrously. Braden accepted my comments and seemed to agree with my thought that we should go after the Nazis, and not Perón and the government—but he had his dander up and did not shift course. (Cabot 1979: 23–24)[15]

Kelly also talked with Braden, who said that the United States "had been on wrong lines playing ball with other dictatorships and disreputable governments in Latin America, thus creating the impression that the Argentine Government was singled out for reasons different to those alleged." Braden added that his policy was not "open attack but steady pressure until they had no alternative to handing over to democratic regime." Kelly asked if Braden were sure that support was continuing from Washington, and Braden replied that "he had only accepted Embassy on condition of full backing and secondly, that Mr. Nelson Rockefeller had that morning telephoned him expressing warm approval of his line."[16]

The question of fascism was important because so much of Braden's position depended on fear of it: "Perón as the one outstanding leader now on Argentine scene is embodiment of present Fascist military control (*FRUS* 9 [1945]: 392).[17] That Perón was Fascist however, was pooh-poohed by Kelly: "There is not the faintest sign that Perón has ever tried to build up such a doctrinaire party or to form a bodyguard of party toughs such as put Mussolini or Hitler in power, or that he could do it if he tried." He thought that "a study of Perón's personality" would lead "to the conclusion that he is potentially just another South American dictator ('Caudillo') without the political philosophy of the totalitarian States, without the gift of binding to himself a band of devoted followers, and without the power to convince either the Argentines or anyone else that he has a mission or indeed any aims except to further his own personal ambitions." Although "a crook and a nuisance, he cannot personally be a serious danger."[18]

Braden had "complete support" for his position from the Department of State (ibid.: 404).[19] His appointment as assistant secretary of state was recognition of "his accurate interpretation of the policies of this Government in its relations with the present Government of the Argentine." Secretary of state James Byrnes said it would be Braden's "duty to see that the policies which he has so courageously sponsored in the Argentine are continued with unremitting vigor" (*DSB* [26 August 1945]: 291).

Braden's appointment meant the resignation of Rockefeller, who had done little or nothing to curb his impetuous ambassador in Buenos Aires. As late as August 14, he had told Braden of his "admiration for the outstanding work you have done under difficult circumstances, feeling which the Ambassador professes to share" (*FRUS* 9 [1945]: 404).[20] And on 24 August (the evening before his resignation), Rockefeller made a speech to Boston's Pan American Society in which he said that "all of us admire the way in which Ambassador Braden has represented the United States in Argentina" (*DSB* [26 August 1945]: 285–289). This speech, called by the British Rockefeller's "road to Canossa," was in effect an admission that Argentina had betrayed the confidence given it at the time of the Mexico City Conference and had not fulfilled the commitments undertaken in signing the Final Act of Chapultepec. Rockefeller, undoubtedly influenced by the press's criticism of letting "fascist" Argentina into the United Nations, was "lying low" but "still tenaciously sticking to the essential correctness of his policy—Economics before Ideology."[21]

Rockefeller saw Byrnes on August 23 to discuss the upcoming speech. Byrnes said there was no use talking: "The President is going to accept your resignation." Rockefeller gave Byrnes the speech he would make the following evening. Joe Alex Morris reports that Byrnes said, "Oh, no; because you'll no longer be Assistant Secretary." "'All right, that will free me to make it as a private citizen and to tell the true story.' Byrnes was not happy at this prospect. 'All right,' he said, 'the President won't accept your resignation until after your speech'" (Morris 1960: 230). Rockefeller told Truman that he did not want to resign, but Truman said he would have to back Byrnes. "When telling the story of this White House meeting to friends later, Nelson would end by saying, as if still incredulous, 'He fired me!'" (Collier and Horowitz 1976: 243).

The Foreign Office was unhappily observing Braden's activities, because it could find no alternative to Perón who would keep order and so keep on providing the essential food exports. Hadow wrote that "U.S.A. is in no mood to brook competition on this Continent; and Argentina has obstinately refused to do Poojah. So that the 'Fascist-Menace' cry unconsciously fits into the picture of this '20th Century Empire' and gives the wherewithal 'righteously' to beat down a rival. That, I fear is the real truth; and it makes any presentation of the other side of the picture by us doubly difficult. For the reply is always 'selfish interests' or 'blindness to the Fascist-Menace.'" The issue, to Hadow, was "that bane of old-fashioned Chancelleries," a question of prestige.[22]

Following Braden's departure, Kelly assessed his term as ambassador:

> It has not been possible to give you a real picture of the unprecedented character of Mr. Braden's four months' campaign against the Government to which he was accredited. The whole episode at times resembled a circus with United States Ambassador and the Vice President [Perón] as principal performers; but whatever secret humiliation many Argentines may have felt (and will certainly feel in future) at this unprecedented intervention by a United States Ambassador, it made them realise the moral weakness of a Government which was apparently powerless to react other than by vulgar proclamations such as the leaflets about 'Cowboy Braden'; and a seemingly overwhelming chorus of criticism and abuse and demonstration was thus launched and daily stimulated against the Government before the normal party activities had been restored, or dates fixed for elections, or any leaders had appeared. This premature campaign was direct cause of General Rawson's stupid attempt at revolt which has given Perón the excuse for which he was probably hoping, to restore state of siege. He really had no choice between this and resigning.
>
> For long before Mr. Braden left the country, and especially at

the moment of his leaving, he had become a national hero and temporarily made United States popular in Argentina for the first time in living memory.[23]

Later Kelly wrote,

Mr. Braden's period as United States Ambassador in Buenos Aires from the 19th May until the 23rd September was perhaps the most remarkable diplomatic episode of which I have had personal experience. The analogies which come to mind of British High Commissioners in Egypt or American Ambassadors in Central American States do not offer any real parallel since he was dealing with a wealthy and in most respects self-contained country, with a very strong economic situation, and which had long been well known for the special stress which its governors and public opinion had attached to their independence, with particular reference to the United States.[24]

On the support Washington gave Braden, Stettinius cabled Rockefeller that he had seen Braden's report on Argentina's failure to live up to the Final Act of Chapultepec: "I am terribly disturbed about this whole situation and think we should do something about it immediately." He asked Rockefeller to work up some specific recommendations, but the reply he got was only that "I am following this matter very closely with Spruille Braden and I am very optimistic about the progress which he is making."[25]

Stettinius was disturbed presumably because Argentina's noncompliance brought into question the whole policy that had brought it into the United Nations. It is curious, however, that Rockefeller put his faith in Braden's confrontational tactics, which were so different from the friendly, cooperative impression the Warren visit gave. Rockefeller may have known at this time that Stettinius would be relieved of his duties as secretary of state before June was out (apparently because Truman did not wish to have him where he would be a possible successor to the presidency), so Rockefeller decided he would go along with Braden, whose tenure was more secure. He may, in addition, have been affected by the newspaper stories and editorials that were charging that the Farrell regime was "Fascist."[26] In any case, his support of Braden meant that he was repudiating the policy that he had followed since becoming assistant secretary.

He must have changed his mind again about Braden, since Balfour reported that "Rockefeller and his advisers express great apprehension at Braden's apparent intention to continue his drive against Perón at any cost," and until Byrnes "has confirmed or changed his advisers on Latin America no one dare curb Braden."[27] Braden remained "uncurbed"; indeed, he was promoted because of his policies, having accurately interpreted the policy of the United States, and Rockefeller left office, on record as favoring Braden's line in Argentina.[28]

The question of whether Braden was "intervening" in domestic Argentine politics was appreciated in Washington at a fairly early stage. Rockefeller's attention was drawn to the matter on July 6,[29] and his anxiety about the ambassador's activities was demonstrated by his informing Braden that the department was "reviewing the Argentine situation with a view to reaching a decision about the desirability of consultation with the other American republics looking toward possible inter-American representations to secure from Argentina a standard of performance under inter-American commitments that would be the equal of performance by any other republic." A "strong and well-documented factual presentation of cases" that would satisfy the other republics of Argentine noncompliance with its obligations was needed.[30] Walter Thurston, the ambassador in La Paz, expressed further concern: "There is reason to believe that while it is generally conceded in Latin America that the regime in control of Argentina is disreputable, our forceful policy toward it is arousing a feeling of uneasiness." Thurston continued:

Regardless, therefore, of the success that may be achieved by our policy toward the regime in control of Argentina (which is surmised to be its removal by collapse, overthrow, or elections), and regardless of the applause with which that success would be greeted by the American press and even the Argentine press and public, the policy would appear to be defective in its present unilateral form.

As currently applied, the policy has these disadvantages: 1. It places our Government, and in particular our Ambassador, in the onerous position of engaging in single combat with the Argentine regime. 2. Should it fail we would be made to appear impotent and ridiculous. 3. If it succeeds, we shall have resumed the role of self-appointed policeman of this hemisphere.

He suggested that other states should "share with us the burden of the corrective policy which is required"; the Argentine policy of the United States should be given the "aspect of a joint undertaking." The Peruvian ambassador, also, had recently said that "our policy in

Argentina may alarm other Latin American states who may reason that if we attempt to set Argentine affairs in order we may later attempt to correct other situations of which we disapprove."[31]

On his arrival in Washington, Braden's first action was to persuade acting secretary of state Dean Acheson that the conference to draw up a security treaty, scheduled to convene at Rio de Janeiro on October 20, should be postponed. Acheson and Braden spent the afternoon of September 29 conferring with Cordell Hull, who concurred in their recommendation. "We felt that our own position would be utterly compromised if we should sign a treaty with the Argentine Government before the situation was cleared up or that Government changed. We also felt that to sign such a treaty would greatly weaken the forces in Argentina opposed to the Government." Truman and Byrnes agreed, and the announcement postponing the conference was made on October 3 (*FRUS* 9 [1945]: 159–160).[32]

At Senate hearings on his confirmation, Braden met a good deal of hostility. Chairman Tom Connally (D-Texas) said: "I just do not want to see Mr. Braden as Assistant Secretary with a 'big stick' in each hand waving it around over them down there. I do not think it is in the national interest. I do not think it is in the national welfare. I do not think it is consistent with our obligations and our pledges." Braden replied, "I have never wielded a 'big stick' in all my experience."[33] He was asked by the chairman, "Is it your purpose if you are confirmed, to adhere to the non-intervention policy in internal affairs of Latin American countries . . . ?" Braden responded, "Absolutely, I am fervently in favor of non-intervention and will adhere strictly to that commitment which we have." Again the chairman asked if Braden had consulted with the Department of State about his speeches in Argentina. Braden answered, "I did not submit the drafts of the speeches to them before I made them; no." Connally replied, "I do not think so. I think, if you had you would not have made them."[34] Braden said that if the American republics were agreed on economic sanctions, "that would mean losing the food products of the Argentine for the starving people of Europe. It is something we would have to have British cooperation on, and the British simply say that they cannot cooperate on that, that they have got to have the food." In general, the senators were critical of Braden, and of Acheson, for not having consulted both with them, and with the other American states before asking Brazil to call off the conference.[35] The confirmation was duly voted by the Senate, but Braden found himself limited to other than military or economic sanctions, as Hull had been for the same reasons, but stricter ones, since he had expressly abjured them in his testimony.

Acheson announced that it was the intent of the United States to consult with the other American republics about the Argentine situation. It was the view of the department that "consultation might be best carried out through diplomatic channels."[36] This "consultation" was the first step in the publication of the so-called Blue Book on the Argentine situation, which appeared two weeks before the election in February 1946 and was intended to point out dealings with the Axis by Perón and other Argentine officials.

The United States' request for a meeting of the Governing Board of the Pan American Union on October 5 to deal with the postponement of the Rio Conference was a source of anger for Gustavo Herrera, the Venezuelan foreign minister, who said there was no time for communication. "There is evidently the feeling, at least in Venezuela, that we are inclined to expect the other American Republics to jump to attention quickly when we speak and possibly to ratify our own conclusions, rather than to reach their own decisions after mature deliberation."[37]

The Foreign Office was deeply concerned about the Argentine affair: "Argentina for a number of practical and straightforward reasons is a country in which Britain is keenly interested." The United States had taken steps affecting British interests there without prior consultation, and things might have gone better with such consultation. On August 21 foreign minister Ernest Bevin had asked John G. Winant, U.S. ambassador in London, to tell Byrnes that Bevin hoped that "he would be able to give us a year's stability in Argentina and to leave political considerations aside for the time being." In October he asked Halifax to tell Byrnes that Braden's actions in Buenos Aires and Acheson's statement on postponing the Rio de Janeiro meeting had created turmoil in Argentina. If the Americans should respond that "non-intervention by the democracies" allowed European dictators to gain power, "I can only reply that the best information that reaches me, coming in many cases from persons of distinction and of liberal views in countries neighbouring Argentina, is to the effect that Argentina psychologically requires a cessation of intervention from outside, and that she is in no position to be aggressive."[38]

At this moment, Perón was forced from office by a group of army officers led by Gen. Amaro Avalos. Perón was detained for a week, during which Argentine politicians and the army vainly debated. Finally on October 17, Gen. Avalos presented Farrell with a list of civilian ministers, which Farrell rejected. Kelly reported that "civilian politicians, who last week and probably until October 16th had the ball at their feet, have by arguing, disunity and procrastination, let the chance slip, as I warned them would happen. During the last two days their preference for talk instead of action has given a walk-over to Perón's supporters who a week ago were cowed and bewildered. Admiral Lima, although honest, lacked strength of character and General Avalos was handicapped by division of opinion in the Army." Perón returned on October 18, after labor disturbances, made a speech to a great crowd of mostly workers, and gave up his post in the government and went off to Patagonia for a rest.[39]

Kelly gave a dramatic account of the events of October 17 and 18. As late as October 16, "the Conservative leaders held out for the elimination of General Avalos and the Radicals flatly refused to accept anything less than the transfer of the presidency to the president of the Supreme Court." On October 18, a general strike was called "as part of the campaign to bring Colonel Perón back into power . . . as a demonstration of his command over the workers and, no doubt, as a warning to any who still felt inclined to take action against him." Kelly concluded:

> In various telegrams and despatches I have stressed that the United States Government, in considering their policy towards Argentina, ought first to answer three questions: first, is the Argentine Government under the Farrell-Perón régime a menace to hemisphere defence? Secondly, have the United States the power to overthrow Colonel Perón? Thirdly, could he be replaced by a more satisfactory civilian government? Whether or not the present régime here is a menace to hemisphere security is still a matter of opinion, but the other two questions have been clearly answered by the events of the last few weeks. Despite all the effervescence that Mr. Braden was able to stir up during his brief stay in Buenos Aires, the politicians, the business men and the society leaders to whom he addressed his appeals showed conclusively that they were not ready when the opportunity occurred to act quickly and effectively enough against a man as determined as Colonel Perón. It is true that the general excitement produced by Mr. Braden's campaign created the situation in which the army eventually decided to act; but it is most important to remember that it was the army and not the civilian "Democrats" who turned Colonel Perón out of office. After this had been achieved the interminable arguments and procrastination of the politicians showed clearly that there was nobody among them of sufficient stature to lead the civilians in dealing with an abnormal situation. I have also frequently pointed out that the United States policy of keeping Argentina in a constant state of turmoil plays into the hands of the extremists here,

whose greater resolution always gives them the advantage over the moderates at any time of crisis. This has once again proved to be the case.[40]

Braden told the counselor of the British Embassy that "the Senate opposition . . . left him hamstrung in the task of encouraging resistance to Perón by which alone Argentina could be brought to democratic Government. Economic and military sanctions were both alas impracticable and there remained only moral sanction of collective Pan American denunciation of the Perón Government's misdeeds."[41]

It does not appear that officials in Washington took any measures toward assisting Perón's opponents in coming to a decision. In the face of senatorial resistance, Braden chose to "back down and both his special advisers, Wright and Spaeth, told me [Hadow] categorically, in front of each other, that economic sanctions were 'out,' as were 'pin-pricking' moral sanctions."[42] Balfour assessed the new turn in U.S. policy in a memorandum: "The restrictions which the Senate have apparently imposed upon the State Department are tantamount to an endorsement of the policy of conciliation pursued by Mr. Rockefeller which the liberal and left wing press had recently declared to be defunct. No criticism of this turn of events has however as yet appeared: a proof, if such be needed, of the mercurial nature of policy and public opinion in this country." The department was apparently following two somewhat divergent policy lines:

(a) On the economic side: to placate United States commercial and economic interests. United States trade with Argentina will no longer be restricted or hampered.

(b) In the political field: Braden's advisers will concentrate upon exposing all possible proofs of Perón's connections with Nazi-Fascist leaders in Germany or Italy.

An attached memorandum by Hadow said that Braden had come to Washington determined "to pursue the policy of attrition" he had followed in Buenos Aires:

His departure from Argentina coincided in a remarkable manner with the unsuccessful *coup* of General Rawson; to which some officials in the State Deparment believe him to have been privy. He is also reliably stated to have flirted with a cabal of rebellious Argentine Naval officers who had agreed to show their hand once Rawson's *coup* had brought out the Córdoba garrison against Perón. Behind his "open diplomacy" further lay the extensive back-stair connections between Braden's closest adviser, a Republican Spaniard named Agusto [*sic*] DURAN, and the emigrés of Montevideo; the Socialist Party of Argentina under Americo Ghioldi; and the so-called Communists under Ghioldi's more resolute brother.[43]

Balfour's two points freed most exports to Argentina, but the State Department continued to oppose the sale of armaments. This aroused more difficulty with the British, who were, of course, in a position to supply Argentina in this area. On the exposure of Perón's Nazi connections, which Halifax called "a rod in pickle for Perón," Braden's assistants "made a somewhat piteous appeal to the Counsellor for proofs wherewith to reinforce their disclosures."[44] On this point Perowne noted: "We shall have, on the one hand, to avoid any suspicion that we are not revealing all that we know, and on the other, after the unusual convenient 'leakage' avoid revealing so much that we can be pilloried for having prevented justice being done to people whom we were in a position to know were all that their American critics said they were, and even worse!"

In a speech at Rutgers University, Braden said that, "while the good-neighbor policy governs all our international relations, it is especially associated with our relations with the other American republics where it is a cornerstone, comparable in importance only to that foundation of our policy—the Monroe Doctrine." The American republics "desire democracy. . . . They have realized that they cannot hope to succeed in those particulars unless this hemisphere can be made secure against aggression from both within and without. As a result, the inter-American system has come into being and has functioned with much success" (*DSB* [28 October 1945]: 693–695). A few days later, on 31 October, Sec. Byrnes told the *Herald Tribune* Forum in New York, "We have discovered that understanding and good-will cannot be bought and cannot be forced. They must spring spontaneously from the people. . . . In the Inter-American system the members do not *interfere* in the internal affairs of their neighbors nor do they brook interference in those internal affairs by others." However, "The policy of *non-intervention* in internal affairs does not mean the approval of *local tyranny*. . . . If, therefore, there are developments in any country within the inter-American system which, realistically viewed, threaten *our security*, we consult with other members in an effort to agree upon common policies for our mutual protection" (ibid. [4 November 1945]: 709–711; emphasis mine).

Commenting on this speech, J. D. Murray of the Foreign Office noted that Braden "in identifying himself with the good-neighbour policy and in emphasizing non-intervention (which is now supposed to apply to Argentine as to all the other republics) sounds two notes; and these will be the theme of U.S. 'inter-American' policy, I think, so long as he is its interpreter: (a) 'The peoples (of America) desire democracy'—i.e., liberty, justice, order and self-government. (b) 'This cannot be attained unless the Hemisphere can be made secure against aggression from within and without.'" Murray added,

> Here is the justification for recent U.S. "intervention" in the Argentine—the Argentine "people" welcomed his actions, Mr. Braden can say, so where was the intervention? And it is the security argument that, so far as we know, the Americans intend to use on the other republics—perhaps also on the Argentine voters; hence their desire to obtain evidence linking Perón and his friends with Nazi Germany.
>
> Thus non-intervention is upheld, but the U.S. dislike of Fascism in South America can still be expressed in no uncertain terms in official quarters, when necessary. Of course, it could be remarked cynically that if you satisfy the State Department that you recognize Uncle Sam as boss, and that you are not really a Fascist, but only an old-fashioned paternal dictator in the good old South American tradition (Batista, Trujillo, Vargas), you can get away with it. Perhaps—but there is a genuine desire in the U.S.A. and in the State Department to promote the development of democracy—government by popular consent, not force—in South America . . . so they may be expected to continue the work against dictators and would-be dictators, in so far as they can stretch "non-intervention."[45]

The apparent contradictions here seemed to depend on one's definition of intervention and interference.

> While the policy of non-intervention has been upheld and restated in Washington, Mr. Braden reserves the right to speak his mind about governments of which the U.S. does not approve. . . . One has the impression that though "intervention" is officially ruled out, Mr. Braden will spare no effort to ensure that when the Argentine people go to the polls in the Presidential election, they will be in possession of all the adverse information which the State Department can assemble and in possession also of the knowledge that Perón's election would be unwelcome to the U.S. Government.[46]

Braden's views, when combined with those of Byrnes, which con-
fused interference and intervention and said that neither implied
approval of "local tyranny," allowed enough latitude at least for consultation with other American republics about threats to "internal
affairs" of an American state.

It was therefore no accident that such consultation was proposed
at this point by Eduardo Rodríguez Larreta, the Uruguayan foreign
minister. Pointing out that the "great advance" made by acceptance
of the principle of nonintervention should be affirmed, but "it must,
however, be harmonized with other principles the operation of which
is of fundamental importance for the preservation of international
peace and security." These include (1) "parallelism between peace and
democracy," (2) "peace is indivisible," and (3) the defense of "minimum human liberties within a civilized continent—wherever they
are notoriously and persistently infringed or ignored." Such harmo-
nization was possible: " 'Non-intervention' cannot be converted into
a right to invoke one principle in order to be able to violate all other
principles with impunity" (ibid. [25 November 1945]: 864–866).

Immediately, Sec. Byrnes gave the principles of the Uruguayan
note "unqualified adherence," saying that "violation of the elemen-
tary rights of man by a government of force and the non-fulfillment
of obligations by such a government is a matter of common concern
to all the republics. As such, it justifies collective multilateral action
after full consultation among the republics in accordance with established procedures" (ibid. [2 December 1945]; 892).

A statement by William Dawson, ambassador to Uruguay, that
Rodríguez Larreta's statement should "contain no specific mention
of Argentina although obviously directed against Farrell-Perón regime" (*FRUS* 9 [1945]: 188),[47] emphasized the idea that the appearance of the Uruguayan "doctrine" was related to Braden's campaign
against Argentina.

Through the diplomatic type of consultation then in vogue, however, it was quickly learned that only a very few of the smaller republics accepted the idea so enthusiastically and rapidly endorsed by
Byrnes. The Mexican foreign minister, Francisco Castillo Nájera,
said on 20 December that "the basic attitude of the Mexican Government was that the principle of non-intervention in the internal affairs of other countries had been one of the most precious achievements of inter-American relationships and that it was a principle
which had, at all costs, to be safeguarded and consolidated" (ibid.:
214). The Argentine Foreign Office on 30 November called the doctrine "the proposed intervention policy" and said that "there is no
'good neighbor' policy—the most precious legacy left by President

Roosevelt for the relationship between American peoples—that can resist interferences such as that proposed in the note of the Uruguayan Foreign Minister. Nobody can ignore that as a natural consequence of its power and greatness, the control of the intervention policy would fall upon the United States, thus invalidating the efforts of the great President Roosevelt who with his conduct banished the fears of those who attributed to his country a 'hard-handed' policy" (ibid.: 198–203).

The United States, recognizing the weight of the attack based on the desire of Latin American countries to preserve the nonintervention policy, pointed out that "in view of fact that intervention is popularly held to mean use of force and hence actual entry into the country involved, it is noteworthy that Uruguayan proposal avoided use of phrase collective 'intervention.' Collective 'action' was phrase used in Uruguayan note which avoids connotations associated with 'intervention.' To critics of proposal who will probably continue to speak of intervention, the obvious reply is that machinery for collective action must include both procedural and substantive safeguards against abuse" (ibid.: 204–206).[48]

Such efforts to salvage the proposal were unsuccessful, and though the hope was held for a time that it might be discussed at the forthcoming Rio de Janeiro Conference, disapproval by the other republics was so general that the idea was quietly dropped, nor was it revived at Bogotá, when the Organization of American States was formed. On the contrary, the injunction against intervention in domestic politics of another state was made more explicit than before.

The comments of British officials were critical. Murray wrote that the Rodríguez Larreta doctrine "can be taken as part of Mr. Braden's campaign against the Argentine government in general and Col. Perón in particular. If adopted, the principle might come in useful elsewhere—e.g., Nicaragua, and the Dominican Republic—but I think the other countries will not exactly welcome it and may take refuge in lip-service only."[49] Hadow noted that "an excellently informed American friend—lately of the State Department and now a well placed Consultant on Latin American affairs [Duggan?] tells me that this threat of active intervention in the internal affairs of a Latin American country has so infuriated even the docile Chileans with whom he is dealing that he considers the statement as merely another piece of 'futile bluff.'"[50]

The United States' formal reply proposed that Rodríguez Larreta continue informal discussions, since it was doubtful that a wide enough area of agreement could be established before the Rio de Janeiro Conference was held. The opportunity was taken, noting, however, that the Uruguayan proposal contemplated intervention, to say that "there is no principle of the foreign policy of the Government of the United States that is more firmly established than the doctrine of non-intervention by a state in the internal or external affairs of any other state. It is the cornerstone of the inter-American system. It is vital to the Good Neighbor policy. The Secretary of State would not have expressed adherence to the principles of your note had he not been convinced that you were entirely correct in maintaining that those principles could be reconciled with inter-American agreements against intervention."[51]

At about this time, John M. Cabot, the U.S. chargé in Buenos Aires, evinced some doubt about certain aspects of the Department of State's policy:

> In short, although there is much evidence of the growth of aggressive Fascism in this country, I doubt that it is conclusive. While we assert with the greatest assurance that this Government is fascist, there are many people in other parts of the world who may by no means be convinced of this. More particularly, and this I wish to stress, I do not believe that we can justify avowedly coercive measures, even multilateral, on the basis of the comparatively nebulous proof we now have that Perón is plotting aggression. Unless we are to act on the basis of the available material regarding the Bolivian Revolution, and I see serious objections to such a course, I think we must await clearer proof of contemplated aggression.

Similarly, with respect to Argentine "dalliance" with Nazism, Cabot thought that "if you read the picture of Argentina as described in 1941 and -42 and compare it with the present I think that you must be convinced of the great progress which has been made in suppressing Nazi activities." No case against Argentina appeared for noncompliance with economic warfare measures, nor any case regarding subversive activities under Mexico City resolutions, and Spaeth was said by Braden to feel "that we did not have a good court case" based on documents found in Germany.

In a letter to Ellis O. Briggs in mid-November, Cabot said that "the old families here make New York bankers sound like William Z. Foster [head of the Communist party in the United States]. He warned that the Argentine government was going to "extraordinary lengths to insist upon its intention to give fair elections," and added that the United States could not "afford altogether to eliminate from our calculations the possibility that Perón may win in reasonably fair elections. . . . You may think that all of the above adds up to a plea for appeasement à la Rockefeller." This was not his intention: the point he wanted to make was that "we should not carry our crackdown policy to such extremes that it becomes *contraproducente*." In view of the lack of a satisfactory basis for a crackdown, "I do not see how we can justify the very serious risks that we are running of wrecking the inter-American system and the Good Neighbor Policy which are inherent in any effort to achieve an effective crackdown on Argentina" (ibid.: 426–434).

In a later despatch, Cabot said that it appeared "probable" that Perón would "attain his ambition to be elected President of Argentina," because of his strong labor constituency and because he enjoyed "the covert support of the Catholic hierarchy." In addition, "The wealthy clique in this country, who can only splutter when Perón's name is mentioned, are evidently not willing to contribute substantially to his defeat, even from the money which may well be taken from them if he wins." Just as the United States had "opposed England when in the Napoleonic wars she was fighting the Hitler of her day," and when "twisting the lion's tail was the favorite American political sport," one of the

favorite Argentine political sports is likely to be plucking the eagle's feathers. . . . A social revolution has been started in Argentina. . . . Reform is necessary and inevitable: Our problem, then is to oppose fascism effectively without giving the impression to the Argentine people as a whole that our purpose is to block reform and stifle any show of independence towards us on the part of the Argentine Government. If we do not handle this situation wisely we are likely to aggravate the very situation which we seek to remedy.[52]

These communications, raising serious doubts as to Braden's policy, and echoing those of Thurston in La Paz, seem to have had no effect in Washington; Spaeth continued to make his case against the Nazi connections of Perón and his colleagues that was to be published in the so-called Blue Book on 11 February 1946.[53] Braden continued his anti-Argentine campaign in vigorous fashion, recalling the diatribes of Hull:

The good neighbour policy continues but it would be the grossest perversion to pretend that it requires us to respect Fascism in any of its guises anywhere at any time.
Now a fascist government anywhere is a standing menace to

world peace and therefore to our security. . . . We American Republics, because of our common aspirations, our similar histories
and our geographical propinquity have established ourselves as a
community of neighbors. When a fascist government arises within that community the danger and the evil have an immediacy
that we and the other American Republics cannot possibly afford
for one moment to disregard. This sickness threatens all of us.

Despite some assertions I have heard to the contrary, there is
nothing in the book of diplomatic etiquette that requires us to
embrace the enemies of our way of life.[54]

The British had been asked to make available the results of the
Hellmuth interrogation, which they did, and they cooperated in October 1945 by agreeing not to sell certain categories of arms to Argentina. However, as Perowne wrote, "We do not claim to intervene
directly in inter-American matters, and we have no wish to champion the Argentine Government, even if we do not ourselves consider all the charges which have been leveled against it, and against
Colonel Perón, as 100% proven. But Argentina is a country which is
most important to us, for a variety of perfectly straightforward and
inescapable reasons of which we are not in the least ashamed."
Further,

Argentina is important to us for three reasons: (a) food, (b) mar-
kets, and (c) capital investments, and in order that our interests
under these three heads may be properly safeguarded, it is indis-
pensable that political stability should exist where Argentina is
concerned. This we believe to be ultimately just as much in the
American interests as our own; while it may be admitted that
American pressure on Argentina has not been without some
useful results, they must be as well aware as we are of the restiveness of the other Latin American countries at the policy of
intervention.[55]

The Blue Book, despite its formal title, was the result of what may
be called "distant consultation," since there was no meeting of foreign ministers involved. In October the department proposed such
consultation because of Argentina's failure to fulfill its obligations
under the Mexico City agreements; the other republics approved.
Nothing happened until, two weeks before the Argentine elections
of 24 February 1946, copies of the Blue Book were given to the governments. Braden said that there was no intent to intervene in internal Argentine politics;[56] the Blue Book's only purpose was to show

that Argentina had collaborated with the Nazis to harm the United Nations war effort and that Nazi agents had "combined with Argentine totalitarian groups to create a Nazi-Fascist state."[57] There was no thought that the Blue Book might affect the Argentine elections (*FRUS* 11 [1946]: 6–7).[58] However, the timing of publication was widely interpreted as an effort to defeat Perón's candidacy and therefore to interfere in Argentina's domestic affairs. The fundamental question raised by the evidence in the Blue Book was "whether the military regime, or any Argentine government controlled by the same elements, can merit the confidence and trust which is expressed in a treaty of mutual military assistance among the American republics."[59]

On being asked for his views at a late date, Cabot responded negatively: "To throw 'atomic bomb' directly at Argentine Govt. in present supercharged atmosphere is to court incalculable results. Opinion will be universal that we are trying to influence election results. . . . Under circumstances, I recommend against official release of document at present" (ibid.: 201–202).[60] However, once the Blue Book had appeared, Cabot indicated that his own "reaction was entirely favorable. He stated that he thought a splendid piece of work had been done and that he was glad the memorandum was issued at this time. So far as he has been able to ascertain there is no resentment among democratic elements about the publication of the memorandum" (ibid.: 209–210).[61]

The publication created a sensation throughout the hemisphere. However, the response of most governments, except for the (to be expected) Dominican Republic, Nicaragua, Honduras, and a very few others, were that the department had not made its case that Argentina could not be trusted to make a treaty of mutual assistance. The Ecuadoran ambassador was quoted: "Whatever the outcome of the Argentine elections, Roosevelt's Good Neighbour Policy and the work of the Pan American Union were now a dead letter. . . . Neither Ecuador nor any self-respecting Latin American government would attend an inter-American Conference without Argentina."[62]

The issue, even before Perón's election, was whether a mutual security conference should be held, with or without Argentina. The United States was ready to go to such a meeting and draw up a treaty with the other American republics, but would refuse to complete a treaty if Argentina attended the conference. The other American republics, or most of them, refused to draw up a treaty unless Argentina were present at the conference. The solution was found in postponing the conference, which was not held until August 1947.

By April 1, responses to the Blue Book had been received from fewer than one half of the other republics, and these did not agree. However, on April 8 Byrnes expressed the "fervent hope" that the new Argentine government would implement the Final Act of Chapultepec: "Those undertakings are plain and unequivocal. They require the elimination from this hemisphere of Axis influences which have threatened the security of the inter-American system. . . . But there must be deeds and not merely promises" (*DSB* [21 April 1946]: 666–667). Such implementation would pave the way to concluding a treaty that the Americas strongly desired.

The policy in Washington thus became one of watchful waiting—a period that Braden reckoned as about three months—to see how well Argentina complied. However, he resisted a Brazilian proposal that the conference be convened on September 7 and thought the fixing of any date would be premature (*FRUS* 11 [1946]: 21).[63]

When it appeared that Perón had won the election—an honest one—the "intolerable defeat" Braden suffered did not cause him to resign. He did, however, change his tactics. According to Hadow, "having to give up his public bludgeoning of Perón or get out, Braden has—on the advice of Duran—turned to the more profitable, if less spectacular, method of 'boring from within' for the destruction of his enemy, with the help of the 'Democratic Institutions' through which Perón must of necessity govern or be branded a dictator." He added, "So long as Braden occupies the stage and Duran is hanging about in the wings, you must expect a continuation of the intrigue by which an ill-advised and, I am beginning to believe, ill-informed as well as sharp, rather than intelligent, Assistant Secretary hopes by hook or by crook to settle a personal vendetta."[64]

Hadow reported that he had learned "from a good Argentine source" that Duran, Gil, and Braden were discussing "how Argentine deputies could, with outside aid, box in and gradually strangle Perón"; he added that "this continued interference in the internal affairs of another country is, to my mind, the most catastrophic feature of Braden's policy; but I cannot see him giving it up so long as he has Duran at his side, and the more subtle line of approach now suggested may be infinitely more dangerous to Perón than public bludgeoning to which Braden has hitherto been given and in which he has of late ceased to indulge."[65]

Perón Is Accepted

Summarizing the situation at the beginning of April 1946, Perowne noted that "the State Department's efforts to isolate, discredit, and overturn the Argentine Government continued ever more openly with the passage of the months." The aim of the Blue Book was "(a) to exclude the present Argentine Government from participation in inter-American defence talks; (b) to influence the Argentine electorate away from Colonel Perón; and (c) to make more difficult, if not impossible, the international acceptance of any Government emerging from the elections which might be headed by Colonel Perón." However, "The Blue Book has signally failed of all its objects." It was rejected by most Latin American countries and was described by a U.S. journalist in Buenos Aires as "the most signal defeat that U.S. diplomacy in Latin America has undergone for many years." Although the fairness of the election prevented the United States from quarreling with the results, "Perón or no Perón, the State Department still need to show they can bring Argentina to heel." The appointment of George S. Messersmith, "well known for his anti-Fascist views" suggested that Braden's policies would be continued by his ambassador.[66]

An Argentine view of Braden is given by the Canadian ambassador in Buenos Aires, who reported that foreign minister Cooke had told the ambassador's wife, "Can you imagine Braden having anything to do with culture? That man of the street! He has no idea of diplomacy, or of manners. Can you imagine what he said to me? He actually said: 'Perón will never be President, because I shall stop him.' When I asked, 'Who are you, a foreigner, to speak like this?' he answered: 'It does not matter who I am. Perón is not going to be President.'"[67]

In a memorandum Hadow emphasized that the section of the U.S. press "which reflects U.S. business and financial opinion, has . . . been unsparing in its denunciation of the low ebb to which Braden's policy has brought United States prestige throughout Latin America, and the utter failure of his interference in the internal affairs of a sovereign country. Those pursuing this line of argument state bluntly that United States must, without further ado, bury the dead past and resurrect the Good Neighbour Policy; in the mutual interests of U.S. and Latin American trade, defence and development."[68] Henry Morgenthau was quoted as saying that "One of our greatest setbacks was the election of Col. Perón in Argentina" (*PM* [9 May 1946]).

Sumner Welles expressed incredulity that Braden should hold his position after the Blue Book disaster. The answer may be that Braden had the strong support of the Congress of Industrial Organizations (CIO): "Braden took with him to Argentina the support of the CIO, which, a spokesman said, considers him one of the ablest diplomats in the State Department." George Michanowsky, executive secretary of the Latin American Affairs Committee of the CIO, was reported as displaying a letter from Dean Acheson "expressing thanks for CIO support for Braden in Argentina."[69]

In Buenos Aires the British ambassador, Sir Reginald Leeper, and Messersmith had established an excellent relationship, and Messersmith began working cautiously with Perón and his aides to bring about full compliance in terms of Byrnes's statement of April 8, which demanded deeds, not promises, by Argentina before the United States would agree to a treaty of defense against aggression.

> The deep-seated American antagonism to Argentina, and particularly the presence of Mr. Braden at the State Department, account for the present U.S. official policy of keeping Argentina in the doghouse, despite the efforts of the U.S. Ambassador at Buenos Aires to restore normality to U.S.-Argentine relations, the patent desire of the U.S. Service Departments to get Argentina into the hemisphere defence arrangements, and the urge of U.S. Big Business to dominate the valuable Argentine market.[70]

The definition and interpretation of "deeds" required more than a year and gradually evolved into an acrimonious dispute between Messersmith and Braden that culminated in their simultaneous dismissal in June 1947. Messersmith claimed that Argentina had complied with its obligations under the Chapultepec agreement, that it was not a Fascist country, and that Braden had "intervened in an improper manner in the internal affairs, and particularly I mean in the internal electoral affairs of the country."[71] Braden took the opposite position on each of these points and at first was supported by both Byrnes and Truman.[72]

In the course of this dispute, Messersmith committed the egregious error of sending to Byrnes a copy of a letter to Arthur Hays Sulzberger of the *New York Times* in the hope of gaining a public hearing for his case against Braden. He did not get it, but he did get a telegram from Byrnes: "Immediately desist from writing to representatives of the press to be used by them for background purposes letters criticizing the Assistant Secretary of State, Mr. Braden."[73]

Messersmith went to Washington for consultations, and Leeper said he was now "fighting his battle with Mr. Braden . . . but he is confident that he will win. He knows that we are on his side in this." If he should win, his influence in Argentina would be greatly increased, "as the personal element plays an important part in the President's outlook." Leeper felt that the British would face "a difficult period ahead in dealing with the arrogant nationalism of this country." He did not think, however, that Perón was a follower of

Nazi ideology; he was simply making appointments and so exploit-
ing victory over his opponents. All this was explainable in Latin
American terms, and it was unnecessary to use German ones. "It is
not for us to take sides in Argentine internal disputes, and with the
recent example set by Mr. Braden before our eyes, it would be highly
dangerous to do so."[74]

There is little information available on Messersmith's talks in
Washington. Although both Braden and Byrnes claimed that Argentina had not yet complied with its agreements,[75] Messersmith went
back to Buenos Aires to "the most rapturous welcome ever received
by a representative of the United States in Argentina," given to him
as "a champion of Argentine–United States reconciliation." He was
met at the airport by Perón and his wife, the minister for foreign affairs, and other members of the cabinet. It was generally believed
that his return meant that he had won out against Braden, and he
told Perón that "he was very happy with the solution reached regarding Argentine relations with the United States." Lord Inverchapel,
the new British ambassador in Washington, reported that, "although
the State Department appears likely to progress in the direction
favoured by Messersmith, there is nothing to indicate that the influence of Braden has been seriously affected by the recent contre-
temps." Looking to the future he said: "There is little doubt that the
whole field of American relations with Latin America—the rejuvena-
tion of the good neighbour policy and the strengthening of hemisphere defence—will figure prominently in the minds of both State
Department officials and the public during the coming months. . . .
One of the objects of the renewed concentration on Latin American
affairs will also be to counteract the spread of communism in Latin
America."[76]

The British government at this point came down hard on Messersmith's side by stating that Argentina was "now fulfilling its obligations in respect of enemy aliens, property and interests at least as
well as the majority of Latin-American Governments," and that Britain therefore planned to treat Argentina "in all respects on the same
footing as other Latin-American countries." "Acheson was upset,"
reported Inverchapel; he hoped that no public announcement would
be made "because if we did the whole American plan would be pretty
well cooked."[77] Britain was denouncing the "Gentlemen's Agreement" of October 1946, in which both governments undertook not
to sell armament of any type to Argentina. On 27 January 1947
Leeper told Perón about Inverchapel's *aide-mémoire*, of the same
date, and Perowne thought "we need not be unduly troubled" by
Acheson's reaction: "The American Chargé d'Affaires at Buenos

Aires has reported to Washington that he thinks the Argentines have now not only worked their passage but arrived home and if the State Department will want more they must be perfectionists indeed, or stand exposed as determined to maintain their quarrel with Argentina for ideological rather than practical reasons."[78]

Messersmith told Leeper that, as a result of his talks with Truman and Marshall, he was "confident that his Government intend to clear up their relations with Argentina as soon as possible. The Senate are equally determined that this shall be done. His instructions are to get some more Germans out as quickly as possible in order to silence press criticism in the United States."[79] Messersmith summed up the situation shortly afterward by saying of Argentina, "This proud country has gone a long way in humiliating itself. It has done it, I believe, because the present Government is so convinced of the desirability of inter-American collaboration and of collaboration with us. . . . After all, there is a degree to which we can intervene in the internal affairs of another country and there is a measure which must be put to the demands which we can place upon another country. The Argentine has taken her medicine, I believe, on the whole very gallantly."[80]

Truman, on a visit to Mexico in early March 1947 gave a splendid tribute to the Good Neighbor policy in saying that it applied "the same standards of conduct that prevail among self-respecting individuals within a democratic community. . . . The good-neighbor policy specifically includes the doctrine of non-intervention. This assures each nation freedom for its own development" (*DSB* [16 March 1947]: 498–499).

Perhaps acting under senatorial pressure, and with Marshall in Moscow, Truman took the Argentine affair into his own hands and arranged a meeting with the Argentine ambassador, Oscar Ivanissevich, at which were present, Sens. Connally and Vandenberg, and acting secretary of state Dean Acheson. Braden was not there. Truman said that he regretted the problems between the countries, but there remained now only one, that of the deportation of "some 20 to 30 dangerous Nazi agents" who remained in Argentina. Ivanissevich protested that he must mean Argentine citizens whose cases were in the courts, but Truman and Acheson said they were talking about "German agents," and since this was the last problem outstanding, Truman said that it was his "earnest desire that this action be taken promptly." The senators were present to indicate congressional support for Truman's position, and the ambassador was impressed (*FRUS* 8 [1947]: 186–187).[81]

Truman was also influenced by complaints from Latin American ambassadors about the stalemate with Argentina, which was preventing the completion of security arrangements at Rio de Janeiro. Messersmith had reported that the breach with Argentina was hampering efforts to contain the influence of communism, and, no less important, Vandenberg "had grown openly critical of the 'tough' policy which Mr. Truman formerly followed."[82] For "Truman" here, read "Braden."

Following Ivanissevich's return from Buenos Aires, with assurances, a decision was finally made in Washington. Braden's resignation was accepted on June 5, and on the same day Messersmith was thunderstruck to receive a cable from Acheson saying that his resignation was accepted and that he should return to Washington. He cabled that he was sure that the president was not unmindful of the fact that he had "carried through, I believe, with success, the primary mission with which he entrusted me which was to secure compliance by the Argentine with her inter-American commitments and my reports show that in this I have had the full collaboration of the present govt. of the Argentine." Having received no answer, Messersmith cabled again on June 6, "I am completely in the dark as to what has been happening and the reasons therefor. . . . As I have not submitted any resignation to the President, has my 'resignation' been accepted by him?"[83]

Messersmith found it hard to believe that such a successful mission could be rewarded by the acceptance of a resignation that he had not offered. He had not realized that Acheson had recommended to Marshall that "the situation and the relations between the two men, and between each of them and the Department, having become intolerable, I be permitted to deal with the problem by eliminating it— that is, by acting in his [Marshall's] name to recall and retire Messersmith and to ask for Braden's resignation" (Acheson 1969: 190; also see Braden 1971: 370). Messersmith had presumably not read press accounts of Truman's unsettling statements that Messersmith had been sent to Buenos Aires "for the accomplishment of a definite assignment, the end of which was not yet in sight," and that he was sent to Argentina only temporarily, since he was not in the best of health and accepted the post "as a favor" to the president and Byrnes (*New York Times* [16 May 1947]). The Department said that Truman and Marshall had not changed their policy calling for holding Argentina to compliance with the Chapultepec agreements; it was only after Ivanissevich "demonstrated to the President and Secretary Marshall that these conditions had been met, that the President issued his statement seeking to fill the breach" (ibid. [8 June 1947]). The policy had not changed, but its aim had been achieved—an admission Braden was unwilling to make.

Both Braden and Messersmith received high awards on leaving public office—but from different governments. Acheson conferred the Medal of Freedom, the highest civilian award in the United States, on Braden. Perón gave the Argentine Order of the Grand Cross of the Liberator General José San Martín to Messersmith, and he accepted the "$4,000 decoration as a symbol of closer relations between our countries and peoples" (ibid. [19 June 1947]).[84] When he left on the *Del Sud* on June 21, there were some ten thousand persons to see him off, including Perón and Evita, and the ship's sailing was delayed by the throng. He was, however, given no such attention on his return to the United States, and Truman did not offer him "a better assignment," as Messersmith said he had been promised; he retired from the foreign service and went into private business in Mexico. In a memorandum to Sec. Marshall, when Messersmith was about to call on him, Armour said that he had told Messersmith "very clearly that you, the Department and many of us felt that he had gone too far in carrying his case through personal letters to the press, the Hill, and elsewhere."[85]

The removal of both the assistant secretary and the ambassador cleared the air and left the way open for a fresh start. James Bruce was named to succeed Messersmith, and he arrived in Buenos Aires with an open mind: "I had no prejudices, and I was under instructions from President Truman and Secretary of State Marshall to be as friendly as possible with the Argentines" (Bruce 1953: 343).

As the British saw it, according to an FO Minute by Murray,

> The thing that has really caused the trouble over the years, in Argt.-U.S. relations is the proud Argentine assumption that in Pan American affairs the two countries meet as equals. The more Washington has sought to extract some sort of acknowledgement of U.S. leadership, the more stubbornly the Argentines have maintained their position; and by and large they have won the round just ended (because Mr. Braden's attempt to have Perón and his people perform to the U.S. word of command and demonstrate that they were not Fascist beasts is part of the whole). Now U.S. policy towards Argentina will be in the hands for a while of people who know Latins, and who will deal with them realistically. It is sad that only the need to close the hemisphere ranks against the arch-enemy [U.S.S.R.] has brought about the rapprochement, but perhaps Mr. Armour can gradually build up a

basis of trust and mutual respect and understanding as a more durable foundation for U.S.-Argt. relations in the future. The removal of Mr. Messersmith (presumably only to give the newcomers a fair start) and (perhaps to save Mr. Braden's face) will not exactly make the task easier.[86]

Perón was successful in "weathering the passing storm of Mr. Braden's attempts to bring him to heel. From this tussle he emerged, indeed, as leader of a covert Latin-American revolt against the United States which Washington has ever since sought to stem by granting financial favours to its favourites—especially Brazil—and doing homage once more to the Good Neighbour policy."[87]

The Argentine experience, in which he was intimately involved, was no doubt behind Cabot's later judgment that "there are two essential reasons why we can not interfere in the internal affairs of other nations. First, our treaty obligations bind us. However, behind these obligations is our feeling that it is unwise to attempt such interference. When we have attempted it the results have been countereffective, having harmed the democratic groups we wished to help."[88]

7. A Diplomatic Aberration

The difficulties of managing a policy of restraint are made evident by the circumstances surrounding the speech by Amb. Adolf A. Berle, Jr., on 29 September 1945, at Petrópolis, Brazil. Berle had, of course, been present since the creation of the Good Neighbor policy. The new assistant secretary of state, Nelson A. Rockefeller, desired Berle's advice, but from a distance, and he persuaded Pres. Roosevelt to appoint Berle ambassador in Rio de Janeiro. Berle at first refused the appointment, later accepted it, and arrived in Brazil in January 1945. In February he was approached by Maj. Juracy Magalhães, a political figure in Bahia, who began to talk of a change of regime in Brazil. Berle's response was entirely correct in terms of the good neighbor tradition: "I said he realized, of course, that the United States Government could not intervene in local politics, nor could an Ambassador. . . . The non-intervention policy of the United States was well-established and would be scrupulously adhered to" (Berle 1973: 522–523).[1] It was thus clear that the ambassador could be held blameless in talking with a Brazilian who might be thinking in terms of an armed revolt.

Berle took a very different view of intervention, however, when it looked to him as though he might bring about a change in government by expressing confidence that the president of Brazil would continue to follow democratic principles. On 4 September Berle wrote to Pres. Truman, saying that "some in Brazil, and possibly in the United States, suggest that the Embassy here should attack President Vargas as Braden has attacked Perón." However, "under quiet encouragement from this Embassy" Brazil had in 1945 made good progress toward democracy, with elections set for December 2. "As long as Vargas keeps going in this direction, quiet encouragement towards democracy seems to me the best policy. If he changes course or does something violent we can re-examine the position." To this

Truman replied on 13 September that "it would be disastrous to interfere with the internal affairs of Brazil at the present time."[2]

Perhaps before receiving this letter from Truman, Berle cabled the Department of State to warn that Vargas might postpone elections and issue a decree setting up a constituent assembly: "This would squarely present us with problem of what attitude to take." Berle suggested that the department prepare a statement expressing pleasure at Brazil's recent democratic steps, and that it especially "welcomed President Vargas' declaration that he had no intention other than to preside over peaceful elections." Speed in making the statement would be necessary, but "time for making such statement public has not come yet and wisdom of making it needs careful consideration."[3]

Berle's cable gave rise to a memorandum in the department that stated that, if properly timed, the statement "could not be considered an act of intervention since no preference would be made for any candidate." This was not true, since the purpose of the statement would be to exclude Vargas himself from being a candidate. The memorandum continued, "If we wait until we have notice that the Brazilian Government is to postpone the elections, which nobody is going to give us, a statement by this Government would probably produce the wrong effect and might easily be labeled as 'intervention.'" The statement should be made soon, therefore, "preferably by the Secretary at one of his press conferences. It could be made in reply to a planted question. We feel it would be preferable for the statement to be made in Washington for two reasons: it would seem less like intervention than if made on the scene, and there would be no risk of weakening Ambassador Berle's position."[4]

However, the department took no positive action, and on 27 September Berle cabled that a decree postponing elections seemed likely, with the aim of continuing Vargas in power. "Rising tempo of agitation and controversy here. Unless Dept. perceives objection it seems desirable to take action along lines last two paragraphs EMBTEL 2905 [note 3] and Braden agreed while here"[5] (Braden was on his way to Washington to become assistant secretary of state).

Berle noted in his diary that "after much sweating I had come to the conclusion that the only way to have democracy was to have it, and that the United States was beginning to be expected to express a view" (ibid.: 549). Hearing nothing from Washington, he went ahead and gave a speech to a group of journalists on the twenty-ninth. Before doing so, however, he showed it to Vargas, who "had no objection and on the whole seemed pleased. Subsequently he seems to have discussed it with two of his ministers, one of whom has just called me to say that the govt. is very happy it is being made."[6]

The speech expressed the satisfaction "of the United States" at the freedom of the press, political amnesty, and the free organization of political parties in Brazil, and added, "The pledge of free Brazilian elections, set for a definite date, by a Government whose word the United States has found inviolable, has been hailed with as much satisfaction in the United States as in Brazil itself. Americans have not agreed with some who tried to misrepresent straightforward pledges and declarations as insincere, or as verbal trickery" (ibid.: 552).

Berle noted that the speech was "going to cause a good deal of political comment and in a sense takes the Embassy off the pedestal and puts it into the firing line." Further,

> It is made on the theory that everything the Brazilian Government has done to date has been done in good faith and it rejects the charges of the enemies of the Government that the Government is secretly fomenting a Fascist coup d'état. I personally think this is true; but it is very difficult to wrestle with the grim fact that probably the worst elements in the Government are proposing a coup d'état, and that many of the men behind it were most active in opposing the United States and cheering Italian Fascism in 1937. (Ibid.: 551)

On October 4, after noting the press comments on the speech, Berle admitted that he had been "in a good deal of mental turmoil, because, being natively a timid soul, I don't like to get into political controversy and always torment myself with wondering whether I did the right thing":

> For the speech is being referred to as the "atomic bomb that ended *Queremismo*." The many hundreds of telegrams and the very kindly support which has been accorded by most of the press are perhaps the best answer; but primarily I think diplomacy has changed. The public opinion in any country is necessarily a factor in the affairs of every other country; the worst thing a diplomat can do is to leave anyone in doubt. Certainly if on October 3, these boys had pulled off their coup d'état and the tide of public opinion in the United States had dealt with it as it dealt with Perón, our situation would have been strikingly unpleasant. But this form of diplomacy means that the easy life of the diplomat is gone forever. (Ibid.: 553)[7]

Berle did not refer to the Good Neighbor policy, nor did he use the term "intervention." However, former ambassador Willard L. Beaulac recalls that first secretary in Rio de Janeiro, Paul C. Daniels, said on being shown the text, "It is an excellent speech, but it is intervention."[8]

On October 3 demonstrations for the Constituent Assembly had been scheduled, and Berle noted that his "own speech of September 29 was designed if possible to head off violent moves in either direction. The good sense of President Vargas prevailed and he told the demonstrations that he was not going to depart from the democratic path he had marked out" (ibid.: 554).

However, the plotting continued and when, on October 29, the army learned that Vargas had appointed his brother Benjamin as chief of police of Rio de Janeiro, the military leaders insisted on Vargas's resignation and the transfer of power to the president of the Supreme Court, José Linhares (this was in accordance with the 1937 constitution). Elections were held as promised on December 2 and Gen. Eurico Gaspar Dutra was elected president.

Vargas's appointment of his brother to be chief of police of Rio de Janeiro demonstrated his misjudgment of the political situation. His plan was "to foment confusion and disorder and in due course to stage a general strike which would have given him the opportunity of declaring a fresh 'state of emergency' and cancelling the elections." For this he needed "a pliant and unscrupulous Chief of Police."[9] Benjamin's reputation did not otherwise recommend him for this post. Gainer called him "probably the worst thug in Brazil."[10] Berle cabled, "Benjamin Vargas was outstanding *Queremista*, known to have urged Vargas to maintain his dictatorship. He further is one of the most unpopular men in Brazil since even men in street believe him to have become millionaire through shady operations involving government influence."[11] His reputation was so bad that even the president's best friends "could not stomach him, while the whole country realised at once that his appointment meant civil disturbance on a grand scale, which might eventually lead to civil war."[12]

Assessing the gains and losses from the speech of September 29, Berle thought that it had contributed "materially to stabilizing situation. It has been widely supported by at least 80% of press and more than that number of telegrams, etc." The extremes of right and left had trouble in attacking the speech, since it "merely amounted to encomium of announced policy of government. On whole I think informed opinion believes results were worth effort. Certainly position of US and of this Embassy in case of coup d'état would have been extremely difficult. Chief end to stabilize situation along legal and constitutional lines seems to have been achieved for time being."[13]

Was Berle's speech authorized by the Department of State? Certainly not by the officers in charge, but they decided to let the matter ride, awaiting further word from Berle. The department cabled after the speech was given:

> Frankly, there was considerable skepticism of the wisdom of making any statement at all. Other questions raised were concerning the place and person to make such a statement, the general view here being that it might be desirable to keep the Embassy out of it and have such a statement made by the Acting Secretary, or possibly Mr. Braden. However, no decisions were reached. . . .
>
> When we received your 2992, September 27, informing the Department that Mr. Braden had agreed to the taking of some action, it was decided to let the matter ride until Mr. Braden arrived in Washington, since it was felt that the decision, so far as the Department was concerned, was largely one for Mr. Braden himself.[14]

The British assumed that Berle had not delivered the speech on instructions from the department, "since it constituted a definite and flagrant intervention in Brazilian internal affairs." However, Berle had contemplated issuing a "warning" to Vargas and he had "discussed his intention and the actual text of his speech, with Mr. Braden when the latter passed through Rio de Janeiro recently on his way back to the US from the Argentine." Although Vargas "was deeply wounded by the incident," Amb. Gainer thought the speech "was not only justified but has served a useful purpose, though Mr. Berle's popularity with the Brazilian Government, already somewhat shaky, will assuredly have suffered a further decline."[15]

Later, Gainer reported a talk at which Berle said, "I am no professional diplomat, and thus I have none of the usual fears and inhibitions of the diplomat; and while I regretted the necessity for having to take this action, once I had overcome my hesitation I went straight ahead." Gainer congratulated Berle on "his courage," and Berle said that he "had been convinced that disturbances were about to break out but he now thought the immediate danger had receded and he liked to think he had contributed to this."[16]

Berle thus had not heard from the department and had consulted with Braden, who was not yet confirmed as assistant secretary of state. He decided to go ahead, with Braden's approval, as a nondiplomat in a situation in which, as he himself said, "diplomacy has changed." This situation led to misunderstandings. Gainer reported that "presumably Mr. Berle must have acted on instructions, though he is a fearless and outspoken personality, who delights in being considered a strong man and is quite capable of weighing on his own account." He added,

> Brazilian papers have publicized a despatch from Washington stating that "well informed U.S. circles" described the speech as expressing the personal opinion of the U.S. Ambassador and did not represent the views of the U.S. Government. This might, if reported accurately, appear to be an official *démenti* of Mr. Berle.
> On the other hand we learnt from other sources that Mr. Berle was asked by the Brazilian M.F.A. [minister of foreign affairs] if he had acted on instructions: he affirmed that he had and was told that if this had not been the case his recall would have been requested.[17]

In the circumstances, both these reports had some justification, for Berle's action had not been approved in Washington, although it had been by the not-yet-confirmed Braden. It is not impossible that Berle, impressed by Braden's apparent success in Buenos Aires, decided to follow his new chief's tactics in Brazil, as he had foreshadowed in his letter of September 4 to Truman.

Berle's speech does not appear to have had much effect on Pres. Vargas, who continued to receive delegations of *queremistas*, "and the speeches he makes them are masterpieces of obscurantism."[18] A member of the staff of the British embassy in Rio de Janeiro, Jack Greenway, wrote to Perowne that he did not believe a story being put out by the American colony that Berle "showed the draft of his speech to the President before delivering it." In London, R. H. S. Allen minuted, "At this rate it is difficult to believe that Mr. Berle will be able to continue in his post much longer. His pedantry and lack of tact were already sufficiently evident in his early dealings with Sir D. Gainer, but now that he has been publicly pilloried by the Brazilians for these defects it will be extremely difficult for him to make his way smooth again. The reputedly difficult Mr. Caffery was quite a success in comparison." Perowne added, "I don't believe that Mr. Berle has any motive stronger than that of self-advertisement—though he may kid himself that his words and actions are dictated by 'higher motives.'"[19]

The American colony was, however, correct. "Later Vargas blandly explained (to [Gen.] Góez Monteiro) that Berle had read the speech to him beforehand in such 'badly masticated Portuguese' that he couldn't remember if it was the same version as the speech Berle subsequently delivered" (Skidmore 1967: 349, citing Coutinho 1955: 430–432). Berle had not deterred the president's efforts to continue in office, but he may have had a secret role in avoiding a military dictatorship, which would have put Brazil in the same category as Argentina, with a military government.[20]

Gainer reported that it was strange that Vargas "should disregard the warnings he had received both from the army and from the United States Ambassador and from his own friends such as Salgado Filho, Minister for Air," but commented that this showed "how out of touch with public opinion he really was." The "public warning" given by Berle strengthened the hand of the army, "but only so long as it did not try to form a Government itself. . . . The United States Ambassador told me himself that he had been approached by the generals immediately after Vargas was deposed, and that he had advised them strongly to support a civil Government and pursue a moderate course."[21]

In partial defense of Berle's speech, Gainer wrote to Hadow that

> It may have been indiscreet of Berle to intervene in Brazilian affairs but it is perfectly clear that both Brazilian and USA interests did demand elections here and that a continuance of Vargas' regime, without some reference to the electorate was bound to provoke civil disturbance which might have ended in a military junta governing the country and a rapprochement with the Argentine Government. Berle by his action has made himself hated here especially by Vargas and his adherents (who are many) but also by those even of the Opposition who for political reasons praised his action. In addition he is personally thoroughly disliked and he harries the Government and Ministers intolerably.[22]

In a later letter to Hadow, Gainer said that Berle "is consumed with vanity and reduces everything to the personal aspect. . . . I think Berle and Dutra will work together well enough, though Dutra may not trust him too far but after all it was to some extent due to Berle that elections were held (or so he likes to think) and these elections made Dutra (or Dona Santinha, his wife) President."[23]

Commenting on Berle in his annual report, Gainer said,

> He has a restless, brilliant and independent mind, with a Messianic complex and an utter conviction that he was born to set

the world right. Ready to defy the State Department at any moment and in any connection, but trusting ingenuously that he can control them, he must at all times hold the centre of the stage. The Brazilians were at first flattered by the appointment of so distinguished a man; but his superior moral attitude and his constant interference in their doings soon caused his popularity to fade and by the end of the year he was almost a man without a friend. This was indeed unjust, for he had done much for Brazil; but gratitude was never the most marked characteristic of this country.[24]

Berle resigned in the middle of February, recalling that Truman had agreed that he might do so after Dutra's installation. "To Brazil and Brazilians I am indebted for one of the happiest and most interesting years of my life" (Berle 1973: 565).[25]

In March Hadow reported, after a talk with Brazilian ambassador Carlos Martins, that "the Berle incident would long live in Brazilian memory; in contrast to the 'courteous, conciliatory and highly intelligent attitude of the British Ambassador at Rio,' which Martins went out of his way to tell me was very much appreciated both by President Dutra and by the new minister of foreign affairs." Berle had insisted on the competitive entry of U.S. oil companies into Brazil, much to the irritation of Standard of New Jersey; he had "asked and failed to receive Braden's support against the SOCNJ; in return for the fatal outburst against Vargas which Berle had made at Braden's instance." In an FO Minute on this letter, J. McQuillen wrote that "Mr. Berle indulged in some very plain speaking against Standard Oil and the oil monopoly in Brazil; whatever his failings he has fought hard for a fair deal over oil in Brazil, and, apparently, from disinterested motives. He never lived down his Petropolis speech, and, as far as spreading goodwill was concerned, his mission to Brazil was a failure."[26]

This last judgment was apparently shared by the Department of State. Daniel M. Braddock, an officer in the department, noted that "we should endeavor discreetly to repair the cooling of relations between the USG and Getulio Vargas which I felt had occurred and progressively increased following Ambassador Berle's Petropolis speech." He had talked with Berle's replacement, William D. Pawley, who said that "Vargas felt bitter against the US, which he had befriended so much during the war, for its having apparently repudiated him. Vargas was reported by his intimates to have said that he would never in his life set foot on U.S. soil because of this ungrateful treatment." Pawley had sent word to Vargas "that the US would never forget nor cease to appreciate the fine cooperation received from Vargas during the war, regardless of the well-known and general disapproval felt by Americans on the subject of dictatorships." Pawley was subsequently invited to Vargas's home and had a "friendly conversation" with him.[27]

Vargas, however, still nurtured animosity toward Berle for his speech. On 4 December 1946 he made a statement amplifying his recent charge that "international financial interests" were responsible for his downfall in 1945: "I do not need any other proof of my contention than the inopportune attitude of the Ambassador of the United States (Mr. Berle) as was noted in a book of Mr. Sumner Welles." Asked if Berle had showed the speech to him before it was delivered, Vargas replied, "Yes, he showed me the text of the speech in advance and I disagreed with it, being surprised that he was even disposed to deliver it. Besides at the time I referred in a speech to that intervention of a North American representative."[28] Vargas had apparently forgotten that he had made no objection to the text of Berle's speech. Berle's response to Vargas was, "That is ridiculous. Nobody who knows my career has ever accused me of being an agent of international finance. Further, Brazilian politics are a matter for Brazilians, and no one who knows Brazil believes that Brazilians will ever be influenced politically by any outsider" (*New York Times* [5 December 1946]). Berle here denied the very objective of making the speech in the first place.

Thirteen years later, Berle was invited to lunch at the Brazilian Foreign Office.

> Assis Chateaubriand told some of the old stories including my famous speech that in legend (though not in fact) ended the dictatorship. Affonso [Arinos] confirmed the fact that I had shown it to Vargas and got his approval first. . . . This was one of those things that happened. It may have been a breach of diplomatic form. But the Brazilians did not resent it as "intervention" but appreciated it as a contribution to history and here was the Foreign Office saying so with bell, book and candle. It is true the old Vargas crowd was not there. They wouldn't agree. (Berle 1973: 697–698)

It is interesting to note that at no time did Berle admit that he was violating the Good Neighbor policy—the speech was merely "a breach of diplomatic form." There is little real basis for judging whether this "breach of diplomatic form" had any significant effect on Vargas and the *queremistas*. Moreover, there was little likelihood that there would have been any significant change in the actions of the U.S. government toward Brazil if Vargas had perpetuated himself in power. The move toward democracy was the Brazilian army's, not Berle's.

The last official comment I have found on Berle's speech is in a memorandum prepared as background for Pres. Truman's speech before the Pan American Union:

> There is a widespread feeling in Latin America that the Good-Neighbor Policy is being shelved. They point out that Ambassador Berle dared, in a public address, to interfere with the domestic problems of Brazil. They feel, right or wrong, that since their champion, the late President Roosevelt, passed away, the Good-Neighbor Policy has taken a secondary place in the scheme of international relations, and they point out that neither the President of the United States nor the Secretary of State have made any major pronouncements on Latin America, nor have they stressed the Good-Neighbor policy.[29]

It may well have been this memorandum that spurred both Truman and Acheson to their rehabilitation of the Good Neighbor policy.

8. Reaffirmation of the Good Neighbor Policy

Acheson Restates the Good Neighbor Policy

At the beginning of 1949, when Dean Acheson became secretary of state, the inter-American system appeared to be well established. The Organization of American States (OAS) was given its constitutional structure at Bogotá in 1948, and the Inter-American Treaty of Reciprocal Assistance, completed at Rio de Janeiro following the departures of Braden and Messersmith, provided for previously lacking political and security arrangements. In 1948 the OAS successfully applied the terms of the Rio Treaty to stop Nicaraguan intervention in Costa Rica. In the economic field, Pres. Truman's announcement of the Point Four Program for assistance to developing nations was intended to lighten the deep gloom that had settled over Latin America when Sec. Marshall told the delegates at Bogotá that nothing like a Marshall Plan was possible for their countries. Still, there was disappointment in Latin America that the level of wartime consultation had not been continued, and there existed a pervasive feeling that Washington was "neglecting" Latin America in comparison with the close attention that was being given to Europe and Asia.

It was therefore decided to "re-define the so-called Good Neighbor Policy. This Policy in the course of the past fifteen years has, according to my [D. G. Clark, a State Department officer] way of thinking, become flexible and has inevitably been subjected to interpretation and application as of the immediate problem in hand." The new statement should indicate that there are limitations on the responsibilities of the United States, and that the policy is not a "one-way street" but requires help from the other American republics, if it is to represent "a hemisphere cooperative effort."[1]

Consequently, an instruction was sent to American diplomatic officers in the form of a preliminary draft, which became the basis for a speech Sec. Acheson made in September.[2] Reference was made to Roosevelt's original statement of the Good Neighbor policy, still valid in the department's approach to inter-American relations. Emphasizing the continuity of the Good Neighbor policy, this important document stated:

> During recent decades, the US has almost completely succeeded in persuading the other American republics that it has renounced, first, additional territorial ambitions and, second, domination or direct interference in their domestic affairs. This, in combination with the great increase in US power, has greatly strengthened the conviction in the other American republics that cooperation with the US is the most effective insurance for their national independence. Moreover, the great relative success of the US political and economic system in providing high living standards and civil liberties, combined with increasing knowledge of this through accelerated communications, has been an important factor in maintaining support in the other American republics for democratic ideals and the private enterprise system.

The view was widely held, however, that there had been "overemphasis on the political and security aspects of inter-American relations and that the economic needs of the area have been neglected," and this opinion was combined with the attitude that government had a "direct responsibility" for the peoples' welfare.

The heart of the problem was set forth in paragraph 16:

> Since dictatorial governments always have existed and still exist in some Latin American countries—although democratic principles are the expressed basis for the Organization of American States—and since non-intervention is an accepted principle of the American republics, the US should continue to use present means and try to find new means to persuade the governing and privileged classes of the Latin American countries to accept their direct responsibility for more rapid progress toward representative, stable and honest government as an important factor affecting hemisphere security and welfare. The withholding of recognition of anti-democratic governments probably is not an effective or appropriate means to deter the establishment and maintenance of such governments. To publicly state US support of democratic institutions and principles is desirable, although there should be no insistence upon "model USA." The Latin American peoples themselves must solve their political problems.

Responsibility for the growth of communism was laid at the door of "the governing and privileged classes," since the department took the view that "all actions, governmental or private, which ignore the legitimate demands of the people both for basic human rights and for better standards of living will inevitably lead to the unrest and misery that contribute substantially to the spread of Communism." Church and youth groups were cited as being of value in combatting communism, and Latin American governments were urged to give "special attention to strengthening the positions of non-Communist workers in trade unions."

The responses provide the views of senior members of the foreign service toward the Good Neighbor policy in 1949. They strongly backed the policy of nonintervention. Three ambassadors submitted alternate drafts of paragraph 16, softening the reference to "governing and privileged classes." Beaulac said that his was intended "to lessen the possibility that our cooperation in the promotion of representative, honest and stable government in Latin America will partake of the nature of unilateral intervention, which we are pledged not to indulge in and which experience has shown is harmful to the cause we are trying to promote."[3] The chargé in Quito, Maurice M. Bernbaum, stated:

> There is no question regarding the invaluable contribution of the Good Neighbor policy in our relationships with the other American republics. . . . There has invariably been encountered a feeling of confidence, engendered by the continued and constant exercise of the Good Neighbor policy, that such power will not be abused. This feeling has been accentuated by the Department's policy of strengthening the Pan American system to the point where each country considers that it has an equal vote with the others in the formulation of hemispheric policies. . . . Whereas, in the past, we were often prone to take matters into our own hands, we are today firmly wedded to the Good Neighbor principle that effective and durable results can only be achieved through cooperation.

Deploring the danger that "our adherence to the norms of diplomacy involving sometimes close and cordial relations with unrepresentative governments may be at the expense of the peoples of this area," he suggested that "the Pan American system so laboriously created by us is the logical vehicle for the application of any corrective measures. Whereas in the past, unilateral action by the United States was attacked as unwarranted intervention, collective action through the Organization of American States may have prospects of success."[4]

"Even now faith in our word is the greatest advantage which the United States enjoys in the Western World today," wrote Amb. Fletcher Warren from Paraguay. "The United States no longer desires a single foot of land or any other material possession which they have and because it does not desire to impose in any measure its governmental, intellectual, economic, or military system upon them. We are ready and prepared to negotiate as equals for whatever we may desire." In his thoughtful review, Warren noted that the United States was "meticulous in the avoidance of any appearance of intervention (in the 1920 sense of the word) in the internal affairs of any of the other American Republics." It had always been hard to define nonintervention so as to make it "jibe with the facts of international relationships. . . . There has been and always will be intervention in the internal affairs of other nations. What the United States, in its own interest and in the general interest of democracy and good government, must be careful to do is never to go further than will accord with public opinion in the other American Republics. In truth, the United States, if it is to promote to the fullest the growth of good government and democracy in the other American Republics, must go as far as public opinion will permit." Since, conceivably, nonintervention could be as censurable as intervention, the "all-important considerations are the general welfare, the justice of our actions. These basic considerations should take precedence over the tenuous theory of non-intervention."[5]

Others put the case for nonintervention more precisely. Amb. H. S. Bursley said that "we should both preach and practice nonintervention and . . . we should not at any time sacrifice the principle for questions of temporary expediency. This feeling is based primarily on my belief that we should at all times adhere to high principles, with the possible exception of such times as those when we are under armed attack."[6]

The only reference to communism as a menace in this connection was made by Amb. Monnet B. Davis in Panama, who said that, "as we understand it, our immediate policy objective is to discourage and present if possible the use of force in Latin American countries to effect political change. It would seem of even greater importance to present the successful use of such methods by Communist-influenced and other elements engaged in active political warfare against the United States and democracy in general."[7]

Giving the opinion of the embassy as a whole, Beaulac said that it considered that "the four most important aspects of our policy toward Latin America should be 1) non-intervention; 2) cooperation (in every field in which it is feasible and helpful for governments to cooperate); 3) reciprocity (not necessarily in kind but certainly in willingness to cooperate); and 4) reliance upon and stimulation of private effort as the principle source of social progress."[8]

These views were echoed by most of the other ambassadors. There were a few, however, who maintained the view that, despite the failure of nonrecognition in the Argentine case, attention should be given to its value in the case of smaller countries. Two or three lamented the Rodríguez Larreta doctrine's failure to gain Latin American favor and were hopeful that the application of sanctions might be safely entrusted to the OAS.[9] Several respondents raised the topic of treating democratic and nondemocratic regimes differently, but the prevailing view was that such action would become known and give rise to resentment, that it would create an unworkable "two-class" system in the hemisphere, and that it might prevent development of the least advanced countries.

With intervention, discrimination, and nonrecognition ruled out by the majority, there appeared to be fairly general acceptance of the view expressed by the ambassador in Quito that "we should encourage in every way the democratically-inclined elements in these countries but it must be recognized that in many cases even this is not sufficient to change overnight the revolutionary and anti-democratic traditions embedded in the minds of Latin Americans over a long period of time." The absence of true liberalism, the lack of an educated middle class, and the colonial tradition inherited from Spain made the spread of democracy "an uphill fight."[10] In view of these problems, many of the ambassadors pleaded for assistance in education, especially through fellowships for study in the United States, for road building and agricultural aid, and for help in bringing about a rise in the standard of living. These measures would only be effective in the long run, but they appeared to be the only ones available, and time and again reference was made to Point Four, whose funds, although useful, were inadequate for the type of program contemplated. "Effectively handled, it [the Point Four Program] can become precisely the sort of rallying point and inspiration that the present situation demands."[11]

Finally, several replies pointed to the importance of the military in Latin American governments. "In many Latin American countries the use of the Armed Forces as a political instrument and their active participation in politics militate seriously against the application of democratic principles of government. Every effort should be made to eliminate this pernicious system."[12] One method, it was suggested, would be to exchange military instructors to indoctrinate the young officers "in the advantages of democratic institutions."[13] Warren strongly supported this view and declared that "we shall not see the desired growth of democracy in the other American Republics until their military change their attitude toward the government and the people. The military must become the servant of the constituted authorities and the people before Latin America can become democratic." He hoped that the sending of military missions by the United States would have a democratic influence on Latin American military attitudes.[14]

Consideration of these and other replies resulted in the preparation of a new document: "Paper on Principles to Govern U.S. Policies Relating to Inter-American Affairs."[15] This document appeared to be a distillation and a restatement of the responses to the instruction of April 19. It does not appear that it was issued to embassies, but it employed some of the language of the April 19 document and was the basis for Sec. Acheson's speech of 19 September 1949.

In a "Statement of Principles" from the document Dean Acheson declared to the Pan American Society of the United States that "the U.S. should continue to support the principle of non-intervention in the internal or external affairs of an American state by other American states; but also should support the principle of such collective action to safeguard the common peace and security as is explicit or logically implicit in inter-American treaties, conventions, and other agreements." Further, "Wherever undemocratic conditions exist in Latin America, the U.S. should encourage the growth of representative and honest government by all suitable means, but without unilateral intervention in the affairs of another country. Public statements of our support of democratic institutions and practices are desirable, although there should be no effort to impose our own particular form of government and institutions upon other peoples." Something approaching Beaulac's language was used in the statement that "reciprocity is essential in inter-American relations; not necessarily reciprocity in kind but in the sense of willingness to contribute to the creation of conditions which give the greatest promise for the general security and welfare." Finally, because the resources of the United States were limited, it "should give priority to those countries which make a genuine and effective contribution toward the establishment of those conditions which we deem essential to security and welfare." Pres. Truman confirmed Acheson's statements on 12 October 1949 (*DSB* [26 September 1949]: 462–466).

This speech "constituted the most complete restatement of Latin

American policy in many years" and may be regarded as representing the mature understanding of the policy of the Good Neighbor by the Truman administration, including the foreign service (*FRUS* 2 [1950]: 590).[16] The secretary began by declaring certain principles on which policy in the hemisphere "must rest." These included faith in the worth of the individual, preservation of the American way of life but without trying to impose it on others, "protection of the legiti-mate interests of our people and government, together with respect for the legitimate interests of all other peoples and governments . . . nonintervention in the internal or external affairs of any American Republic," freedom of information and exchanges in all fields, and "the promotion of the economic, social, and political welfare of the people of the American Republics." He noted that the security sys-tem was being tested by turbulent events in the Caribbean area and said that the United States found this political turmoil "repugnant." He put his faith in the Rio Treaty to prevent armed attacks in the Caribbean.

Acheson repeated the views of the department on the meaning of recognition and said, "We always deplore the action of any group in substituting its judgment for that of the electorate. We especially de-plore the overthrow by force of a freely elected government." In con-cluding, he summarized the experience of the preceding seventeen years:

> These then are our three major objectives—the security of our nation and of the hemisphere; the encouragement of demo-cratic representative institutions; and positive cooperation in the economic field to help in the attainment of our first two objectives. . . .
>
> We can take satisfaction in the stability of our policy in the hemisphere. The good-neighbor policy as we practice it today is, for us, an historic, bipartisan, national policy. It has been wrought by Democrats at both ends of Pennsylvania Avenue— President Roosevelt, Secretary Hull, and Senator Connally, and also by Republicans at both ends of the Avenue—President Hoover, Secretary Stimson, and Senator Vandenberg. And this by no means exhausts the distinguished list who have contributed to this great policy.
>
> It is the firm intention of President Truman, as it is of myself as Secretary of State—of the entire personnel of my Depart-ment and, I believe, of the people of my country—to work for ever closer relations between the nations of this hemisphere. We seek by positive good will and effort to strengthen the Organiza-

tion of American States, within the more extensive design of the United Nations, as the most effective expression of law and order in this hemisphere.

We and the other American Republics have determined and pledged ourselves to carry on our common policy of the Good Neighbor as a living and constantly growing reality.

Acheson described this as a "ritualistic" speech and said that he had said nothing new (1969: 330). This of course was in line with what he had called "the stability" of policy in the hemisphere. However, in using words taken from the Charter of Bogotá to describe the commitment to nonintervention, by denouncing the use of force in upsetting freely elected governments, and in promising to strengthen the OAS, he gave a policy line that lasted throughout the Truman administration.

The Good Neighbor Policy Is Applied

This policy line was not mere rhetoric, for Acheson's actions were in accord with his words. This is evident in the three fields of economic policy, recognition, and nonintervention.

Economic Policy

It was an objective of U.S. policy "to protect the rights of private citizens of the United States and privately-owned American companies in the area, defending them against abuses and discrimination and trying, where appropriate, to enlarge on a non-discriminatory basis opportunities for United States trade and investment." This involved "vigorously" defending American interests and "pointing out that wide-scale economic development cannot be achieved except through private enterprise—*but of refraining always from interfering in the legitimate rights of other countries.*"[17] It also involved, for Latin Americans, the kind of restraint and reasonableness demonstrated by the Mexicans in the oil controversy in the late 1930s, together with comparable qualities manifested by the American companies concerned. For the latter, the Department of State looked to them to act "in a responsible manner" and to take "an enlightened attitude towards the welfare of the country in which the business operates, including paying an adequate local rate of taxation and conducting forward-looking industrial and public relations programs."[18]

The government of the United States used various means to provide economic assistance. These included continuation of work on the Inter-American Highway, adequate funding to allow the Export-Import Bank and the International Bank to finance development projects, fair treatment for Latin America with regard to availability of scarce materials in the United States, tax incentives to private capital investment abroad, and other measures such as the completion in October 1954, with the aid of U.S. funds, of the Santa Cruz– Cochabamba highway in Bolivia, which provided the first link for motor traffic between the plateau and the low-lying eastern regions of the country.[19]

At the same time, the United States employed economic sanctions to try to persuade Guatemala to change its attitude toward communism. In July 1951 the department initiated a program of stopping work on the Inter-American Highway in Guatemala, making no loans, not expanding aid under the Point Four Program, and exerting pressure by refusing to allow export of scarce materials. The policy was to be carried out "in the strictest secrecy," so that Guatemala would not have grounds for accusing the United States "of discriminating against Guatemala for political reasons or of attempting to intervene in her internal affairs." This policy was ineffective, and it was later found impracticable to attempt to restrict Guatemalan exports of coffee, but it was carried out by the Truman administration anyway.[20]

Recognition Policy

In accordance with Resolution 35 of the Bogotá Conference, the United States, following consultation, recognized the government formed by the military who overthrew the Gallegos government of Venezuela at the end of 1948. The department deplored the undemocratic character of the coup, but considered that nonrecognition "as a unilateral sanction is interventionist" and therefore "undermines confidence in the Good Neighbor policy, which is based on mutual respect and voluntary cooperation for common interests."[21] Thus the department did not regard nonrecognition as a suitable instrument for strengthening the democratic framework of Latin American countries.

Nonintervention

The department recognized that Latin American countries were "in the midst of a social revolution, strongly nationalistic in character," and that this not only reduced "their will and ability to cooperate," but also presented "a threat to United States positions that are vital to our security." At the same time, the United States had "lost leverage" in the area by renouncing the use of force. Therefore the United States should draw Latin America "into closer association with us in the pursuit of the foreign policy we want them to support." This could be done by identifying the United States more clearly as a member of the OAS and by instilling in Latin America "a feeling that the United States is a trustworthy, mature, and just nation which will act in its own national interest but with a sense of loyalty and fair play to other countries." U.S. adherence to agreements concerning the doctrines of sovereign juridical equality and of nonintervention, which were "the corner stones of the inter-American system," would reinforce such a feeling.[22]

As late as 3 October 1952, the department learned that Pres. Anastasio Somoza of Nicaragua had the impression that a "military venture" against Guatemala would "have the blessing of the United States." However, both assistant secretary of state Edward G. Miller and Thomas C. Mann had told the Nicaraguan ambassador "as clearly as possible" that the United States "could never condone military intervention on the part of an American State against one of its neighbors, pointing out that non-intervention was one of the very keystones of the Inter-American system and that there are treaty commitments against such action."[23]

The same response was given to North American business executives who proposed that the United States "invoke the Monroe Doctrine," even though this might mean "the use of military force to deal with the problem in Guatemala." They also suggested that economic sanctions such as an embargo on coffee might be applied. To these suggestions, Miller explained why the United States could not, given its commitments, "intervene directly into the affairs of other states." An embargo would "constitute intervention just as much as would direct military action—at least in the eyes of other Latin American states. The repercussions of such action by the United States in the Hemisphere and elsewhere would be so serious . . . as to render the cost prohibitive in terms of the United States national interest."[24]

Earlier, to Thomas Corcoran, whose law firm represented the United Fruit Company, Mann had said that the department did not have "any program for bringing about the election of a middle-of-the-road candidate in Guatemala. . . . Any attempt by the Government to intervene would not only be counter-productive, but would meet with opposition in Guatemala, in the other American republics and in the United States itself." Although he agreed that "Arbenz, like Macbeth, could not last," Mann did not agree that any

action should be taken by American companies to bring about "political stability and social tranquility." Corcoran said he thought "it
would become increasingly necessary for the U.S. to exercise a
greater degree of control over Latin America and that there would be
a growing demand in the U.S. for a Latin American policy which
would open up the way for larger investments. It was Mann's view
that Guatemalans should be allowed to work out their own problems, although he added, "I would not like to try to guess what the
policy in the future might be if it were definitely determined that
the Guatemalan Government and people had fallen under the totalitarian control of Communist elements."[25]

If both nonrecognition and economic sanctions were ineffective,
and intervention was prohibited, the ability of the United States to
exert pressure on a country like Guatemala was limited indeed. The
issue was raised in 1950 in a memorandum by George F. Kennan,
counselor to the department, who, after noting that the United States
had become "deeply involved in a tremendous network of multilateral engagements within the inter-American community," stated
that this sort of thing had about reached its limit "in committing
our freedom of action. . . . Success in the conduct of foreign policy,
particularly in the Latin American area, rests ultimately . . . with
the power and will to discriminate, wisely, prudently and in ways
that cannot be labelled as offensive, in the application of our national power. . . . In matters of security, our fate already formally
rests, for better or for worse, with the enlightenment and wisdom of
a majority of the American family, modified by whatever moral as-
cendency we are able to exert at a given moment." Kennan, in a suggested statement to Latin America for the secretary of state, said
that never before in world affairs had a great power offered

> the most scrupulous respect for your sovereignty and indepen-
> dence, the willing renunciation of the use of force in our rela-
> tions with you, the readiness to join with you at any time in a
> large variety of forms of collaboration which can be of benefit to
> us both. But you will appreciate that the payoff for this unprece-
> dentedly favorable and tolerant attitude is that you do not make
> your countries the sources or the seats of dangerous intrigue
> against us, and that you recognize that relationships no longer
> governed by the sanction of armed force must find their sanction
> in mutual advantage and mutual acceptability. (*FRUS* 2 [1950]:
> 598–622)[26]

Louis J. Halle, a member of the Policy Planning Staff, opposed Kennan's view and stated,

Our policy in this century has been to assume the responsibility of leadership in developing a regional international system on which we can place reliance for our security and for the maintenance of order within the Hemisphere. The Rio Treaty is an indication of the progress we have already made in this direction, and our non-intervention commitment is a demonstration of the degree to which we rely on this progress. Our policy . . . is to have the community take action as such to deal with any common danger (whether from Guatemala, say, or from overseas). That does not mean that, in case of a major crisis, we would not respond to necessity by taking action on our own. Such action, however, would be equivalent to a suspension of civil rights under a decree of marshal [*sic*] law. Only extreme emergency could justify it.[27]

Halle's views prevailed, and for the duration of the Truman administration, although the United States discriminated against Guatemala, it did so secretly and relied on the OAS to respond to threats against U.S. security. The basic ideas expressed in the Pearson memorandum of 2 April 1952 were repeated in a memorandum for Pres. Truman at the end of the year, although Mann also struck an ominous note for inter-American affairs:

To sum up, an objective appraisal of the forces currently at work in Latin America, and of the bargaining power which we possess within the framework of the existing international organizations, suggests that the prevailing complacency concerning the area is based on criteria which are now obsolete. The next decade may be a critical one; certainly it will present important and difficult problems requiring a high degree of comprehension, consistency and skill to avoid a crisis in inter-American relations.[28]

The executive secretary of the National Security Council proposed this same policy line for the United States in a report in March 1953. Opting for a policy of cooperation, rather than one either of compulsion or of detachment, the secretary noted that the United States was bound by the prohibition of intervention in the OAS charter. On the other hand,

Non-intervention does not preclude multilateral action by the inter-American system. It is probable that the majority of Latin American governments do not yet favor even limited multilateral intervention, except where it is aimed at preserving the peace and security of the hemisphere. Collective action to preserve the peace in recent Caribbean disturbances has been of proven utility and a great step forward. *In addition, if a clearly identifiable communist regime should establish itself in the hemisphere, collective action, with our leadership, would probably be supported in Latin America.*[29]

With regard to the last sentence in the preceding quotation, R. Richard Rubottom, Jr., noted that the problem of communism had reached "a critical point" for the new administration. However, he believed that "the inter-American system is strong enough to withstand a debate over communist influence in Guatemala, assuming that we can carefully document the record and actions of the persons involved, and that it would be proper, and perhaps even helpful, to settle it once and for all."[30]

In the last months of the Truman administration, Miller took an optimistic view of the present and future of the Good Neighbor policy. In an address on 19 January before the Chamber of Commerce of Portland, Oregon, he emphasized the policy of nonintervention and also pointed to the concern of the United States for "scrupulous reciprocity" on the part of Latin America with regard to North American rights and interests. Balancing these claims, he noted that the department occasionally had to make "very difficult decisions" involving "putting the national interest ahead of a specific local interest" in the United States. On the whole, however, he felt that the United States could "assure our friends to the south that the policies which we pursue with regard to them will be stable." U.S. policy had been tested over twenty-five years, and

> the Good Neighbor Policy as we practice it today is for us an historic bipartisan national policy. It has been wrought by Democrats as well as by Republicans and the names of Hoover and Stimson in the Republican Party can take their place along with those of Roosevelt and Hull. This is the greatest guarantee that we can offer to our friends of the Americas, that, regardless of how hard fought may be our ensuing political campaign, they can look forward with confidence to working with us in the future as they have in the past. (*DSB* [11 February 1952]: 208–210)[31]

The Good Neighbor policy was firmly ensconced in both the minds and actions of the political leaders and their diplomatic officers as the time approached for turning the making of policy over to the new administration.

9. Bolivia and Guatemala

The Setting

At the end of World War II, Latin American diplomats desired to conclude both a collective, mutual security treaty and a charter for the inter-American system as the means for controlling both Argentina and the United States and for making a new institutional start on economic cooperation. The United States also desired the treaties, although its emphasis was on their usefulness as a defense against external aggression, which gradually came to mean against the Soviet Union. This difference in purpose led to differences in attitude and action that were ultimately fatal to the Good Neighbor policy.

Sen. Vandenberg said in January 1947 that the conference promised for Rio de Janeiro in 1945 should now be held "to renew the joint new world authority which is the genius of our new world unity. There is too much evidence that we are drifting apart . . . and that a Communistic upsurge is moving in."[1] He made this statement at a time of transition in policy that was nicely described by John Balfour:

> Accumulating evidence of Communist penetration in Latin America has in any case done much to promote the idea that the Administration would be well advised to return to the tactics of the good neighbour policy in its dealings with Argentina. Considerations of hemisphere defence and the need for a campaign in Latin America to combat the Communist virus are now tending to weigh more heavily in the public estimation than the desire to uphold United States prestige or to cold-shoulder an Argentina believed to be still tainted with fascism.[2]

The very different policies the Eisenhower administration followed in Bolivia and in Guatemala provide interesting comparisons between the continuation of the Good Neighbor policy in Bolivia, and the beginning of its dismantling in Guatemala.

Bolivia

The Bolivian revolution of 9 April 1952 was led by the same party and by some of the same men who had taken part in the revolution of December 1943. The 1943 movement had not been recognized by the United States and most of the other American republics for six months, until the revolutionary government had given unequivocal proof of its cooperation in the war effort by maintaining the flow of tin, rubber, and cinchona and by turning over enemy aliens to the United States.

From 1952 to 1953 the government of Bolivia, directed by the Nationalist Revolutionary Movement (MNR), expropriated the three large tin companies (Aramayo, Hochschild, and Patiño) that had long dominated the production and export of tin ore, instituted a drastic land reform program, greatly reduced the status of the army, and established universal suffrage. The government had the support of the small local Communist groups, and one of its principal members, Juan Lechín, minister of mines and petroleum, "an extremely radical, ambitious and violent individual,"[3] was thought by some to be a member of the Communist party. The new president, Víctor Paz Estenssoro, was one of those who had been forced to leave the government in 1944, in part because of pressure from the United States. It was the view of one officer in the Department of State that "the MNR has accepted Communist support and might collaborate with the Communists or even fall under their domination if it came to power."[4] The Chilean government believed that the revolution in Bolivia would have been impossible without the help of Perón and the Communists and that the Communists would influence the new government.[5] As late as December 1952, the archbishop of Acre, José Clemente Maurer, warned that "there is a danger of the advent of a communist regime in the country." Evidence included the creation of a Communist party, "criminal agitation of the Indians of the farms and mines," the holding of a pro-peace congress, and the "passive or active complicity of certain legal authorities in the Communist campaign."[6]

However, the Truman administration, personified in assistant secretary of state Edward G. Miller, Jr., viewed the Bolivian scene calmly and cautiously, and at the end of a month indicated that the United States looked favorably on recognizing the Paz Estenssoro government. In a cable to La Paz Miller noted that there appeared to have been no Communist participation in the revolution and that Communist domination of the new government was not an immediate danger; that the MNR government enjoyed a greater degree of popular support than any recent Bolivian administration; that the only alternative to the present government was one headed by Lechín, and Paz Estenssoro was preferable; and that a point had been reached at which delay might increase the disadvantage of nonrecognition and would operate against the interests of the United States. The State department felt that the new president would give assurances that Bolivia intended to honor all its international obligations (including compensating the nationalized enterprises) and that the tin-purchasing policy of the United States was the best instrument for influencing Bolivia's decisions on the issue of nationalization.[7] Miller added in a later telegram that the department would not "consider changes in Cabinet as condition precedent to recognition." The department did not use recognition as an "instrument of coercion," but it did have to be certain that "established criteria for recognition have been met."[8]

By the first week in June, after consultation with other countries, notably Brazil, Miller concluded that continued nonrecognition was equivalent to "withholding influence and preventing ourselves from helping moderate elements."[9] On June 6, the United States joined seventeen other republics in recognizing the MNR government.

In the autumn, the nationalization of the tin companies was completed. The United States did not object to the fact of nationalization, but it did insist on compensation for the owners of the tin mines, including some U.S. citizens who had invested in the Patiño company. Because Bolivia depended on tin exports for 70% of its foreign exchange, and because the United States purchased much of this strategic material, the Bolivians desired a long-term contract; so although the United States agreed to two spot purchases of tin, it delayed signing such a contract until June 1953, when agreement on compensation was reached.

The Bolivians needed a secure market for tin in order to obtain essential imports, including food, but U.S. officials in the new administration felt themselves under certain restraints in dealing with Bolivia: "Since a change of government might well bring in a more extremist regime and since we are concerned about the security of the tin mines, which would have strategic importance in wartime as the only source of tin in the Western Hemisphere, we have considered it in our interest to support the present government to the extent feasible."[10] A "more extremist regime" might well be a Communist one, which would entail "severe blows to United States prestige and to hemisphere solidarity." Bolivia offered an opportunity "for possibly successful cooperation with a popular government, as distinguished from the various dictatorial governments which we are accused of favoring." Further, assistance would be a "dramatic demonstration to Bolivia and the rest of the hemisphere that the Good Neighbor policy is still a practical and important reality."[11]

Assistant secretary John M. Cabot adopted these ideas and received approval from undersecretary W. Bedell Smith to offer assistance to Bolivia if an agreement were reached providing compensation for shareholders in the nationalized tin companies.[12] Agreement was reached in June, but Cabot had no success in getting consent from the Reconstruction Finance Corporation to sign a three-year contract for tin purchases, from the Treasury Department or the International Monetary Fund to allow Bolivia to draw the remainder of its quota from the fund, or from the Export-Import Bank for a loan of up to ten million dollars. He therefore asked secretary of state John Foster Dulles to take up with Pres. Eisenhower the question of the aid Bolivia so urgently needed. Cabot pointed out that, "if the economy and the present Government collapse, the extremists of Communist affiliation may gain control." The proposed assistance would be "a comparatively low price to pay if, as we believe, it can be instrumental in preventing a total breakdown and give Bolivia a reasonable chance to bring about at least a moderate degree of stability."[13]

The position Dulles took is evident from a letter he wrote on September 2 to Harold Stassen, director of the Foreign Operations Administration. In the letter he said that Bolivia faced "economic chaos":

> Apart from humanitarian considerations, the United States
> cannot afford to take either of the two risks inherent in such
> a development: (a) the danger that Bolivia would become a focus
> of Communist infection in South America, and (b) the threat to
> the United States position in the Western Hemisphere which
> would be posed by the spectacle of United States indifference
> to the fate of another member of the inter-American community.
> (*FRUS* 4 [1952–1954]: 535)

Milton S. Eisenhower, the president's brother, strongly supported the decision to aid the MNR government. He toured South America in the summer of 1953 and vouched for the non-Communist character of the MNR leaders and for the dire need of the Bolivian people for food. In early October Pres. Eisenhower decided in Bolivia's favor: food was shipped immediately and the way was opened for the massive amounts of economic aid that continued through 1968.

It was this aid that made economic progress possible and that ensured that the social goals of the revolution would be achieved. These aims were primary in the thinking of Presidents Paz Estenssoro and his successor, Hernán Siles Zuazo, both of whom submitted to many U.S. actions that would have been regarded as intervention in other countries at other times. For example, Amb. Edward J. Sparks reported that a Communist named Francisco Lluch held a government position during the Siles administration, but he added: "The Foreign Minister has stated that if the Embassy really feels that Lluch's presence is an embarrassment, that he can be removed. The Embassy has so indicated."[14] Lluch's appointment to teach in the newly opened military academy was therefore canceled.[15]

Again, Pres. Siles accepted the presence and recommendations of George J. Eder, an economist sent down by the U.S. government to stop inflation and stabilize the currency. Finally, following the disbanding of the army in 1952, it was at the urging of the U.S. government that civic action groups were organized. Hundreds of officers were trained in Panama and elsewhere, and the army was equipped with post–World War II weapons. Later, this new army was able to replace Pres. Paz with a general in its coup of 1964.

These were concrete evidences of the working of the principle of reciprocity, which was essential to the operation of the Good Neighbor policy between the United States and the individual American republics. These were the price of U.S. aid for the policies of the MNR government. The nature of the situation became clear in November 1953, when Cabot noted that there was evidence of "a concerted campaign" to arouse public opinion in the United States concerning communism in Bolivia. "The best estimate that we can make on the basis of available intelligence is that the Bolivian Government is not communist and that it is probably the only practical alternative to a communist-dominated regime under present circumstances."[16]

The strength of the campaign "to convince the American people that the Bolivian Government is communist dominated" was pointed out by Cabot on November 23, along with suggestions as to how the Bolivian regime might demonstrate its non-Communist orientation. Cabot's suggestions were to be made "in a spirit of helpfulness," not to be regarded as "interfering in purely domestic Bolivian affairs because (a) communism is a matter of common danger and common concern and (b) the communist activities which the Bolivian Government has tolerated and in some cases even furthered have been activities hostile to the United States, which is a friendly neighbor nation." Suggestions included an unequivocal break with Communist groups and the dismissal from public service of officers affiliated with Communist organizations. The Bolivian government should avoid increased relations with Communist countries and the "granting of haven" to "members of the international communist conspiracy, such as Luis Carlos Prestes."[17]

It is of interest to note Washington's concern with making anti-communism compatible with nonintervention, and La Paz's interest in following the State Department's suggestions with a view to securing support beyond the eleven million dollars provided in 1953. Both motivations met and blended, so that in 1954, the department was "convinced that we must proceed vigorously to eliminate the conditions which are conducive to the growth of communism by promoting stable and healthy economies in the Latin American Republics," and that the Bolivian government was "a nationalistic, reform movement which accepted communist collaboration when it seized power in April 1952 and has since tolerated communist activity, but has become increasingly hostile to communism and is now anti-communist."[18] It was with these ideas in mind, involving predictions that proved accurate, that the department went ahead and persuaded the Congress to vote credits for Bolivia in the succeeding decade.

Bolivia and Guatemala Compared

A brief review of policy toward Bolivia offers the opportunity to compare it with U.S. policy toward Guatemala. The Bolivian revolution was the first major upheaval in the Americas since Mexico's in 1910. At the end of the 1952 revolution, there was no alternative to the MNR government: there was no army, nor was there another party capable of governing. The only alternative appeared to be chaos, with advantage, if any, to the Communists. Therefore, the United States recognized the MNR government in the hope of exerting some influence over it. The United States did not, however, offer any economic aid until after the Bolivian government had completed arrangements to compensate the North American and other owners of the tin mines. The emphasis here was on the *principle* of compensation, since the North American investors were few in number and held few shares.

In Guatemala, North American firms, notably the United Fruit Company and the International Railways of Central America, were of great importance to the country's economy; they were able to exert influence on public opinion in the United States through the Bernays firm (see Bernays 1965), and their relationship to the officials in the Department of State was of a close and personal nature.[19] The United States formally proposed negotiation of legal issues in the dispute over expropriation of land owned by the United Fruit Company, but Guatemala did not reply.[20]

Communication about mutual problems was free and easy both in La Paz and with Bolivian ambassador Víctor Andrade in Washington, whereas exchanges of views in the Guatemala case were strained and formal.

Bolivia was far from the United States and from the Panama Canal, and there was no chance to train an army of émigrés to invade the country to establish another government. Guatemala was nearby; it had a seacoast; there was an available alternate regime; and local satraps in Nicaragua and Honduras could be suborned or persuaded to provide help for an invasion.

Practical pressure could be brought on Bolivia in the form of a refusal to purchase tin ore. Bolivia did not possess a tin refinery, and the ore could be refined only in Britain, where the Patiño interests controlled the facility, or in Texas, where the Reconstruction Finance Corporation maintained the refinery. Toward Guatemala, although the Truman and Eisenhower administrations tried to discriminate in aid and trade, there was no such easy method of exerting pressure through limitation of Guatemalan exports of bananas or coffee.[21]

Finally, but no less important, it was necessary for Bolivian and Guatemalan leaders "to know how to treat this imperial Troy"— the United States (Marroquín 1955 [?]: 187). The issue here went to the heart of reciprocity. What was vital to the United States, and what was the response to be? What were the conditions for "survival politics"?

After the Guatemalan invasion, Juan Lechín was quoted as telling his followers among the miners that, "in contrast to United States hostility to the Communist-influenced regime of Arbenz, the United States had helped the indigenous regime in Bolivia" (Alexander 1955: 258–259).[22]

The Bolivian leaders dealt first with the issue of compensation, and then with the matter of communism. Declaring their independence from Moscow, they eliminated all Communists from government offices. Other elements of reciprocity, such as the U.S. demand for currency stabilization, were easy to accommodate. The Guatemalan leaders showed no such flexibility, no comparable understanding of the obligations of neighborliness, no recognition of the fact that, to avoid destruction, they must evict Communists from their administration. The presence of such Communists, their frequent visits behind the Iron Curtain, and the clandestine purchase of arms from Czechoslovakia seemed to be evidence of Soviet penetration into America, even though the Communists in Guatemala were numerically weak. This combination of factors was unacceptable to the Eisenhower administration following the Korean War and in the atmosphere created by the activities of Sen. Joseph McCarthy.

Guatemala

The makers of the Good Partner policy began the dismantling of the Good Neighbor policy. Dwight D. Eisenhower, who took office in January 1953 as the first Republican president in twenty years, could hardly have been expected to use the term "Good Neighbor," which the Democratic party had applied to Latin American policy, although members of both parties had supported the policy in the previous two decades. Within the year, the old policy was on its way out, and others were being framed.

In 1953, economist Simon G. Hanson pointed out several areas of economic relations that indicated that "a change of heart" had taken place in the new administration: curtailment of imports as indicated by the countervailing duty on wool tops from Uruguay and by the tariff on oil from Venezuela; the transfer of development financing from the Export-Import Bank to the World Bank in May; the harsh terms of a loan to Brazil; and the down playing of Point Four because of Truman's initiation of it (Hanson 1953: 3–49). "It was a warm, self-generated identification of our interest with that of Latin America, which is the essence of the good-neighbor policy" (ibid.: 11). Hanson felt that "the good will and good faith and sympathy and understanding that had been the core of this very great policy" had evaporated, not only with the actions taken, but also with the unconvincing explanations given for them (ibid.: 15). To Brazil's charges that the United States was refusing to carry out its commitments for a program of loans, Hanson commented: "Under the good-neighbor policy a commitment had been worth something. One recalls, for instance, Sumner Welles' cold insistence to the wartime requirements committee that regardless of the alternative uses for materials the United States had pledged certain assistance for Volta Redonda and that as long as he was in charge of Inter-American relations the commitments of this committee to Brazil would be carried out (ibid.: 45).

If these developments gave Latin Americans in general cause for concern about the future of the Good Neighbor policy, there were far greater causes for concern in the course of relations with Guatemala.

In June 1944, the dictatorial regime of Gen. Jorge Ubico y Castañeda had been overthrown, and under his successor, Juan José Arévalo, an educator, Guatemala embarked, beginning in March 1945, on a program of political and economic reform that involved political freedom, a social security system, an institute for economic development, and a national bank. Besides his internal reforms, Arévalo had ambitions "to become the founder and head of a united Central America."[23] He had sent arms to Cuba for an expedition against Trujillo in the Dominican Republic; he had provided support for José Figueres in Costa Rica; and it was expected that Guatemala would assist revolutionary efforts against the dictators Tiburcio Carías Andino and Anastasio Somoza, in Honduras and Nicaragua, respectively.[24]

However, despite the fact that several cabinet members had "given cause to believe that they are 'party liners,' it must be recognized that Arévalo was popularly elected, appears to enjoy the support of the Guatemalan people, and on the whole is democratic in spirit and action. Accordingly, the United States would regret the overthrow of the Arévalo Government by unconstitutional means and the danger such overthrow would involve of retrogression in the advance toward full democracy of the Guatemalan people."[25]

In mid-1949 the department was concerned about both Guatemala's "rendering of cooperation and assistance to pro-Communist elements in Guatemalan national life," and its "disregard of the rights of legitimate American interests established in the country." It asked Amb. Richard C. Patterson, Jr., to talk with Pres. Arévalo and explain to him that the department planned to take measures "to protect its interests and to place relations between the two countries on a sounder and more even footing." However, the ambassador

> should carefully refrain in any way from conveying the impression that this Government is assuming, or intends to assume, a threatening posture toward Guatemala, which is not the case. However, the Department feels, and you may so state to the President, that it cannot continue to conduct its relations with the Guatemalan Government in that cordial and cooperative spirit that has inspired it in the past unless there is a reciprocal desire on the part of the Guatemalan Government to contribute likewise to mutual understanding, fair treatment, and friendly cooperation. (*FRUS* 2 [1949]: 650–654)[26]

Patterson talked with Arévalo and came away with the impression that "he fully understands our view point." According to Patterson, Arévalo said that "the difficulties and apparent harassments due fundamental nature Guatemalan revolution resulting inevitably conflict between capital and labor effects of which felt by Guatemalan capital as well as US private interests. Policy his government precisely one of social and economic betterment as only long range means remove maladjustments that now unfortunately provide fertile soil Communist propaganda" (ibid.: 654–655).[27]

The United Fruit Company and its subsidiary, the International Railways of Central America (IRCA), were the foreign firms chiefly affected disadvantageously by the Arévalo labor legislation. The companies asked the department "to intervene officially in this matter and to stop the confiscation of our property through the acts of the so-called labor tribunals." To a United Fruit Company suggestion that "economic sanctions" be employed against Guatemala, Assistant Secretary Edward G. Miller, Jr., "pointed out the impossibility of using this obvious weapon and emphasized that irrespective of the justice of the case, the result would be 100 per cent censure by every other nation in Latin America and probably of many other nations in the world." The most he would offer was to make clear the pressing nature of problems with Guatemala "before high-ranking officials of the Department."[28]

This adherence to the Good Neighbor policy is similar to the advice given to Ben Moseley, vice-president of EBASCO, a company with interests in Costa Rica. Moseley suggested "sending armed forces into Costa Rica." For the department, M. M. Wise said that "this would require a major decision contrary to the policy which this Government has followed in recent years and . . . I had most serious doubts that any official of this Government would make a decision of this nature at this time." Continuing, Wise noted:

> Moseley then withdrew from his position a little by saying that he was not necessarily referring to the dispatch of armed forces to Costa Rica but rather to sending in a few planes for the purpose of "showing force." I said that this also would be contrary to our policy. Moseley then withdrew further from his original position and said that the maneuver he suggested would not necessarily have to be a "show of force," but that planes should be sent in for the purpose of evacuating Americans if that became necessary. Moseley stressed the importance of saving American lives.
>
> In conclusion, I let it be known to Mr. Moseley that the Department felt it was following the Costa Rican situation carefully and adequately and was doing everything proper to bring the turmoil to an end.[29]

The United Fruit and IRCA cases were temporarily settled in early September 1949, and a memorandum by Wise indicated both the moderate attitude of the department and its closeness to that of the Roosevelt administration in similar cases. Wise wrote that the department should try to impress

> upon the Guatemalan Government, and labor unions through such contact as is possible, and U.S. firms, the desirability of approaching labor problems fairly and impartially, and in accordance with law. Magnifying the issues into questions of sovereignty and removing them from their true significance as management-employee problems, can only be detrimental to both sides. . . . As a basis for continuation of this missionary work, we have two glaring examples (the United Fruit Company, and IRCA cases) of how improper handling and magnification of labor issues has done nothing but force dubious face-saving settlements after provoking a vast amount of lasting ill will.[30]

This tone was maintained throughout the Truman administration. Under-secretary James E. Webb told Guatemalan ambassador Ismael González Arévalo on 14 September 1949 that the United States "had gone all out for cooperation as a philosophy of government," and that "American business has a lot to learn and . . . the State Department is aware of this and is not the blind advocate of American private enterprise abroad" (ibid.: 665–667).

This, however, was not Patterson's view. He regarded his purpose as the protection and promotion of American interests. Pres. Arévalo said that Patterson was more a representative of the United Fruit Company than of the United States. When, in March 1950, Patterson asked that seventeen officials be dismissed for being Communists, the Guatemalan government asked the State Department to recall him, without, however, declaring him persona non grata (Immerman 1982: 99).[31] This was done immediately and, to make amends, chargé Milton K. Wells talked with Col. Jacobo Arbenz, who was then a candidate for the presidency, and

> I tried to disabuse Arbenz of the notion the United States in any shape or form is departing from a strict policy of non-intervention in the internal affairs of Guatemala; that this policy carries with it disapproval of any interference or meddling in local politics by American companies and citizens; that we seek no special privileges, only fair treatment. . . .
> The United States under no circumstances is going to meddle in Guatemalan internal affairs, nor take sides in the coming electoral campaign. Also, . . . American business concerns are al-

ready warned to abstain from contributing to campaign funds or otherwise involving themselves in politics. (*FRUS* 2 [1950]: 870–874)[32]

Finally, assistant secretary Miller, visiting Guatemala, spoke "forcefully and frankly" on "the overt anti–United States propaganda of extremists identified with the Government, and our determined policy of non-intervention in the internal affairs of this country." Pres. Arévalo replied that Guatemala was with the United States, that communism was not adaptable to the agrarian population of the country, and that it would be "stupid" for Guatemala to take a pro-Soviet position (ibid.: 905–907).[33]

The assassination on 18 July 1949 of Col. Francisco Javier Arana, the chief of the armed forces, cleared the way for the election of Arbenz in 1950. Identified with conservative elements in the revolution, Arana was undoubtedly Arbenz's principal rival for the presidency. Arbenz is widely believed to have been responsible for the killing. British ambassador C. C. H. Lee reported that Arana's death made it possible for Arévalo "to achieve his object of subjecting Guatemala to Moscow's plans," since Arana had been the "sole moderating influence on the more extreme members of this government." He considered Guatemala to be "on the point of becoming the first 'iron-curtain' state in this continent"; and, "unless the United States Government adopt a very strong attitude towards the leaders of the Guatemalan State, we shall be confronted with a Kremlin-controlled focus in Central America of incalculable potential danger. The unblushing hypocrisy and the dastardly treachery of the present top men of Guatemala in this murder of Arana warrant the development of our future policy towards them upon a premise that their avowed object is to make Guatemala one of Moscow's satellites."[34]

Arévalo left office early in 1951 in an atmosphere of rising tension between the two countries. The United States had not appointed a successor to Patterson; no arms had been sold to Guatemala since 1948; influential members of Congress and leaders of the national press had taken positions favoring the United Fruit Company and defending the former ambassador.

Following Arbenz's election, the department expressed a view that "there is at least some reason to believe that it [the Arbenz administration] may take steps to end Guatemala's procrastination on the Communist question. If it does not, a re-consideration of Guatemalan policy in the light of world events will be in order. At this date, no Guatemalan who is genuinely interested can have any doubt of the U.S.'s attitude toward international Communism and its manifestations in that country." The department would have to manage policy toward Guatemala skillfully, possibly through consultation with the American republics, since "even though Latin American states might feel a deep concern with developments in Guatemala there would doubtless be many which would censure any United States act or policy which was or appeared to be interventionist (*FRUS* 2 [1950]: 928–930).[35]

The tension was increased when Pres. Arbenz proclaimed a new Agrarian Reform Law on 17 June 1952. It expropriated uncultivated lands and offered compensation in government bonds. The United Fruit Company lost a substantial portion of its fallow lands as a result of the act, which, of course, also affected large Guatemalan landowners. The Department of State protested the expropriation, alleging that United Fruit had been discriminated against and that the Payment in government bonds was not fair compensation under international law.[36]

Arbenz also constructed a highway and a port at Santo Tomás that offered competition to the monopolistic privileges formerly enjoyed by the IRCA, and he built power facilities to open up a market largely controlled by North American interests. The dispute over the land expropriations was still going on in 1954, when the invasion led by Col. Carlos Castillo Armas took place.

The Eisenhower administration took office in January 1953. In September of that year it began to dismantle the Good Neighbor policy by financing an invasion and planning to install its own man as successor to Arbenz. This course would require armed intervention and interference in domestic politics on a scale that had not been seen in the Americas since the Marines invaded Nicaragua in 1926. Four factors made this sudden transformation of policy possible: (a) willingness to employ force; (b) development of a two-track policy; (c) cooperation of certain other American republics; and (d) secrecy of operations.

Willingness to Employ Force

The new men who came to office with Pres. Eisenhower were uncommitted to the Good Neighbor policy. They were members of the Republican party, which had taken no position, as a party, on the Good Neighbor policy, although some of its prominent members, such as Sen. Arthur Vandenberg, had supported it. The new administration repudiated the name "Good Neighbor" and spoke of a "Good Partner" policy. However, it was obligated by the Bogotá Charter to continue the policy of nonintervention, which "perhaps represents the greatest conquest of Pan Americanism. No other international principle has had such deep roots in the juridical conscience of the American states or had greater importance in the life of the hemisphere" (Castañeda 1970: 168–169).[37]

John Foster Dulles, secretary of state, had, as a member of the law firm of Sullivan and Cromwell, served as an attorney for IRCA and had taken a strong anti-Communist line in the 1952 election. In this campaign, he had criticized the Truman-Acheson policies as being merely "reactive" and had favored the liberation of countries of Eastern Europe from the domination of the Soviet Union (Blasier 1976: 165, 229).

His brother, Allen Welsh Dulles, who became director of the Central Intelligence Agency (CIA) in January 1953 when its former director, Gen. Walter Bedell Smith, became undersecretary of state, had enjoyed a successful career in the wartime intelligence service of the United States. Writing in the *New York Times* on 29 April 1966, Tom Wicker said:

> As long as his brother, John Foster Dulles, was Secretary of State, Allen Dulles had no need to chafe under political "control." The Secretary had an almost equal fascination for devious back-alley adventure in what he saw as a world-wide crusade. . . .
>
> Thus in the Dulles period at the C.I.A. there was a peculiar set of circumstances. An adventurous director, inclined to rely on his own extremely good and informed intuition, widely traveled, read and experienced, with great prestige and the best connections in Congress, whose brother held the second highest office in the administration, and whose President completely trusted and relied upon both, was able to act almost at will and was shielded from any unpleasant consequences.

The fact that Allen Dulles was able, in private talks in a car or at home with his brother Foster, to clear his plans without having them monitored by Foster's Department of State, meant that the CIA was nearly independent of the department's regular procedures in its dealings with Guatemalans.[38]

Uninhibited by the twenty-year-old tradition of nonintervention in the American republics, Eisenhower, Smith, and the Dulles brothers were faced in Guatemala with a government they regarded as "soft" on communism, a government that permitted the open organization of a Communist party, and appointed Communists to important government positions, although there were none in the cabinet. In addition there was the expropriation of United Fruit Company land and, finally, the government's encouragement and support of efforts to bring down dictators such as Trujillo in the Dominican Republic.[39]

Confronted by similar problems with regard to Guatemala, the Truman administration had protested, refused to provide arms to Arévalo and Arbenz, and limited financial and other aid. Beyond this it did not go. In writing to Truman on 3 May 1961 about the Bay of Pigs fiasco, Acheson said: "Why we ever engaged in this asinine Cuban adventure, I cannot imagine. Before I left [the department] it was mentioned to me and I told my informants how you and I had turned down similar suggestions for Iran and Guatemala and why I thought that this Cuban idea had been put aside, as it should have been" (1980: 207).[40]

The "suggestions" for action had presumably come from the CIA. They were turned down by men who had made a commitment to the Good Neighbor policy and who would not entertain notions that were different from those that had been worked out by Roosevelt, Hull, and Welles in dealing with Mexican land and oil expropriations from 1938 to 1941. Their views, on the whole, were shared by the officers of the Department of State, for the great majority of whom nonintervention was not only a treaty obligation, but a traditional, nearly sacrosanct, principle for dealing with Latin American governments. As John M. Cabot, assistant secretary of state for American republics affairs under Sec. Dulles wrote, "I had been brought up on the doctrine of non-intervention and I could recall various episodes in which intervention had ended disastrously" (1979: 23—24).[41]

Cabot recalls that soon after his installation as assistant secretary he talked with undersecretary Smith about Guatemala. Smith "suggested a coup against the Arbenz government, pointing out that the coup against the Mossadegh government in Iran had been staged by the CIA and the British secret service and that our involvement had not become public at the time." Cabot suggested that "it would be better to act through the Organization of American States if that were possible, and he [Smith] acquiesced" (ibid.: 90). Cabot's position would almost certainly have been taken by nearly all the staff in the Latin American area of the department.

This point is an important one, and necessary to indicate the extent of the contrast between the style of the officers in the foreign service and that of the new men in the Republican party and the CIA. As Robert F. Woodward, who was deputy assistant secretary of state from July 1953 to October 1954, has stated, "A few months after Braden's departure, all of his immediate lieutenants had left

the Bureau of Inter-American Affairs and the Bureau was manned
throughout with Foreign Service Officers steeped in the tradition of
nonintervention and just as dedicated to maintaining this policy as
before World War II. However, gradually, this attitude was affected by
the alienation of the Soviet Union and steadily increasing polariza-
tion of relations between the communist nations and the West."[42]
Further,

> So far as "indoctrination" is concerned, there was no delib-
> erate, planned or systematic training in policy for the FSOs
> who were working on Latin American relations. But "non-
> intervention" was so much the centerpiece of all relations with
> Latin America that it loomed like Mount Hood or Mount Rainier
> on the landscape. It was just there. You took it for granted as
> being something big and immovable. Charles Evans Hughes had
> taken a big step, in Habana, by almost committing the U.S.
> Then, in Montevideo, Hull had added to it. And President Roose-
> velt's visit to BA put the seal on it. And then, in any situation
> where an attitude was shown—and in speeches—deference was
> shown to the policy and commitment. The big test came when
> the Mexicans seized the oil properties—and non-intervention
> prevailed.
>   In all these circumstances, the generality of FSOs who had
> gone through these years in Latin America thought that Braden
> was a veritable idiot to get so mixed up in the internal affairs of
> Argentina.[43]

It was men with these ideas who concluded the Rio Treaty of 1947,
a treaty intended to provide a genuinely inter-American method of
dealing with security problems that unilateral intervention had previously addressed, and it was these men who wrote the principles of
nonintervention and juridical equality into the Charter of Bogotá.
They thought they had created a new type of international system
that, within the Charter of the United Nations, would defend and
promote the interests of all Americans.

Thus Cabot was entirely within this tradition when he suggested
to Smith that the Guatemalan question should be taken up in the
OAS, and he was presumably pleased when Smith "acquiesced."
Such "acquiescence" was the initial step in a long series of deceptions, and attempted deceptions, first of the Department of State,
and second of the U.S. public and press, that characterized the policy
directed by the CIA in coming years.[44]

In late April 1953, probably after his conversation with Bedell Smith, Cabot went to Guatemala for talks with officials. He wrote later, "My talks in Guatemala were highly unsatisfactory. The Foreign Minister [Raúl Osegueda] was a complete jackass who talked endlessly without making any sense. President Arbenz had the pale, cold-lipped look of the ideologue and showed no interest in my suggestions for a change of course in his government's direction. He had obviously sold out to the Communists and that was that" (ibid.: 87; and Blasier 1976: 160).

That Smith's "acquiescence" was a sham was discovered by Cabot in September 1953. He says that in that month he realized that action through the OAS was not even remotely possible. "After much soul-searching I went to Bedell Smith and said that I thought that a CIA-organized coup was the only solution. He nodded and smiled, and I got the impression that the plan was already under way." He added: "An officer in ARA was designated liaison with other agencies involved in developing the plans. For the rest of my tour as Assistant Secretary I was in constant touch with this officer, but I never knew the details of the planned operation, nor did I want to know them; my principal concern was to keep secret any United States involvement in the projected coup" (Cabot 1979: 87).[45]

It was in this way that the traditional policy of nonintervention was changed. The assistant secretary of state for inter-American affairs went over to the other camp; he agreed that a "CIA-organized coup" was the only solution to the Guatemalan problem and then endeavored to keep the "projected coup" a secret from all but one other officer in the Department of State.

There was no debate on the issue in the Department of State because none but one of the officers below the level of the assistant secretary was aware of the president's authorization for the CIA to organize an invasion. The secret was well kept: "Only one or two of the highest officers of the Department of State were aware of all the important activities of this agency [CIA], and I doubt if they could be sure that they knew for certain what the agency was up to."[46] And even earlier, Robert F. Woodward said,

> I can testify that, as Deputy Assistant Secretary of Inter-American Affairs from July 1953, to October 1954, I did not have any inkling until about April, 1954, that the effort to overthrow Arbenz in Guatemala was planned. . . . The background for this intervention was of course the growing fear of communist subversion or takeover efforts. Secretary Dulles was particularly

convinced that the strong dictatorial governments in Latin America were key elements in providing the U.S. with the cooperation
it needed in unpredictable emergencies.[47]

This change in attitude reflected U.S. policy worldwide. Had the
Communists been successful in Guatemala, they would have under-
cut Dulles's attempts to induce governments in other areas to take
strong action against Communist movements. In October 1953 the
British government had taken decisive action in British Guiana by
landing troops and suspending the constitution in order to prevent
the People's Progressive party from organizing a Communist state.
This landing of troops offered Sec. Dulles an example of ways of dealing with Guatemala.[48]

Development of a Two-Track Policy

Once it had been determined in the late summer of 1953 that force
might be used to unseat Arbenz, the acceptance of the CIA as the
planner demanded the adoption of a two-track policy.

The "radioman" of the invasion, David Atlee Phillips, writes that
he had thought about his part in the Guatemalan revolution:

> It was clear that the Guatemalan operation of CIA was brazen
> intervention. After reviewing the documents left behind by Ar-
> benz and his collaborators, I was more inclined to agree with
> those who saw the endeavor as a justifiable act of American for-
> eign policy. The documents revealed a paradigm of Soviet Cold
> War expansionism, a program clearly designed to establish a
> power base in the Western Hemisphere. Certainly President
> Eisenhower had reached that conclusion. He considered Gua-
> temala a CIA success, and did not have, I am sure, any moral
> qualms about sponsoring it. (1977: 53)

It appears, however, that Eisenhower had two qualms about openly
"sponsoring" the CIA. One, a nonmoral one, was that it was essential to protect the CIA from publicity in order to maintain secrecy
about its methods and resources. The other, more "moral," was that
it was necessary, or seemed so, to be protective of the inter-American
system; it would not do simply to shrug off the obligations and traditions of twenty years and to ignore the institution of consultation.
Therefore, on one track the CIA was secretly dispatched, carrying
advice to Castillo Armas, and men, supplies, arms, and aircraft to
Honduras and Nicaragua. On the other, the Department of State

moved openly and sedately in traditional fashion, respectful of its obligations to the OAS, and to the established consultation procedures.

The Dulles brothers, however, did not expect the second track to get rid of Arbenz. They used it to throw observers off the scent and to give the impression that the United States was trying to do everything possible to make a persuasive case that would justify the OAS's taking effective action against Guatemala because it had permitted Communist penetration into the hemisphere. Evidence of this tack is provided by a talk between Foster and Allen Dulles in which the former said that "he did believe that, as a minimum, proceeding along the lines of the resolution (that is calling a meeting of consultation) would give a subsequent armed intervention a more legitimate appearance. He [Foster] explained to the CIA director, 'If something like this [some action along the lines of the resolution passed down there] got underway, it might make other things more natural'" (Immerman 1982: 155).[49]

The first track was a secret to all but a very small number of officers in the department, at least until April 1954. From that date, until 18 June 1954, most of the officers dealing with Latin America were given the impression that they were preparing a case against Guatemala for presentation to a meeting of consultation of the ministers of foreign affairs of the American states. This was also the impression given to Latin American governments and to the North American public. Within their own organization, the Department of State, the officers who had been brought up as noninterventionists found no place to make their case. See, for example, the telegram from a distressed Francis White, U.S. ambassador to Mexico, who explained the reasons why a number of Mexicans were forming the opinion that the government of the United States was "implicated" on the side of Castillo Armas. He thought the United States was "slow and uncertain" in refuting "false charges" and suggested that it would be wise to put "the full weight and prestige of our Government" behind a statement that "we are not responsible for or involved" in the Guatemalan affair. "This assumes that the Department can safely assert that the fruit company's hands are clean and knows that no agency of our Government has been concerned. It also presupposes that our shipments of arms to Honduras in particular could be shown not to have aided the insurgents."[50]

None of the officers of the "old school" resigned from the department or the foreign service over the issue of the Guatemalan invasion, once the full extent of the CIA's part in Arbenz's overthrow was known. They were busy making the case for an OAS resolution; many of them felt that the arrival in Guatemala of a disguised cargo of arms from the Soviet bloc was proof that the threat of communism was real. In any case, by staying in the "system" it might be possible to mitigate the effects thereon of the violation of the Good Neighbor policy. Members of a "new school" were now in the ascendancy, and they were across the Potomac River, in the CIA. The Department of State had been secretly superseded, and the secretary of state was a party to the secret.

The First Track.   Organized in 1947, the CIA had three types of function: (1) intelligence gathering and analysis; (2) the protection of its own integrity—counterintelligence; and (3) political intervention. The last is "a tool of middle resort, lying somewhere between a note of diplomatic protest and sending in the Marines" (Powers 1979: vii). The "adventurers" in the CIA "thought of the world as being infinitely plastic; they thought they could do anything with funds and a broad okay from the top, and they offered policymakers in the late 1940s and early 1950s an irresistible promise: that they might achieve secretly what the United States government felt it could not attempt openly" (ibid.: 37). The renewed and expanded authorization for the CIA's actions was contained in "National Security Council Directive on Covert Operations" (NSC 5412), approved by Pres. Eisenhower on 15 March 1954.[51] The report of the Hoover Commission in that year provides an informal statement of the meaning of the agency's covert activities:

> There are no rules in such a game. Hitherto acceptable norms of human conduct do not apply. If the U.S. is to survive, long-standing American concepts of "fair play" must be reconsidered. We must develop effective espionage and counterespionage services. We must learn to subvert, sabotage and destroy our enemies by more clever, more sophisticated and more effective methods than those used against us. It may become necessary that the American people be acquainted with, understand and support this fundamentally repugnant philosophy. (Stockwell 1978: 251).[52]

The CIA was able to operate nearly without budgetary restrictions or congressional oversight. Its funds, which grew rapidly in the 1950s, were hidden in various categories of appropriations for the military services. (Serious questioning of the agency's operations began only after its failure at the Bay of Pigs in 1961.)

The adventurers had, in "a classic of quiet political subversion," removed Mohammed Mossadegh, prime minister of Iran, in August 1953 (Powers 1979: 85).[53] This success encouraged Eisenhower and the CIA to undertake the overthrow of Arbenz in Guatemala. In this they were seconded by John Foster Dulles, who was determined to halt the establishment of Communist regimes in the Western Hemisphere, and who "wanted an activist CIA" (ibid.: 83). "Once Arbenz's exact political coloration had been identified—a shade of pink made up of reformism, which inconvenienced American commercial interests, anti-Americanism, excessive tolerance of Communists— there was not much question what Foster Dulles's policy toward Guatemala would be. The question was not whether to remove him, but how" (ibid.: 85).

Since it was not regarded as possible to deal with Arbenz by sending in the marines, the "job of his removal was turned over to the CIA" (ibid.). The method, which cannot yet be described in full documentary detail, was to bypass the Department of State by authorizing the CIA to support Castillo Armas in the training of troops, in their supply, and especially in their support with airpower.[54]

The CIA's plan of action involved the provision of arms to Castillo Armas and his men (variously estimated at 200 to 450), their training, and air support when they entered Guatemala from Honduras. United States ground troops were not involved. The planes were piloted by private fliers, under contract, most of whom were U.S. citizens. Jerry De Larme was one of these; he later flew aircraft for Somoza in the Nicaragua–Costa Rica affair in 1955–1956.

In the process of bypassing the department, Amb. Rudolph E. Schoenfeld, "a correct and reserved career diplomat of the old school" (Blasier 1976: 163), was replaced by John E. Peurifoy, a former army officer who had made a career as an administrator in the department and had served as ambassador in Greece.[55] Special arrangements must have been made for handling some of Peurifoy's dispatches. They may have been received only by the officer mentioned by Cabot (1979: 87); it is apparent that some of his cables went to the CIA over its private facilities, rather than to State. Allen Dulles, asked by his brother if there was "anything new," replied "There are a lot of messages,—with several very good ones from Peurifoy."[56] It is possible that the officer in question was Henry F. Holland, who succeeded Cabot as assistant secretary in January 1954. Holland, an able Texas lawyer, fluent in Spanish, is reported to have been "horrified" to learn that twenty million dollars had been set aside for "Arbenz's overthrow." Undersec. Smith overruled his protests, but Holland "continued to object to both the Americanization and the militarization of the projected coup." However, Holland is reported not so much to have opposed "the goal of Arbenz's overthrow as he did the ostentatious scale of the CIA's role" (Powers 1979: 86).

It has also been suggested by Edward A. Jamison, a State Department officer concerned with OAS affairs at the time, that the principal person in the department on whom Sec. Dulles relied for day-to-day liaison with the CIA was Raymond G. Leddy, chief of the Central American Division in the Bureau of Inter-American Affairs. And Corson states that "in the Arbenz operation" John Foster Dulles "handed the ball to Raymond G. Leddy, the officer in charge of Central American–Panamanian Affairs," and that Leddy "had put together the CIA's operational system in South America." He states further that R. Richard Rubottom, director of middle American affairs from 1952 to 1953, "had gotten wind of Leddy's plan. As a result, Undersecretary of State Walter Bedell Smith told Rubottom, in effect, not to stick his nose into matters of no concern to him" (Corson 1977: 356). Rubottom was transferred to Madrid in 1953, and Leddy succeeded him. Rubottom, however, does not think there was any connection between his move and the Guatemalan affair, since he had been in the department for three years in 1953, so his reassignment was probably a routine matter.[57] By replacing Cabot, Rubottom, and Schoenfeld, however, the way was cleared for establishing a system that, below the assistant secretary, excluded the Department of State from any influence over events in Guatemala until the end of June 1954.

The *Alfhem*, a British vessel chartered by a Swedish company, with a cargo of about two thousand tons of small arms and ammunition manufactured by Skoda in Czechoslovakia and disguised as optical equipment, loaded at the Polish port of Szczecin and reached Guatemala on 15 May. The Department of State in commenting on the shipment merely said, "Because of the origin of these arms, the point of their embarkation, and destination, and the quantity of armaments involved, the Department of State considers that this is a development of gravity" (*DSB* [31 May 1954]: 835). Sec. Dulles asked his brother: "Does this [the shipment of arms] invalidate [your] program?" The director of the CIA "said no, but he doesn't know if we can pull it off next month. We can't do much unless a large or substantial section of the army is with us. Campbell went down, and got back last night, but AWD does not yet have his report. They are planning to work right ahead, but will take a reappraisal."[58]

Whether the "army is with us" appeared to depend in part at least on bribery by the CIA. "Guatemalan Army officers who could not be convinced that Arbenz was a Communist were bought off by direct bribery" (Ambrose 1981: 229). Authors "such as [Guillermo] Toriello, [Raúl] Osegueda, and [Luis] Cardozo y Aragón, stress the corruption of the military by the United States Embassy in Guatemala" (Cehelsky 1965[?]: 49).[59]

Although Guatemala could not buy arms in the United States, the U.S. Army and Air Force missions remained in the country, and Woodward reported that the U.S. military wished to use the missions to inform the Guatemalan army "of the extent of Communist penetration in an effort to shape their attitudes against the Government. Leddy stated that the CIA project on this line started in January had produced no results to date."[60]

The secretary planned a press conference for June 15 and called his brother for suggestions. Allen Dulles called back "and said the Sec. should say the situation in Guatemala is getting very critical as a result of repressive and communist dictatorial activities of the government, and that we hope and expect that the army and the loyal anti-communists in the country which constitute the vast majority of the people will clean their own house. The Sec. questioned the use of 'army' as it implies we want a revolution. AWD said he hadn't thought of it that way, and they agreed the Sec. would not use that word."[61]

Castillo Armas moved into Guatemalan territory on June 18. On the previous day, Holland had said that secretary of war Anderson had told him "that he has a military telegram from Honduras that Armas (?) 'is moving.' The Secretary said he did not know what that means, but he supposes it means something. H. said A. is a revolutionary individual lurking in the forest."[62]

The Guatemalan army put up only token resistance, although it greatly outnumbered the invading force. U.S. planes, based in Nicaragua and piloted by North Americans, appeared over Guatemala City and dropped numerous small bombs.[63]

When Castillo Armas lost two of the three planes delivered to him originally, the CIA was able to obtain assistance for him on short notice. On June 22, Pres. Eisenhower held a meeting with the Dulles brothers and Holland.

> The point at issue was whether the US should cooperate in replacing the bombers. . . . Holland made no secret of his conviction that the US should keep hands off, insisting that other LA republics would, if our action became known, interpret our shipment of planes as intervention in Guatemala's internal affairs. Others, however, felt that our agreeing to replace the bombers was the only hope for Castillo Armas, who was obviously the only hope of restoring freedom to Guatemala.

> I [Pres. Eisenhower] considered the matter carefully. I realized
> full well that US intervention in Central America and Caribbean
> affairs earlier in the century had greatly injured our standing in
> all of LA. On the other hand, it seemed to me that to refuse to
> cooperate in providing indirect support to a strictly anti-Commu-
> nist faction in this struggle would be contrary to the letter and
> spirit of the Caracas resolution. I had faith in the strength of the
> inter-American resolve therein set forth. On the actual value of a
> shipment of planes, I knew from experience the important psy-
> chological impact of even a small amount of air support. In any
> event, our proper course of action—indeed my duty—was clear
> to me. We would replace the airplanes. (Eisenhower 1963: 426)

As Eisenhower indicated, "Delivery of the planes was prompt and
Castillo successfully resumed his progress" (ibid.). Further, "The air
support enjoyed by Castillo Armas, though meager, was important in
relative terms; it gave the regular armed forces an excuse to take action in their own hands to throw out Arbenz. The rest of Latin America was not in the least displeased. . . . By the middle of 1954, Latin
America was free, for the time being at least, of any fixed outposts of
Communism" (ibid.: 426, 427).[64]

The CIA's radio station in Honduras exaggerated both the success
of Castillo Armas and the size of his army.[65] As the result of an ultimatum from the Guatemalan army, Arbenz resigned on June 27,
while Castillo Armas was still at Chiquimula, some seventy-five
miles from the capital (see Blasier 1976: 172–177). Arbenz and some
770 of his closest associates were accepted in nine Latin American
embassies.

Dulles's interest in finding ways of breaking the time-honored
Latin American custom of giving sanctuary to political refugees in
embassies provides a striking indication of the intensity of feeling in
Washington. There was discussion in the Department of State of "an
OAS detention center," of denying international Communists "the
traditional benefits of asylum," and of the granting by Guatemala
of safe-conducts "for dangerous asylees conditioned on their being
transported to and accepted by an Iron Curtain country."[66] The tradition was too strong, however, and those given asylum were allowed
to leave Guatemala with no restrictions.[67]

On the twenty-seventh, Toriello told Peurifoy that he knew that
the United States could stop the fighting "in fifteen minutes" if
it wished. But the bombings did not stop until Guatemala accepted
the leadership of Castillo Armas (*FRUS* 4 [1952–54]: 1188–1189).[68]
There was no further fighting. The Communists, said to number

four thousand party members, failed to mount any kind of opposition and did not organize any sort of guerrilla activities in the hills: "AWD said the Commies have proved to be yellow."[69] One of the Communist responses to such a charge might have been that they had not received any of the arms from the *Alfhem*; the army took control of them on arrival and would not release them following the invasion. A second response might have been that the strength of the anti-Communist, pro–United States Guatemalan army prevented Communist organizations from training or equipping any mass movement that might have opposed the army. In any case, the absence of even token resistance raises serious questions about the reality of a "Communist menace" in Guatemala.[70]

The interest of the department and the CIA, however, did not end with Arbenz's resignation. For ten days there was pulling and hauling that involved six ambitious colonels, Amb. Peurifoy and his staff, and representatives of the CIA. The Dulles brothers had agreed that they could not let Castillo Armas down, and this became the primary purpose of U.S. maneuverings.

The first objective was to get rid of Col. Carlos Enrique Díaz, to whom Arbenz had surrendered power on condition that he not negotiate with Castillo Armas. Peurifoy had at first accepted Díaz.[71] However, Díaz referred to Arbenz as his friend and pledged himself to follow his policies in his speech that followed Arbenz's address of resignation. This angered Peurifoy and, more important, two CIA agents: John Doherty and Enno Hobbing. These two met with Díaz; a portion of their conversation follows:

"Wait a minute, Colonel," Hobbing suddenly interjected. "Let me explain something to you," he said sternly, pointing a finger at Colonel Díaz. "You made a big mistake when you took over the government."

Hobbing paused to let his words sink in. Then he continued: "Colonel, you're just not convenient for the requirements of American foreign policy."

Díaz was taken aback. "But," he stammered, "I talked to your ambassador. He gave me his approval."

"Well, Colonel," Hobbing said, "there is diplomacy and then there is reality. Our ambassador represents diplomacy. I represent reality. And the reality is that we don't want you."

"You mean I can't stay in office?" Díaz meekly asked.

Hobbing shook his head. (Schlesinger and Kinzer 1982: 206–207)

Díaz asked if he could hear the ambassador confirm Hobbing's statement, and Peurifoy, routed from bed at about 3:00 in the morning of June 29, told Díaz that he was "amazed and astounded at fact that he had permitted Arbenz in delivering his valedictory to charge that US was responsible for supplying aviators to forces attacking Guatemala, and for his general line to say we had used 'pretext of Communism' to unleash aggression on this country." He suggested to the State Department that Díaz name Col. Elfego Monzón, "well-known for his anti-Communist feelings, as President" (*FRUS* 4 [1952–54]: 1192).[72] It should be noted that Peurifoy in this telegram to the department gives no indication that CIA officers had met with Díaz, nor that this was the reason for his being called at 3:00 A.M., as Richard H. Smith suggests (cited in Schlesinger and Kinzer 1982: 206–207). After further discussions Díaz informed Peurifoy that "he and Col. [José Angel] Sánchez had decided resign from Junta since it appeared they were unacceptable to Castillo Armas" (*FRUS* 4 [1952–54]: 1197).[73] Allen Dulles told Foster that he did not "like Díaz—he was put in by Arbenz. They are maneuvering to get him out and get a better army officer in."[74]

Monzón became head of a junta that he formed with Cols. José Luis Cruz Salazar and Maurice Dubois of the army in Guatemala City. Monzón then went to San Salvador to negotiate with Castillo Armas. He was about to return without reaching an understanding when Peurifoy joined them and arranged for a new junta of five, adding Castillo Armas and Col. Enrique Trinidad Oliva, of the liberation forces. This plan was part of an agreement signed on July 2.

Holland had originally proposed that Peurifoy not go to San Salvador, because "it would inflate propaganda against U.S. for alleged complicity in movement against Arbenz government. Present anti-U.S. feeling serious on this issue."[75] On June 29, Holland still hoped for backing from the Council of the OAS and he asked Peurifoy to arrange for requests from both the junta and Castillo Armas for a meeting that would bring about the end of fighting and a meeting of the two groups with the council in San Salvador to arrange a settlement.[76] However, Peurifoy was unable to arrange for a cable from the Monzón junta,[77] nor did the junta desire that the Inter-American Peace Committee move from Mexico City to Guatemala. Thus when negotiations between Monzón and Castillo Armas seemed on the brink of failure, Peurifoy went to El Salvador in response to telephoned instructions from Holland. On his arrival at the office of the president of El Salvador (on July 1), Peurifoy received a telephone call from Sec. Dulles, "who emphasized the importance of bringing the

negotiations to a satisfactory conclusion and that, if it were necessary, I was authorized to 'crack some heads together.'" He avoided
such bashing, however, and reported only that after he had talked for
a half hour with each man, he emerged with the agreement (ibid.:
1202–1208).[78]

Monzón's two colleagues resigned almost immediately to take diplomatic posts in the United States, and each was reported to have received $100,000 in addition, presumably from the CIA. Cruz Salazar
was appointed ambassador of Guatemala in Washington on July 25,
and on the same day Dubois was named as Guatemalan consul general in New York (Cehelsky 1965[?]: 63–65; Dept. of State Diplomatic List, 1954f; Paul Kennedy, *New York Times* [9, 26 July 1954]).
On July 7, after their resignations, Castillo Armas was elected provi-
sional president by the remaining three-man junta—Monzón, Trinidad Oliva, and Castillo Armas himself.[79] The United States recognized the new regime on July 13 and followed this with substantial
economic and technical assistance. Castillo Armas, for his part, declared the Communist party illegal, restored the expropriated land
to the United Fruit Company, and opened the country to foreign con-
cessionary interests.

The Second Track.   Sec. Dulles decided to make use of the Tenth
Inter-American Conference, held in Caracas in March 1954, to secure joint action against communism in the Americas. He proposed
a resolution that declared that "the domination or control of the political institutions of any American State by the international Communist movement, extending to this Hemisphere the political system of an extra-continental power, would constitute a threat to the
sovereignty and political independence of the American States, endangering the peace of America, and would call for appropriate action in accordance with existing treaties" (U.S. Dept. of State 1955).

However, the Latin American representatives, knowing that Dulles
had Guatemala in mind, insisted on amending the resolution so that
it would call at the end for "a meeting of consultation to consider the
adoption of appropriate action in accordance with existing treaties."
This satisfied the amenders that no unilateral action could be taken
by the United States under inter-American treaties. On his return on
14 March, Dulles said of the "Declaration of Caracas," "In effect it
makes as the international policy of this hemisphere a portion of the
Monroe Doctrine which has largely been forgotten and which re-
lates to the extension to this hemisphere of the political system of
despotic European powers" (*DSB* [22 March 1954]: 429). If this were
the case, of course, the hemisphere would have to relate a given in-

stance to the doctrine through a collective decision, which it got no chance to make.

Suggesting that this should be done, Dulles said in a speech on 16 March entitled "The Declaration of Caracas and the Monroe Doctrine" that "it would be appropriate for the American States to unite to declare the danger to them all which would come if international communism seized control of the political institutions of any American State. I believe that this action, if it is properly backed up, can have a profound effect in preserving this hemisphere from the evils and woes that would befall it if any one of our American States became a Soviet Communist puppet. That would be a disaster of incalculable proportions (ibid. [29 March 1954]: 466).[80]

The references to the Monroe Doctrine brought back to inter-American relations a notion that had not been influential for some time. The term "Monroe Doctrine" had even gone out of style in Good Neighborly discourse. The implication of its renaissance was that the United States would oppose the imposition of European rule in the American continents. To justify recourse to the doctrine, though, it was necessary to demonstrate, or to invent, a threat to an American state from the Soviet Union, or from local communism.

The local Communists were noisy, abusive of the United States, supportive of Arbenz's expropriations, quick to accept invitations to Communist party conferences in the Soviet Union and elsewhere, and influential in a number of government posts. How strong were they? Even Peurifoy suggests that they were weak: "The carefully contrived Communist machine collapsed overnight; its leaders ran, snatching on the way as much cash as they could from the public till" (ibid. [6 September 1954]: 335–336).[81]

The Department of State itself at first thought the Guatemalan Communists were weak. In a pamphlet published by the department in August 1954, the following statement was made: "The thinking of Guatemala's intellectuals during the 1930's and the early 1940's became covered with a glaze of nationalism and Marxism, a scrambled compound which was short of the full strength of militant communism" (U.S. Dept. of State 1954: 44). This statement, contained in a report prepared apparently by the Department's Office of Intelligence and Research, was regarded as not giving sufficient support to Sec. Dulles's assertion in his address on 30 June that "the growth of communism in Guatemala was 'an intrusion of Soviet despotism.'" The department therefore issued a second pamphlet, in 1957, on the Guatemalan Communist party, which contained, verbatim, much of what had been said in the 1954 pamphlet, but without making any reference whatever to the existence of the earlier one. Among many changes made for the 1957 version, the foregoing statement was eliminated, and the claim was made that the Guatemalan affair was "the brazen attempt of international communism to establish a Soviet satellite in the Western Hemisphere" (ibid.: 1957: 2). The secretary's speech and the Monroe Doctrine were thus brought into line, however covertly (Wood 1968).

The difficulty with the department's citing the Monroe Doctrine in this fashion is that the decision to give the CIA authority to assist Castillo Armas was made in the late summer of 1953, at least six months prior to the "intrusion" represented by the disguised cargo of arms at Puerto Barrios aboard the *Alfhem*. This was not the first case of a Latin American country's purchasing arms from Czechoslovakia, but it was the first such case involving a government in whose councils Communists were influential. As such, it exacerbated the tension between Guatemala and the United States and was probably the most important factor affecting the attitude not only of Congress and the public, but also of the officers in the Department of State, nearly all of whom were still ignorant of the planned role of the CIA in the invasion proposed for the following month (Chardkoff 1967: 351).[82] It should be remembered that the Cold War was at a serious stage following the Korean War, and the worst would readily be thought of any actions or presumed actions of the Soviet Union.

To the official view that there was a Communist "beachhead" in Guatemala, Blasier replies:

> Familiarity with John Foster Dulles' personal and political objectives are essential to understanding the Guatemalan intervention of 1954. Dulles' policies toward Guatemala were in part a religious crusade against atheistic communism, in part an ideological struggle on behalf of free enterprise, and in part a political battle with Soviet expansionism. . . . He regarded this "victory" as one of the major constructive achievements of the Eisenhower administration and used it as a rallying cry in the 1954 and 1956 elections. This background helps explain why he was deaf to arguments that the Arbenz government was not, in fact, a Communist beachhead in the Americas. (1976: 229)[83]

At the Caracas Conference Dulles stated, "I believe that there is not a single American state which would practice intervention against another American state." At a news conference on 25 May, asked whether the United States would act alone or under the Rio

Treaty of 1947, Dulles replied, "We would expect to act under the Rio Pact and in full conformity with our treaty obligations. No member of the Rio Pact gives up what the Charter of the UN calls the inherent right of individual or collective self-defense; that right is reserved. Nevertheless, it is contemplated that, if the circumstances permit, there should be an effort, a sincere effort, at collective action and we would expect to comply with both the letter and spirit of our treaty obligations" (*DSB* [7 June 1954]: 874). On June 8, Dulles told a press conference that an exchange of views was under way with other American states as to whether or not a foreign ministers' meeting should be held on Guatemala; the United States was "disposed to feel that the situation is one which calls for such a meeting," but the outcome of the exchange of views was awaited (ibid. [21 June 1954]: 950). Finally, in a speech at Seattle on June 10, Dulles said he hoped "that the Organization of American States will be able to help the people of Guatemala to rid themselves of the malignant force which has seized on them." He thought that the evil design of communism to destroy the freedom and independence of Guatemala would "be thwarted by peaceful, collective processes. If so, the Organization of American States will attain a new stature and assert a new influence. The American Republics will have shown that diversity can unite so that it produces, not confusion but enlightened action" (ibid.: 938, 939).

Holland, the assistant secretary, on being informed by Sec. Dulles of the CIA's plans for an invasion of Guatemala, told his deputy, Robert F. Woodward, about the project. This was near the first of May 1954. Holland said that "when he accepted appointment as Assistant Secretary he had not contemplated carrying out relations by such methods." He told Woodward that he was "seriously considering resigning and returning to his law practice in Houston." Holland then asked Woodward "to think about his situation for a couple of hours and come back to advise him what he should do." Woodward advised Holland not to resign. Instead, he should

> make a determined effort to find some other method, within the inter-American organization, to try to solve the problem of the trend of the Guatemalan Government toward communist affiliation. A day or two after that, Holland told me that he had had another conversation with Secretary Dulles and that the Secretary had told him that Holland could have until December, 1954, to find some other method of solving the problem. Holland then held a series of meetings with a group of Latin American Ambassadors to the OAS, presumably to find such a method. These

meetings were closed and I did not take part nor was I informed about what was said.[84]

Holland also held at least nineteen meetings of what came to be known in the Department of State as the "Guatemalan Group" between 10 May and 2 July 1954. He said at the first of these that "he had been authorized by the Secretary to move to obtain OAS action against the Communist problem in Guatemala . . . to do nothing would be to admit that we are powerless to solve the problem; in the present world situation this would be intolerable. We should move toward application of the Caracas Resolution to Guatemala"[85]

Holland wrote to Dulles that in Guatemala "the test is whether the world Communist organization has the strength to establish a satellite nation in this hemisphere and, conversely, whether the free nations have the power to resist that attempt." If a satellite were established in the Americas, it "would enable Russia to claim throughout the world that the power of communism lies in its appeal to men's minds and not in fear or force." Since "the greatest significance of the Guatemalan test [lay] in its effect on all regional organizations similar to the Organization of American States," Holland judged that the policy of expressing a concern about communism had been "ineffective," that unilateral action by the United States would be "inconsistent with our treaty obligations and the firm policy which we have followed in this hemisphere for more than 20 years," and that action through the OAS was clearly the line that the United States "must follow" (*FRUS* 4 [1952–54]: 1107–1108).[86]

Holland proposed to take a "straw vote" of American republics on a resolution that would condemn Guatemala and apply sanctions. He would approach Brazil first and he hoped that by June 15 he would know whether the U.S. position was strong enough to call a meeting. John C. Hill would be recalled from Guatemala to prepare the case.

Action was immediate. On May 11, Dulles and Holland met with the Brazilian ambassador, João Carlos Muniz. Dulles said "he had come to the conclusion that the time had arrived when we must consider joint action regarding the Guatemalan problem." It appeared to him that "the penetration of communism in that Government was steadily extending and that it appeared to be spreading to surrounding countries." Muniz agreed to go to Rio de Janeiro and submit the problem to the president; Dulles warned that it would "be impossible to produce evidence clearly tying the Guatemalan Government to Moscow, that the decision must be a political one and based on our deep conviction that such a tie must exist."[87]

Holland also met with Alberto Lleras Camargo, secretary general of the OAS, who said that "opinion generally was not ready" to invoke the Caracas resolution, but that "it could be prepared in such a way that we could hope for success." Lleras thought that Holland could make several speeches expressing confidence "that the nations of America would not permit the establishment of a satellite nation here by the communist organization," but he also said that Holland should "refrain from any indication that the United States would act unilaterally."[88]

Further preparations were made with a meeting between Muniz, Holland, and Joe Martin, speaker of the House of Representatives. Holland said that "a point of frontal contact" between the Communists and the free world existed in Guatemala, "where the communist organization was undertaking to establish a satellite state." Further, "We felt the time had come to invoke the Caracas resolution and to apply against Guatemala those sanctions which might be necessary to eliminate the communist penetration there." Anti-Communist elements in Guatemala had "lost control of the situation," and if the Soviet Union could "establish a puppet state in this hemisphere it would destroy the argument that communism can capture governments only where it is supported by the threat of the Red Army and would win a tremendous propaganda victory."[89] A memorandum of May 14, attached to the record of the conversation, concludes: "Unless action is taken the establishment of the first Soviet-controlled 'People's Democracy' type of State in the Western Hemisphere is in sight. This would be the first occasion that a Communist-controlled state had been established outside of the area adjacent to Soviet military power and would represent a breakthrough of Soviet aggression into the inner defenses of the democratic community."[90]

Holland prepared for Dulles a document recommending that "the U.S. invoke consultative procedure under Rio Treaty to consider problems of international communism in Guatemala" (ibid.: 1108–1110). It was also presented to Muniz, who said that, "of the three courses of action mentioned in the document, i.e., inactivity, intervention and invocation of the Organ of Consultation, the last is clearly the best road. . . . It is time that the Organization of American States demonstrates that it is an instrument capable of meeting and solving problems." Muniz added that he was not sure that he could gain the support of his government or carry the hemisphere, but he felt "that the issue and the time justify our making the effort." In addition, Muniz said this was a good time to approach his government, "because he has been sending it reports emphasizing what he considers to be a decision on the part of the United States Government to revive the particularly close relationships that it sustained with Brazil during the war."[91]

The Guatemalan Group varied in size from seven to fifteen persons. Regular members were Holland, Dreier, Jamison, Leddy, and Woodward; others included John W. Fisher, Guatemalan desk officer, John C. Hill of the United States embassy in Guatemala City, Ambs. Walter J. Donnelly and William Pawley, and directors of offices such as E. G. Cale, H. S. Atwood, C. H. Burrows, William A. Wieland, Norman M. Pearson, and others. Beginning on June 7, Frank Holcomb of the CIA attended nearly all the meetings.[92]

On the ambassador's return, Brazil's support was announced for "a proposal to convoke the Organ of Consultation to consider the Guatemalan problem," although emphasis was given to "the necessity for a strong statement distinguishing between the United Fruit and the Communist problems in Guatemala."[93] On May 29, a circular telegram was sent "outlining our determination to call or support a call for an OAS meeting to deal with Communist penetration in Guatemala and arms shipments to that country. A meeting will not be called unless at least fourteen votes are assured."[94] Brazil's full support was now certain, and the United States had no desire "to impose any sanctions stronger than necessary to eliminate Communist penetration in Guatemala." The U.S. ambassadors were instructed to sound out the governments to which they were accredited.

This telegram marked a change in Washington's tactics, as John C. Hill explained:

> If we obtain a resolution requiring the prevention of movements of arms and Communist agents to Guatemala, this will enable us to stop ships including our own to such an extent that it will disrupt Guatemala's economy. The idea is that this will accelerate one of two developments: either it will encourage the Army or some other non-Communist elements to seize power or the Communists will exploit the situation to extend their control. If the latter occurs, it is thought, it will justify the American community, or if they won't go along, the U.S. to take strong measures.

> With this in the back of the policy making minds, a decision crystalized gradually over the past week to retreat from the former intent to call an OAS meeting to haul Guatemala up under the Caracas Resolution which in effect would have called for a finding by two-thirds of the States that Guatemala's political in-

stitutions were under the "domination and control of international Communism." With the Alfhem case fresh, it was thought more Latin Americans would go along under Article 6 of the Rio Treaty on a case of threat to the peace, based on "extensive penetration" of Guatemala by international Communism plus the arrival of arms from the Soviet orbit. It was also thought that a resolution calling only for prevention of movement of arms and agents would get more votes than one calling for economic sanctions or other tough action.

The opinion here seems to be that we have the necessary fourteen votes.[95]

On being asked what the United States would require "to give Guatemala a clean bill of health," Holland said, "The only action that would be required of Guatemala would be that she eliminate all Communists and Communist sympathizers from all public offices including labor organizations."[96] The United States proposed a resolution that would "prevent Guatemala from obtaining further armaments from communist sources, and . . . restrict the travel of communist agents to and from Guatemala. Actions taken by the members of the OAS in response to the resolution should include the inspection of shipping to Guatemala, the detention of armaments so found, and the control of international passenger traffic to and from that country."[97]

To Amb. Francis White, who had talked with the Mexican foreign minister, who "was strongly opposed to armed intervention," Holland said that if the measures proposed were not sufficient, the United States would "go further at a later meeting," but that he "felt certain that it would never be necessary to reach the point of armed intervention."[98]

Commenting on the resolution prepared for the OAS, the *New York Times* of June 13 said that, "because the State Department has all but decided on that course of action rather than on more drastic measures, it has apparently won the support of the other American republics except Guatemala. . . . What has also impressed the American republics, it is understood, is the earnestness with which the United States has prepared its case against Guatemala, a case that despite a fairly skeptical response at the start, has won wide support." This editorial is a remarkable tribute to the politics of deception Dulles followed at the time and to the sincerity of those officers of the department who were following the OAS track.

As early as the meeting of June 4, Holland said that he thought the United States should "call the OAS meeting sometime next week," which indicated that he was fairly certain that at least fourteen votes were secure.[99] However, no action was taken, despite Holland's views that the meeting should be held on June 21, in view of "insistent rumors" that additional shipments of arms were heading toward Guatemala.

In an official, but informal, letter dated 5 June, Leddy gave Peurifoy a more explicit explanation of the reasoning behind the new line adopted:

> First, by asking for advance OAS concurrence on a specific resolution, it is hoped that we may be assured of the votes in advance of a meeting and limit the meeting to the mere formality of approval, thereby avoiding a long drawn out debate and resulting bitterness and disunity. Second, by limiting the resolution to one authorization, believed to be the minimum step in the present circumstances, and one on which general concurrence is most likely to be obtained, it is hoped that success will be certain. Third, since the resolution is so drawn as to permit examination of traffic in both directions, it will be possible to halt effectively the normal flow of commerce. Fourth, this halting or interruption will be as effective as the most specific economic sanctions, which if proposed on their own would fall into certain opposition. Thus, in total, it is expected that we will achieve the ends desired by an easier and quicker route.

Using language quite distinct from that employed by Holland, Leddy said that "we are on the road of settling this problem, either by the means now devised or by some other means should these not succeed. There is 100 percent determination here, from the top down, to get rid of this stinker and not to stop until that is done. For this reason, our morale is rather high and I am sure the Embassy's will correspond as the methods utilized become more understandable" (ibid.: 1156–1157).

The U.S. tactic was to present a resolution that would have the agreement of the required majority of states in advance of the meeting, so that debate would be limited. By June 16, twelve countries had given their approval, and every effort was being made to bring Brazil into line, with the probability that Bolivia, Chile, Paraguay, and Uruguay would follow Brazil's lead.

The invasion of Guatemala on June 18 did not change the purpose of those charged with the approach through the OAS.[100] "Holland indicated that if Arbenz were overthrown, we would still go ahead with the Montevideo meeting but extend the date."[101] The Guatemalan

Group also thought that "the meeting was more necessary than ever and that the current Guatemalan revolution should be handled separately." Holland noted that Castillo Armas had no more than six hundred men, "that he counted on the defection of the Guatemalan Army, that since this defection did not occur he would probably lose." [102] Should this occur, the prestige of the United States would suffer in Latin America. Since "Guatemala is more than ever the underdog, and hence has very great appeal to all Latin Americans," the United States should take all steps possible to change that position, and "to take the stigma surrounding the revolution off the U.S." (ibid.: 1180).

At this same meeting of 23 June, it was noted that "Secretary Dulles would not approve sending notes to the Foreign Ministers in an effort to get their agreement in advance that no changes would be made in the draft resolution without the unanimous approval of the sponsoring group. He indicated that it would damage his prestige if some of these countries did not accept." Therefore, oral arrangements were proposed, and "when a total of fourteen countries, including ourselves, have approved this proposal the meeting will be called."

On June 25 Holland noted that Dulles "had not yet approved his recommendation that the OAS meeting be called." It was the secretary's view that, should Castillo Armas fail, Arbenz and Toriello would become heroes, and the United States might not then secure the passage of the resolution. "Such a major diplomatic defeat would be a great blow to the U.S. prestige." After discussion within the group, Holland decided that despite the risk he would recommend again that the meeting be called (ibid.: 1186). This time the secretary was more amenable, and on Saturday, June 26, Dreier, on behalf of eleven countries, asked that the Council of the OAS call a meeting of foreign ministers under Articles 6 and 11 of the Rio Treaty to consider "the demonstrated intervention of the international communist movement in the Republic of Guatemala" (*DSB* [5 July 1954]: 31–32). [103]

On Sunday, June 27, Arbenz resigned, and the following day the council voted to call the foreign ministers into session. It heard Dreier state that "the international Communist movement has achieved an extensive penetration of the political institutions" of Guatemala, as demonstrated by Guatemala's efforts to prevent action by the American states to restrain the progress of the international Communist movement, by the "open association" of Guatemala with the Soviet Union, by the affair of the *Alfhem* and its shipment of arms, by Guatemala's efforts to prevent the OAS from dealing with its charges of aggression, and by the support of the Soviet press and radio for Guatemala. Dreier noted the recent news that the Guatemalan government had been changed on June 27, but said that this did not mean there should be no meeting. It was necessary to prevent "the complete subordination of one of our Member States to Soviet communist imperialism. For when one State has fallen, history shows that another will soon come under attack" (ibid. [12 July 1954]: 45−47).[104]

The OAS Council voted to hold the meeting in Rio de Janeiro on July 7, but in view of events in Guatemala, it was never convened. The fact of the vote, however, gave Dulles the opportunity to praise the OAS in a speech on June 30: "The events of recent months and days add a new and glorious chapter to the already great tradition of the American States. . . . We are grateful that the Organization of American States showed that it could act quickly and vigorously in the aid of peace. There was proof that our American organization is not just a paper organization, but that it has vigor and vitality to act" (ibid.: 45).[105]

Had the United States desired a discussion in the OAS about the Guatemalan problem, it had an opportunity on June 16, at a meeting of the council. It did not take advantage of it, nor did any other government. Asked at his news conference on June 15 about a discussion in the OAS, Foster Dulles said there had been an exchange of views about an OAS meeting on Guatemala, but he had "no knowledge that it would be brought up" on the sixteenth at the meeting of the council. "The exchanges of views that have been taking place have been brought through diplomatic channels" (ibid. [28 June 1954]: 980).[106]

At the time of the invasion Guatemala appealed to the U.N. Security Council, charging intervention by Nicaragua and the United States; Henry Cabot Lodge said that his information "strongly suggests that the situation does not involve aggression but is a revolt of Guatemalans against Guatemalans." He added that Soviet charges that "the United States prepared this armed intervention were 'flatly untrue'" (Blasier 1976: 169−170).[107] The United States was able to delay action by the Security Council, and finally to prevent it. The Guatemalan government as early as June 19 invited the Inter-American Peace Committee (IAPC) to help restore peace. However, the next day Guatemala asked that the IAPC suspend the trip it had planned to make on June 20, since the U.N. Security Council "had taken cognizance of the Guatemalan complaint." The original appeal to the committee had apparently been taken to soften criticism of Guatemala for going to the United Nations, to get its appeal before the IAPC in case Guatemala were not satisfied with action in the Security Council, and to take advantage of the fact that Argentina and Mexico, which had voted against the Caracas resolution, were members of the IAPC (*New York Herald Tribune* [20 June 1954]). The committee remained on the alert, and Dreier said that the view of the United States "was that the Committee should proceed with investigation" of the "very serious" Guatemalan charges of "foreign aggression." This view was approved by Argentina, Brazil, and Cuba, which were members of the IAPC (ibid. [22 June 1954]).

On June 25, "in the teeth of a 69–1 United States Senate vote" to bring the case before the OAS, Guatemala "flatly refused" to accept a visit by the IAPC. However, on June 27, it agreed to accept the presence of the IAPC team. The group flew to Mexico City on June 29, stayed there overnight, and returned to Washington almost immediately on being informed by Guatemala, Honduras and Nicaragua that the threat to peace and security had been eliminated (ibid. [26 June, 9 July 1954]).[108] It is interesting to note that an appeal could be made to the IAPC without any involvement by the Council of the OAS.

It was thus evident that the United Nations, the OAS, and the IAPC had been prevented from taking any significant action on Guatemala. This, of course, was precisely what Eisenhower and the Dulles brothers desired. In view of the prevarications, denials, subterfuges, and evasions that were rife at the time, it is difficult to avoid concluding that, from the standpoint of the top policymakers, their request to the OAS was simply play acting.

Assuming that the CIA was able to pick its time to start Castillo Armas into Guatemala, and that Holland, knowing of plans for such an invasion, did not know anything about their maturation but anticipated that he had until December to work out an arrangement through the OAS, it was an easy matter for Sec. Dulles to seem to support him while really stringing him along and delaying the actual calling of a meeting of foreign ministers. This he did until June 26, the day before the Arbenz resignation. Coming when it did, rather than immediately after disclosure of the *Alfhem*'s cargo or on the heels of the invasion, it appeared that some members of the U.S. government were well aware that the Arbenz regime was on its last legs. Gordon Connell-Smith says that "the record suggests that the convocation of this meeting [of consultation] was no more than a smoke screen; that the United States had no wish to have the affair discussed in the OAS either" (1974: 71).[109]

This suggests that the effort by the Department of State, below Dulles and Smith, was an honest one. Holland and the Guatemalan

Group apparently believed that they would be able to rid Guatemala of Communists by means of the trade restrictions they would ask the OAS foreign ministers to ratify. If not, additional measures would be taken, but action would occur within the OAS, as Holland indicated. The best evidence to support this important point is offered in a June 15 memorandum from Holland to Dulles. In it Holland said that he would "most vigorously oppose" the use of a proposed press statement prepared by the CIA for the president:

> Our whole plan for an OAS meeting on Guatemala is based upon the principle that the United States is undertaking to solve this problem without unilateral intervention, whether political or economic, in Guatemalan affairs. I have reiterated this again and again to every Latin American Ambassador and so have our Ambassadors in those capitals.
>
> The CIA very understandably wants to bring both political and economic pressure to bear in Guatemala at this time. From their point of view I can see that this is logical. I object strenuously, however, because *by following this course we will demonstrate that our assertions regarding the OAS meeting are not true.* On the one hand, we would be avowing a laudable determination to forbear from all unilateral action and on the other hand, through the President of the United States we would be indulging in the most direct unilateral political intervention.
>
> The results, in my judgment, would be disastrous to our proposed OAS meeting. (*FRUS* 4 [1952–54]: 1168–1169; emphasis mine)[110]

Both Dreier and Holland indicated that the meeting called for July 7 should be held whatever the outcome of the Castillo Armas invasion. It was needed to clarify the views of each country and to test the ability of the OAS to deal with such a fundamental issue. How far would reciprocity take the Latin Americans in support of the fears of Eisenhower and Dulles regarding communism in the hemisphere? We do not know whether Latin America had ever really accepted the implications of collective security as understood in Washington, and we shall never know in the Guatemalan case, where the balance between collective security and reciprocity would have been struck.

It is probable that some of the members of the Guatemalan Group were aware of CIA sponsorship of the invasion; if so, they turned their backs on that policy and followed their own track to its futile and frustrating end. They may well have agreed with Cabot, whose "principal concern was to keep secret any United States involvement in the projected coup" (Cabot 1979: 90–91).

Since secrecy on the part of the CIA was total, the onus of deception lay primarily on Sec. Dulles, whose speeches indicate the degree to which he protected the department's efforts via the OAS and then welcomed the movement "by the Guatemalan people themselves" to oust Arbenz. Although Dulles may have congratulated himself on the outcome of the affair and for having kept the secret for the time being, there must have been certain costs to him. One was presumably the sympathy of his subordinates, to the extent that they were misled by him. More important, perhaps, must have been the feelings of the Brazilian ambassador, Muniz, whom Dulles had asked directly "to undertake a very delicate and secret mission" in going to Rio to submit the Guatemalan problem to his foreign minister and president, since Dulles did not want to "invoke the consultative procedure without first consulting fully with the Government of Brazil." This renewed Muniz's impression that the United States was ready to reassert the close friendship with Brazil that had developed during World War II, and he must have felt badly used as a result of subsequent events.[111] He presumably told Latin American colleagues how he had been deceived. This was all the more important, since Brazil was the traditional ally of the United States, and as Thomas C. Mann had written as recently as 11 December 1952 to Pres. Truman: "our policy should take account of Brazil's great importance to us and, to the extent possible within the framework of the principles of the inter-American system, should seek to help Brazil to achieve its aspirations and thus to convert it into a friendlier, stronger ally."[112]

The outcome of the affair had two aspects: the first concerned the aid given by the CIA, and then by Peurifoy, in Castillo Armas's victory; the second the nature of the regime that would emerge as successor to Arbenz. As P. Trezise stated in a perceptive estimate dated 17 June 1954:

If the Communist-infiltrated Arbenz government were to be replaced by a regime of the traditional Guatemalan cast, if the "reforms" of the post–1944 period were to be junked, and if it could be made to appear that the United Fruit Company had regained its former preeminent position in Guatemala, then a large and very articulate segment of Latin American opinion would accept the proposition that US imperialism had, in the interests of

United Fruit, seized on a false issue to destroy a reformist Guatemala government.[113]

Sec. Dulles's deceptions were adequate to cover the first of these aspects, at least for nearly a decade, but the second could not be hidden, and it was on this that Latin American and other opinion fastened, when criticizing the United States.[114]

Cooperation of Certain Other American Republics

A movement by Castillo Armas had been under way since March 1952, when, after escaping from a Guatemalan jail, he had signed an agreement in El Salvador with Miguel Ydígoras Fuentes on political arrangements following a successful coup. Pres. Trujillo of the Dominican Republic provided some funding, but the principal help from Central America came from Presidents Anastasio Somoza of Nicaragua and Juan Manuel Gálvez of Honduras. Trujillo and Somoza apparently provided financial aid before the United States had made up its mind to support Castillo Armas, and Gálvez allowed the training base for the Castillo Armas troops to be moved from Nicaragua to Honduras, which, unlike Nicaragua, was contiguous with Guatemala (Blasier 1976: 160–161; on aid from Trujillo, see Crassweller 1966: 335–336).

The United States made military assistance agreements with Nicaragua and Honduras in early 1954 that provided for cooperation "in missions important to the defense of the Western Hemisphere."[115] In addition, the CIA set up a radio station in Honduras that broadcast messages of doom to Guatemala City at the time of the invasion. Without these local advantages, the United States would not have been able to support the training of troops in secrecy, nor would it have had the use of air bases from which the highly effective bombing planes could operate. On the other hand, collaboration with such unsavory characters as Gálvez, Somoza, and Trujillo may be one of the reasons that induced the Eisenhower administration to keep most of its actions secret, at least from the American people.

Secrecy of Operations

Allen Dulles once called the CIA "the State Department for unfriendly countries." It was "a weapon available to the Commander in Chief for the life or death struggle for freedom and democracy around the world" (Ambrose 1981: 178).[116] Its operation was secret. As one of its directors has written:

Until the Bay of Pigs . . . the Agency had enjoyed a reputation
with the public at large not a whit less than golden. After all, we
were the derring-do boys who parachuted behind enemy lines,
the cream of the academic and social aristocracy, devoted to the
nation's service, the point men and women in the fight against
totalitarian aggression, matching fire with fire in an endless
round of thrilling adventures like those of the scenarios in James
Bond films. . . .

The total secrecy surrounding the CIA added the appropriate
touch of mystery to its romantic reputation and, what's more, it
was perceived as an altogether necessary condition of its dangerous occupation. From the public's point of view, it was more
than sufficient to know in a general way that the CIA's spies and
counterspies were out there somewhere . . . engaged in such cun-
ning coups as ousting the pro-Communist Arbenz government in
Guatemala or restoring the Shah to the Peacock Throne in Iran.
(Colby 1978: 180–181)

Secrecy had worked well in the case of the Shah. In Iran the job
had been done with funds, a few associates including some British
agents, and a part of the army. The CIA's "adventurers," therefore,
proposed secrecy for Guatemala, where local force would also have
to be used. Since the local force, except for North American airmen,
would be composed of Guatemalans and other Latin Americans, the
CIA thought that secrecy could be observed here, too, especially
since the training of troops would be done on the territory of com-
plaisant, neighboring dictators. Secrecy was also essential to the
CIA's method of covert operation. It does not appear from available
documentation that the issue was ever thought out or debated within
the Eisenhower administration.

Secrecy involves deception. In January 1954 the Presidential Information Office of Guatemala had charged that "the U.S. Government had acquiesced in a plot by other nations against Guatemala.
The charge is ridiculous and untrue. *It is the policy of the United
States not to intervene in the internal affairs of other nations.* That
policy has repeatedly been reaffirmed under the present administration" (*DSB* [15 February 1954]: 251; emphasis mine).[117] "The accusa-
tion, of course, caused a sensation in Latin America, and when several months later troops crossed the borders with air support as
outlined in the revelations of 29 January 1954, the credibility of the
U.S. government reached zero" (Dinerstein 1976: 7).[118]

An interesting method for maintaining secrecy was for the spokes-
persons of the administration to adopt a uniform language in refer-

ring to Guatemala. Sec. Dulles in his speech to the U.N. General Assembly on June 30 said that "the situation is being cured by the Guatemalans themselves." Later he said that "the American States exchanged views about this danger and were about to meet to deal with it collectively when the Guatemalan people themselves eliminated the threat" (*DSB* [4 October 1954]: 471–472).[119] Peurifoy said in a speech on August 28 that "the Guatemalan people themselves rose up and gave their support to a courageous leader, Col. Carlos Castillo Armas" (ibid. [6 September 1954]: 335).[120] Pres. Eisenhower noted that when a Communist threat had arisen in Guatemala, "the American states were preparing to act together to meet it when the Guatemalans themselves removed the danger."[121] In his presidential campaign against John F. Kennedy, Richard M. Nixon said, "We quarantined Mr. Arbenz. The result was that the Guatemalan people themselves eventually rose up and they threw him out" (*New York Times* [22 October 1960]).

Eisenhower in 1954 stated that "the majority of the Guatemalan people rose to defeat the first specific attempt of Communist imperialism to establish a beachhead in this hemisphere."[122] This statement may be compared with the account of a celebratory session held by CIA officials and Pres. Eisenhower: "The President's final handshake was with Allen Dulles. 'Thanks Allen, and thanks to all of you. You've averted a Soviet beachhead in our Hemisphere'" (D. Phillips 1977: 51). Peurifoy in his speech of August 28 (already noted) said that after the Caracas resolution, "determined to push through its thrust into Guatemala before the inter-American machinery could be invoked against it, the Communist conspiracy last April loaded up a ship." In this speech, Peurifoy went further in misdirection of his audience than either Dulles or Eisenhower: "In proving that communism can be defeated, we relied on the traditional American principle of honesty in the conduct of foreign affairs and the American doctrine of continental liberty from despotic intervention, first enunciated by President Monroe 131 years ago."

Each of these men was aware, of course, of the limited veracity of their statements. It is amusing to find that "Colonel Amadeo Chinchilla [Arbenz's ambassador in Honduras] openly discussed support to the Liberation Movement and described how he pleaded with the American ambassador in Tegucigalpa to have his government hold back the invasion to permit the Guatemalans to deal with the Communist problem themselves" (Blasier 1976: 161).

If, however, there are reasons for criticizing U.S. policy toward Guatemala, there are also good reasons for criticizing Guatemala's policy, as has been done by Guatemalan journalist Clemente Marroquín Rojas. In a book of articles replying to Guillermo Toriello's account of the affair, Marroquín derides the Arbenz regime for misjudging its position. The Guatemalan government knew that the Republicans in the United States supported the United Fruit Company, but "instead of getting out of trouble cleverly, they stood firm and allowed themselves to be rolled over like real blockheads" (Marroquín 1955[?]: 87). "It is necessary to know how to treat this imperial Troy," (ibid.: 187), and if, before Caracas, Arbenz had changed his cabinet and expelled the Communists from the country, something could have been arranged with the United States. Arbenz and Toriello apparently thought that if the United States attacked them the Russians would attack New York with atomic weapons (ibid.: 33). However, the Russians did nothing; the other American states did nothing; the army did not arm the people, for they were the army's enemy (ibid.: 121).[123]

The United States had certainly made its position clear. Rubottom told Toriello, then the Guatemalan ambassador, that "the American people learned the terrible truth that there is no such thing as cooperating with communists"; Leddy added that "in the midst of the life and death struggle with world communism in which we are engaged we find it difficult to ignore the established fact of the existence of communist influence in Guatemala."[124] Later, Thomas Mann told Toriello that "there was only one basic matter preventing solution of all the other problems existing between our two Governments. That was the Guatemalan Government's belief that it could successfully cooperate with the communists. . . . This Government knew that communists the world over were agents of Soviet imperialism and constituted a mortal threat to our own national existence."

To Toriello's statement that the president and government of Guatemala were "against communism," and their policy was "to let the communists discredit themselves rather than force them underground with the repressive measures used by his country's hated dictatorships," Mann replied that the government could exclude the Communists from political influence if it so desired and concluded that "there obviously could be no improvement of relations between our countries as long as the Guatemalan Government insisted on cooperating with the communists."[125]

Finally, Peurifoy in a talk with Arbenz noted that the president "reiterated his views that Communism was no threat." Peurifoy came away "definitely convinced that if the President is not a Communist, he will certainly do until one comes along. . . . Also, I am convinced further that the normal approaches will probably not work in Guatemala. Furthermore, the longer we remain idle and do nothing, the more difficult it is going to be to change the situation. This very small group of Communists is strongly entrenched and is strangling the nation day by day. The candle is burning slowly and surely, and it is only a matter of time before the large American interests will be forced out completely."[126]

Here was the nub of the problem. Guatemala had decided to defy the United States, a great power. In these circumstances, it was Guatemala that should have sought methods of compromise, of disarming the United States, of separating itself from the Soviet Union, as Bolivia had recently done. This would have blunted charges that it was a beachhead for communism and the Soviet Union and paved the way to a compromise on the United Fruit Company issues—Mexico in the petroleum negotiations was the model here.

Both sides committed errors. The United States responded like an outraged great power, but through its effort at secrecy it appeared to be a great power with a bad conscience. Latin Americans did not require archival documentation, twenty years after, to believe the CIA was responsible for Castillo Armas's victory:

> Helms, several sources say, felt the price had been high—the CIA was more notorious than ever, its role being far too great to hide from any other intelligence agency, even if the American press had been deceived; and the scale and publicity surrounding the operation had inevitably compromised many CIA assets. If the Dulles brothers considered the operation a victory for the Free World, many Latin Americans did not agree. If anything they liked the CIA even less than they liked the Marines. When Lyman Kirkpatrick made a tour of Latin America in 1956 he found resentment of the Agency for the coup wherever he went. (Powers 1979: 88)

At the time of the conflict, it was reported that in Latin America "all the old doubts about intervention will be raised," and it was "felt that hemisphere policy-makers in Washington were willing to risk some resurgence of old Latin American fears in view of the primary purpose: To make absolutely clear the United States attitude on Communist maneuvering in the heart of the Americas."[127]

The Eisenhower administration commenced the dismantling of the Good Neighbor policy in three ways. First, the Good Neighbor policy's "inviolate" principle of nonintervention was violated. Second, the United States' word was broken: "Even now faith in our word is the greatest advantage which the United States enjoys in the Western World today," as Amb. Fletcher Warren had said in 1949.

Third, the obligations of the United States to consult and to use the inter-American treaties of Rio and Bogotá were unfulfilled.[128] The new policy direction was indicated by a revision of NSC 144/1, which now stated that

> in the event of threatened or actual domination of any American state by Communism, the US. should pursuant to Resolution 93 of the 10th Inter-American Conference [Caracas], promote and cooperate in application of the sanctions, including military, provided for in the Rio Treaty to the extent necessary to remove the threat to the security of the hemisphere, all sanctions being applied in collaboration with other OAS members *to the extent feasible, and unilateral action being taken only as a last resort.*[129]

Pres. Kennedy continued the dismantling process with his acceptance of the CIA's plans for the invasion of Cuba at the Bay of Pigs; Pres. Johnson continued it with his noncovert invasion of the Dominican Republic. Pres. Carter completed it verbally, and there is no sign of a return to Good Neighbor principles in Pres. Reagan's policy. These cases, however, are for later and much briefer consideration.

10. Conclusion

The Good Neighbor Policy as Method

The common element in Washington's reaction to the events in Argentina and Guatemala was fear of the external threat from a foreign power and ideology. Once fascism became established in Argentina, or communism in Guatemala, Washington anticipated that the virus would spread into nearby countries and menace either continental solidarity, or the security of the United States, or both. Other elements, such as Hull's antipathy to Argentina and the impact of Guatemalan legislation on the United Fruit Company, entered the picture but were of secondary importance.

Hull tried a wide range of ways to change Argentine foreign policy and, later, to oust Perón. He asked his own military if force could be used against Argentina, and he once sent Adm. Ingram to display the fleet in Montevideo. He tried public browbeating and economic sanctions—all in vain. The wartime needs of both the U.S. Army in England and Britain's own civic population were brakes on his impetuosity that could not be released.

The British position was consistent with the Good Neighbor policy, but Hull constantly tried to circumvent it, despite his having been a major force in its definition and creation. When he was about to charge Argentina with responsibility for the Bolivian revolution in 1943, the British, for the only time in the whole affair, exerted critical pressure via the Hellmuth evidence to bring about Argentina's break in relations with the Axis, and so defuse Hull's contemplated offensive. Finally, the British, by lending their chargé as the carrier of Rockefeller's final offer to Perón, made possible Argentina's entrance into the United Nations and its rejoining the American family.

Braden's struggle against Perón—which he might have won had he remained for another month in Buenos Aires, through the week during which Perón was incarcerated and politicians dithered—was doomed to failure. The Senate reimposed the restraints of the Good Neighbor policy on him, and his greatest effort, the Blue Book, was, if anything, counterproductive as a method of defeating Perón in the 1946 election. He was able to stay on for over a year, largely because the CIO and certain elements of the U.S. press supported him and because of the distractions provided Truman, Byrnes, and Marshall by the far more demanding problems of settling the terms of peace in Asia and Europe. Braden's dismissal made possible the Rio and Bogotá treaties, the inauguration of a five-year period during which the OAS was successful as a peace keeping agency, and the slow rehabilitation of the Good Neighbor policy as the basis for U.S. action in the Americas.

In the Guatemalan affair, the fear was of communism and of its spread to other countries as far away as Panama. The domino theory, traceable as far back as George III, was invoked, as it was in the case of Argentina, to intensify the fear. Ten years' experience with Soviet operations in international politics, the Korean War, the tension wrought by the McCarthy hearings, and the predilections of Eisenhower, Smith, Peurifoy, and the Dulles brothers, created a situation in which it was easy to misjudge the amount of communist influence in Guatemala.

It is of the greatest importance to note that, in both cases, Hull, Braden, and Dulles avoided the Good Neighbor policy's method of consultation. They did utilize various rudimentary forms of "consultation." Hull, for example, had recourse to "diplomatic consultation" in the nonrecognition of the Farrell regime. Braden employed a type of "distant consultation" while the Blue Book was in preparation. And Dulles, after Caracas, and through apparent consultation, made outwardly valiant, but actually obstructive, efforts to secure support for the meeting of foreign ministers that was finally scheduled for 7 July 1954, and then never held. U.S. leaders shunned consultation in the shape of a formal meeting of foreign ministers and were primarily concerned with the foreign threat. It was as though they were uncertain of their own judgment, or felt their case against the enemy was too weak to place before the other American republics for purposes of securing advice and cooperation. The urgings of Bonsal and Duggan for a meeting of foreign ministers and, later, those of Cabot, Holland, and Woodward, went unheeded at the level of the secretary of state.

The Good Neighbor policy was unique. A great power obligated itself not to use force in its dealings with twenty smaller powers and not to interfere in their domestic politics. The policy, with some perturbations, endured for twenty years. Was it inevitable that it should fail, even after its principles had been embedded in the treaties of Rio de Janeiro and Bogotá? In the heyday of the policy Welles wrote, "As I have said on other occasions, the 'good neighbor' policy is essentially a reciprocal policy. I believe that the recognition of the inherently reciprocal nature of its principles is widespread throughout the continent" (1937: 5). Woodward, however, says, "It was too much to expect that the other American Republics would understand that there was an implicit obligation of reciprocity to the Good Neighbor policy and that the admittance into an American government of an alien ideology dedicated to the eventual destruction of the democratic system would constitute a denial of that reciprocity and therefore compel the United States to take defensive measures" (letter to me, 27 October 1981). Another view held that,

> under the stress of the Cold War, the United States seemed to be reverting to her traditional policy of intervening to prevent extracontinental intervention. . . .
>
> The United States is bound to use her power to promote her interests as her government and people interpret these. It would be surprising if there were a true community of interests between the most industrially advanced and militarily powerful nation in the world and the twenty mainly underdeveloped, militarily weak republics to the south. The record shows unmistakably that there does not exist a community of interests between the United States and Latin America in the field of peace and security. On the contrary, as the record again indicates, the promotion of United States peace and security appears, in the last analysis, to be incompatible with the exercise of sovereignty by the Latin American countries. (Connell-Smith 1974: 88, 90)

Similarly, Welles's "hope for non-intervention was always illusory, although it still lingers on in some Latin American circles and among those holding extreme 'disengagement' sentiments in Washington today" (Ferguson 1972: 101).[1]

Braden developed one of the arguments permissive of "intervention": "Admittedly, whatever we *do* or *don't do* in this hemisphere is, in some degree, by reason of our preeminent position, an intervention" (see chap. 6). C. Neale Ronning echoes this statement:

> Thus *absolute* nonintervention becomes an impossible and utopian objective as far as the United States is concerned. The political and economic power of the United States is so great that anything it *does or does not do* in relation to another American

republic influences the political affairs of that republic. Responsible persons in the United States and Latin America will have to
face the fact that it will be a matter of deciding *how* and *with
what objective* to intervene rather than taking an utterly impossible and unrealistic "non-intervention" position. (Ibid.: 102)

The United States, however, for twenty years following 1933 explicitly and avowedly followed the Good Neighbor policy and did not
intervene in any Latin American country. It seems clear that what
Braden and Ronning meant was really *interference*, and not intervention, which, of course, is military action. Braden's purpose was to
widen the range of measures by which the United States might interfere with dictatorships and disreputable governments. He did not
intervene in Argentina, and he refrained from both intervention and
interference in Nicaragua in 1947. With his speeches in Buenos Aires
and by means of the Blue Book he tried to interfere in Argentina, but
his efforts were dismal failures.

This issue, of course, is related to the complaint that the Good
Neighbor policy permitted the continued existence of notoriously
dictatorial regimes in the Dominican Republic, Nicaragua, and elsewhere at a time when the United States was preaching the advantages and promise of democracy in the Americas. The inconsistency
was clear, but the need for military action against dictators, at least
as long as they were not opposing U.S. foreign policy, was not apparent to the Department of State. Besides, the department was unsure
that the ousting of a given dictator would result in the establishment
of a democratic system of government; earlier experiments along
this line had resulted in enduring dictatorial regimes in the Dominican Republic, Haiti, and Nicaragua.

The challenge of World War II was, on the whole, well met by the
Good Neighbor policy and the Latin American response. Chile joined
the company led by Brazil in support of the United States, and even
Argentina continued without fail to send its precious products to
Britain. This satisfied the British, but Sec. Hull, obsessed by his antipathy to Argentina, by his fear of the propagation of fascism in
America, and by his solicitude for the unity of the American system,
experimented vainly with methods of forcing Argentina to follow his
lead. Hence his exaggeration of the evidence of fascism in Argentina,
his insistence on Argentina's treason of hemispheric solidarity, and
his overestimation of Argentina's capacity to form a bloc of like-
minded states in South America. Britain pooh-poohed all of these,
saying that Perón was a Latin, not a European, phenomenon, that
hemisphere solidarity was an unrealistic creation as compared with

the realities of Argentina wartime trade with Britain, and that Argentina was too weak to form a bloc with its neighbors. Baffled, Hull retired, having severely and unsuccessfully tested the limits of the policy of interference in trying, first, to bring Argentina back into the fold, and then to unseat the Farrell-Perón regime. That Hull's sanctions were imposed in wartime was reason both at home and abroad to view these breaches of the Good Neighbor policy generously and to regard them as less than irremediable infractions.

That this was the case became clear when Rockefeller became assistant secretary of state. In 1941 Perowne had regarded Welles as "a champion turner of the other cheek as far as Latin America is concerned," even though he adopted the policy of "the cold shoulder" in dealing with Chile in 1942. However, Rockefeller, in striving to close the breach with Argentina and unify the Latin American states as a voting bloc in the United Nations, not only turned the other cheek, but even bowed his head in reducing the terms for Argentina's acceptance of the Chapultepec agreements, in arranging for its entry into the new world organization, and in secretly employing the British, instead of the U.S. embassy to persuade Perón to declare war on Germany and Japan. Between the "vendettas" of Hull and Braden against Perón, Rockefeller's success in reducing the pressure on Argentina by noninterference in that country's domestic politics represented a high point in the growth of the Good Neighbor policy.

However, Rockefeller's policy toward Argentina was simply an admission that Hull's efforts at interference were misapplied. "The 'reality' and the value of a regional system cannot be measured in terms of a negative principle such as non-intervention. It must be measured in terms of the positive aspects of coexistence" (Castañeda 1970: 168). During the war, the United States had purchased supplies, made loans, sold arms on easy terms, and engaged in various cultural activities in Latin America. With the end of World War II, it was to be expected that a new restiveness in Latin America against the leadership of the United States would be accompanied by a relative lack of concern in Washington for that region, as compared with the demands being made for peace settlements in Asia and Europe. As British minister Campbell put it in 1944: "the honeymoon of Pan-Americanism may be drawing to a close, leaving behind the problems of day-to-day matrimony."

If Latin American states tried thus to escape from the demands of the Good Neighbor, the United States also endeavored to restrict the scope of previous limitations imposed upon it by its own policy. Thus Hull argued that Argentina had no right "to invoke the doctrine of intervention to protect a seething mass of German intrigue and plotting within its boundaries"; and the Department of State proposed that Latin America should consider it a "joint concern" when the nature of the regime in power in a country presented a "threat to the peace or stability of the hemisphere." Collective action was regarded in the department as "the wedge of returning to intervention," and therefore Sec. Byrnes offered his support to the Rodríguez Larreta doctrine that favored multilateral collective action to reestablish human rights and maintain peace. Latin America decisively rejected the doctrine. Argentina called it "the proposed intervention policy," and Castañeda held that it would amount to intervention: "The modern form of intervention is through collective action obtained by votes in international meetings" (Castañeda 1948: 171).

Dreier expressly contradicted this and other views:

> However, the intervention which the doctrine outlaws should be understood to consist of arbitrary acts of any government to impose its will on another by the use of force or other coercive measures that violate the sovereignty of the other state. The emphasis should be on the *arbitrary* and *coercive* character of the measures, which are taken by *unilateral* decision. The concept of intervention should certainly not apply to action taken by the O.A.S. pursuant to established procedures. This view is explicitly stated in the Charter, which exempts from the nonintervention rule "measures taken for the maintenance of peace and security in accordance with existing treaties." (1962: 132–133; original emphasis)

The sharp opposition between these two views concerning the limits of nonintervention would have been brought out with clarity had the Eisenhower administration agreed to their discussion at a meeting of foreign ministers of the OAS in July 1954. Had the Mexican view prevailed, the OAS would have been emasculated as an instrument of hemisphere peace and security a decade before the invasion of the Dominican Republic. Dreier put the dilemma very well.

> [The United States] has placed its confidence in the proposition that its vital interests in this hemisphere can and will be protected and pursued in collaboration with Latin America. . . . The United States cannot, therefore, take the O.A.S. lightly or ignore what it stands for, even when it is a cause of frustration or acts as a brake on necessary action. On the other hand, the Latin American states must take account of the vital importance of the

O.A.S. to them. If they attempt irresponsible use of their numerical strength in the O.A.S., if they carry to extremes the doctrine of nonintervention, if they leave the United States no alternative but to act unilaterally to protect itself, they will have destroyed not only the basis of hemispheric cooperation for progress but all hope of a secure future for themselves. (Ibid.: 114)

This, then, was the situation as the Western Hemisphere faced the postwar period. The United States asserted that if there were in any country a situation affecting the security of the hemisphere or the United States, consultations would be held to develop common policies for mutual protection. The formal bases for such consultations were laid at Rio de Janeiro in 1947 and at Bogotá in 1948, with Mexico's approval and despite Castañeda. The basis for policy was laid by the rehabilitation of the Good Neighbor policy under Truman and Acheson.[2]

In 1953, when power passed to Eisenhower and Dulles, it was not inevitable that the Good Neighbor policy should not still be followed. It had met the test of Argentina and had emerged with flying colors, after some tribulations. A more subtle doctrine had replaced the simple notion of nonintervention, for it was obvious that a more dangerous foreign force than fascism might make an attempt on the security of the hemisphere. In such a case, if there were sufficient agreement on the threat to security, then consultation as to how to meet it would be explored. If the signers of treaties and the ties of good neighbors were strong enough, then the threat would be met with joint and adequate countermeasures; if not, the probability was that the United States would have had to act alone to protect what it regarded as its own security. In that case the Good Neighbor policy would have failed.

In 1954 the United States, having agreed not to intervene, had also agreed, with the support of Latin American governments, to collective security with the specific provisions of the Rio and Bogotá treaties. This looked like a balanced equation. However, the outcome, given in general terms in the treaties, remained to be tested in actual practice. Nonintervention was clearly understood, but what was the occasion for measures of collective security? Dulles claimed that the occasion had arisen in Guatemala, but he would not risk a negative response from the members of the OAS. Would Latin America have given sufficient reassurance to Dulles's fears so that the equation would still have held, and the balance been maintained? It would have been a severe test for the new OAS, and for the new administration in Washington.

In fact, however, the policy was never given this ultimate test, for Eisenhower and Dulles avoided consultation in favor of a covert invasion of Guatemala. The nature of this test of policy was never plumbed; Latin America's understanding of reciprocity was not explored. This creation of the United States—of Roosevelt, Welles, Rockefeller, Truman, Acheson, and Miller—was not allowed to be carried to its conclusion. A noble experiment by a great power and its smaller neighbors was terminated at the moment of trial.

The Good Neighbor policy did not fail, but the persons entrusted to carry it out failed to follow it through to its logical conclusion— consultation in the event of a threat to security as perceived by the Unied States. Their substitute—covert action—was temporarily successful in Guatemala, but was shown to be faulty at the Bay of Pigs. In the Dominican Republic, the United States disavowed secrecy and returned to the interventions of the 1920s and to their justifications. The multilateral approach to limits on the use of power by the United States was abandoned; consequently, the OAS has never been fully utilized to try to establish the foundations of a society in which the use of power by all member states has been circumscribed. The dismantling of the Good Neighbor policy and the enfeeblement of the OAS began simultaneously in 1954.

The Good Neighbor Policy and Communism

The dismantling of the Good Neighbor policy occurred in a period of great change and tension in the relationships of the superpowers, in which essentially territorial spheres of influence were being defined and their boundaries tested.

The Good Neighbor policy of the 1930s, with its absolute prohibitions against intervention and interference, was a denial of the imperialism that had marked U.S. policy since the war with Spain. The question of what to do to face the menace of changing times was not a new one. Pres. Roosevelt had said at a press conference on 20 April 1938, "If European governments were to do in Mexico what they did in Spain, . . . do you think that the United States could stand idly by and have this European menace right on our own borders? Of course not. You could not stand for it. . . . We probably all agree that we could not stand for a foreign nation doing that under the guise of a Mexican flag" (Wood 1961: 349). However, when William S. Paley of the Columbia Broadcasting System formally proposed on 7 January 1941 that consideration be given to "a policy under which the Americas will not tolerate the control of any American republic by a foreign nation, irrespective of the methods used to gain and maintain such control," (ibid.: 350), Roosevelt sent the letter to Sumner Welles, who replied in a letter to the president that the "whole structure of inter-American cooperation" would be endangered if the United States itself should decide that the government of an American state "were subservient to Nazi or Fascist influence" and therefore "undertook to intervene directly in order to correct that situation." Welles thought if such a "danger spot" should appear, "our neighbors would join with us to remove it" (ibid.: 350). Welles clearly was confident that any external threat could be handled collectively.

The Department of State recognized at an early date that Communist influence in the Americas might possibly endanger the security of the United States, but did nothing specific about it until the Bogotá Conference in 1948. On 1 November 1947 the CIA reported in "Soviet Objectives in Latin America" that Soviet penetration in Latin America was capable of withholding from the United States "its normal peacetime flow of strategic raw materials from Latin America, and to precipitate economic crises in several key Latin American countries." Although the army and air force approved this report, the Department of State and the Office of Naval Intelligence disagreed with it. The department's view was that "Latin America for the present seems to be low on the Soviet target list"; and the navy's opinion was that "the real or latent danger from Communism in Latin America, as expressed in the CIA paper, seems exaggerated."[3] Further, "It is extremely important, always with our own national security in mind, to concentrate upon the defeat of international Communism. As a corollary, it is essential to follow policies and to adopt measures calculated not only to command the very valuable support of anti-Communist labor, liberal and Socialist elements, but also to persuade sufferers from reactionary forces in the American Republics that the United States is a better and more promising hope than Communism or the Soviet Union." Finally, "The policy of the United States was to stand upon the inter-American principle of non-intervention, but without derogation from the right of the community of States to concern itself with any matter bearing upon its peace and welfare—a right which is inherent in the inter-American principle of consultation and in the Charter of the United Nations" (*FRUS* 9 [1948]: 197).

Brazil and other countries offered support prior to Bogotá. "President Dutra informed me [U.S. ambassador Pawley] yesterday that he felt that Communist Parties in American Republics were not political parties in usual sense of term but rather that they constituted groups headed by a 'fifth column' whose main purpose was to create chaos and undermine every government's effort to maintain political stability." Dutra thought the time had come "when action in this hemisphere against Communists should be taken on a joint basis . . . to eliminate this great menace from the Americas." The occasion would be the Bogotá Conference.[4] Such an initiative from Brazil offered a great opportunity, but it was missed. The department's official position was that the United States believed that sound economies were the greatest defense against Communist ideology, and if communism were to become a threat to the peace, the Rio treaty of 1947 provided the mechanism for joint action.[5]

At Bogotá the American republics declared that "the political activity of international communism or any other totalitarian doctrine is incompatible with the concept of American freedom, which rests upon two undeniable postulates: the dignity of man as an individual and the sovereignty of the nation as a state"; they condemned "interference by any foreign power or by any political organization serving the interests of a foreign power" in the Americas, and they resolved "to proceed with a full exchange of information concerning any of the aforementioned activities that are carried on within their respective jurisdictions."[6]

The Department of State agreed that the CIA was the proper body to take responsibility for coordinating such an exchange of information and instructed its missions to appoint an officer, in consultation with the existing CIA senior representative in each country, for liaison with the government.[7]

George F. Kennan, the counselor of the State Department, expressed a hopeful note in a 6 January 1950 memorandum to the secretary, reminiscent of Welles's statement a decade earlier:

> As for international frictions, the *Organization of American States is beginning to function effectively*. It will soon have the task of smoothing down trouble which has arisen between Haiti and the Dominican Republic. We have strong hopes that from now on, by this means, a sense of collective responsibility among all nations of the area will suffice to handle such instances of international friction and *to save us from dilemmas which in the past often caused us to resort to unilateral U.S. intervention*.
>
> In both of these matters—the problem of stability and liberality of domestic institutions as well as the problem of inter-American relationships—firm, vigorous but tactful U.S. leadership will continue to be essential to real progress. (Ibid. 1 [1950: 134–35; emphasis mine])

This note was echoed in the well-known NSC 68 (ibid.: 234ff). Noting that "it is quite clear from Soviet theory and practice that the Kremlin seeks to bring the free world under its dominion by the methods of the cold war," and that "the preferred technique is to subvert by infiltration and intimidation," NSC 68 said that the policy of the United States was "to foster a world environment in which the American system can survive and flourish." This meant two policies: (1) developing a healthy international community, and (2) containing the Soviet Union. "The policy of striving to develop a healthy international community is the long-term constructive effort which we are engaged in. It was this policy which gave rise to our vigorous sponsorship of the United Nations. *It is of course the principal reason for our long continuing endeavors to create and now develop the Inter-American system.*" Further, "We must lead in building a successfully functioning political and economic system in the free world. It is only by practical affirmation, abroad as well as at home, of our essential values, that we can preserve our own integrity, in which lies the real frustration of the Kremlin design" (ibid.: 241, 252, 263; emphasis mine).

The theme of developing the inter-American system even in the face of Communist subversion held a prominent place in a policy proposed to Pres. Eisenhower as late as March 1953 by the National Security Council. The NSC report took into account "hemisphere solidarity in support of our world policies, particularly in the UN and other international organizations," and "the reduction and elimination of the menace of internal Communist or other anti-U.S. subversion." To accomplish these aims:

The United States should achieve a greater degree of hemisphere solidarity by:
a. A greater utilization of the Organization of American States as a means of achieving our objectives, which will avoid the appearance of unilateral action and identify our interests with those of the other American states.
b. Consulting with the Latin American states, whenever possible, before taking actions which will affect them or for which we wish their support, explaining as fully as security permits the reasons for our decisions and actions.
c. Evidencing greater consideration of Latin American problems at the highest levels of government by according sympathetic attention to representatives of Latin America, by exercising care in public statements relating to the area, and through such methods

as visits by high government officials and distinguished private citizens to Latin American states.

d. Refraining from overt unilateral intervention in the internal political affairs of the other American states, in accordance with existing treaty obligations. This does not preclude multilateral action through the inter-American system.

The United States should also "*a*. Encourage through consultation, assistance and other available means individual and collective action against internal subversive activities by communists and other anti-U.S. elements."[8]

This document could have been written by Sec. Acheson, with the possible exception of the first sentence of "*d*"; the term "overt" implies that the way was clear for "covert" intervention. This is the first suggestion available that someone in the NSC might have been aware of possible CIA plans for Guatemala at this early stage.

Sec. Acheson recognized the Soviet threat. He told the American Society of Newspaper Editors on 22 April 1950 that the Soviet Union was "a threat to the very basis of our civilization and to the very safety of the free world" (*DSB* [1 May 1950]: 674). Negotiating with the Russians would be very difficult, but

we have reached a situation in the Western Hemisphere where negotiation is the normal way of settling disputes. The normal way for the American republics to settle all their differences—and there are very grave and serious difficulties—is by negotiation and reasonable settlement. That has taken nearly 60 years to work out. It has taken all of that time to build up the trust of the American republics among themselves and between them and us. For years we were called the "Colossus of the North" and we took actions from time to time which made the other American republics apprehensive of us, but I think that no longer exists. I do not believe there ever took place in the world a more harmonious or constructive meeting than the recent meeting between the Foreign Ministers of the American republics, in which all sorts of questions vitally affecting all our countries, were taken up and discussed. . . . . On one very tough economic question it took staying up all night for three nights to get people to realize that there was a good deal in common between them! But we solved that question and we will solve other differences in the Hemisphere in that way. (Ibid. [23 July 1951]: 127–128)

Looking back, Acheson said that the central aim and purpose of the lines of policy developed under Truman were "to safeguard the highest interest of our nation, which was to maintain as spacious an environment as possible in which free states might exist and flourish. Its method was common action with like-minded states to secure and enrich the environment and to protect one another from predators through mutual aid and joint effort" (Acheson 1969: 727).[9]

A progress report on NSC report 144 noted that Cabot in a speech in October had dealt with the issues in Guatemala—expropriation of American property and Communist influence—in such a way as to indicate "the seriousness with which the United States views the course of events in that Republic."[10]

In the summer of 1953, the Eisenhower administration made a fateful decision. Truman had carried on the policies of which Acheson had spoken—over sixty years had been devoted to building up "the trust of the American republics among themselves and between them and us." A fourth "harmonious and constructive" meeting of foreign ministers had recently been held, and the Truman administration was determined through "common action with like-minded states . . . to protect one another from predators through mutual aid and joint effort." Acheson had testified at the hearings preceding his confirmation that he knew "something of the need in American foreign policy for steadiness and continuity."[11]

The Truman Doctrine had been publicly discussed, and congressional appropriations were obtained to carry it out in Greece and Turkey (Jones 1955). It was a doctrine of "intervention on a massive scale, upon the request of the Greek government, to make Greece a strong, independent, self-supporting, democratic state" (ibid.: 77).[12] When Truman decided to defend South Korea, arrangements had to be made through the Security Council of the United Nations for authorization of an international force, and this was done with a maximum of publicity. This also was a case of collective intervention to limit the territorial expansion of Communist control.

In the Guatemalan situation, however, the Eisenhower administration followed a radically different procedure and policy. At a small, secret, and historic meeting of the so-called 54/12 committee, which had been charged with supervising covert operations, the official decision to topple the Arbenz regime was recommended. The members of the committee included Allen and Foster Dulles, Walter B. Smith, C. D. Jackson, Eisenhower's psychological warfare adviser, an aide to Charles Wilson, the secretary of defense, and Robert Cutler, the president's assistant for national security affairs. However, Cutler was not present at this meeting and "did not know about the operation" (Schlesinger and Kinzer 1982: 108).[13] Eisenhower approved the plot against Arbenz, but he "hedged on a final commitment. His *modus operandi* since World War II had been to prepare forces and then decide at the last moment whether to use them or not."[14] There are no documents or memoirs available that describe the meeting. We know it was small because the assistant secretary of state for American republics affairs, Cabot, did not even know it had taken place; he got the impression that the matter had been decided, however, in September.

It would be of great interest to know what consideration was given at this meeting to the building of trust in the Americas over the previous sixty years, to use Acheson's terms. In this last moment of credibility, was no attention given to the value and fragility of that trust? Eisenhower, Smith, and Allen Dulles probably had little knowledge of that history and little appreciation of the potential of the institutions that it had created. John Foster Dulles, however, with his background as an internationalist, fortified by his experience at the San Francisco Conference of the United Nations, should have shown greater awareness. Why was the OAS not tried before a decision was made to prepare for a basically unilateral, covert intervention? The "steadiness and continuity" that Acheson regarded as necessary, as well as the good experience with the OAS over the preceding five years should have counseled at least a test of the inter-American system; an amalgam of the techniques used in the Greco-Turkish and Korean cases might have been found for Guatemala.

One reason for bypassing the OAS was that the CIA had successfully arranged for the upsetting of Mossadegh in Iran in 1953. A second reason was that John Foster Dulles did not trust all the professional officers of the Department of State. Third, an appeal to the OAS would have given rise to public discussion, and to the suspicion that the United States had defense of the United Fruit Company as much in mind as opposition to Communists in Guatemala (Westerfield 1963: 427). Fourth, the prospects of a quick, fairly inexpensive covert operation by the CIA looked promising. Fifth, no arrangements were made for the participation in consideration of the policy decision by those who had been involved in the development of the OAS. Acheson says that during the eight years of the Eisenhower presidency, he was "never invited into the White House or to the State Department or consulted in any way. However, this involved no invidious discrimination, since my chief, President Truman, was treated in the same way" (Acheson 1969: 691). The decision was taken with full knowledge that the position of the Department of

State, below the secretary, would have favored action through the OAS, as Cabot's and Woodward's statements indicate (Cabot 1979: 90; Woodward, letter to me, 12 December 1979). It was a decision by new men determined to act in new ways that would not be influenced by any of their predecessors, whether politicians or professionals, and the latter group was excluded from any part in the decision. They were acting, of course, under the influence of the intellectual atmosphere of NSC 68 and the outbreak of the Korean War, but in this regard they were in a position similar to that of Truman and Acheson.

This tendency of an administration to start off as though the world were new, especially after a long run by the other party, results in what has been called "the institutional amnesia, resulting from frequent changes in administrations, and in part the political pressures on each new administration to differntiate its policy from that of its predecessor."[15] Flora Lewis has compared the American system unfavorably with the British, where continuity is provided by the fact that former officeholders continue to sit in Parliament: "The lack of a respected, organized forum with which to honor distinguished public servants and make continued use of their experience has come to bother many people involved in national affairs. It is particularly poignant when administrations change and the outs are simply out."[16]

Sixth, the CIA, possessing fiscal independence and a separate communications system, was available as a new facility, competing with the Department of State, that offered Eisenhower " a range of policy instruments that competitive co-existence requires. Some forms of political intrigue are needed to supplement other programs of assistance and influence" (Westerfield 1963: 440).

Seventh was the matter of timing. The CIA operation looked as though it would oust Arbenz before the Communists developed a solid power base in Guatemala, and especially before they were able to infiltrate the army in serious fashion.

Finally, in this series of necessarily speculative reasons for not trying the OAS, the CIA offered Castillo Armas as an individual who might be more amenable to U.S. policy in bringing about change, than some other person who might emerge as president from another procedure.[17]

Presumably, this small group gave attention to other options. Some of them have been put succinctly by a retired U.S. ambassador, Willard L. Beaulac: "Guatemala, I suppose, posed a typical dilemma. If we intervene overtly we are criticized, and if we intervene covertly it is found out, and we are criticized not only for intervening but for being sneaky about it. If we do nothing and the country goes communist we are denounced as helpless" (letter to me, 26 January 1980).

There was an additional alternative. As Amb. Beaulac also wrote, "It is not a corollary to non-intervention that others should be permitted to intervene freely." In other words, the Monroe Doctrine, which expresses the primacy in policy of U.S. national security, takes precedence over any system of treaties and traditions, such as those the curators of the Good Neighbor policy cherish. As Sec. Dulles put it in his speech of 30 June 1954, "This intrusion of Soviet despotism was, of course, a direct challenge to our Monroe Doctrine, the first and most fundamental of our foreign policies." Further, in a speech on November 29 Dulles said that the Caracas Declaration "may serve the needs of our time as effectively as the Monroe Doctrine served the needs of our nation during the last century. It made clear that collective action to eradicate international communism is not an act of intervention but an act to uproot intervention" (*DSB* [13 December 1954]: 892). This statement was reminiscent of the Rodríguez Larreta Doctrine, which had been supported by Sec. Byrnes, but turned down by the Latin American states in 1945.

As to the alternative, Pres. Eisenhower might simply have said that the growth of communism in Guatemala menaced the security of the United States and that the United States thought that OAS action was necessary to eliminate the threat. In conformity with the Declaration of Caracas, he would have consulted with the other American republics immediately before or after making this statement. In this way, the United States would have brought the intervention within the requirements of the Charter of the OAS, the Good Neighbor policy, and its own security, as it perceived them. As Woodward has put it,

> The policy of restraint is not dead. I believe it is still pretty
> consistently followed until there develops a general conviction
> in whatever administration is in office in Washington that a
> situation is being created in which a chink of significance is
> being opened in the security belt around the U.S. In proportion to
> the seriousness of such a "chink," I believe the policy of non-
> intervention can be considered, proportionally, a "dead letter."[18]

A balance was required among the legality of treaties, the tradition of policy, and the demands of self-interest; this would have been achieved by the proposed statement by Eisenhower, if not by the debate and OAS action.

This is not to say that the policy would not have had disadvantages. It would have been criticized by international lawyers, and by such purist advocates of the Good Neighbor policy as Sumner Welles. The United States would have been accused of "imperialism" and of being "hegemonic." This was the first occasion for the assertion that the Monroe Doctrine took precedence over both the Charter of the OAS and the Good Neighbor policy, and the debate would have been noisy and prolonged. However, it would not have involved charges that the OAS had not been consulted or that the United States was engaged in covering up its intervention. There would have been a single issue: Did the influence of Communists in Guatemala pose an overriding threat to the security of the United States? This was a "judgment call" and it could have been argued openly on its merits, rather than furtively, as in the case of the two pamphlets issued by the Department of State. It may be noted that in a speech on 10 June 1963, Eisenhower "for the first time conceded, for all practical purposes, that the United States had overthrown the government of Guatemala in 1954. 'There was one time,' he said, 'when we had a very desperate situation, *or we thought it was at least,* in Central America, and we had to get rid of a Communist government which had taken over, and our early efforts were defeated by a bad accident [presumably Castillo Armas's loss of two CIA-supplied aircraft] and we had to help, send some help right away'" (Wise and Ross 1964: 166; emphasis mine).

What Eisenhower thought was a "very desperate situation" came about after the invasion by Castillo Armas had started—not before. The situation was not desperate until it appeared that Castillo Armas and the CIA might be beaten after the invasion had begun. Before the invasion became public, the opportunity to follow the Good Neighbor policy and use the OAS treaties remained open. There does not appear in any of the available memoirs any suggestion that any of the four principal planners wavered in their support of the CIA's plans, or that they thought seriously of presenting the case to the OAS for its deliberation. Henry Holland wavered in his acceptance of the CIA's policy, but he was tricked by John Foster Dulles into thinking that he had another six months to achieve results from his approach to the OAS.[19]

The conclusion seems unavoidable, therefore, that the Eisenhower administration, having received a Good Neighbor policy that was being practiced and having inherited the obligations of an OAS that was vital and full of promise, commenced the dismantling of the policy and of the OAS—at least so far as that organization's capability to restrain the United States was concerned. I use the term "dismantling," since the policy was complicated and sophisticated: "termination" would be too abrupt; "wrecking" would be too complete; "supersession" would imply replacement by an alternative.

The Guatemalan operation was largely secret, but it was recognized as being managed by the United States. As Carlos Fuentes has put it, "The residue of good feeling left by the Roosevelt era had died in Guatemala; the majority of universities and scientific and cultural organizations in Latin America had sided with the Guatemalan revolutionaries and had decided to shun their U.S. counterparts after the invasion of 1954. This was the result of disillusionment, of outrage, and even of a certain confusion" (1981: 29).

The dismantling continued when, previous to the Cuban affair, there was only an ineffective effort to involve the OAS. The difference was that the Bay of Pigs was a disaster, as compared to a kind of success in Guatemala; the CIA lost prestige and its director, Allen W. Dulles, was fired. In the Dominican Republic intervention in 1965, the United States at first scorned the OAS and openly sent in troops. The cooperation of several states—Brazil, Costa Rica, El Salvador, Honduras, Nicaragua, and Paraguay—with small military forces and the formal multilateralization of the intervention by a bare two thirds of the members of the OAS may be regarded as an effort of the other American republics to restrain the extent of the United States' military operations and of the United States to undo the damage of unilateral intervention, rather than to eliminate the effects of the intervention itself. From that point, it was obvious that the United States would not be deterred by any provisions in the Rio or Bogotá treaties from intervening in the Caribbean in the interests of what it considered its national security. The expenditure of funds from 1970 to 1973 to "destabilize" the regime of Salvador Allende in Chile indicated the lengths to which the United States would go in South America to defend what Richard M. Nixon and Henry Kissinger regarded as the country's interests.[20]

The process of dismantling the Good Neighbor policy was completed under the administration of Jimmy Carter. Zbigniew Brzezinski, who was national security adviser, said in an interview with James Reston:

> To me the central problem is that because we and the Latin Americans have a divergent view of our common past we may confront the risk of divergent futures. Americans tend to be very proud of the Monroe Doctrine. To most Latin Americans it is a document expressing American domination.
>
> This Administration, I think I can boast, has made two very important and positive innovations, at some real pain and cost.

We got the Panama Canal treaties through and *we have aban-doned a 40-year-old tradition of creating a slogan to describe a single American policy for Latin America. We have deliberately chosen not to label our policy toward Latin America* and instead to pursue a policy of treating Latin American countries as mature partners on a bilateral basis in most cases, as we do with Europe and Asia; on a regional basis when needed (and we have made real strides in developing Caribbean cooperation); and on a global basis in regard to those problems which Latin America shares with other developing countries. I think we have made real prog-ress. (*New York Times Magazine* [9 January 1979]: 47, emphasis mine)

Finis: Good Neighbor policy. And an end also to its rhetorical, syn-thetic successors, the policies of the Good Partner and of Special Relationship.

This is not to say that the United States would not carry on ordi-nary, friendly relations with some Latin American countries, nor that it would refrain from helping establish the Inter-American De-velopment Bank, or discontinue its contributions toward the ex-penses of the OAS. The United States could, however, no longer claim to be acting in the spirit of the Good Neighbor policy, for by its own actions it had flouted the principles that it once embraced.

Beginning with Guatemala, the United States gradually dismantled the Good Neighbor policy, and with it the political features of the OAS and the inter-American system. It avoided the crucial test of the policy by refusing to submit its judgment of the strength of a foreign threat—communism in Guatemala—to the formal consideration of the other members of this society that had been formed by its uni-lateral renunciation of intervention, and by the treaties of Rio de Ja-neiro and Bogotá.

The "warm, self-generated identification of our interest with that of Latin America" that Simon G. Hanson had recalled in 1953 disap-peared in the preoccupation with the interest of the United States alone. In the process there were three losers: the United States gov-ernment lost credibility and an honorable reputation in Latin Amer-ica and elsewhere that it has not regained; the Guatemalan people lost the opportunity for a freer and fairer social and economic order (which they are still fighting for); the American states jointly lost a chance to face a Soviet threat and to forge a new political order in America. After 1954, the voice of the Good Neighbor was no longer heard in the land.

Notes

Introduction

1. Compare, for example, Lowenthal and Fishlow (1979: 71), in which the Good Neighbor is lumped with other "policies" as "one U.S. administration after another has promised to improve U.S.–Latin American relations."

2. John Balfour, FO Minute, 28 April 1941. A3463/47/26. Vol. 26062.

3. Desp. 1160, from V. A. L. Mallet, Washington, 30 December 1938. FO Minute by Geoffrey H. Thompson. A258/51/51. Vol. 22752.

4. Alberto Ulloa y Sotomayor, no friend of the United States, expressed a Latin American view:

> There is no denying that the Good Neighbor policy has been loyally carried out. Since President Roosevelt's ascent to power his statements and acts in that connection have revealed that it not only serves to give steady direction to his ideas but is a sentiment deeply rooted in his spirit. He has let pass no opportunity of demonstrating that the foundation of United States international policy toward the South American republics has undergone a fundamental alteration and that continental solidarity can no longer be the work of a hegemony that reduces frightened peoples to the same level below itself, but must derive from a voluntary understanding between states fully aware of their community of interests and risk. (*La Prensa* [Lima], 26 March 1941)

5. J. V. Perowne, head, South American Department, FO Minute 8 May 1941. A3407/.2810/51. Vol. 26012.

6. Letter, R. H. Hadow, counselor, British Embassy, to Perowne, Washington, 15 February 1946. AS992/235/2. Vol. 51904.

1. Setting the Stage

1. It is ironic to recall in this connection that, commenting on the Lima conference in 1938, Hull wrote, "Unanimity, as always in the Pan American Conference, was my aim. I could have had a vote of 17 to 4 or 18 to 3 or perhaps 20 to 1 on my original draft at any time, but such was not our method of procedure. That would have shown the outside world that there was a split in the Pan American front" (1948: 1: 609).

2. Welles had talked with Roosevelt on the eve of his departure for Rio de Janeiro, and they had apparently reached conclusions rather different from, and more flexible than, those Welles had accepted in staff meetings with Hull and other officials (*FRUS* 5 [1942]: 36–39). No other record of this talk has been found, except in Welles (1951: 105–106), in which Welles said to Roosevelt, "The expedient course was for us to lay the facts before our American neighbors, and to avoid taking any action that would break the unity of the hemisphere and thereby give the Axis a chance to fish in muddy waters." Welles wrote, differently, to Hull on 16 January that he completely shared Hull's "own feeling that every effort should be made to preserve unanimity, but that if the Argentine Government is unwilling to join in a continental declaration for a severance of relations with the Axis Powers, Argentina should be allowed to proceed alone" (ibid.: 27)

3. "Hull's Tennessee mountaineer background showed through in his vocabulary on the frequent occasions when he became irritated, and especially when the White House was bypassing the Department of State" (Bohlen 1973: 129). "The relations between the Secretary and his new Under-Secretary were strained from the start, which demoralized the internal administration of the department. . . . The Hull-Welles feud adversely affected the conduct of our foreign relations for several years" (Phillips 1952: 186; see also Hooker 1956: 378).

4. See also Dallek (1979: 421), who says that "rumors about alleged homosexual activities on Welles's part, made Hull determined to act" in requesting that Welles be asked to resign. See also Gellman (1979: 176f), and Woods (1979: 103f), who say that Sens. Tom Connally and James Byrnes demanded of Roosevelt that Welles be ousted.

5. "As at so many previous inter-American conferences, Argentina preferred the role of opposing the United States" (Hull 1948: 1: 823).

6. J. V. Perowne, head, South American Department, FO Minute 7 January 1942. A266/266/2. Vol. 30320.

7. Cable from Amb. Lord Halifax, Washington, 21 January 1942. A822/1/51. Vol. 30475. This view is difficult to reconcile with Berle's statement that he and Laurence Duggan thought that the "revised resolution was disastrous," as accepted by Welles at Rio (Berle 1973: 398).

8. FO Minute, 28 January 1942. A974/266/2. Vol. 30475. "It is of course true that unanimity is an essential requirement of Mr. Welles' Pan-American policy. It has been attained, at the cost of considerable concessions, at all previous Pan-American conferences, and once it had been breached, the way would have been open to successful recalcitrance by any Latin American country on almost any issue" (R. A. Gallop, FO Minute, 21 January 1942. A778/266/2. Vol. 30320).

9. Letter, Sir Noel Charles, Rio de Janeiro, to Perowne, 13 February 1942. A3078/1/51. Vol. 30476.

10. Cable from Halifax, Washington, 8 February 1942. A1344/1/51. Vol. 30476; and letter from Charles to Perowne (see note 9), in which Welles was reported as telling Argentine foreign minister Enrique Ruiz Guiñazú that

the USSR, then England, and then Brazil had first calls on U.S. war matériel. When Ruiz Guiñazú complained that Brazil was "singled out," Welles said that the United States "could not very well act differently towards the country which had been their friend."

11. Tel. 266, 24 February 1942. DS835.00/1145.

12. Tel. 21, from Amb. Sir Esmond Ovey, Buenos Aires, 5 January 1942. A196/1/51. Vol. 30474; and tel. 2, Welles, Rio de Janeiro, to the secretary of state, 13 January 1942. DS 710. Consultation (3)/304.

13. The memorandum was in reply to one sent to the president by the Treasury, and the Department of State was understandably huffy at being bypassed by Morgenthau, whose access to the White House was better than Hull's.

14. Letter, R. A. Humphreys, adviser to the FO to Perowne, 21 November 1941. A9694/8362/51. Vol. 26028.

15. Gallop, FO Minute 14 December 1941. A10298/15/2. Vol. 25704. N. A. P. Sands took a similar view and said that Britain desired that Argentina declare war on the Axis, but "everything must be left to the U.S.A. (as part of the good neighbour policy) and to the influence of Brazil. The U.S. is now responsible for that part of the world and we must not interfere. Pressure by us would be far more likely to scare off Argentina than to assist U.S. efforts (FO Minute on tel. 911, from Ovey, Buenos Aires, 20 December 1941. A10482/15/2. Vol. 25704).

16. FO Minute on tel. 6039, 25 December 1941, from Washington. A10635/10529/51. Vol. 26036.

17. FO tel. 6077, 27 December 1941. A10669/10529/51. Vol. 26036.

18. FO memorandum by Perowne, 19, 21 April 1942. A3971/23/2. Vol. 30314. See, however, Woods (1979: 58), who says that the British had proposed collaboration with Washington "in toppling those Latin governments that were proving less than enthusiastic about doing battle with Hitler and Mussolini. He [Sir Ronald Hugh Campbell, minister in Washington] mentioned Argentina and Brazil specifically. . . . The Americans, however, would have no part of it." The only reference to this is the Berle diary, box 213, 24 January 1942, p. 3. In the diary is the statement that the British "through their military intelligence people, proposed just before Welles went to Rio that they should assist us in working up a series of Latin American coups d'état. They specifically mentioned, I believe, the Argentines, to Duggan. We turned the idea down promptly." There is no reference to Brazil in this diary entry. I have found no way of reconciling Berle's statement with Perowne's "minor forms of pressure."

19. FO Minute to tel. 6077, 27 December 1941. A10669/10529/51. Vol. 26036.

20. Desp. 13/64A/42, from Washington, 30 April 1942. A4424/3188/2. 30333.

21. FO Memorandum, by Gallop, 23 February 1942. A1817/234/51. Vol. 30504. Compare FO Minute by Perowne, on letter from Charles to Sir David Scott, 5 February 1942. A2674/2674/6. Vol. 30365: "It seems to me natural

for the Americans to wish to regard the whole Western Hemisphere as their oyster." Compare also FO Minute by Francis Edward Evans to above memorandum by Gallop: "I find the U.S. attitude consistent with American tradition and reasonable in the light of American experience. It is an extension—indeed, no more than a continuance—of the policy which has been followed by the U.S. for 120 years. . . . Europe, in the Pan-American view, must be allowed no part in the politics of the Americas, for so long as Europe produces imperialism, Europe is suspect." In commenting, Perowne agreed with Evans, but said that "pressure of war circumstances will *drive* the Americans into much greater collaboration with us in the Latin American as in all other spheres than their primary predisposition would probably make seem likely. . . . The State Dept. is at last turning to us to help put pressure on Argentina" (FO Memorandum, by Gallop, 23 February 1942. A1817/234/51. Vol. 30504).

22. Desp. 75, from Sir Charles Orde, Santiago, 27 May 1942. A5656/52/9. Vol. 30436. Orde expressed the hope that the Chilean government might "realise that they can sell a rupture with the Axis for more armaments (the acquisition of which by Peru seems to be causing apprehension) and for commercial advantages both during and after the war, if they act before the increasing strength of the Allies makes it a matter of indifference to them what policy Chile pursues. The difficulty is probably that they wish to be sure of their price before taking action; the generous gesture and faith in an eventual reward does not appeal to the Chilean mind." Similarly, Gallop believed "that while Argentina is not 'for sale' Chile *is*. There will be ups and downs but a break with the Axis, and possibly war, will come some day" (FO Minute on desp. 95, from Orde, Santiago, 26 June 1942. A6607/52/9. Vol. 30437).

23. Gallop, FO Minute, 17 July 942. A7017/52/9. Vol. 30437.

24. Tel. 885, from Bowers, Santiago, 2 June 1942; and tel. 649, from Hull to Bowers, 6 June 1942, *FRUS* 6 (1942): 22–24.

25. Desp. 113, from Santiago, 23 July 1942. A7478/52/9. Vol. 30437.

26. Ibid.

27. Samponaro says that the CPD was "an instrument of the United States that was used to pressure the governments of Argentina, Chile, and Bolivia to realign their policies in accordance with Washington's wishes" (1979: 38).

28. Perowne and Sir David Scott, FO Minutes on desp. 135, from Orde, Santiago, 18 September 1942. A9217/52/9. Vol. 30437.

29. Perowne, FO Minute on tel. 388, from Orde, Santiago, 10 October 1942. A9364/1702/9. Vol. 30440. Gallop said that "President Rios is notoriously a weak character, and his hesitations, coupled with the fact that his last visit was to Buenos Aires, have raised doubts of the sincerity of his assurances in Mr. Sumner Welles' mind, which have been translated into this characteristically impetuous action." He added, "Nor is this example of the Good Neighbour Policy likely to be lost even on those countries whose conduct Mr. Welles commended in his speech."

30. Tel. 973, from Rio de Janeiro, 12 October 1942. A9412/1/51. Vol. 30476. Gallop commented, "Mr. Sumner Welles is as unfortunate in his use of the

big stick as of the velvet glove." Perowne feared that Welles was, in general, "a danger to our interests in Latin America, as well as (sometimes) to those of the U.S.A. I have long thought that we should get on better without him in his present position of influence and authority: but he may have hidden charms."

31. Tel. 5089, from Halifax, Washington, 13 October 1942. A9469/1702/9. Vol. 30440. Gallop noted in an FO Minute that Welles felt that Ríos would not break relations before his visit to Washington "and that he should not be allowed to obtain the kudos of the latter without delivering the goods first." Perowne agreed, saying that the lack of a break in relations would, in Welles's view, "take 'all shine' out of the Presidential visit to Washington."

32. Tel. 5093, from Halifax, 13 October 1942. A9470/3188/2. Vol. 30333. Gallop commented that the Welles speech "can only have been regarded in the Argentine as a display of U.S. petulance and bad manners. This tends to strengthen our view that the speech was one of the most striking examples we have yet seen of Mr. Sumner Welles' ineptitude in dealing with his Latin American 'good neighbours' the moment their standard of 'goodness' falls short of perfection." Perowne noted that Argentina was "enraged." and no statement by Britain at this point would advance the common aim. A Peruvian deputy visiting in Brazil called the Welles speech "disastrous" and deplored "the tactlessness of Mr. S. W. and his tendency to treat South Americans as if they were Cubans, than which no greater mistake could possibly be made" (tel. 997, from Charles, Rio de Janeiro, 20 October 1942. A9676/1/51. Vol. 30476).

33. Tel. 394, from Orde, Santiago, 14 October 1942. A9493/1702/9. Vol. 30440.

34. Orde, FO Minute on tel. 404, Santiago, 18 October 1942. A9554/1702/9. Vol. 30440.

35. Gallop, FO Minute on tel. 440, from Orde, Santiago, 5 November 1942. A10280/1702/9. Vol. 30440.

36. Perowne, FO Minute on tel. 5986, from Halifax, Washington, 9 December 1942. A11586/52/9. Vol. 30438.

37. DS740.0011, European War 1939/27117. Documents attached to memorandum of conversation between Welles and Amb. Morales, 22 December 1942. The documents are headed "Solely for the Secret and Personal Information of His Excellency the President of Chile and His Excellency the Minister of the Interior of Chile."

38. See p. 18 and note 11.

39. Desp. 11, from Orde, Santiago, 27 January 1943. A1481/7/9. 33750A.

40. In February 1945, Chile, under strong pressure from Washington, declared war on Japan. Ríos stated to Roosevelt that he was declaring "the state of belligerency existing between Chile and Japan" (Francis 1977: 144).

2. Relations with Argentina to 4 June 1943

1. Letter, Dean Acheson, assistant secretary of state, to Winfield W. Riefler, minister to London, 19 June 1943, *FRUS* 5 (1943): 333.

2. The memorandum was in response to a memorandum of protest from Argentina of 8 June 1942.

3. Letter, Lord Drogheda to Sir David Scott, 8 May 1942. A4605/4031/51. Vol. 30516.

4. Amb. Courteney Forbes, FO Minute on tel. 107, Lima, 16 May 1942. A4605/4031/51. Vol. 30516.

5. Ibid.

6. Letter, Charles to Perowne, Rio de Janeiro, 11 May 1942. A5146/5146/6. Vol. 30369.

7. Gallop, FO Minute on ibid.

8. Maurice Butler, FO Minute on ibid.

9. Tel. 3266, from Halifax, 14 June 1942. A5693/5146/6; and tel. 637, from Charles, Rio de Janeiro, 29 June 1942. A6131/5146/6. Vol. 30369. An FO Minute by N. A. P. Sands on tel. 637 wondered whether Aranha "dropped a hint" to Caffery, since Aranha had been concerned about the "lack of cooperation" between the United States and Britain.

10. Memorandum, 9 July 1942. A6602/4031/51. Vol. 30516.

11. Letter, Sir Ronald Hugh Campbell, minister in Washington, to Scott, 31 July 1942. A6602/4031/51. Vol. 30516. The FO sent an instruction along the same lines to its missions, 25 August 1942.

12. Desp. 125, from Gainer, Caracas, 27 August 1942. A8542/8542/47. Vol. 30760. In an FO Minute, Sands said that he thought that Gainer had here "hit the nail on the head."

13. Letter, Hadow to Perowne, Buenos Aires, 27 January 1943. A1758/4/2. Vol. 33507.

14. Letter to Scott, Rio de Janeiro, 15 November 1942. A11219/5146/6. Vol. 30369.

15. "Summary of Reports on Public Opinion," Buenos Aires, 3 February 1943. A1257/1257/2. Vol. 33565.

16. FO Minute, 30 March 1943. A3068/4/2. Vol. 33507.

17. Ibid. In May the Argentine minister of interior was asked to obtain from the British a "complete list of all sinkings." Henderson noted that "we have hitherto drawn a complete blank from Admty. in regard to evidence which would have convinced the Argentines of Axis espionage being responsible for sinkings of H.M. ships. . . . The implication behind all this appears to be that Sr. Castillo has at last become convinced as to who is winning the war and that he is looking for a good enough excuse to join the winning side before it seems *too* obvious. If so, it is rather a bolt out of the blue." However, Butler said he would be surprised if the admiralty provided the information, "either because they haven't got it; or because they may see no point in confirming to the Axis sinkings of which the latter may well be doubtful" (tel. 336, from Kelly, Buenos Aires, 17 May 1943, and FO Minutes thereon. A4594/283/2. Vol. 33546).

18. Gallop, FO Minute, on letter from Kenneth B. Grubb, Ministry of Information, to Perowne, 17 March 1943. A2710/483/2. Vol. 33558.

19. See n. 16. Gallop's remarks are worth quoting, since they show an understanding of the reasons for the "thwarted rage" of the United States:

If the Americans were moved only by considerations of enlightened self-interest, it would no doubt be a simple matter to ask them what real benefit they expect to get out of Argentine belligerency. Since, in point of fact, we believe them to be moved by thwarted rage, such an enquiry would only increase the suspicion, which our attitude towards Argentine-Swedish and Argentine-Spanish trade may already be sowing, that we are out to shelter the Argentines and curry favour with them. Moreover, the Americans have in any case more solid grounds than we have for wanting Argentina to come to heel. It is not only disagreeable but dangerous for them, if one Latin American country is able successfully to defy the Pan-American and Good Neighbour policies. The rot may spread, if not now, then after the war. (Source, n. 18)

20. Tel. 1216, Buenos Aires, 6 June 1943. One problem in this connection was that of knowing who "the army" was. Kelly talked with Dr. Eduardo Labougle, who headed a group of people who called on Ramírez to advocate press freedom and who said that "the whole trouble of this present Government is central group of German-trained colonels whose saturation by German influences he [Labougle] had watched and lamented while Ambassador to Berlin" (tel. 716, Buenos Aires, 14 September 1943. A8505/11/2. Vol. 33516). "The large majority of the Army are still behind the Government and want to continue sitting on the political fence. . . . The Argentines wanted freedom and were not going to be 'bossed about' by the United States, either now or after the war." One army officer asked if Argentine policy, "which was gradually reducing her to a position of inferiority as a nation in South America instead of being a leader as she formerly was, was a good one. He said: 'No, we now realize our mistake, but no one seems to know how to effect a change'" (letter, Hadow to Perowne, Buenos Aires, 1 October 1943, and A. A. Walser, air attaché of Britain, FO Minute, 1 October 1943. A9362/4/2. Vol. 33509).

21. Desp. 160, from Kelly, Buenos Aires, 18 June 1943. A6530/11/2. 33514. Henderson commented that "the manner in which the movement was carried out was in the best Nigger-Republic style."

22. Desp. 489, from Halifax, Washington, 14 June 1943. A5895/11/2. Vol. 33513. Henderson's comment was that "the new order in Argentina has been responsible for a breakdown in the Pan-American front which augurs ill for the post-war period. This episode seems to show that Pan-Americanism when put to a real test, has not been able to stand up to it."

23. Tel. 46, from Rio de Janeiro, 13 July 1943. A6952/5521/2/ Vol. 33598. Aranha criticized the United States for "waiting to obtain joint action of the American republics or in wishing to impose conditions on Argentina" and added that he had wished to recognize before the Axis powers.

3. Relations with the Ramírez Administration

1. Letter to Armour, 28 June 1943. This letter was drafted by Bonsal, reviewed by Duggan, and approved, with the addition of the above paragraph by Welles. Hull reiterated the statement on 23 July (*FRUS* 5 [1943]: 443).

2. Tel. 1506, from Buenos Aires, 6 July 1943 (*FRUS* 5 [1943]: 429).

3. Tel. 509, from Kelly, Buenos Aires, 14 July 1943. A6658/4/2. Vol. 33508.

4. Tel. 515, from Kelly, Buenos Aires, 16 July 1943. A6670/4/2. Vol. 33508. This information came from the "democratic and pro-Ally Bishop Andres who is a most intimate friend of the President and the Minister for Foreign Affairs."

5. Letter, Perowne from Kelly, Buenos Aires, 4 August 1943. A7605/483/2. Vol. 33560.

6. Memorandum, "Economic Policy towards Argentina," 3 February 1943, *Memoranda on Argentina*, vol. 3, NA.

7. Tel. 889, to Buenos Aires, 18 June 1943.

8. Desp. 10961, from Buenos Aires, 13 July 1943.

9. Tel. 1113, to Buenos Aires, 27 July 1943.

10. Text, 5 August 1943. Ramírez drastically changed Storni's original draft (Conil Paz and Ferrari 1966: 107). Kelly reported that Storni had told the Brazilian ambassador that his letter was "originally intended as a memorandum to protect Mr. Armour's personal position in consequence of the President's light-hearted promise that relations would be broken within five weeks, but the memorandum was turned into a letter which was redrafted by the President himself, whose amendments (grp. undec. ? constituted) the most vulnerable targets" (tel. 695, from Buenos Aires, 9 September 1943. A8403/11/2. Vol. 33516).

11. Letter, Hull to Storni, 30 August 1943.

12. Tel. 2481, from Buenos Aires, 20 October 1943. In this talk Ramírez followed a well-known Argentine line by asserting that, since the Rio resolution had "left it to each country to decide when and how it would proceed to carry out the terms of the Resolution . . . it therefore could not be considered as a commitment which had not been fulfilled."

13. M. Butler and Sir Maurice Peterson, FO Minutes on tel. 4081, from Campbell, Washington, 10 September 1943. A8413/4/2. Vol. 33508.

14. Statement attached to tel. 4235, from Campbell, Washington, 21 September 1943. A8731/4/2. Vol. 33508.

15. Letter, Campbell to Kelly, Washington, 12 September 1943. A8670/483/2. Vol. 33560.

16. Tel. 2483, from Buenos Aires.

17. Tel. 1644, to Buenos Aires, with text of telegram to Hull in Moscow, 24 October 1943; and tel. 1647, to Buenos Aires, 25 October 1943. This discussion referred to a general freezing order; an earlier blocking of funds in the United States had been applied only to the Banco Nacional and Banco de la Provincia, owing to their sending funds to Europe and other activities for the benefit of Axis governments or nationals.

18. Memorandum to the secretary, from Bonsal, Duggan, and Emilio G. Collado, "The Argentine Situation," 11 November 1943. DS835.00/2184.

19. Tel. 901, from Buenos Aires, 15 November 1943, and FO Minutes by Perowne and Scott. A10437/483/2. Vol. 33561.

20. Desp. 1025, from Halifax, Washington, 1 December 1943. A11230/483/2. Vol. 33561.

21. Desp. 1073, from Washington, 12 December 1943, and FO Minutes by Gallop and Scott, AS117/59/51. Vol. 38159. Sir Alexander Cadogan added: "Mr. Hull is not a very apt pupil."

22. Desp. 1064, from Halifax, Washington, 17 December 1943. A121/59/51. Vol. 38159.

23. Tel. 5776, from Washington, 22 December 1943. A11561/346/5. Vol. 33611.

24. Tel. 5777, from Halifax, Washington, 22 December 1943. A11524/483/2. Vol. 33561. In an FO Minute, Perowne lamented: "(O! the relative simplicity of Greek and Yugoslav imbroglios!)"

25. Tel. 1042, from Kelly, Buenos Aires, 26 December 1943, and FO Minutes by Butler and C. E. Scott. A11713/483/2. Vol. 33561.

26. Tel. 669, from Charles, Rio de Janeiro, 24 December 1943. A11579/346/5. Vol. 33611.

27. George Vereker, ambassador in Montevideo, FO Minute on desp. 137, 27 December 1943. AS433/433/2. Vol. 37737.

28. Tel. 16, from Washington, 3 January 1944. AS78/78/2. Vol. 37698, and FO Minutes thereon.

29. Gallop, FO memorandum, "The Lesson of the Argentine Case," 4 January 1944. AS130/78/2. Vol. 37698. Perowne did not, however, think that fascism represented "a very great danger to us or to the Americas." Gladwyn Jebb, one of Gallop's colleagues, thought that "there is only one criterion which can govern and justify interference in the internal affairs of a foreign State, and that is if there is a declared and acknowledged danger that the Government concerned may be about to disturb the peace." Paul Mason, another of his colleagues, thought that "the full machinery of Pan-American meetings . . . so carefully integrated by Mr. Sumner Welles" would continue "to be the methods whereby the US sought to be a, if not the, leading influence in Latin America." Donald St. Clair Gainer reported the Venezuelan foreign minister as saying that "the Argentine in her fear of Brazil and of isolation in America had first tried to provoke a coup in Chile and then Uruguay, both of which attempts had proved abortive but that now she seemed to have succeeded in Bolivia, where the German element had always been strong and influential" (desp. 9, Caracas, 10 January 1944. AS678/503/51. Vol. 38178).

30. Tel. 14, from Buenos Aires, 7 January 1944. AS191/76/2. Vol. 37698. Kelly recommended that Britain insist on an "expert examination" of the possibility and purposes of trade sanctions: Was it the "overthrow of the Argentine Government?" His recommendation was approved in London, but no immediate action was taken.

31. Tel. 134, from Halifax, Washington, 9 January 1944. A209/4/2. Vol. 37666. See on the question of coordination in the United States, the memorandum by Gallop, "Notes on a Visit to Washington," 8 March 1944, AS1538/901/61. Vol. 38185.

32. Tel. 139, from Washington, 10 January 1944. AS254/78/2. Vol. 37698.

33. Tel. 285, to Halifax, Washington, 12 January 1944. AS254/78/2. Vol. 37698.

34. Tel. 1264, 13 January 1944. AS254/78/2. Vol. 37698.

35. Tel. 357, to Washington, 14 January 1944. AS294/78/2. Vol. 37698. Perowne had written that the United States "seem to believe that if only you shout loud enough, the enemy's walls will collapse—as at Jericho" (Halifax, FO Minute on tel. 157, Washington, 11 January 1944. AS286/1/5. Vol. 37805).

36. Memorandum to the secretary, "Argentine Policy." 18 January 1944. DS711.35/212.

37. Memorandum to the Secretary, "Bolivian-Argentine Policy," 10 January 1944. DS710.11/3221.

38. Text in desp. 44, from Washington, 14 January 1944. AS630/1/5. Vol. 37807. Noted was a dinner given for Paz Estenssoro at the Club del Plata, attended by Gen. Basilio Pertine, mayor of Buenos Aires "and a ringleader in Nazi activities in Argentina; by Carlos Ibarguren, whose writings have conspicuously associated him with pro-German and anti-democratic ideas; by Julio and Rodolfo Irazusta, publishers of the pro-Nazi *Voz del Pueblo*; and by other prominent supporters of the Ramírez government."

39. Tel. 99, 12 January 1944.

40. Tel. 257, from Washington, 18 January 1944. AS423/78/2. Vol. 37698. Halifax added that Roosevelt "appeared to assent to this general thought and I hope this rather casual exchange may act as some slight brake if Mr. Hull wants to be more active than you [i.e., the Foreign Office] would approve."

41. Text in tel. 315, from Halifax, Washington, 21 January 1944. AS496/1/5. Vol. 37806. Robert F. Woodward, chargé in La Paz at the time, has written that Bolivian production and trade in tin, tungsten, and cinchona continued uninterrupted, and he argued in cables to Washington "that the Bolivian revolution was totally unrelated to the war effort and we should resume normal relations." The foreign minister asked Woodward what the U.S. reaction would be if he "offered to round up some of the key Germans in the country." Woodward informed Washington, and immediately Amb. Avra Warren was sent down to assist Woodward in receiving the Germans. Nine DC-3 Dakotas came from the Canal Zone to take the deported persons. Woodward does not recall whether the United States asked for "the removal of specific Cabinet officers" as a means of securing recognition (letter to me, 29 January 1982).

42. Tel. 468, to Washington, summarized in FO memorandum, "Argentine Situation," 20 February 1944. AS615/78/2. Vol. 37699. This memorandum was used as the source for certain subsequent messages, which I did not find in the files of the Public Record Office.

43. Tel. 288, from Washington, 20 January 1944. AS615/78/2. Vol. 37699.

44. Tel. 545, to Washington, 21 January 1944. AS615/78/2. Vol. 37699.

45. Tel. 546, to Washington, 21 January 1944; and tel. 317, from Washington, 22 January 1944. AS615/78/2. Vol. 37699. See also "Memorandum from Combined Chiefs of Staff," 29 January 1944. DS835.50/165. Essentially the same message was conveyed by the combined chiefs of staff, which, basing its view on studies by the Combined Boards, said that the situation had not changed between January and May: "Irrespective of the effect upon civilian economies, any cessation of supply from Argentina of meat, wheat, fats,

oils, leather, and quebracho, would have unfavorable military implications" ("Proposed Economic Sanctions with Respect to Argentina," reply to letter from Acheson and Hadow, 4 May 1944. RG218, Box 542, Argentina, CCS091.3. NA).

46. Tel. 357, from Washington, 23 January 1944. A573/4/2G. Vol. 37677. Duggan saw eye to eye with Hull, for he was reported as saying that the department "did not anticipate that these proposed measures would result in the overthrow of the Argentine Government; the opposite effect would probably result for a time. He did not believe that there was any chance of the Argentine interfering with exports. The object was to demonstrate U.S. disapproval of the behaviour of Argentina" (tel. 366, from Washington, 23 January 1944. AS615/78/2. Vol. 37699).

47. Tel. 552, from London, 23 January 1944. RG218, Box 542, CCS091.3. Paraphrase, NA.

48. Tel. 60, from Kelly, Buenos Aires, 21 January 1944. AS615/78/2. Vol. 37699. Kelly said that "Argentine action was due (apart from Hellmuth case, which offered a perfect opportunity) to *threat* of pressure" (tel. 70, from Buenos Aires, 25 January 1944. AS615/78/2. Vol. 37699).

49. Tel. 358, from Halifax, Washington, 23 January 1944. AS615/78/2. Vol. 37699.

50. Eden was careful in a statement to Parliament, to avoid chronological specificity. Sometime between 29 October 1943 and 22 January 1944, the British government furnished information to Argentina that led to a decision in Buenos Aires "to hold an investigation into the existence of an enemy espionage organization on Argentine territory." London had been "in the closest touch throughout" with Washington, and "the exchange of information and views between our two governments has been of the fullest, frankest, and most cordial nature" (*FRUS* 7 [1944]: 379, quoting from Eden's statement in the House of Commons, 27 January 1944). In a memorandum prepared for Eden's statement Perowne noted that "information from most secret sources indicated unmistakably that the [Bolivian] revolution had been largely organized from Buenos Aires, with the backing of the Argentine Government and possibly also of German elements there as part of a scheme to create a bloc of totalitarian Governments in opposition to the U.S. in South America." He noted that only Argentina had recognized the Bolivian regime and that the U.S. ambassador had been withdrawn: "This procedure is somewhat unusual, and amounts to something very like interference in the domestic affairs of another country, contrary to the spirit of the Atlantic Charter" (FO Minute for the secretary of state, 25 January 1944. AS693/1/5. Vol. 37807).

51. FO Research Department, memorandum, "The Totalitarian State in Argentina," 13 March 1944. AS3323/4/2. Vol. 37675. When the United States refrained from mentioning Argentina in its message on nonrecognition of Bolivia, the Argentines breathed deeply and thenceforward claimed full credit for the "discovery" of German and other espionage groups and the finding of clandestine radio transmitters (tel. 499, from Armour, Buenos Aires, 19 February 1944. DS800.20235/409).

52. Letter from Adm. William D. Leahy, chief of staff, to Hull, 29 February 1944. DS835.01/176. On the letter in Leahy's file (RG218, Box 542, File CCS092, Argentina, NA) is the notation, "No record received from Secy. State. Presumably handled orally."

53. Tel. 201, from Buenos Aires, 24 January 1944.

54. Circular tel., and tel. 205, from Buenos Aires, 24 January 1944.

55. Tel. 266, from Armour, Buenos Aires, 29 January 1944. The Junta Revolucionaria Nacionalista charged that the United States menaced Argentina by (1) threatening to publish documents imputing intervention by Argentines in the Bolivian Revolution, (2) withdrawing diplomats, and (3) dispatching ships of war to Uruguayan ports. Gilbert was asked at a meeting if the break was due to pressure from the United States: "The Minister, visibly confounded, gave a blow with his fist on the table, replying: 'Yes, sir, relations with the Axis were broken in the face of pressure from the United States.'" This caused a great commotion in the hall (taken from a memorandum by the junta, contained in desp. 14352, from Armour, Buenos Aires, 1 April 1944. DS835.00/2769).

56. Tel. 467, from Armour, Buenos Aires, 17 February 1944. Gilbert resigned on 15 February. The State Department was reported as "worried at the leakage of their memorandum on the Bolivian coup, with its implications of Argentine complicity, which played into the hands of the Nationalists" (tel. 517, from Washington, 2 February 1944. AS863/145/2. Vol. 37725).

57. Tel. 70, from Kelly, Buenos Aires, 25 January 1944. AS615/78/2. Vol. 37699.

58. Desp. 3820, from William Dawson, Montevideo, 25 January 1944. DS811.3333/49.

59. Memorandum of conversation, 30 December 1943.

60. Tel. 5, to Montevideo, 4 January 1944.

61. Tel. 78, from Montevideo, 16 January 1944. *La Razón*, Montevideo, was quoted as saying that "presence in River Plate waters of powerful United States vessels will remind those who forget of the irrevocable will of world democracy" (*FRUS* 7 [1944]: 1592).

62. Tel. 636, from Montevideo, 1 July 1944.

63. Letters, 11 January, 1 February 1944. Box 165, Box 4, Papers of Fleet Admiral Ernest J. King. Naval Historical Library.

64. "At the same time Washington decided to increase pressure on Buenos Aires to break relations with the Axis . . . Admiral Ingram steamed to Montevideo in his flagship, the cruiser USS *Memphis*. The Argentines' nerve weakened and they severed relations with the Axis on Jan. 25, [sic] 1944" (F. McCann 1973: 323). It seems probable, however, that the Argentine break on 24 January was due more to other British and American pressures.

65. Letter, Charles to Scott, Rio de Janeiro, 17 February 1944. AS1499/51/6. Vol. 37842.

66. Memorandum of conversation, by James H. Wright, 28 January 1944.

67. Tel. 194, to Buenos Aires, 2 February 1944. Gilbert had proposed that Argentina might act as an intermediary to bring about certain changes in the Bolivian government.

68. Letter, Hull to Roosevelt, 8 January 1944.

69. Memorandum from Roosevelt to Hull, 12 January 1944. For portion of letter omitted from *FRUS*, F. McCann (1973: 323).

70. R. H. S. Allen, FO Minute on letter to H. Blake-Tyler, FO, from Cdr. R. D. Coleridge, 18 January 1944. AS878/59/51. Vol. 38159.

71. FO memorandum, "The Anglo–United States–Argentine Triangle," 28 January 1944. AS425/78/2. Vol. 37698.

72. K. P. Kirkwood, Canadian Legation, Washington, contained in letter from Campbell to Scott, 29 January 1944, AS974/59/51. Vol. 38160.

73. Tel. 51, from Rio de Janeiro, 27 January 1944. AS759/446/6. Vol. 31859. Perowne commented that "'kindly liaison' will apply in the case of Bolivia also, and here we may be able to make use of Sr. Aranha."

74. Letter to Scott and Charles, Washington, 20 January 1944. AS631.31/6. Vol. 37842.

75. Tels. 152, 164, from Kelly, Buenos Aires, 15, 17 February 1944. AS1108/4/2; AS1189/4/2. Vol. 37668.

76. Tel. 266, to Buenos Aires, 12 February 1944.

77. Tel. 49, from Halifax, Washington, 21 February 1944. AS1326/4/2. Vol. 37669. The origin of this telegram was a talk Gallop and a member of Halifax's staff had with Duggan and Bonsal. The Combined Chiefs of Staff at this time emphasized their concern about "serious military implications" that would make it necessary to "reexamine the feasibility of undertaking military operations on the scale now planned," if any question arose about a cessation of supplies from Argentina (memorandum from Combined Chiefs of Staff to Acheson and Campbell, "Economic Sanctions against Argentina," 29 January 1944. DS835.50/165).

4. Failure of Nonrecognition

1. Circular tel. to the American republics, except Argentina, Bolivia, and Chile, 4 March 1944. Bolivia and Chile had already recognized the Farrell regime; they were soon joined by Ecuador and Paraguay.

2. Memorandum by J. Kenly Bacon, 6 March 1944. DS835.01/209. Bacon added that Chile "had been displeased at not receiving larger handouts" from the United States and that it might have wished "to keep Argentina out of the so-called happy family of American Republics."

3. "Statement on Argentine Situation," 4 March 1944. DS835.00/2620. Woods has used this difference of view in exaggerated fashion, in my opinion, to distinguish between "internationalists" and "Latin Americanists" in the Department. The first were typified by Hull and Breckenridge Long; the second by Welles, and later Bonsal and Duggan. There is something to the distinction, but it is vastly overdrawn, as may be seen by an analysis of Welles's note to Armour of 28 June 1943. See Woods (1979: 97–98) and the analysis here (pp. 43–44). Incidentally, the statement about the Storni note is erroneously attached to n. 65, p. 97 in Woods.

4. Tel. 998, from Halifax, Washington, 28 February 1944. AS1356/4/2. Vol. 37669. In an FO Minute, Henderson said these remarks were "as surprising as they are inexplicable." Perowne thought it was best not to take up the

question with Stettinius, but to "let the brake be put on, as it certainly will be put on, by the other American States."

5. Tel. 140, from Rio de Janeiro, 10 March 1944. AS1568/4/2. Vol. 37670. Henderson noted in an FO Minute that the Brazilians were "unwilling to do anything liable to upset their relations with Argentina"; and Gallop noted that "apparently, a neighbour is not the same as a Good Neighbour."

6. Memorandum of conversation with Sen. Eduardo Cruz-Coke, Cecil B. Lyon, and Duggan, 11 March 1944. DS835.01/268.

7. Tel. 128, from Washington, 14 March 1944. AS1672/51/6. Vol. 37842. FO Minute by Scott: "This kind of talk shows that the Good Neighbour Policy is less than skin deep in the average American."

8. Tel. 118, to Montevideo, 1 March 1944. DS811.3333/5DA; and tel. 222, from Montevideo, 2 March 1944. DS811.3333/51.

9. Tel. 652, 6 March 1944. DS811.333/52.

10. Tel. 240, from Montevideo, 6 March 1944. DS811.3333/53.

11. Tel. 133, to Montevideo, 6 March 1944. DS811.3333/53.

12. Tel. 248, from Montevideo, 7 March 1944. DS811.3333/55.

13. Tel. 865, from Rio de Janeiro, 7 March 1944. DS811.3333/56. By "bolstering up," Caffery presumably meant that Washington did not wish Uruguay to recognize the Farrell-Perón regime.

14. Tel. 674, from Buenos Aires, 8 March 1944. DS835.3333/58.

15. Memorandum, Duggan to Bonsal, 8 March 1944. DS811.3333/56. In transmitting this to Bonsal, Duggan said, "Before we call Captain Colclough [Navy Department] I would like to speak with you about this over the phone" (DS811.333/56).

16. Memorandum to Stettinius, acting secretary of state, 8 March 1944. DS811.3333/62.

17. Tel. 141, to Montevideo, 9 March 1944. DS811.3333/56.

18. Tel. 144, to Montevideo, 10 March 1944. DS811.3333/56.

19. Memorandum to Duggan, "Argentine-Bolivian Policy," 14 March 1944. DS710.11/3221.

20. Quoted in desp. 44, from Orde, Santiago, 21 March 1944. AS2055/4/2. Vol. 37673. The *Daily Mail* was quoted as saying that "in any case the revolt against American domination is spreading now and the whole of Mr. Sumner Welles's policy has been prejudiced" (ibid.).

21. Memorandum of conversation, "Uruguayan Action with Regard to Argentina," 20 March 1944. DS835.01/325. This same statement is given verbatim in a memorandum of conversation between Hull and Rodolfo Michels, ambassador of Chile, 20 March 1944. DS835.01/325.

22. Letter to Gallop, Washington, 24 March 1944. AS1993/59/51. Vol. 38160.

23. Tel. 557, to Armour, 3 April 1944.

24. Tel. 905, from Buenos Aires, 4 April 1944. DS835.01/323.

25. Tel. 1654, from Halifax, Washington, 2 April 1944. AS1980/78/2. Vol. 37700. Gallop differed from Kelly and Armour on point (2) because Armour emphasized that the cabinet changes would be related to "hemisphere secu-

rity." Later Kelly cabled that, whereas "it would be practical to urge the wisdom of early elections it would be extremely dangerous to impose as *conditional* such a demand amounting to direct and radical intervention in internal politics which could be described without difficulty as impairing national independence" (tel. 337, from Buenos Aires, 3 April 1944. AS1989/78/2. Vol. 37709). Hull's mood seemed to be that, because the Bolivians were making cabinet changes in response to U.S. suggestions, the same technique would work in Buenos Aires, an assumption that was seriously doubted elsewhere.

26. Undersec. Stettinius had sent to Armour early in March a list of five points that would have to be accepted as conditions of recognition of the Farrell-Perón regime: (1) internment of Axis diplomats; (2) elimination of Axis spy rings; (3) prevention of smuggling of platinum and industrial diamonds; (4) control of communications with the Axis; and (5) prevention of transactions by Argentine entities that benefited Axis interests (FO memorandum, "South America," by Gallop, 10 April 1944. AS2120/78/2. Vol. 37701). Armour does not appear to have presented these points to Argentine authorities, and no mention of them is offered in *FRUS* 7 (1944).

27. Letter from H. B. Blake-Tyler, Washington, to J. Dalton-Murray, La Paz, copy to Gallop, 27 April 1944. AS2363/1/5. Vol. 37809.

28. Tel. 1095, from Armour, Buenos Aires, 29 April 1944. DS835.01/362. Armour had earlier reported a talk with Alonso Irigoyen, an associate of Perón's. Armour had suggested "that appointment of a good Foreign Minister and certain Cabinet changes, particularly replacement of Perlinger would seem essential preliminary steps to create confidence in Farrell's regime" (tel. 678, from Buenos Aires, 8 March 1944. DS835.01/203).

29. Memorandum, 3 May 1944. DS835.00/2824.

30. Memorandum to the secretary, "Argentine Policy," 12 May 1944. DS835.00/5-1244.

31. Hadow offered a glimpse of the "dog-fight that is going on in the State Department." He said that Walmsley believed on May 12 that everything was "cut-and-dried," and he and Duggan believed that Hull would send off "reasonable instructions."

On Saturday 13th (an ominous date for the superstitious) he [Walmsley] asked me to walk down with him at 8 am and on the way (for greater security in case of being watched) gave me the details I sent off; saying that it was now he hoped "all over bar the shouting," though the opposition had been strengthened by one WENDELEN [*sic*], just up from the Embassy in Buenos Aires who "fortunately over-played his hand" in urging Mr. Hull to have no truck or trade with the Military in Argentina.

However, on May 15,

everything was "in reverse"! . . . WALMSLEY . . . was so "fed up" with the results of the Secretary of State's week-end thinking that—according

to himself—he *ordered himself* back to his Brazilian desk alone and told
WENDELEN that he could take over Argentina and do what he liked
with it till SPAETH . . . came back! . . .

Walmsley is a forthright, honest and able official, whose return to the
Brazilian desk I regret. . . .

DUGGAN . . . is "slated" by every gossip-writer as leaving shortly—
some say because one by one the Welles men are being cleared out. . . .

If he [Spaeth] is thus promoted over Bonsal's head . . . Bonsal will go
abroad again. (Letter to Gallop, Washington, 16 May 1944. AS2758/78/2.
Vol. 37702)

Duggan resigned in June, and Bonsal was transferred to Madrid in July 1944.

32. Tel. 1543, 17 May 1944. DS835.01/406A. This was an effort to stiffen
the backs of some of the Latin American countries:

The Brazilian Government seems to place the Argentine problem in one
compartment; and its cooperation with the United States and the United
Nations in the war in another. The history of South America as the Brazilian views it reveals a constant effort, sometimes conscious and sometimes unconscious, to maintain equilibrium between the two most
powerful countries, Brazil and Argentina. With blandishment, coercion,
and cries of United States intervention, Argentina is endeavouring to
build up a bloc ostensibly to counteract United States influence; and in
long-range effect to belittle Brazil as a means of belittling the United
States, Brazil's "champion." (Memorandum to the secretary, by Joseph F.
McGurk, 16 May 1944. DS732.35/150)

33. "Memorandum of Conversation with the Argentine Foreign Minister,
General Orlando Peluffo," 23 May 1944. DS835.00/2900. This memorandum
is not signed, but it must have been written by Armour, since he had earlier
reported that he and Peluffo were alone.

34. Tel. 1414, from Buenos Aires, 3 June 1944.

35. Tel. 1420, from Buenos Aires, 5 June 1944. DS835.00/2868.

36. FO Minute on tel. 344, 17 May 1944, to Kelly. AS2571/78/2. Vol.
37702.

37. Desp. 147, from Kelly, Buenos Aires, 17 May 1944. AS2948/144/2. Vol.
37723. Kelly added that "when a foreign representative is deprived of his personal contacts with members of the Government in the country where he
resides, the situation is more likely to deteriorate than otherwise."

38. Desp. 287, from Halifax, Washington, 19 May 1944. AS2773/78/2. Vol.
37702. Halifax quoted Eric Johnston, president of the U.S. Chamber of Commerce, who had given his recent blessing "to a Good Neighbour industrial-
isation of Latin America"; and Berle, who had said that "the foundation of
the foreign policy of the United States must be the policy of the Good
Neighbour," without, however, explaining how the " 'Good Neighbour' is to
be squared with Mr. Hull's 'toughness' towards recalcitrants."

39. Tel. 2859, from Halifax, Washington, 30 May 1944, and tel. 4931, to

Washington, 2 June 1944. AS2855/78/2. Vol. 37702. Scott commented, "I have little hope that anything said to Mr. Hull, who seems to be as ignorant as he is obstinate about the Argentine, will make him change his mind, and we are precluded from taking a line of our own . . . so long as the course of the war is not injured by U.S. policy" (FO Minute on Hadow letter to Gallop, Washington, 3 June 1944. AS3040/78/2. Vol. 37702).

40. Desp. 175, from Kelly, Buenos Aires, 19 June 1944. AS3627/4/2. Vol. 37675.

41. Tel. 3378, from Halifax, Washington, 22 June 1944. AS3303/78/2. Vol. 33702.

42. The original of this telegram carries the notation that it was seen and approved by Berle, Long, Hackworth, and Duggan (DS835.01/535A).

43. Tel. 3377, from Washington, 23 June 1944. AS3298/78/2. Vol. 37702. Welles was writing weekly columns in the *Washington Post* and *New York Herald Tribune*.

44. Tel. 3479, from Washington, 27 June 1944. AS3381/78/2. Vol. 37703.

45. Tel. 575, from Pres. Roosevelt to prime minister, 30 June 1944; and tel. 723, PM to FDR, 1 July 1944. AS3562/78/2. Vol. 37704. Roosevelt had been told by Hull of Eden's refusal to recall Kelly.

46. FO Minute by Gallop, on tel. 3494, from Halifax, Washington, 26 June 1944. AS3408/78/2. Vol. 37703. Scott commented: "So long as there was a Japanese or German threat to their independence or to the stability of the existing regimes or so long as they could expect arms or economic etc. advantages, these countries would put up with a good deal of 'leadership' from the U.S. Now that the enemy threat has disappeared and the U.S. are shewing signs of retrenching on the economic side, they are far less amenable."

47. Parts 1, 5, 6, and 7 are given in *FRUS* 7 (1944): 324–327. Parts 2, 3, and 4 are taken from the original document: DS800.20235/6-2444.

48. Letter, Washington, 22 June 1944. AS3425/59.51. Vol. 38162.

49. Letter to Gallop, Washington, 20 June 1944. AS3350/78/2. Vol. 37703.

50. Tel. 865, to Duggan, 19 May 1944. DS123 Bonsal, Philip W.71.

51. Memorandum of conversation with Diógenes Escalante, Venezuelan ambassador, 3 July 1944. DS835.00/7-344.

52. Desp. 10,107, from Santiago, 3 July 1944. DS835.00/7-344.

53. No. 10 (Com:) Tel. 575, 30 June 1944 from Pres. Roosevelt to prime minister; minute to PM from Eden, 13 July 1944. AS3562/78/2. Vol. 37704.

54. Letter to Gallop, Washington, 7 July 1944. AS3690/78/2. Vol. 37704.

55. Letter from Hadow to South American Department, Washington, 10 July 1944. AS3779/59/51. Vol. 38162.

56. Tel. 412, to ambassador in Montevideo, 12 July 1944. DS733.35/7-1244. A few days later, Uruguay recalled its ambassador, Eugenio Martínez Thedy, from Buenos Aires.

57. Memorandum of conversations between Hull and Armour, and Kelly and Campbell, 17 July 1944. Notes by Armour. DS835.01/7-1744. See also tel. 3867, from Campbell, Washington, 17 July 1944. AS3820/78/2. Vol. 37705.

58. FO Minutes on tel. 3867, from Campbell, Washington, 17 July 1944. AS3820/78/2. Vol. 37705.

59. Tel. 3903, from Campbell, Washington, 19 July 1944. AS3851/78/2. Vol. 37705.

60. Letter to Gallop, Washington, 27 July 1944. AS4237/78/2. Vol. 37707. Hull was reported as thinking that Berle was also an appeaser, and his views were strengthened by Stettinius's report that "he had been given Carte-blanche over Argentina" in his talks with Eden in England. Hadow asked that Duggan not be given away on this conversation, "as he was 'sticking his neck out' as you will realise and rightly fears the long hand of an Elephantine memory." Duggan's position, it should be noted, was parallel to Britain's. On Stettinius's remark, Butler commented that Eden's response "did not mean and could not mean that we were content docilely to follow policies vis-à-vis Argentina of which we were merely informed. We were allowed no real time to tell Mr. Hull our views after recalling and consulting Sir D. Kelly (at his suggestion) before he came out with his terrific indictment of Argentina" (FO Minute on tel. 4081, from Campbell, Washington, 29 July 1944. AS4091/78/2. Vol. 37706). The reference here is to Hull's statement of July 26, which was published in Buenos Aires, where it was regarded as "much too strong," and as "unusual and inappropriate to the ideal of continental solidarity" (*La Prensa*; tel. 773, from C. A. E. Shuckburgh, chargé, Buenos Aires, 31 July 1944. AS 4131/78/2. Vol. 37707).

61. Memorandum to Hull from Spaeth, 4 August 1944, "Argentina." DS835.01/7-2044. Some governments were deterred "by considerations of possible reprisals by Argentina" (circular tel., 2 August 1944. DS835.01/8-244). A vague statement of approval by Brazil, which renewed its appeals so that Argentina might "bring the assistance of the greatness, the power and the solidarity of its people to the security and the victory of America in the world conflict," was regarded by Aranha as "a definite departure for Brazil." He was surprised that Vargas had authorized it: "Brazil has always had very much in mind her proximity to Argentina and, in the past, has always had something of an inferiority complex in regard to the Argentine Army and Navy, especially the Navy which is, of course, considerably more powerful than the Brazilian. In other words they have felt that the Argentine Navy could sink the entire Brazilian Navy in no time in case of hostilities" (tels. 2706, 2718, from Caffery, Rio de Janeiro, 28, 29 July 1944. DS835.01/7-2844, and 835.01/7-2944).

62. Stettinius heartily approved these fine words, and it is ironic that within a year, at San Francisco, they were to be repudiated by Argentina's election to membership in the United Nations. The form of Stettinius's congratulations were queried by Gallop, however, who thought they were an attempt to commit Britain "to a policy of indefinite non-recognition" (Prime Minister Minute M. 924/4, 5 August 1944. AS4348/78/2. Vol. 37708). Eden prepared a draft of a reply by the prime minister to a note from Roosevelt that said, "I would not do anything in the world to cut down the supply of meat to England. Heaven knows that it is already quite short enough. We would do nothing to prevent your getting a new contract." Roosevelt hoped

that Churchill would let Argentina know in "very firm, clear, disgruntled tones of voice . . . that we are all fed up with her pro-Axis sentiments and practices" (tel. 588, 22 July 1944; *FRUS* 7 (1944): 333–334). Eden's draft said that the United States should "ignore the Colonels for a good many weeks, thus giving both of us an opportunity to examine a common policy and the Argentines a chance to mend their ways, which they can never do under the glare of public indictment" (ibid.).

63. Memorandum, Spaeth to John C. Dreier, 4 August 1944. DS835.01/ 8-444.

64. Tel. 4378, from Halifax, Washington, 14 August 1944. AS4369/78/2. Vol. 37708. The Brazilian ambassador was reported as saying that "Hull was utterly unapproachable about Argentina"; he had found Stettinius "equally intransigent, and he felt at a loss as to how the door of compromise might be pushed upon ere some incident created widespread trouble" (tel. 4611, from Halifax, Washington, 27 August 1944. AS4594/78/2. Vol. 37709).

65. Memorandum from Bonsal to Armour, 26 August 1944. DS835.00/ 8-2644. This was Bonsal's "swan song" as he shortly left to become first secretary at the Madrid embassy.

66. Letter, from Buenos Aires, 10 August 1944. AS4539/78/2. Vol. 37709. Shuckburgh concluded that the American chargé, Edward Reed, had complained that some of his own people at the embassy were "taking the Sumner Welles line quite openly. My impression is that the U.S. Embassy itself is very critical of Hull's handling, and that there is *more*, rather than less appreciation of our methods."

67. Tel. 4865, from Halifax, Washington, 8 September 1944. AS4782/78/2. Vol. 37710. Interesting is a letter to the South American Department from the Rio de Janeiro Chancery 9 September 1944. AS5064/95/6. Vol. 37847), in which it is stated that Vargas "has been careful to keep, in key positions, all the old fascist minded generals and strong men." R. H. S. Allen commented that the Vargas regime was "every bit as bad as that of the Argentine Colonels . . . but . . . the Americans persist in cherishing [it], because it suits them to do so." Butler added that the Vargas regime was "nothing like as 'bad' as the Argentine, if only because it has military forces and bases against the Axis, and has not intrigued with Nazis to foment revolutions in other countries."

68. Tel. 900, from Shuckburgh, Buenos Aires, 14 September 1944. AS4894/ 78/2. Vol. 37710. Henderson commented that "we know that Mr. Hull will be content with nothing but unconditional surrender and the disappearance of 'this gang of crooks'—to use his words. Thus it seems quite impossible to hope for a break of the *impasse*." In Buenos Aires, Peluffo said that Hull's "direct attack . . . unusual in diplomacy" must mean that there "must be grave errors of opinion and understanding unless you [Hull] were misquoted." It was "absurd to think Argentina would be selected as haven by Axis refugees," and the suggestion was "disagreeable" (tel. 2343, from Reed, Buenos Aires, 9 September, 1944. DS835.01/9-944).

69. FO Minute by Butler on letter from John G. Winant, U.S. ambassador in London, to Butler, 15 September 1944. AS4901/78/2. Vol. 37710. Hull felt,

said Winant, that "the Argentine Fascist threat . . . is a matter of major policy, and if the U.S. should fail in implementing that policy a powerful center in this hemisphere would become available to the Axis from which they could renew their fight politically, economically, and, eventually, in a military way." [Marginal comment: "Argentina cd. not provide this."]

70. Letter to Perowne, Washington, 16 September 1944. AS5141/78/2. Vol. 37711.

71. Letter, Hull to George S. Messersmith, ambassador in Mexico City, 19 September 1944. This letter was apparently drafted by J. F. Matthews and Eric C. Wendelin and approved by Joseph F. McGurk. Hull was attempting to get Mexican foreign minister Padilla to make a statement supporting the U.S. position on Argentina.

72. Memorandum of conversation between Hull and Halifax, 16 September 1944.

73. Tel. 5038, from Washington, 16 September 1944. AS4909/78/2. Vol. 37710.

74. "Memorandum for the President," from Hull, 28 September 1944. DS835.01/9-2944; and declaration by Roosevelt, 29 September 1944. Reed reported that "on the whole we feel that effect [of Roosevelt's statement] has been beneficial. Coming on top of suspension of our shipping, President's vigorous condemnation of regime has created awareness of gravity of Argentina's international position. For first time implications of Churchill's warning to neutrals are being fully grasped" (tel. 2526, from Buenos Aires, 3 October 1944; *FRUS* 7 [1944]: 357).

75. Tel. 1378, from Hull to Buenos Aires, 4 September 1944.

76. Tel. 5176, from Halifax, Washington, 22 September 1944. AS5007/78/2. Vol. 37711. The ambassador added that Brazil "could no longer admit either United States right to forbid her trading with the Argentine in vital exports such as coal, or 'vexatious' United States pressure such as cutting off vital imports if Brazil did not comply promptly with these sanctions." He said that he had already spoken in vain to Armour, "who was impotent, and to Berle."

77. From *The Pacific Shipper* (25 September 1944), in desp. 1120, 5 October 1944, from Halifax, Washington, AS5361/2681/2. Vol. 37764. Hadow stated that both Spaeth and Wendelin had used the statement in italics, and he had no doubt that one of them had given the warning (letter to Perowne, 6 November 1944, AS5361/2681/2. Vol. 37764).

78. Hull to Winant, 10 October 1944.

79. Memorandum, "Summary of Developments Relating to Argentina for Meeting of Policy Committee," from Spaeth to Armour, 13 October 1944. DS835.00/10-1344.

80. Memorandum, "Anglo-United States Policy towards Argentina," 31 October 1944. AS5857/78/2. Vol. 37715.

81. 31 October 1944. DS710 Consultation 4/10-3144.

5. Recognition of the Farrell Government

1. Letter to Perowne, Washington, 9 November 1944. AS5983/78/2. Vol. 37715.

2. Memorandum for the president, "Subject: Our Policy toward Argentina," 21 November 1944. DS835.01/11-2144. This was drafted by Spaeth and initialed by Armour. On the same day Armour, in talking with the Venezuelan ambassador (Escalante) said, "We consider that Argentina's failure to cooperate with us has cost American lives as well as material resources, and . . . we see the Fascist-military government of Argentina as a threat to the peace and security of this Hemisphere" (memorandum of conversation, 21 November 1944. DS Memoranda on Argentina, Box 18. NA).

3. Memoranda of 7, 9, 28 December 1944, by E. C. Wendelin. DS Memoranda on Argentina, Box 19. The Argentines used this story as part of a campaign to gain support among other Latin American countries.

4. "Next Steps with Regard to Argentina," memorandum, Lockwood to Rockefeller, 13 December 1944. DS711.35/12-1344; and "Further Proposals with Regard to Argentina," memorandum, Lockwood to Rockefeller, 15, December 1944. DS835.00/12-1544.

5. See, for example, "Fascist-Totalitarian Character of the Present Argentine Regime," by John C. Dreier, transmitted to Stettinius by Armour 15 Dec, 1944. DS835.01/12-1544. This memorandum concluded: "It is hoped that this report will not only serve to clarify and confirm the fascist-totalitarian character of this regime but will suggest the nature of the changes which must occur in the Argentine situation before there can be any prospect of genuine cooperation between Argentina and other members of the family of American nations."

6. Memorandum for the president, "United States Policy toward Argentina," 2 January 1945. The memorandum was written on Department of State stationery but it was neither signed nor initialed (it bears the notation, "OK. FDR.").

7. "Memorandum under Date of January 2 for the President on 'United States Policy toward Argentina,'" from Spaeth to Lockwood, 3 January 1945. DS811.35/1-345.

8. Letter, Perowne to Waldemar Gallman, U.S. Embassy, 8 December 1944. AS6336/78/2. Vol. 37716. With regard to the appendix, Hull in his telegram to Winant of 10 October 1944 had said that "the power which in the final analysis controls the Government of Argentina today is vested in the Campo de Mayo and Club del Plata military-Fascist combine." Apparently Gallman never did get a copy of this letter, but Hadow gave one to Rockefeller about 30 December 1944.

9. Letter to Perowne, Washington, 26 December 1944. AS20/12/2. Vol. 44684. Earlier Hadow had reported that "Spaeth will be given a post outside the State Department 'because he cannot get on with Rockefeller nor agree with the latter's appeasement policy'" (letter to Perowne, Washington, 15 December 1944. AS74/12/2. Vol. 44684).

10. See DS835.00/2-2745. Memoranda were entitled e.g.: "Axis Psychological Warfare in Argentina," and "Argentina's Penetration and Interference in the Internal Affairs of Neighboring Republics."

11. DS835.00 F. W. 7 December 1944. It is of interest to compare the Strong memorandum with the "Memorandum on the Argentine Problem," prepared for the Mexico City delegates in the department:

> If Hemisphere unity is to be more than an empty form without real substance, it must be based on action which demonstrates a common purpose, common ideals and a practical spirit of cooperation among both the governments and the peoples of America. Such unity can be achieved only through the conscientious support and active defense of the principles that underlie Hemisphere solidarity as they have been enunciated and put into practice by the American republics which have cooperated in the war effort. There would be grave danger in the creation of a façade of unity behind which hostile forces can work to undermine and destroy everything for which we have been fighting. (*FRUS* 9 (1945): 451)

This memorandum also took care of the charge that nonrecognition constituted "intervention in the affairs of the Argentine nation" by stating that this view "overlooks completely the fact that the exclusive basis for the policy of the American republics is their concern with the international conduct of the Farrell government. . . Neither this Government nor any other American republic has suggested that this collective emergency action should be employed in time of peace to induce domestic or internal action beyond the competence of the family of nations" (ibid.: 450).

12. Tel. 230, from Mexico City, 22 February 1945, to Joseph C. Grew, acting secretary of state, for the president. DS835.00/2-2245. Stettinius added that if Argentina declared war on the Axis it might well "receive support from the European members of the United Nations and thereby place us in a most unfortunate position in our relations with the inter-American system."

13. Tel. 324, from Mexico City, 6 March 1945. DS835.00/3-645.

14. Tel. 523, to Stettinius, 7 March 1945. DS835.00/3-645.

15. Text of Resolution 59, 7 March 1945, in *Report* of the U.S. Delegation, 1946, 133–134.

16. Letter to Perowne, Mexico City, 8 March 1945. AS1589/1/2. Vol. 44683.

17. Ibid. Allen here referred to Washington tel. no. 1623 of March 13 which I did not find in the files at the Public Record Office, and which apparently is reserved. No record whatever has been found in the National Archives of this "direct approach" by Rockefeller.

18. FO Minute, 10 March 1945. AS1631/1/2. Vol. 44683.

19. Gellman states that Rockefeller had Roosevelt's approval for sending Oreamuno to Buenos Aires, although it was done without Stettinius's knowledge. When Stettinius heard about it at Mexico City, he was annoyed because he knew that Hull would regard the effort as appeasement.

20. Tel. 167, from Buenos Aires, 15 March 1945. AS1586/92/2. Vol. 44709. The "Vice President" was, of course, Perón.

21. Circular tel. to U.S. diplomatic representatives in the American Republics, 3 April 1945.

22. A year later Hadow sent to London a copy of a Drew Pearson column from the *Washington Post* containing the text. AS2019/235/2. 4 April 1946. Vol. 51811. Hadow added: "Nelson Rockefeller once showed me a photostat copy, which he had had the foresight to have made; for the necessary purpose, as it afterwards transpired, of proving President Roosevelt's personal agreement to his policy of bring [*sic*] back Argentina to the fold." In an FO Minute, H. V. Livermore wrote: "This document is quite important. In Latin American eyes it proves that Roosevelt never abandoned the GNP, and would not have countenanced Mr. Braden's antics."

23. Desp. 71, from Buenos Aires, 22 March 1945. AS1964/92/2. Vol. 44709.

24. Tel. 176, from Buenos Aires, 21 March 1945. AS1673/92/2. Vol. 44709. Mandl was an Austrian industrialist who went to Argentina at the beginning of the war and became a leader at Industria Metalúrgica y Plástica Argentina (IMPA), a firm on the U.S. Proclaimed List.

25. Desp 71, from Buenos Aires, 22 March 1945. AS1964/92/2. Vol. 44709. This despatch was received in London on April 9; neither of the two telegrams Noble refers to, 1623 or 2505, is currently available in British or American documentary sources.

26. Tel. 176, from Buenos Aires, 21 March 1945. AS1673/92/2. Vol. 44709.

27. Tel. 185, from Buenos Aires, 23 March 1945. AS1707/92/2. Vol. 44709. On Japan, Perón had remarked that "Chile was at war only with Japan, with whom on the contrary Russia was not at war. I [Noble] stamped firmly on the idea that Argentina could get away with a declaration of war on Japan only, pointing out that everyone would say that it was pure bluff and that the Argentine Government were making a last effort to protect Nazi interests. I do not think Vice-President thought this idea to be very well received and he did not press it" (tel. 176, from Buenos Aires, 21 March 1945. AS1673/92/2. Vol. 44709). In the end Argentina declared war on Japan and added only that, since Germany was an ally of Japan, war was declared on it too.

28. FO Minutes on tel. 177, from Buenos Aires, 21 March 1945. AS1679/92/2. Vol. 44709.

29. FO Minute on desp. 71, from Buenos Aires, 22 March 1945. AS1964/92/2. Vol. 44709.

30. Biographers of Rockefeller and Stettinius such as Gervasi (1964), Collier and Horowitz (1976), J. Morris (1960), and Campbell and Herring (1975) have nothing on this exploit; nor do Gellman (1979) or Woods (1979). The last two have made extensive researches into oral histories, diaries, and private papers of persons associated with Latin American affairs at the time. I assume here that Stettinius knew of Rockefeller's activities, although this is uncertain.

31. Tel. 334, from Kelly. Buenos Aires, 28 March 1946. AS1786/235/2, Vol. 51811.

32. Desp. 17,605, from Reed, Buenos Aires, 23 March 1945. DS835.00/3-2845.

33. Tel. 955, from Rio de Janeiro, 28 March 1945. DS835.00/3-2845.

34. Letters, 27 and 28 March 1945. DS740.0011 EW/3-2745.

35. Tel. 2176, from Washington, 2 April 1945. AS1864/317/51. Vol. 45017. Halifax added: "For Foreign Office aid and 'patience,' as he put it, Rockefeller also expressed his gratitude and that of Stettinius."

36. Letter to Perowne, Buenos Aires, 3 April 1945. AS2238/92/2. Vol. 44709.

37. Copy of Hadow's letter enclosed with letter to Perowne, Washington, 9 April 1945; and letter from Noble to Hadow, Buenos Aires, 26 March 1945. AS2251/12/2. Vol. 44686. Noble was distressed that "having insisted so much on my desire to play straight with him [Reed]" he had been forbidden by the State Department "to take him into my confidence." Rockefeller had told Hadow he planned to remove Reed at the first convenient opportunity, since he considered "Reed to be a foolish fellow and unfit for the job."

38. Note from Rodolfo García Arias to the director general of the Pan American Union, 28 March 1945, emphasis mine.

39. Tel. from the acting secretary of state (Acheson) to the diplomatic representatives in the American republics, 4 April 1945; emphasis mine.

40. Memorandum, "The Foreign Policy of the United States, (Revised as of April 1, 1945)," by the Department of State. President's Secretary File, Harry S. Truman Library.

6. Failure to Oust Perón

1. Tel. 3877, from Washington, 2 June 1945. AS2937/12/2. Vol. 44686. Halifax based his report on a despatch by Arnaldo Cortesi to the *New York Times* from Buenos Aires (June 1), charging that Argentina was following Fascist policies.

2. Memorandum to G. H. Butler and Dana Munro, "Internal Situation in Argentina," 23 April 1945. DS835.00/4-2245; emphasis mine. One relevant declaration from Chapultepec was, "The American states reiterate their fervent adherence to Democratic principles which they consider essential for the peace of America."

3. Circular, 28 May 1945. DS711.00/5-2845. Braden's despatch was no. 9103.

4. Desp. 922, from Asunción, 7 July 1945. DS711.00/7-745.

5. Desp. 453, from Guatemala, 3 August 1945. DS711.00/8-345.

6. Desp. 3416, from Lima, 7 June 1945. DS711.00/6-745.

7. See memorandum from Dreier to Roland D. Hussey, 19 October 1945, stating that he had read the report on no. 9103. DS835.00/1-1945.

8. Desp. 104, from Buenos Aires, 17 April 1945. AS2471/.92/2. Vol. 44710.

9. Tel. 1498, from Buenos Aires, 11 July 1945.

10. Tel. 382, 7 June 1945, from Buenos Aires. AS2997/12/2. Vol. 44686. Kelly said,

> The first point on which the United States Government ought to make up its mind once and for all is whether the Argentine Government is so obnoxious that it must be overthrown even at cost of abandonment of "good neighbor" policy in favour of specific intervention in Argentine

internal affairs. . . . The wisest policy for United States would be to leave Argentines to manage their own internal affairs but at the same time to continue to press the Argentine Government to fulfill their international obligations as signatories of the Act of Chapultepec and as belligerents. We could give full support to such a policy, which would not rally support to the Argentine Government, as United States intervention in internal affairs has done in the past.

11. Desp. 186, from Buenos Aires, 23 June 1945. AS3584/12/2. Vol. 44687.

12. Tel. 4419, from Halifax, Washington, 26 June 1945. AS3325/12/2. Vol. 44687.

13. FO Minute on tel. 462, from Kelly, Buenos Aires, 2 July 1945. AS3471/12/2. Vol. 44687.

14. Tel. 7251, from FO to Washington, 7 July 1945. AS3545/12/2. Vol. 44687. If the United States were determined on a showdown, said Henderson, ships and planes would have to be sent to Buenos Aires to force Perón to resign, or "it could be arranged for Col. Perón to become involved in a motor car accident by subtle enough means to avoid an open display of force" (ibid.).

15. Cabot does not give dates here, nor have I found a copy of Lockwood's letter in the archives. There does not appear to have been any attempt by Rockefeller to protest Braden's policy, and his support and praise for Braden continued throughout his career as assistant secretary.

16. Tel. 480, from Buenos Aires, 7 July 1945. AS3557/12/2. Vol. 44687.

17. Tel. 1498, from Buenos Aires, 11 July 1945.

18. Desp. 212, from Buenos Aires, 21 July 1945. AS4042/92/2. Vol. 44712. Apparently Perón later did arrange for organizations like those in Germany and Italy. John Cabot reported that the "Fascist nature of Perón regime [was] again emphasized by yesterday's events. Manifestations showed excellent organization of hoodlums on Fascist lines like Brown Shirts and Black Shirts. Events again indicate that Perón plans a proletarian, totalitarian dictatorship with army and police support" (tel. 2598, from the chargé in Buenos Aires, 19 October 1945, *FRUS* 9 [1945]: 422). In his telegram, Kelly was certainly wrong in saying Perón could not "convince either the Argentines or anyone else," since he had convinced the Department of State that he had a mission.

19. Tel. 1085, to Braden, 14 August 1945.

20. Tel. 1085, to Braden.

21. Letter from Hadow to Perowne, Washington, 2 August 1945, AS4150/12/2. Vol. 44688. "This rather shameful speech [in Boston] was of no avail, since Mr. Rockefeller's resignation was accepted shortly after it" (P. F. Hancock, FO Minute on United States Embassy [Communicated], 24 August 1945. AS4446/12/2. Vol. 44688). One can only wonder whether the speech would have been regarded as more "shameful" had Hancock been aware that Rockefeller made it knowing that on the following day he would be fired. "The State Department officials indicated yesterday that Hull now reigned supreme; the officials brought in by Rockefeller having all resigned

except Warren. A return to Hull's negative policy is therefore expected as soon as Braden arrives here" (tel. 5885, from Balfour, Washington, 28 August 1945. AS4485/12/2. Vol. 44688).

22. Letter to Perowne, Washington, 31 July 1945. AS4185/12/2. Vol. 44688. Perowne commented that "when *prestige* comes in at the door, commonsense, or at any rate objectivity, is apt to fly out of the window" (Kelly, FO Minute on tel. 578, Buenos Aires, 10 August 1945. AS4143/92/2. Vol. 44712). Hadow in a letter to Perowne said that Oscar Ibarra García of the Argentine embassy " 'warned' us that Braden's vigour had captured Argentine imagination and that he was genuinely popular for 'doing something' even though that something was gross interference in the internal affairs of a sovereign state" (letter, Washington, 8 September 1945. AS4738/92/2. Vol. 44713).

23. Desp. 711, from Buenos Aires. 1 October 1945. AS5117/12/2. Vol. 44689. Kelly noted that Braden counted on Truman's support: "His recommendations were accepted with enthusiasm immediately and his initiative praised." In addition, the five U.S. press correspondents "displayed fanatical admiration for his activities, and these received front page headlines in Washington and New York." Neville Butler commented: "While Gen. Rawson's failure shows that Mr. Braden was not quite an Ambassador Plenipotentiary, it does at least reveal him as an Envoy Extraordinary" (Halifax, FO Minute on tel. 6616, Washington, 4 October 1945. AS5165/12/2. Vol. 44689).

24. Desp. 292, from Buenos Aires, 5 October 1945. AS5469/12/2. Vol. 44690. "It is perhaps a pity that he [Braden] did not stay in Argentina a few weeks longer, as his dynamic personality might have produced—or at least hastened—the formation of a Govt. strong enough to have prevented the return to power of the Peronistas" (J. D. Murray, FO Minute, ibid.).

25. Memorandum, San Francisco, 13 June 1945, and Rockefeller's reply, 21 June 1945. DS835.00/6-2145.

26. Notable among these were a despatch by Arnoldo Cortesi to the *New York Times* (1 June 1945), and an editorial in the same paper (21 June 1945).

27. Tel. 5686, from Washington, 18 August 1945. AS4251/12/2. Vol. 44688.

28. Hadow noted that Rockefeller, "broken by the cold shouldering he has received from Byrnes since the latter's return from London," has gone on record against the Argentine regime "in true Hull style. . . . Whether, as promised him, this will 'save him for another day' those who know how hollow are the protestations in his speech of admiration for Braden, 'one of our ablest Ambassadors,' gravely doubt. . . . The speech is therefore, I fear, not one of conviction but of face-saving" (letter to Perowne, Washington, 25 August 1945. AS4475/12/2. Vol. 44688). The letter was written on the day the speech was given.

29. "Ambassador Braden reports that Perón endeavored to distort some of his speeches as being interference in Argentine internal affairs. Perón also added that the Ambassadors of some of the other American Republics thought Braden was intervening. Ambassador Braden claims that in spite of Perón's unwillingness to listen he (Braden) insisted on reviewing his speeches as proof that the facts were directly contrary to Perón's assertion. Ambas-

sador Braden also observes that his diplomatic colleagues have emphatically declared their opinion that Braden is not intervening in internal affairs" (memorandum, "July 5 Interview between Ambassador Braden and Colonel Perón," by Warren and Lockwood, 6 July 1945. DS735.11/7-545). The nearly complete text of Braden's report of this interview is in *FRUS* 9 (1945): 514–517. Lockwood had earlier, in a talk with Col. Luis Manuel de Bayle, director general of public health, Nicaragua, stated that his study of U.S. relations with Latin America had made him a "strong opponent of intervention in any form." He said that the United States was always being requested to intervene by one political group or another in its behalf. Our history had demonstrated that any such intervention generally ended up in trouble for the United States and no great benefit to the country concerned" (memorandum of conversation, San Francisco, 21 June 1945). DS500.cc/6-2145).

30. Desp. 6964, Rockefeller to Braden, 14 August 1945. DS711.35/8-1445.

31. Desp. 1431, 31 August 1945. DS711.35/8-3145.

32. Hadow reported that Braden and Acheson met Senate objections to having negotiated the abandonment of the Conference before securing the approval of the Committee on Foreign Relations. "This, the members of the Committee apparently claim, was in contravention of an understanding between them and the State Department; and, as tit-for-tat, they have refused at the moment to endorse Braden's appointment as Assistant Secretary." Some senators criticized the officials also for not having consulted Latin American governments about the postponement (letter to Perowne, Washington, 5 October 1945. AS5264/317/51. Vol. 45018).

33. RG46. NA. Records of the U.S. Senate, Committee on Foreign Relations, *Nomination of Spruille Braden.* 79th Congress, 3, 10 October 1945, pp. 36–37.

34. Ibid., pp. 53, 54.

35. Ibid., pp. 122, 46, and passim.

36. *DSB* (7 October 1945): 552; and circular tel., 3 October 1945. DS710 Consultation 4/10-345.

37. Memorandum from FSO B. C. Davis to FSOs Joseph Flack and Ellis O. Briggs, 12 October 1945. DS710 Consultation 4/10-445. Flack commented, "From personal experience, I know this reaction to be a strong one."

38. Tel. 10100, FO to Washington, 9 October 1945. AS5263/12/2. Vol. 44689.

39. Tel. 765, from Kelly, Buenos Aires, 18 October 1945. AS5459/92/2. Vol. 44714.

40. Desp. 310, from Buenos Aires, 26 October 1945. AS5887/92/2. Vol. 44715.

41. Tel. 6936, from Washington, 18 October 1945. AS5421/12/2. Vol. 44690. Braden said that Sen. Wherry (D-Wisconsin) had called him an "'unashamed interventionist.' Though not published in the U.S.A. (an interesting indication of the ability of the State Department to restrain its Press when it wishes to do so) these attacks had been telgraphed by the A.P. to Buenos Aires 'where they had contributed materially to Perón's return.'" Hadow said that Braden had brought back as special advisers, "Spaeth—for-

merly of the Argentine Desk and ousted by Rockefeller—and Wright" (letter to Perowne, Washington, 19 October 1945. AS5528/12/2. Vol. 44690).

42. Letter, Hadow to Perowne, Washington, 24 October 1945. AS5668/12/2. Vol. 44690. Hadow noted, "Mr. B's Argentine policy has been an utter flop for him, and a serious disadvantage for us. We shd. take the warning to heart."

43. Memorandum by Balfour, Washington, 26 October 1945, and by Hadow, same date, entitled, "Argentina—Great Britain—U.S.A." Desp. 1370, AS5770/12/2. Vol. 44690. Hadow observed that Braden's action in calling off the Rio Conference without consultation "was not to the taste of a number of Senators who . . . had planned, in company with their wives, to attend the Conference in state travelling there on a United States battleship" AS5770/12/2. Vol. 44690. Balfour later commented on the "personal vendetta" between Braden and Perón (desp. 241, from Washington, 30 January 1947. AS852/1/2. Vol. 61122).

44. Tel. 435, from Washington, 26 October 1945. AS5629/12/2. Vol. 44690.

45. Communication of speech by Braden, 26 October 1945, from U.S. Office of War Information, 27 October 1945. AS5790/317/51. Vol. 45019. Murray added that "many would find it hard to reconcile the praise of the principle of non-interference—which Mr. Braden so strongly upholds—with the recent policy of the U.S.A. towards Argentina."

46. Murray, FO Minute on tel. 861, from Kelly, Buenos Aires, 24 November 1945. AS6118/92/2. Vol. 44715.

47. Tel. 673, from Montevideo, 31 October 1945.

48. Tel. 479, Byrnes to Dawson, Washington, 8 December 1945.

49. Vereker, FO Minute on tel. 357, Montevideo, 26 November 1945. AS6157/317/51. Vol. 45019. Allen commented: "This is, I think, hot air and likely to be completely ineffective. It may well be due to U.S. lobbying."

50. Letter to Perowne, Washington, 29 November 1945. AS6283/317/51. Vol. 45019. Murray commented that "it seems clear that if Perón is elected the recent struggle between the U.S. trading interests, who want to go ahead and deal with any Government in the Argentine and the U.S. Radicals, who fear Perón as a neo-fascist, cannot go on forever" (letter, Hadow to Perowne, Washington, 3 December 1945. AS6378/317/51. Vol. 45019).

51. Instruction 2748 from Braden to the ambassador in Uruguay (Dawson), Washington, 7 January 1946. DS710.11/12-1345.

52. Desp. 1747, "General Survey of the Political Situation in Argentina," Buenos Aires, 9 January 1946. Memoranda Argentina, Box 19, NA.

53. *Consultation among the American Republics with Respect to the Argentine Situation.* Memorandum of the U.S. Government, Washington, February 1946 (hereafter Blue Book).

54. Text in tel. 523, from Halifax, Washington, 23 January 1946. AS560/126/2. Vol. 51801.

55. FO Minute, 2 February 1946. AS698/126/2. Vol. 51801. A telegram (no. 1460) was sent to Halifax on February 14 along these lines, but the Department of State apparently did not respond to Halifax's letter based upon it.

56. Memorandum of conversation, 9 April 1946. DS835.00/4-946.

57. Blue Book, p. 1.

58. Circular tel. 9 March 1946.

59. Blue Book, p. 4.

60. Tel. 430, 8 February 1946. Cabot envisaged certain cases that would justify publication, such as if elections were flagrantly fraudulent, and concluded, "We cannot send ships or planes here without arousing screams of intervention, therefore I see little we can do except warn key Americans Wednesday of what is coming."

61. Memorandum of conversation with FSO George H. Butler, 13 February 1946. In his memoirs, Cabot recalls his opposition to publication of the Blue Book; he said it was a polemic and distorted the source material (1979: 26). His later approval is not mentioned; it may have been influenced by his professional loyalty toward a *fait accompli.*

62. Letter, Hadow to Perowne, Washington, 15 February 1946. AS992/235/2. Vol. 51904.

63. Tel. 615, 10 May 1946.

64. Letters, Hadow to Perowne, Washington, 10, 18 March 1946. AS1547/235/2; AS1616/235/2. Vol. 51810. Hadow here referred to Enrique Gil, "an unscrupulous and neo-leftist Argentine," as being in touch with Braden in connection with a new policy toward Argentina. Duran had recently become an American citizen; "there was apparently, quite a schimozzle about this highly irregular procedure." Braden had insisted that Duran's time spent in Cuba and Buenos Aires as his assistant should be counted as residence within the United States; he also pointed out to Byrnes "the catastrophic result of having to admit that a foreigner had access to the State Department's most secret files" (letter, Hadow to Perowne, Washington, 19 March 1946. AS1670/11/51. Vol. 52078). In an earlier letter to Perowne, Hadow had referred to "backstairs intrigue," which appeared to be a dig by a British army officer at "Braden's apparent dependence upon a Spanish Republican named Gustavo Duran. . . . This man, who did well in the Spanish Civil War appears to have become Braden's inseparable companion and to have been his principal mentor in Buenos Aires" (attached to memorandum, "Argentina—U.S.A.," by Hadow, Washington, 28 September 1945. AS5110/12/2. Vol. 44689). Oddly enough, Duran's name is not listed in the department's *Biographic Register* for 1946, nor does it appear in the indexes to the *New York Times.*

65. Letter to Perowne, Washington, 21 March 1946. AS1724/235/2. Vol. 51810.

66. FO Minute, 9 April 1946. AS2209/235/2. Vol. 51812. This estimate of Messersmith was in error.

67. Desp. 106, from the Canadian Embassy, Buenos Aires, 12 April 1946. AS2883/235/2. Vol. 51814.

68. Memorandum, "Argentina: U.S. Policy," by Hadow, in desp. 856, Washington, 26 April 1946. AS2373/235/2. Vol. 51813. In a letter to Perowne, Washington, 2 May 1946, AS2495/235/2. Vol. 51813, Hadow quoted George Sokolsky in the *New York Sun* of 6 April 1946 as saying that Braden would make the United States into "Uncle Buttinsky." "For what it really means is that we are to be petulant harriers of all peoples, telling them precisely how

to live and what to do and in what manner they must do it. For otherwise we shall be guilty of intervention by inaction. . . . Mr. Braden ought to resign. His policy of intervention in the affairs of a neighbor has proved a costly and ridiculous failure. . . . He made himself an issue. He made the United States an issue. His removal from office would remove the issue."

69. Memorandum, from Buenos Aires, 5 March 1947. AS3826/12/51. Vol. 61296. The memorandum, made available by Hadow, was accompanied by an FO Minute: "The way in which Mr. Hadow serves his information up to us is certainly terrible; at the same time he does get it for us, and from all sorts of sources, in a quite remarkable way. The Service Attachés can't touch him in this respect" (N. Butler).

70. Perowne, FO Minute on tel. 1119, from Leeper, Buenos Aires, 2 December 1946. AS7430/235/2. Vol. 51818. The reference is to the desires of the Departments of War and the Navy to standardize weapons and other equipment throughout the Americas, and to their efforts to secure passage of an act for inter-American military cooperation that would have provided for U.S. military missions in Latin America. Truman proposed the act to Congress in 1946, but it was not passed.

71. Letter to Acheson, Buenos Aires, 16 October 1946. DS835.00/10-1646.

72. See letter from Braden to Pete Jarman, Committee on Foreign Affairs, House of Representatives, 29 July 1946. DS835.00/7-2946, and attached memorandum (portions of this memorandum are printed in *FRUS* 11 [1946]: 270–278).

73. Tel., 29 October 1946. DS111.12. Braden, Spruille/10-2346. Messersmith had sent Byrnes a copy of his letter to Sulzberger.

74. Desp. 520, from Buenos Aires, 12 December 1946. AS7961/235/2. Vol. 51819.

75. See memorandum of conversation between Messersmith, Braden, and others, 21 January 1947 (*FRUS* 8 [1947]: 166–168); and speech by Byrnes, 11 January 1947 (*DSB* [19 January 1947]: 90). The disputed commitments involved German influence in schools, control over German property, and expulsion of certain German nationals.

76. Tel. 26, from Washington, 2 February 1947, and attached "Weekly Summary." AS964/1/2. Vol. 61122. Inverchapel noted, as background, that Argentina had "been a thorn in the flesh of successive United States Governments," because of its resistance to U.S. "hegemony of the western hemisphere, which almost all United States citizens regard as a necessity as well as a right." Argentine attitudes had exasperated American leaders. "Accumulating evidence of Communist penetration in Latin America has in any case done much to promote the idea that the Administration would be well advised to return to the tactics of the good neighbour policy in its dealings with Argentina."

77. Text of *aide-mémoire* of 27 January 1947 in *FRUS* 8 [1947]: 171–172. Inverchapel's report is in tel. 538, from Washington, 27 January 1947. AS615/1/2. Vol. 61122.

78. Tel. 98, from Buenos Aires, 27 January 1947, and FO Minute thereon by Perowne. AS621/1/2. Vol. 61122.

79. Tel. 121, from Buenos Aires, 4 February 1947. AS832/1/2. Vol. 61122. The reference to "the Senate" was presumably to a statement by Vandenberg that the American states should now plan to hold the proposed conference at Rio de Janeiro. "Marshall might have Braden for a short time, but he would certainly have to go," said Messersmith, not realizing that, as Hadow put it, the country was aware that its prestige in Latin America "would be damaged by an appearance of surrender to Perón. Consequently I find even officials who are notoriously against Braden's 'bull-dozing' arguing that Marshall must not sacrifice Braden without at the same time showing disapproval of Messersmith . . . the end of this struggle may be the elimination of *both* Messersmith and Braden in a discreet fashion, for which Marshall was famous when he was Chief of Staff" (letter to Perowne, Washington, 5 February 1947. AS943/1/2. Vol. 61122).

80. Letter to W. L. Clayton, undersecretary for economic affairs, Buenos Aires, 21 February 1947. DS835.00/2-2147.

81. Tel. 252, from Acheson to Messersmith, 2 April 1947. *FRUS* 9 (1947): 186–187.

82. James Reston, *New York Times* (15 April 1947); and Turner Catledge, ibid. (8 June 1947). Reston noted that Braden had become out-of-date, since "the administration is now concentrating not on catching fascists but on stopping communists. Meanwhile, certain 'modifications' are being made in various policies. Argentina has modified her policy toward the Nazis; we are in the process of modifying ours against the Communists." Braden had done the job for which he had been engaged, but the "political pressures that favored his appointment in August of 1945 are now running against him."

83. Tels. 677, 687, 5, 6 June 1947, from Buenos Aires. DS123. Messersmith, George S. Braden concludes: "who was responsible for this mysterious capitulation, who had pulled what strings, I never knew. It was the result of strictly secret diplomacy, and to speculate on its method or motivation would be idle. The important fact is that from that time until Perón was thrown out by the Argentine people in spite of our tacit support, the United States gave him whatever he demanded and intervened on his behalf throughout the hemisphere" (Braden 1971: 369). This last statement is obviously ridiculous.

84. It was said in the Department of State that Messersmith should not, by department regulation, have accepted the decoration, but it was agreed that nothing could be done about it.

85. Memorandum to the secretary, "Ambassador Messersmith's Call on the Secretary," 17 July 1947. DS123 Messersmith, George S.

86. Tel. 125, from Inverchapel, Washington, 7 June 1947. AS3492/1/2. Vol. 61123.

87. "United States Policy in Latin America," memorandum attached to letter from Hadow to Shuckburgh, Washington, 31 March 1948. AS2307/33/51. Vol. 68271. This memorandum was referred to as Hadow's "swan song," and the Foreign Office sent him "a warm rewarding letter" for his five years of work as adviser to the embassy in Washington (FO Minute, AS2307/33/51. Vol. 68271).

88. Memorandum of conversation between Cabot, FSO John F. Fishburn, and Paul K. Reed, international representative, United Mine Workers, 16 March 1953. DS820.06/3-1653. A similar view was expressed by Thomas C. Mann in pointing out that attempts at open intervention, such as those in Argentina in 1946 (via the Blue Book) and in Nicaragua in 1947 (via non-recognition), not only "ended in a failure but . . . actually strengthened the very regimes [they were] designed to weaken" (memorandum to Charles S. Murphy, special counsel to the president, "Latin America and U.S. Policy," 11 December 1952. Harry S. Truman Library. President's Secretary's File. Lent to me by Thomas G. Bohlin, University of Notre Dame).

7. A Diplomatic Aberration

1. At the end of March, Berle wrote that moderate groups in Brazil thought that if Vargas remained in the field or attempted to hold power, "there will be an armed rebellion. There is considerable evidence to support that viewpoint" (1973: 525).

2. Letters in Harry S. Truman Library.

3. Tel. 2905, from Rio de Janeiro, 18 September 1945. DS832.00/9-1845.

4. Memorandum to Philip O. Chalmers, Brazil Desk, by D. M. Braddock and J. G. Mein, 23 September 1945. DS832.00/9-2345.

5. Tel. 2992, from Rio de Janeiro, 27 September 1945. DS832.00/9-2745.

6. Tel. 3008, from Rio de Janeiro, 29 September 1945. DS832.00/9-2945.

7. *Queremismo* was the name of the movement that wanted Vargas to remain, but not hold an election, or to run for the presidency himself. Berle said that the *queremistas* were ex-Fascists—perhaps as a means of justifying his speech. He records that Pedro Leão Velloso, the Brazilian foreign minister, told him on October 6 that "the President was somewhat irritated at my speech," but that after talking with Velloso, Vargas agreed that "it was meant in friendly spirit and so the incident was closed." Berle added, "Doing a thing like this is like using up your capital. Obviously it can be done very, very rarely. To date the results seem to justify the act" (1973: 554).

8. Letter to me, 6 November 1981, from Beaulac. It was reported that the speech was described in Brazil as "only intellectual intervention," and Berle's friends contended "his silence would have been 'negative but tremendously effective intervention' in support of the status quo" (William S. White, *New York Times* [9 November 1945]).

9. Desp. 229, from Gainer, Rio de Janeiro, 6 November 1945. AS6094/52/6. Vol. 44809.

10. Tel. 518, from Rio de Janeiro, 29 October 1945. AS5648/52/6. Vol. 44808.

11. Tel. 3279, from Rio de Janeiro, 30 October 1945. DS832.00/10-3045. Berle added, "Machiavelli observed that Princes fall because they continue to use their old methods in new situations when current and tides of opinion have changed. Basically this was true of Vargas."

12. See note 9. This whole despatch gives a fascinating analysis of the causes for Vargas's resignation.

13. Tel. 3048, from Rio de Janeiro, 4 October 1945. DS832.oo/10-445. The U.S. military attaché reported that the president's brother Viriato had said that if Roosevelt were living, "it couldn't have happened"; that Viriato's wife had said: "Naturally we are surprised, hurt, angry. Our Ambassador in Washington does not take sides in your politics. We consider it undiplomatic and unfriendly" (tel. 7153, to War Department, from Rio de Janeiro, 3 October 1945. DS832.oo/9-2945). Berle's report was that the general effect of the speech "seems to have been to ballast situation" (tel. 3080, from Rio de Janeiro, 8 October 1945. DS832.oo/10-845).

14. Letter from Philip O. Chalmers, to Berle, 2 October 1945, DS832.oo/9-2945.

15. Desp. 196, from Rio de Janeiro, 5 October 1945. AS5517/52/6. Vol. 44808. Hadow in a letter to Gainer said that Carlos Martins, Brazilian ambassador to the United States, had said that "after what Berle has done (for which Martins long ago told me that Brazil would never forgive Berle)" Martins thought there might be some cooperation between Perón and Vargas (letter, Washington, 15 November 1945. AS5517/52/6. Vol. 44808).

16. Letter, Gainer to Perowne, Rio de Janeiro, 9 October 1945. AS5553/52/6. Vol. 44808.

17. Tel. 503, from Rio de Janeiro, 23 October 1945. AS5546/52/6. Vol. 44808.

18. Ibid. Anti-Berle posters similar to those attacking Braden in Buenos Aires, and presumably issued by *queremistas*, appeared on Rio de Janeiro walls, e.g., "Advice to Sr. Adolf Berle. The other Adolf also tried to interfere in the private life of foreign nations"; "Sr. Adolf Berle. Our country can look after itself"; "Sr. Adolf Berle. Brazil came of age 100 years ago" (Chancery, Rio de Janeiro to South American Department, FO, 13 October 1945. AS5538/52/6. Vol. 44803).

19. Letter from Rio de Janeiro, 11 October 1945, and minutes thereon. AS5554/52/6. Vol. 44808.

20. Hadow had earlier reported that he had found the Brazilian ambassador (Martins) "particularly incensed at 'Berle's unwarranted intervention' over Brazil's elections; which he said might easily turn the scale among the Brazilian Military in Argentina's favour" (letter to Perowne, Washington, 19 October 1945. AS5528/12/2. Vol. 44690).

21. See note 9.

22. Letter from Rio de Janeiro, 14 December 1945. AS11/11/51. Vol. 44690; and Skidmore (1967: 349).

23. Letter, from Rio de Janeiro, 28 December 1945. AS220/13/6. Vol. 51899. Gainer noted that Dutra had chosen João Neves da Fontoura for minister of foreign affairs: "Berle will no doubt nobble him—but then Itamarati [Brazilian Foreign Office] is really a dependency of the State Department and horribly inefficient at that" (ibid.).

24. Desp. 11, from Rio de Janeiro, 9 January 1946. AS486/13/6. Vol. 51899.

25. Hadow said that a rumor that seemed a "little sensational" to him was that Dutra had hinted . . . that what had been said of Vargas by Berle would

not make the latter's return welcome to the new Brazilian Government" (letter to Perowne, from Washington, 14 February 1946. AS1072/15/6. Vol. 51904).

26. Letter, Hadow to Perowne, Washington, 8 March 1946. AS1444/15/6. Vol. 51904.

27. Memorandum, "Conciliation of ex-President Vargas," Braddock to Briggs, 14 November 1946. DS711.32/11-1446. Braddock added that Pawley had "suggested that I make this incident a matter of record in the Department."

28. Tel. 1960, from Rio de Janeiro, 4 December 1946. DS832.00/12-446. Gainer translated "atitude intempestiva" as "unseemly attitude" (desp. 395, from Rio de Janeiro, 5 December 1946. AS7733/13/6. Vol. 51903).

29. "Confidential Memorandum on Latin America," March 1947. Harry S. Truman Library.

8. Reaffirmation of the Good Neighbor Policy

1. Memorandum, D. G. Clark to Robert F. Woodward and Paul C. Daniels, 1 February 1949. DS710.11/2-149.

2. "Request for Comments on Draft of Principles to Serve as a Guide in the Formulation of U.S. Policies Related to Inter-American Affairs," drafted by Woodward and signed for the secretary of state by Dean Rusk, undersecretary, 19 April 1949. DS710.11/4-1949.

3. Desp. A-233, from Bogotá, 3 May 1949. DS810.00/5-349. Beaulac added, "A little intervention is like a little pregnancy. It is difficult to stop, it becomes inflated out of all proportion to the intent of those who started it, and someone always feels he has been taken."

4. Desp. 420, from Quito, 22 June 1949. DS710.11/6-2249.

5. Desp. 250, from Asunción, 8 June 1949. DS710.11/6-849.

6. Desp. A-127, from Tegucigalpa, 11 May 1949. DS810.00/5-1149.

7. Desp. A-316, 7 May 1949. DS810.00/5-749.

8. Desp. 329, from Bogotá, 20 May 1949. DS710.11/5-2049.

9. See, e.g., Chargé Philip P. Williams, in Desp. 460, from Managua, 24 June 1949. DS710.11.6-2449; also Bowers, desp. 319, from Santiago, 6 May 1949. DS710.11/5-649.

10. Desp. A-198, from John F. Simmons, 2 June 1949. DS710.11/6-249.

11. Desp. 241, from Ellis O. Briggs, Montevideo, 25 May 1949, DS710.11/5-2549.

12. Desp. A-166, from William E. DeCourcy, Port-au-Prince, 4 May 1949. DS710.11/5-449.

13. Desp. 394, from Walter J. Donnelly, Caracas, 25 May 1949. DS710.11/5-2549.

14. Desp. 250, from Asunción, 8 June 1949. DS710.11/6-849.

15. Memorandum, no author or source given, 29 August 1949. DS810.00/8-2949.

16. "Briefing Material for Secretary" memorandum, unsigned, 4 January 1950.

17. DS611.20/4-252. Memorandum from Norman Pearson, American Re-

publics Affairs, to Miller, "Draft Policy Statement for Discussion at BAC Meeting, Thursday, April 3," 2 April 1952, p. 4; emphasis mine.

18. Ibid., p. 19. This view had been taken a year previously, when the department noted that it had encouraged U.S. companies to undertake "a review and modification of their general policy and *modus operandi* to meet the new and changing requirements of the day. This has been considered by the Department to be a prime necessity for the continuation, in an atmosphere of good will, of their operation in the territory of another sovereign country and for reducing the possibility of expropriation" (DS611.14/5-251, "Policy Statement: Guatemala," Department of State, 2 May 1951).

19. David Green (1971) holds, largely on economic grounds, that the Good Neighbor policy "was a failure," and that the Truman administration completed "the building of an inter-American system which was intended to ratify United States supervision and control of Latin American economic development." It failed, however, to convince Latin Americans that the policy "was really a policy of institutionalized benevolence" (p. 291). He is especially wide of the mark in saying that Truman and his advisers had developed "a postwar policy approach that equated nationalism with communism and instability with subversion in Latin America" (idem 1970: 188–189). He apparently wrote this without considering the policy followed in Bolivia after April 1952.

20. See letter from Miller to Loring K. Macy, Office of International Trade, Department of Commerce, 30 July 1951. DS611.14/7-3051. See also "Notes of the Under Secretary's Meeting," Department of State, 15 June 1951 (*FRUS* 2 [1951]: 1440–1442), where Thomas C. Mann is quoted as saying that he felt economic pressures would be effective, but that the policy would be "a violation of the Non-intervention Agreement to which we are a party. . . . He pointed out that these proposed actions would be the first of its kind since the establishment of the Good Neighbor policy."

21. Memorandum from Paul C. Daniels to the acting secretary of state, 22 December 1948, "United States Relations with Latin-American Countries that Have Military Coups." DS711.20/12-2248.

22. See note 17.

23. Memorandum to Acheson from Mann, 3 October 1952, "Possible Military Action against Guatemala." DS714.00/10-352.

24. Memorandum of conversation between Miller, Mann, and Ernest V. Siracusa of the State Department, and Thomas Bradshaw and M. Bogie of International Railways of Central America (IRCA), 18 February 1952, "Critical Situation of IRCA in Guatemala." DS914.512/2-1852.

25. Memorandum of conversation, 15 May 1950. DS714.00/5-1550.

26. Memorandum to the secretary of state, 29 March 1950. This memorandum was apparently not distributed within the department at the time, and its fate is a good example of "the impossibility of having the planning function performed outside of the line of command." It was this type of action that was responsible for the failure of the Policy Planning Staff, which Kennan had formerly headed (Kennan 1967: 480, 467).

27. Memorandum from Halle to Miller, "Our Latin American Policy," 27

March 1950. DS611.20/3-2750. This date is prior to the issuance of Kennan's memorandum because it is in reply to his views expressed at a meeting of ambassadors in Rio de Janeiro a few days earlier.

28. Memorandum to Charles S. Murphy, special counsel to the president. "Latin America and U.S. Policy," 11 December 1952. Harry S. Truman Library, President's Secretary's File, p. 17 (lent by Thomas G. Bohlin, University of Notre Dame).

29. "A Report to the National Security Council by the Executive Secretary on United States Objectives and Courses of Action with Respect to Latin America," 6 March 1953. Annex to NSC 144; emphasis mine. The enduring value of the Pearson memorandum of 2 April 1952 is shown by the fact that this "report" and Mann's memorandum to Murphy reproduced almost verbatim certain key points without giving credit to Pearson. See, e.g., p. 20, n. 12, and pp. 23–24, from the Pearson memorandum, and paragraph 31 of the Mann memorandum.

30. Memorandum, to Miller and Mann, "Caribbean Situation," 21 November 1952. DS713.001/11-2152.

31. It is of interest to compare this address with Acheson's to the Pan American Society of the United States on 19 September 1949.

9. Bolivia and Guatemala

1. Tel. 46, from R. W. A. Leeper, British ambassador in Buenos Aires, 14 January 1947. AS321/1/2. Vol. 61121.

2. Desp. 241, from Washington, 30 January 1947. AS852/1/2. Vol. 61122.

3. The phrase is used in a letter to Philip B. Fleming, ambassador in San José, 27 May 1952. DS724.00/5-2752. The author is unknown, because the last page of the letter is missing, but it may have been William P. Hudson, who in a cable to the Costa Rican embassy on 6 May had called Lechín "an extremist demagogue" (DS724.02/4-1852).

4. Memorandum from William P. Hudson, to Amb. Edward J. Sparks, "Your Call on the President," 28 February 1952. DS724.00/2-2852.

5. Memorandum of conversation between Chilean ambassador, Félix Nieto del Río, and H. S. Atwood and Milton Barall, 19 April 1952. DS724.00/4-1952.

6. Desp. 401, from Edward J. Rowell, counselor of embassy, La Paz, 11 December 1952. DS724.001/12-1152.

7. Tel. 312, to La Paz, 9 May 1952. DS724.00/4-2752.

8. Tel. 317, to La Paz, 13 May 1952. DS724.00/5-1252.

9. Tel. 418, to Lima, 20 May 1952. DS724.02/5-1952.

10. Memorandum to Walter Bedell Smith from Mann, "The Bolivian Situation," 22 April 1953. DS724.00/4-2253.

11. Memorandum to Atwood from Hudson, "A Suggested Approach to the Bolivian Problem," 30 April 1953. DS824.00/5-3053. This is the last case I found in which the term "Good Neighbor policy" was used officially to buttress an argument for following a particular line.

12. Memorandum, to Smith from Cabot, "The Bolivian Situation," 18 May 1953. DS824.10/5-1853.

13. Memorandum to the secretary from Cabot, "The Bolivian Problem,"

11 June 1953; and attached memorandum for the president, "Action to Forestall Collapse in Bolivia." DS824.10/6-1153.

14. Desp. 258, from La Paz, 23 October 1953. DS724.00/10-2353. This statement may be compared with one by Duggan, who in 1944 said that it would be "neither dignified nor proper" to tell Bolivia what it should to in connection with its own government, but that the junta contained elements that were "wholly unacceptable," and their "Axis taint" precluded recognition by the United States (memorandum of conversation with Fernando Iturralde, representative of the Bolivian junta, 28 January 1944. DS824.01/582). This time, Amb. Edward J. Sparks merely expressed the thought that "the Department would like to see more clearly established the dominance of the moderate elements in the Government," rather than to tell the Bolivians that such establishment was a condition of further aid, since such a statement might be "misinterpreted as the exercise of pressure" (desp. 213, from La Paz, 6 October 1953. DS724.5-MSP/10-653).

15. Memorandum to Cabot from W. Tapley Bennett, Jr., "Evidence of Non-Communist Character of Bolivian Government," 7 December 1953. DS724.00/12-753.

16. Memorandum to the secretary, "Briefing for Call by Bolivian Foreign Minister," 19 November 1953. DS724.5-MSP/11-1953.

17. Memorandum to Cabot from Bennett, "Your Meeting with Foreign Minister Guevara November 23." DS724.00/11-2353. The campaign apparently began with an article by George Shea in the *Wall Street Journal* on November 1, and included letters from the public and members of Congress. It continued with a letter to the *New York Times* from Enrique Hertzog, former president of Bolivia, and reports by Herbert Matthews of the *New York Times* that he had been "deluged by propaganda" charging that the Bolivian government was Communist-dominated. At the interview, Guevara told Cabot that the Bolivian embassy was planning to have its case explained to the U.S. public by "the public relations firm of Selvage, Lee and Chase" (memorandum of conversation, "Bolivian Problems in General," 23 November 1953. DS824.00/11-2353).

18. Letter to Rep. John W. Byrnes from Thruston B. Morton, assistant secretary of state, 13 April 1954. DS720.001/4-354. Similarly defensive was the line Smith took in a note Cabot drafted: "It is natural that the extremely conservative upper class in Peru and the disgruntled Bolivian opposition elements tend quite sincerely to depict as Communism the nationalistic radicalism which undeniably dominates the Bolivian Government" (memorandum for Robert Cutler, White House, "Observations on Letter from Mr. Henry S. Sturgis," 14 January 1954. DS724.001/1-1454).

19. See, e.g., letter to Mann from John C. McClintock, assistant vice-president, United Fruit Company, stating that he and his wife were "looking forward very much to having you and Nancy and your youngster as our house guests over the weekend of the 25th and 26th, and as long thereafter as you can arrange to stay" (10 October 1952. DS714.00/10-1052).

20. See *aide mémoire* of 28 August 1953. DS814.20/8-2753.

21. The difficulties of trying to control Guatemalan coffee exports, which

provided nearly 80 percent of its foreign exchange, are well brought out in a talk by Cabot with coffee importers in the United States: "Guatemalan Coffee," 25 November 1953. DS814.2333/11-2553.

22. Thus "it was the Communist influence, not the revolutionary program, of the Arbenz government which the United States opposed."

23. Desp. 114, from W. H. Galliene, British ambassador in Guatemala City, 6 June 1948. AN2340/436/8. Vol. 67951.

24. Galliene stated:

It may be difficult to understand why Arévalo, an extreme leftist, if not a communist, should support rightists like Figueres against the communists in Costa Rica. My personal opinion is that in most of these countries ideologies and political labels have no real significance, whether communist or fascist, leftist or rightist, liberal or conservative. The real distinction is "in" and "out." Personal likes and dislikes often outweigh public policy: Likes, a little; dislikes a lot. Loyalties are rare, but hatreds are common. Forgiveness and love and charity are weakness: hatred and cruelty and avarice are strength. (Ibid.)

25. Memorandum, "Guatemala," 24 May 1949. DS711.14/5-1349.

26. Instruction 80, 14 June 1949. DS711.14/6-1449. No clearer indication could be given of the department's desire to demonstrate that the Good Neighbor policy was a "two-way street" and to engender the "evocation of reciprocity" on which the policy depended.

27. Tel. 274, from Guatemala, 29 June 1949. In detail, Arévalo said that he stood ready "to use his political influence to right injustices, but where questions of law, the authority of Congress, et cetera, are at issue, he may not intervene as would dictators SOMOZA and TRUJILLO. Surely, the United States does not wish him to adopt that course" (desp. 331, from Guatemala, 30 June 1949. DS711.14/6-3049).

28. Memorandum of conversation with Messrs. John L. Simpson et al., 25 July 1949. DS814.504/7-2549.

29. Memorandum of telephone conversation with M. M. Wise, "EBASCO Operations in Costa Rica," 20 April 1948. DS818.00/4-2048. On "saving American lives," which was a usual last resort of those proposing the use of force, it may be noted that Latin American governments and revolutionaries used extraordinary care to save American lives in their frequent clashes. Apart from one life lost apparently as the result of a stray bullet in the Cuban insurrection of 1933, the only other cases in which lives of U.S. citizens were lost in revolutions after 1920 were when U.S. forces were sent into a Latin American country, as in Nicaragua between 1927 and 1933, and in the Dominican Republic in 1965 (see my letter to the *New York Times* [13 June 1965]).

30. Memorandum, 8 September 1949, from Wise to Willard F. Barber and Edward G. Miller, Jr. DS814.504/9-949. For accounts of activities of the United Fruit Company and its close relationships with the Department of

State, see Schlesinger and Kinzer (1982), chap. 5; and Immerman (1982), chap. 4.

31. See also DS Memorandum of Conversation, 24 March 1950, from *Declassified Documents Quarterly Catalogue* 1:179C.

32. Tel. 395, from Guatemala, 31 March 1950.

33. Desp. 13, from Guatemala, 7 July 1950.

34. Desp. 130, 4 August 1949, from Guatemala. AN2522/1015/8, and letter from Lee to Philip Broad, North American Dept., FO, 4 August 1949. AN2549/1015/8. Vol. 74030. The British "were denouncing Arévalo and his gang as communists earlier and more strongly than we were. They certainly warned Secretary Marshall about the leftward trend of events at the time of the Bogotá Conference, long before most people at the working level in State were prepared to go that far" (letter to me from Edward A. Jamison, FSO retired, 19 September 1981).

35. Memorandum of conversation, "Arms for Guatemala," between Col. Oscar Morales López, Guatemalan representative on the Inter-American Defense Board, and Thomas Mann and Ernest V. Siracusa, 29 December 1950.

36. Text in DS814.20/8-2753.

37. See also NSC 144, 4 March 1953, Report to the National Security Council by the executive secretary, "United States Objectives and Courses of Action with Respect to Latin America," Eisenhower Library: "The United States should achieve a greater degree of hemisphere solidarity by: . . . Refraining from overt unilateral intervention in the internal political affairs of the other American states, in accordance with existing treaty obligations. This does not preclude multilateral action through the inter-American system."

38. This recalls other "escapes" from the department's supervision, such as Rockefeller's acting at the San Francisco Conference as though he were "a separate delegation" (Morris 1960: 210); and Zbigniew Brzezinski's apparently carrying on discussions with the Iranian ambassador "without the knowledge of anyone in the State Department" (Walter Goodman, "The War of the Memoirs," *New York Times Book Review* [29 May 1983], p. 23).

39. For the detailed case, see "Penetration of the Political Institutions of Guatemala by the International Communist Movement: Threat to the Peace and Security of America and to the Sovereignty and Political Independence of Guatemala." DS714.00/7-1954. See also *Intervention of International Communism in Guatemala*, Department of State Publication 5556, and *A Case History of Communist Penetration: Guatemala*, Department of State Publication 6465 (Washington: GPO, 1954 and 1957, respectively).

40. See on this Matthews (1971: 262–264) for an account of a talk with Edward G. Miller, Jr., in which details are given of a plot involving Trujillo, the United Fruit Company, and various Colombian and Venezuelan officials to ship arms to Nicaragua for Somoza to use to "clean up Guatemala." The arms shipment was on the high seas when a CIA representative asked for Miller's signature on a document related to the case. Miller refused and went to Acheson, who went to Truman, who ordered the ship to Panama, where

the arms were unloaded. Truman had originally initialed a document that had gone directly to Gen. Walter Bedell Smith, director of the CIA, without being seen first by Miller. On Iran, see Roosevelt (1979).

41. Cabot here was speaking of his remonstrations in 1945 with Braden over the latter's interference in Argentine politics, but the notion of the principle's penetration of his thought was manifest.

42. Letter to me, 12 December 1979. Woodward did not realize until much later that he was appointed ambassador to Costa Rica because he had not been in sympathy with the military action in Guatemala.

43. Letter to me, 22 January 1980.

44. It may be noted that Smith, following his war experience and ambassadorship in the USSR, had accepted the idea that the Soviet Union was an implacable enemy of the West and would take advantage of every opportunity offered by weakness shown by the United States. See his memoir, W. Smith (1950).

45. Cabot gives his justification in a footnote to the above: "For those who decry the Guatemalan coup as the 'immoral' overthrow of a 'democratically' elected government I would rejoin that Arbenz was elected solely because he had had Aranha [sic]—who would otherwise clearly have been elected—murdered; that Arbenz regime had made several efforts to overthrow the regimes of neighboring countries; and that Guatemala was on a course which would have made it—as Cuba later became—a menace to our national security."

46. On this situation, Woodward wrote to me on 27 October 1981, that

I never felt at any post that I had real supervision as Ambassador, over the CIA Station Chief. . . . So far as information gathering was concerned, the State Department in the Embassy could never be sure that they would be informed of all the CIA reporting, but this was the situation in most Embassies and we were accustomed to it. (When I became Assistant Secretary of State for Inter-American Affairs I had an opportunity to try to correct this problem, as a member of a high-level liaison committee with the CIA. It was impossible to get an effective commitment that Embassies, or even Ambassadors personally, would have complete access to all CIA reporting on substantive—as differentiated from administrative and personnel—matters.)

47. Letter to me, 12 December 1979. Two differing views of the "Communist menace" in Guatemala may be found in memoranda (1) for the president, signed by Smith and drafted by J. W. Fisher, 15 January 1954; and (2) for Henry F. Holland, Cabot's successor, from Woodward, 3 May 1954, both in DS714.001/5-354.

48. See *New Statesman and Nation* (17 October 1953): 449–454. See also NSC 144/1, 20 November 1953, National Security Council, Progress Report on "United States Objectives and Courses of Action with Respect to Latin America," Eisenhower Library, in which it is stated that the Department of State had told Latin American governments that "the establishment of a

communist bridgehead in British Guiana would be a matter of deep concern to all the American Republics and that we considered that the American Republics should regard the measures taken by the British with genuine satisfaction."

49. Immerman cites C. D. Jackson to Dulles, 26 February 1954, "Caracas," JFD Papers; telephone conversation with Allen Dulles, 7 April 1954, Dulles Papers Telephone Conversations, "Telephone Memoranda (Excepting to and from White House) 1 March to 30 April 1954/1."

50. Tel. 1602, from Mexico City, 23 June 1954. DS714.00/6-2354. I found no reply to this telegram in the papers in the National Archives. See also White's letter to Holland, 22 July 1954, in which he raises the question of whether "the Soviet Government's method of intervention and control by infiltration presents a new problem not now covered sufficiently and explicitly." This "lacuna in the present inter-American structure" could be filled through consultation and a conference, and such action might "be very useful at some future time" (22 July 1954. DS720.001/7-2254). No action seems to have been taken on this wise and farsighted proposal.

51. Policy Papers Subseries, NSC Series, Records of the White House Office, Office of the Special Assistant for National Security Affairs (OSANSA) (Robert Cutler, Dillon Anderson, and Gordon Gray). Box 10, Eisenhower Library. The CIA was authorized "to develop underground resistance and facilitate covert and guerrilla operation. . . . in areas dominated or threatened by International Communism." These and other "covert operations" should be planned and executed so that "any U.S. Government responsibility for them is not evident to unauthorized persons and that if uncovered the U.S. Government can plausibly disclaim any responsibility for them."

52. Stockwell comments that this philosophy "created an exhilarating new game where all social and legal restraints were dissolved. . . . The CIA presence in American foreign affairs will be judged by history as a surrender to the darker side of human nature."

53. Kermit Roosevelt was the CIA agent primarily concerned; he was specially praised by Eisenhower and was secretly awarded the National Security Medal.

54. Blasier, writing in 1976, felt it necessary to offer proofs that the CIA was actually involved; he concluded that "the evidence is overwhelming and virtually irrefutable" (p. 161). In the view of later books, such as D. Phillips (1977), Powers (1979), Cabot (1979), Schlesinger and Kinzer (1982), and Immerman (1982), it is safe to assume the CIA's participation.

55. Peurifoy is reported to have been "fairly successful in efforts to influence internal Greek politics." He "appeared to have been collaborating in these efforts with personnel of the Central Intelligence Agency who functioned more or less undercover in and out of the embassy" (Westerfield 1963: 428–429).

56. Telephone call to Allen Dulles, 28 June 1954. Papers of J. F. Dulles. Telephone Calls Series. Eisenhower Library.

57. Letter to me, 25 January 1982. These are examples of what has been called the "dispose-all system." The term has been used by an experienced

retired foreign service officer to describe "a diplomatic appointment—usually but not always of a chief of mission—primarily for a reason other than the logic of the appointment from the point of view of the nominee's qualifications, career or non-career. A prime example would be the appointment of a Latin American politician with whose absence from the domestic political scene the appointing government would feel more comfortable than with his presence. Our government has made such appointments from time to time though I do not recall any involving major political figures."

58. Telephone call to Allen Dulles, 19 May 1954. Papers of J. F. Dulles. Telephone Calls Series. Eisenhower Library. Campbell is not identified, but was apparently a CIA official.

59. Immerman, citing an interview with E. Howard Hunt, states that Henry Hecksher offered bribes to Guatemalan army officers (1980–81: 644). Jonas charges that "the U.S. military mission made up for the lack of overt military aid by paying off (bribing) individual military officers to undermine the Arbenz government" (1974: 85). The source Jonas gives is simply "Interview."

60. Meeting of Guatemalan Group, Minutes, 4 June 1954. DS714.00/6-454.

61. Telephone call to Allen Dulles, 15 June 1954. Papers of J. F. Dulles. Telephone Calls Series. Eisenhower Library. Allen Dulles added that "there is a good rumor the army served an ultimatum on the President [Arbenz] to act by today. The Sec. questioned the tactics reported—beheading. AWD said Dick Bissell will be over with information on that" (ibid.).

62. Talk with Holland, 17 June 1954. Papers of J. F. Dulles. Telephone Calls Series. Eisenhower Library. This quotation is the whole of the secretary's notes of this message and indicates the level of secrecy maintained over the telephone, even within the department. Notes of other calls in this series indicate frequent communication between the Dulles brothers, but are barren of indication as to what was discussed, except on two occasions. Once, "AWD asked if the Sec. were going to get hooked on ground troops. The Sec. said he never had it in mind. He is opposed to it. This is the place to apply his theory. AWD was in agreement" (complete text of conversation, ibid., Box 2, March–April 1954). Again: "AWD will try to be here close to 11 to go over the speech, and he will probably bring a technical man with him to answer questions. AWD suggested a word of praise for the fellow in the wilderness who has been fighting for years. The Sec. thought this was already in" (ibid., 30 June 1954; the speech was that given by the secretary on that day).

63. Richard M. Bissell, Jr., formerly of the CIA, notes that the rebel planes "used to fly over Guatemala and drop a few bombs, and intersperse these quite liberally with empty Coca Cola bottles which made the same sound and were about as effective" (Oral History Project, Columbia University, by permission).

64. Sec. Dulles later said of the CIA's role, "There were a few old crates which flew around and dropped some firecrackers, but they were enough to turn the tide. In these countries, air cover has a tremendous significance" ("Remarks of the Secretary to Western European Chiefs of Mission," 9 May 1958, quoted in Gardner [1972]: 426).

65. As the director of central intelligence, A. W. Dulles, wrote to the president on 20 June 1954, "the use of a small number of airplanes and the massive use of radio broadcasting are designed to build up and give main support to the impression of Castillo Armas' strength as well as to spread the impression of the regime's weakness" (*FRUS* 4 [1952–54]: 1176). A report prepared by the U.S. Information Agency, 27 July 1954, indicates that after a review by Peurifoy, the Department of State, and the Central Intelligence Agency, additional funds became available (probably from the CIA) to establish "a regional servicing operation" to help meet "the problem of communist penetration in the Central American area" (ibid.: 1213).

66. See memorandum from Woodward to Holland, "Problem of Disposition of Principal Communist Leaders in Guatemala," 13 July 1954. DS714.001/7-1354; and memorandum from Holland to Dulles, "Asylum Problem in Guatemala," 10 August 1954. DS714.001/8-1054. Woodward thought that an OAS center would create too much bad publicity to be taken seriously. See also the view that setting up an OAS "prison camp" for the "incarceration of Guatemalan Communists" was neither "feasible or practicable" (memorandum to Holland from C. R. Burrows, "Problems of Disposition of Principal Communist Leaders in Guatemala," 7 July 1954. DS714.001/7-754). See also the view of the Chilean government that it could not adopt the position that Communists "were not entitled to asylum since they represented an international conspiracy and not an indigenous political party" (desp. 16, from Santiago, 9 July 1954. DS714.00/7-954).

67. The matter was settled by Castillo Armas's favorable response to a demand by the Mexican ambassador that all refugees be removed from his embassy before 16 September, Mexico's national holiday. Despite his having agreed with Peurifoy to make a renewed effort to "prevent dispersion of Communists and other undesirables throughout hemisphere," Castillo Armas ordered that safe-conducts be issued to all those who were granted asylum. Peurifoy, angered by this breach of faith and by learning about it through the newspapers, protested vigorously to the Guatemalan foreign minister, without effect (tel. 256, from Peurifoy, Guatemala City, 8 September 1954, *FRUS* 4 [1952–54]: 1227).

68. Tel. 1121, from Peurifoy, Guatemala City, 27 June 1954. Bailey (1967: 97), asserts that "just in case the invasion bogged down (which it did), and it proved impossible to generate an internal *coup*, American Marines were moved from Puerto Rico to the waters near Jamaica to be ready to assist the invading forces." Bailey gives no source for this claim, and I have found no reference to it elsewhere.

69. Papers of J. F. Dulles. Telephone Calls Series. Eisenhower Library. Call to Allen Dulles, 30 June 1954.

70. "Collapsing like a house of cards, the elaborate political structure erected by the Communists over a ten-year period fell on June 27. . . . The regime fell basically because the Army apparently had no heart in a fight to protect the Communists and the populace had even less taste for sacrifice for their cause. Thus, it was demonstrated that the Communists' domination of the country was an artificial thing, built upon merely their control

over the Presidency but lacking a control over the real sources of power"
(Joint Weeka No. 26, from Guatemala, 6 July 1954, from William L. Krieg.
DS714.00(W)/7-654).

71. Tel. 1124, from Peurifoy to Dulles, 27 June 1954, 11 P.M. DS714.00/
6-2754. Tels. 1125 through 1130, all of June 28, are not included in the
papers made available under the Freedom of Information Act.

72. Tel. 1131, from Peurifoy to Dulles, 29 June 1954, 11:15 P.M. Schlesinger and Kinzer erroneously use the word *annoyed* instead of *amazed* in
this quotation. The suggestion in favor of Monzón's appointment may be
contrasted with Peurifoy's earlier statement to Díaz that he "could not (repeat not) attempt to dictate his Cabinet" (tel. 1124, n. 72).

73. Tel. 1146 from Peurifoy to Department of State, Guatemala City, 30
June 1954.

74. Papers of J. F. Dulles. Telephone Calls Series. Eisenhower Library. 28
June 1954, 9:39 A.M.

75. Tel. 1379 to Peurifoy from Holland, 29 June 1954, 8:07 P.M. DS714.00/
6-2954.

76. Memorandum of telephone conversation between Holland and Peurifoy, 29 June 1954, 3 P.M. DS714.00/6-2954.

77. Memorandum of telephone conversation between Leddy and Peurifoy,
"The Guatemalan Change of Government," 30 June 1954, 11:45 A.M. DS-
714.00/6-3054.

78. "Memorandum of Negotiations Leading to Signing of Pact of San Salvador, July 2, 1954," Desp. 5, Peurifoy to Dulles, 7 July 1954. Peurifoy notes
that he was "finally forced to talk with Castillo Armas alone and ask him
point blank whether he was the chief of his 'outfit,' since every time he
agreed on a point he subsequently changed his decision after conferring
with his advisers. I told him that if he was not the top man in his organization, I would appreciate his telling me who was, so that I could deal with
that person. I believe this question was the turning point in the negotiations"(*FRUS* 4 [1952–54]: 1205).

79. In a letter, the two who resigned stated: "We promised we would retire
as soon as the overthrow of communism had been accomplished and peace
re-established. Both objectives have now been accomplished" (Kennedy,
New York Times [9 July 1954]). Details of these resignations may be found in
departmental documentation, 29 June–9 July 1954.

80. Dreier notes that the idea of "domination or control of the political
institutions" of an American state by communism was "a new juridical
barrier behind which the opponents of action can defend a negative policy."
The Caracas Declaration was therefore not used "when the time came to
organize action through the O.A.S.," nor was it used in the case of Cuba in
1962. In both instances, direct reference to the Rio Treaty was made (Dreier
1962: 52–53).

81. Speech of 28 August.

82. Chardkoff suggests that the U.S. Navy would not have allowed the *Alfhem* to dock "unless it were fairly certain that the equipment could be of
little use to the Arbenz regime" (1967: 358).

83. Alexander suggests that "the Communists thus were able to divert the Guatemalan Revolution from its course and convert it into one more weapon of Soviet foreign policy. In doing so they not only brought disaster to the Revolution, but, for the time being at least, oblivion to themselves" (1957: 362). On the other hand, Milton Bracker reported that "the regime of President Jacobo Arbenz is neither Communist nor dominated by Communists. However, it is infiltrated and honeycombed by them to an extent that a showdown would almost certainly be disruptive to the country." Guatemala was not a threat to the Panama Canal, and it was no more than "a bustling outpost of Soviet propaganda in the heart of the Americas" (*New York Times* [3 March 1954]).

84. Letter to me, 27 October 1981.

85. Minutes of meeting of 10 May 1954. DS714.00/5-1054.

86. Memorandum to the secretary, 14 May 1954. Counterposed to Holland's view was the Third Progress Report on NSC 144/1, "United States Objectives and Courses of Action With Respect to Latin America," 25 May 1954, in which it was stated, "It appears from the views expressed that the number of Latin American states (particularly the more influential ones) which at this time regard the growth of communist influence in the Guatemalan Government as a serious threat to their peace and security is not sufficient to bring about OAS action" (*FRUS* 4 [1952–54]: 47).

87. Memorandum of conversation, 11 May 1954. DS714.00/5-1154.

88. Memorandum of conversation, 12 May 1954. DS714.00/5-1254.

89. Memorandum of conversation, 13 May 1954. DS714.00/5-1354.

90. This memorandum was prepared by Hill and given to Muniz on May 14: "OAS Action against Communism in Guatemala," minutes of meeting chaired by Holland. DS714.00/5-1354. See also memorandum from Holland to the secretary, "Call by Dr. João Carlos Muniz, Ambassador of Brazil," drafted by Leddy, 11 May 1954; and memorandum of the same date, "Summary of Communist Influence in Guatemala," by J. W. Fisher. DS714.001/5-1154.

91. Memorandum of conversation, 15 May 1954. DS714.00/5-1554.

92. *FRUS* 4 (1952–54) refers to four of the nineteen meetings of the group. In each case, an omission in those present is indicated, and in each case the omission is "Frank Holcomb (CIA)" (I determined this by comparing *FRUS* with the actual reports of the meetings, which are among the Schlesinger documents). Such care in excluding any reference to the CIA in the official record is probably also reflected in the report of the meeting of June 9, in which several omissions are indicated by ellipsis points in the *FRUS* account (p. 1162), of which no copy was made available under the Freedom of Information Act.

93. Memorandum of conversation between J. F. Dulles, Holland, and Muniz, 24 May 1954. DS714.00/5-2454.

94. "OAS Action Against Communism in Guatemala," minutes of meeting chaired by Holland, 29 May 1954. DS714.00/5-2954.

95. Letter to Peurifoy, 30 May 1954. DS714.00/5-3054. On the last point in this letter, a different view was taken at a high, if uninfluential, level in the

department. At a time when commitments had already been made to act through the OAS, Louis J. Halle, Jr., a member of the Policy Planning Staff, gave the staff's director a memorandum recommending that, since there was not any "imminent danger" to the United States, and since it was "too risky" to attempt collective action through the OAS, it would be preferable "to adopt a policy of watchful waiting in the expectation that if the situation gets worse the chances of getting effective collective action will thereby be increased" (28 May 1954, *FRUS* 4 [1952–54]: 1141–49). This memorandum was written far too late to affect the course of negotiations, and in any case it is not known whether it came to Holland's attention.

96. Memorandum of conversation with Amb. José A. Mora of Uruguay, 31 May 1954. DS714.00/5-3154. Holland added that Mora "seemed quite relieved that we would not require any action with regard to the United Fruit Company."

97. Memorandum of conversation between Holland and Víctor Andrade, ambassador of Bolivia, 3 June 1954. DS714.00/6-354.

98. Memorandum of telephone conversation, 1 June 1954. DS714.00/6-154. For background on this conversation, see letter to Holland from White, and attached memorandum, "Call on President Ruiz Cortines," 26 May 1954. DS714.001/5-2654. See also attached memorandum of May 25, "Conversation with Minister for Foreign Affairs," in which White emphasized that Communist "intervention" in Honduras in promoting strikes and disorders was "intervention in an American country by international Russian communism, using Guatemala as their instrument."

99. Minutes, meeting of Guatemalan Group, 4 June 1954. DS714.00/6-454. It is of interest in this connection that the minutes of the June 4 meeting indicate that "(a) Since Holland is using as his major argument with the Latin American Ambassadors the fact that we are not putting economic pressure on Guatemala, we cannot denounce the trade agreement." Since that agreement requires the ending of concessions to any country, "dominated by international Communism, we do not consider Guatemala 'dominated.' Our view is that it is 'intensively penetrated.'"

100. The official view in the United States was that this was not an "invasion," since the land forces were mainly Guatemalan; I use the term here, however, since the CIA provided the training funds and aircraft, and the aircraft "invaded" Guatemalan air space from bases in Nicaragua and Honduras.

101. Minutes, meeting of Guatemalan Group, 16 June 1954. DS714.001/6-1654.

102. Ibid., 22 June 1954. DS714.001/6-2254.

103. The request was supported by the following governments besides the United States: Brazil, Costa Rica, Cuba, Dominican Republic, El Salvador, Haiti, Honduras, Nicaragua, Panama, and Peru. Eleven was the number of countries required to call a meeting of foreign ministers, but was less than the two-thirds majority (14) required to pass a resolution in such a meeting.

104. Dreier added: "There hang in the balance not only the security of this continent but the continued vitality and existence of the Organization of American States and the high principles on which it is founded. In our

decisions at this hour we may well profoundly affect the future of our American way of life."

105. Eisenhower was reported as saying at his news conference on June 30 that "the recent developments in Guatemala had given great satisfaction. To try to conceal that, he said, would be deceitful" (*New York Times* [1 July 1954]).

106. On June 19, Dulles said that the department had no evidence to indicate that this was "anything other than a revolt of Guatemalans against the Government" (*DSB* [28 June 1954]: 981–982). It was, of course, the CIA that had the evidence, as Dulles well knew; the department had carefully arranged that no documentary evidence could be found in its files.

107. The Department of State on June 19 stated that it had "no evidence that indicates that this is anything other than a revolt of Guatemalans against the Government" (*New York Times* [20 June 1954]).

108. See also memorandum of telephone conversation between Daniels and Holland, 2 July 1954. DS714.00/7-254.

109. Slater's view is that the United States thought the OAS should "take just enough action to justify the exclusion of the UN, but not so much as to endanger the success of the Castillo Armas coup" (1967: 123). Slater adds, with respect to the U.S. proposal for a meeting of consultation, "The belated timing of this move, coming as it did two weeks after nearly unanimous Latin American consent for a conference had been obtained and with an anti-Communist victory in Guatemala imminent, suggests that it was designed only to provide a mantle of legitimacy for a *fait accompli*" (ibid., p. 125). Westerfield rather more cautiously indicates that "American efforts were therefore directed as inconspicuously as possible to the task of preventing Arbenz from getting any early outside aid against the Honduran-based insurrection. In particular, the United Nations and the OAS must be prevented from acting against the invaders until the Guatemalan army chiefs had had ample time to reach a decision against Arbenz" (1963: 435–436).

110. Texts of the CIA draft and of an alternative draft stressing consultation with the other American republics are attached. Eisenhower accepted Holland's view (Cook 1981: 277, and n. 34; also see comment by James C. Hagerty, press secretary to the president, 16 June 1954, *FRUS* 4 [1952–54]: 1169).

111. Memorandum of conversation between Joe Martin, Muniz, and Holland, 13 May 1954. DS714.00/5-1354; and memorandum of conversation between Dulles, Muniz, and Holland, 11 May 1954. DS714.00/5-1154. Dulles wrote a note of thanks to Muniz on 7 July 1954, saying that Muniz had "contributed much to the success of the cooperative measures taken by the Organization of American States. I feel that our regional American organization is stronger and more unified as a result of the trial just past, and Brazil played a leading and constructive role." The file contains no response to this disingenuous letter. DS720.001/7-754.

112. Memorandum to Charles S. Murphy, special counsel to the president, "Latin America and U.S. Policy," 11 December 1952. Harry S. Truman Library, President's Secretary's File. Mann pointed out that in 1939 Gen.

Góes Monteiro, chief of staff of the Brazilian armed forces had dealt directly with Roosevelt and Hull, but when he came in 1952 to negotiate on troops for Korea he dealt with a brigadier general and an assistant secretary of state.

113. "Prospects for and Probable Consequences of an OAS Resolution against Guatemala," Intelligence Report, Office of Intelligence Research, Department of State. DS714.00/6-1754.

114. See, e.g., statement by Marcel Niedergang, reporter for *Le Monde* (Paris) that Guatemala "was a deplorable situation that had two aspects— Communism, where there was evident infiltration, and the interests of the United Fruit with the open intervention of the United States. . . . The result was a terrible blow for the Good Neighbor policy and this fact is recognized not only in this hemisphere, but in Europe. Popular reaction, not in favor of Communism, but against United States' intervention proves it" (quoted in Desp. 75, from Caracas, 23 July 1954. DS714.00/7-2354; the quotation is from *El Universal*, 20 July 1954).

115. From text of agreement with Honduras of 20 May 1954, which is a copy of that with Nicaragua of 23 April 1954: *U.S. Treaties and Other International Acts Series*, nos. 2975 and 2940, "Military Assistance."

116. The CIA "had acquired a power which, however beneficial its exercise often might be, blocked State Department control over the conduct of foreign affairs" (Ransom 1970: 91, quoting Arthur Schlesinger, Jr.).

117. See also press release of 30 January 1954. DS714.00/1-3054.

118. Still, the department maintained its position in dealing with citizens of the United States. For example, to a telegram of 18 June 1954, asking "Is it true that United States is furnishing munitions to the rebels for invasion of Guatemala?" Leddy replied that "the assisting in any way of foreign political movements by the United States Government is contrary to its strictly observed policy of nonintervention in the affairs of other countries. The United States Government accordingly . . . avoids involvement in any way in all such movements" (letter, drafted by J. W. Fisher, to H. H. Scriven, 14 July 1954. DS714.00/6-1854). Was such obfuscation a "necessary art" in the circumstances?

119. See also *DSB* (13 December 1954): 892, in which Dulles says that "international communism had in fact got control of the Government [of Guatemala]. The American States were about to meet with reference to this danger when the Guatemalan people themselves backed loyal elements who cut out the cancer of communism."

120. Continuing this line Peurifoy in testimony before the Latin American Subcommittee of the Select Committee of the House of Representatives on 8 October 1954, stated that "the menace of communism in Guatemala was courageously fought by the Guatemalan people themselves, always against the superior odds which a police state has over the decent, patriotic citizen. . . . They fought the battle which is the common battle of all free nations against communist oppression, and they won the victory themselves" (*Hearings*, p. 696).

121. Speech, 20 October 1954. Public Papers of the Presidents of the United States. Dwight D. Eisenhower (1954), p. 925.

122. Speech, 30 August 1954. Ibid., p. 781. See also Blasier (1976: 177, and n. 98).

123. Lombardo Toledano did not turn up, there was no heroism, no *gritos*, only the general effort to escape on the part of those "who only hours before, were still eating the biggest and most savage jaguars" (Marroquín 1955[?]: 21).

124. Memorandum of conversation, 11 March 1953. DS714.001/3-1153.

125. Memorandum of conversation, 26 June 1953. DS611.14/6-2653.

126. "Conversation between Ambassador John E. Peurifoy and Colonel Jacobo Arbenz Guzmán, President of Guatemala," and their wives, 16 December 1953. DS611.14/12-1353. Later Peurifoy reported that as a result of this interview, "I am convinced Communists will continue to gain strength here as long as he remains in office. My staff agrees fully on this" (tel. 163, from Guatemala City, 23 December 1953. DS611.14/12-2353). Earlier, in a talk with the former Guatemalan military attaché in Washington, Col. Oscar Morales López, Cabot had said that the difficulty seemed to be "the Guatemalan Government's unawareness of the danger of communism." Morales responded that the president's "attitude is that the communists in Guatemala are few, are well known, are easily controllable, and constitute no international problem. . . . He would do something about the communists if somebody would prove to him that they constitute a menace" (memorandum of conversation, 12 March 1953. DS611.14/3-1253).

127. "U.S. Likely to Get the Blame However Latin Revolt Ends," Milton Bracker, *New York Times* (21 June 1954). Similarly, "U.S. prestige with the Latin Americans has suffered a severe blow through the Guatemalan fighting whether the North Americans have any direct responsibility or not. The Latin Americans believe that the United States does have an obvious direct responsibility on moral grounds because they are convinced that the invasion by the Guatemalan exiles would not have been possible without at least the tacit approval of Washington" ("U.S. Prestige Ebbs in Latin America," Sam Pope Brewer, *New York Times* [27 June 1954]). This may be compared with Col. Díaz's remark that "Castillo could not have obtained these arms without US acquiescence," for which statement Peurifoy rebuked him sharply (tel. 1124, from Guatemala City, 27 June 1954, 11 P.M., *FRUS* 4 [1952–54]: 1190).

128. I make this statement despite the fact that "Progress Report on NSC 5432/1," approved by the president, 3 September 1954, states that "the Organization of American States was used as a means of achieving our objectives in the case of communist intervention in Guatemala" (*FRUS* 4 [1952–54]: 92).

129. NSC 5432, 18 August 1954. National Security Council. "U.S. Policy Toward Latin America," p. 7. Eisenhower Library; emphasis mine.

10. Conclusion

1. Ferguson quotes Richard A. Falk as stating that "intervention in some form is an unavoidable concomitant of national existence" (1972: 102).

2. Paul Mason commented that "the Good Neighbor policy of the US to-

wards Latin America . . . has really progressed beyond the stage of Party politics in the US, and . . . it would be carried out by any foreseeable Republican Administration in the US. Indeed, the present Republican leaders are on record on this point." FO Memorandum, "The Lesson of the Argentine Case," by Gallop, 4 January 1944. AS130/78/2. Vol. 37698.

3. Memorandum by George H. Butler, "Problem: To Establish U.S. Policy Regarding Anti-Communist Measures which Could be Planned and Carried out within the Inter-American System, March 22, 1948." DSP.P.S-26. This statement of the department's view was omitted from *FRUS* 9 (1948): 193–201.

4. Tel. 321, from Amb. William Pawley, Rio de Janeiro, to secretary of state, 24 March 1948. DS710.J/3-2448.

5. Circular airgram, "Bogotá Conference Guidance," 25 March 1948. DS710.J/3-2548.

6. Resolution 32, "The Preservation and Defense of Democracy in America," Final Act (1948), pp. 46–47.

7. Circular, 15 October 1948. DS810.00B/10-1548. Problems arose with the liaison because CIA took the position that material from Latin American ministries should not be cleared for transmittal to other governments (memorandum from R. K. Oakley to Woodward and Daniels, 8 April 1949, "Communist Liaison with OAR [Other American Republics] Fails to Progress," DS810.00B/4-849). Oakley later made suggestions for a committee of the OAS Council "to deal with questions concerning totalitarianism of an extra-hemispheric derivation," for a training school under the OAS to study the tactics of international communism, and for the negotiation of agreements for coordination of anti-Communist efforts, but nothing seems to have come from these recommendations (Memorandum from Oakley to Miller, 25 October 1949, "Inter-American Cooperation to Combat Communism," DS810.00B/10-2549).

8. NSC 144, Report to the National Security Council by the executive secretary, "United States Objectives and Courses of Action with Respect to Latin America," Eisenhower Library.

9. This policy was applicable to the Americas, although Acheson had in mind primarily the policies adopted toward Europe and Korea.

10. "Second Progress Report by the Under Secretary of State (Walter B. Smith) on the Implementation of United States Objectives and Courses of Action with Respect to Latin America (NSC 144/1)," 20 November 1953. Cabot was speaking at this time out of both sides of his mouth, however. In an address to Canadian War College students on 28 October he said: "There is, then more or less of a Communist menace in all of the South American republics. Nevertheless, no South American government is today much influenced by Communists; on the contrary, on the government level Communists have unquestionably tended to lose ground in recent years" (Cabot 1955: 118).

11. U.S. Congress, Senate, Committee on Foreign Relations, *Hearing, Nomination of Dean G. Acheson to be Secretary of State,* 81st Congress, 1st Session. 13 January 1949, p. 17.

12. Jones notes that "to Americans in 1947 intervention was an ugly word," and the word "was never used by Will Clayton, Paul Porter, and others" in explaining to Congress how the funds would be administered.

13. Immerman suggests the decision was taken by the "10/2 committee," since the 54/12 committee was not created until 1954, but he has no data on either (1982: 241, n. 3).

14. "Ike vehemently and frequently insisted to his closest associates approval of plans did not mean approval of actual operations. . . . Ike gave the order to go only after the arrival of the Alfhem in Guatemala" (Ambrose 1981: 225). It is evident, however, that an earlier decision had started the Castillo Armas adventure. That 1953 decision might possibly have been taken by the National Security Council itself, but this seems doubtful, since Bissell is reported as saying, "Remember that under Eisenhower the NSC was a whole big roomful of people" (ibid. 241).

15. Joseph S. Nye, *New York Times Book Review* (17 January 1982).

16. "The Memory of Mistakes," *New York Times* (18 January 1982). Lewis proposes the creation of a National Academy for Public Affairs, which, however, would have been of little use in the Guatemalan affair, the plotting of which was done in utmost stealth and with great duplicity. The Guatemalan affair also provides an outstanding contradiction to the views of George F. Will, "The Old Foreign Policy Goes On," *Washington Post* (14 January 1982): "Foreign policy does not trickle down from the highest levels; it rises through the bureaucracy, which defines options, narrows choices and makes continuity hard to escape." This would be partly true if there were only the Department of State and no CIA.

17. Westerfield (1963: 440–441) comments, "If these considerations, together with the possibility of the premature eclipse of Castillo Armas himself, were thoroughly explored by American policy makers, in secret of course, their approach to the problem can be commended as appropriate."

18. Letter to me, 12 December 1979. This statement, of course, does not deal with the legal obligations that remain but are not observed. These, the hope and despair of the OAS, are, however, beyond the scope of this study.

19. John Foster Dulles is described as "that Jesuit in Presbyterian clothing" by John King Fairbank in his recent memoir (1982: 402).

20. The similarity of the Monroe and Brezhnev doctrines has been pointed out by many commentators; see, e.g., Carl T. Rowan, "To the Big Guys Go the 'Spheres,'" *Washington Post* (16 August 1983); and Franck and Weisband's discussion of verbal strategy among the superpowers (1971).

Note on Sources

Five principal sources provide the basis for this study. First are the generally available documents of the Department of State. Some of these are published in *Foreign Relations of the United States* (*FRUS*). Some incidents or stories, however, are not referred to at all in this publication, and documents are frequently incompletely published. It is therefore necessary to read the full texts of all relevant documents in the files of the National Archives (NA), to which the department has sent its collections through 1954. Fortunately, the present manuscript has had the benefit of some of these later materials in considering U.S. policy toward Bolivia and Guatemala. Even so, the files contain many sheets that indicate that a document has been extracted from the files under authority of the FBI, the CIA, or the department itself. In a number of instances, it has been impossible to retrieve these materials from the agency concerned. In the text a reference is given to *FRUS* in all cases in which the citation is available there; if not, the source is given as a Department of State (DS) document.

"The American Republics," *FRUS* 4 (1952–54), was issued in January 1984. Those persons listed as editors of the volume are in fact compilers and annotators. They selected documents to be published, within practical spatial limits, with the intent of providing a clear and complete "story" of the relations of the United States in substantive or country terms. In a sense, the real editors of the volumes are persons in the department, or in other agencies, such as the CIA, who decide which of the selected documents are to be declassified for publication under the authority and with the approval of the executive branch of the government of the United States. Other agencies, and in some cases even foreign governments, may also influence the editorial process. Declassifiers in other agencies may even require the excision of parts of documents that are published in *FRUS*, as in the case of the membership in the State Department's Guatemalan Group (see n. 93, chap. 9).

Additional materials are of course available in the presidential libraries, such as records of telephone conversations between John Foster and Allan W. Dulles.

Secondly, the State Department archives are, in general, open after thirty years. Modifications in this situation have been made under the Freedom of Information Act (FOIA), however, and Stephen Schlesinger by this route obtained in 1979 some fifteen hundred pages of documents on Guatemala for 1953 and 1954. My request to secure copies of this material was granted by the Department of State in 1982, with the exception of six undescribed documents; most of the papers cited in chapter 9 are from this collection.

With respect to the documents available under the FOIA, I selected some eight hundred pages from those made available to Mr. Schlesinger by the Department of State. Subsequently, I offered, and the late William E. Carter, chief, Hispanic Division, Library of Congress, accepted, these materials as part of the vertical file collection of the division, where researchers may have ready access to them.

It should be noted that there is an important difference in documents obtained under the FOIA before and after 1980. In the first group, which includes those obtained by Mr. Schlesinger, the documents released were not individually censored; in the second group, those obtained by me, were, to use the Department of State's term, made available only as "sanitized copy." This meant, specifically, that in the case of Desp. 213, from Amb. Edward J. Sparks, La Paz, 6 October 1953, "Conversations with President Paz and Cabinet Members regarding Special Aid by the United States to Bolivia," DS724.5-MSP/10-653, there were four censored sections of the despatch, officially indicated as "sensitive information deleted." The authority for such deletions as given on the card in the file in the National Archives is "Stat. Pol. Sens."

The third source consists of documents read in the Public Record Office (PRO), Kew Gardens, near London. The PRO follows a thirty-year rule, although it makes it actually a thirty-one-year rule by adding a day to the date of opening materials. The documents from the British Foreign Office are well indexed and are nearly completely available; reserved for at least fifty years are materials relating to the Falkland Islands and Belize, and certain evaluations by British ambassadors of the performance of their diplomatic colleagues. Foreign scholars are welcome in the handsome and efficient establishment of the PRO. Because of Britain's large investments in Argentina, and as a result of its dependence during World War II on Argentine exports, the PRO documents are especially valuable on the Argentine scene, as professional commentaries on the changing facets of the policy of the United States. The access of British diplomats to American officials was often much closer and more intimate than that of journalists. American diplomatic historians would do well to examine the British materials to enrich their understanding of actions taken in Washington and their effects abroad.

Fourth, there are secondary sources, especially those on the CIA. Because of the secrecy surrounding the CIA these materials are necessarily sketchy and, with respect to the Guatemalan policy of the United States, they must be evaluated with care. Whereas one is inclined, for example, to assume that the CIA used bribery to persuade Guatemalan army officers, the evidence is only persuasive and remains short of conclusive because of the desire of both sides to conceal it. In any case, it is believed that the general lines of both the Department of State's and CIA's policy are sufficiently clear, so that doubts about details are not strong enough to modify them.

Finally are the talks with, and letters from, former foreign service officers, as noted in the Acknowledgments.

Bibliography

Acheson, Dean. *Among Friends: Personal Letters of Dean Acheson.* Edited by David S. McLellan and David C. Acheson. New York: Dodd, Mead, 1980.

———. "Peace through Strength: A Foreign Policy Objective." *DSB* (26 June 1950): 1037–1041.

———. *Present at the Creation: My Years in the State Department.* London: Hamish Hamilton, 1969.

———. "Stenographic Transcript of Remarks to a Group of Magazine and Book Publishers." *DSB* (23 July 1951: 125–128.

———. *This Vast External Realm.* New York: Norton, 1973.

Aguilar Monteverde, Alonso. *Pan-Americanism from Monroe to the Present.* Translated by Asa Zatz. New York: Monthly Review Press, 1968.

Alexander, Robert J. *The Bolivian National Revolution.* New Brunswick, N.J.: Rutgers University Press, 1955.

———. *Communism in Latin America.* New Brunswick, N.J.: Rutgers University Press, 1957.

Allison, Graham T., and Morton H. Halperin. *Bureaucratic Politics: A Paradigm and Some Policy Implications.* Washington, D.C.: Brookings Institution, 1972.

Ambrose, Stephen E., with Richard H. Immerman. *Ike's Spies: Eisenhower and the Espionage Establishment.* Garden City, N.Y.: Doubleday, 1981.

Andrade, Víctor. *My Missions for Revolutionary Bolivia 1944–1962.* Pittsburgh: University of Pittsburgh Press, 1976.

Arévalo, Juan José. *Guatemala, la democracia y el imperio.* Montevideo: Marcha, 1954.

Aybar de Soto, José M. *Dependency and Intervention: The Case of Guatemala in 1954.* Boulder, Colo.: Westview Press, 1978.

Bailey, Norman A. *Latin America in World Politics.* New York: Walker, 1967.

Barnet, Richard J. *Intervention and Revolution: The United States in the Third World.* New York: World, 1968.

———. *The Roots of War.* New York: Atheneum, 1972.

Berle, Adolf A. *Diary, 1937–1971.* Hyde Park, N.Y.: Franklin D. Roosevelt Library.

————. *Latin America: Diplomacy and Reality.* New York: Harper & Row, 1962.

————. *Navigating the Rapids, 1918–1971.* Edited by Beatrice Bishop Berle and Travis Beal Jacobs. Introduction by Max Ascoli. New York: Harcourt Brace Jovanovich, 1973.

Bernays, Edward L. *Biography of an Idea: Memoirs of a Public Relations Counsel.* New York: Simon & Schuster, 1965.

Bernstein, Barton J., ed. *Politics and Policies of the Truman Administration.* Chicago: Quadrangle Books, 1970.

Bissell, Richard M., Jr. *Oral History.* New York: Oral History Research Office, Butler Library, Columbia University.

Blackstock, Paul W. *The Strategy of Subversion.* Chicago: Quadrangle Books, 1964.

Blasier, Cole. *The Hovering Giant.* Pittsburgh: University of Pittsburgh Press, 1976.

————. "The United States, Germany and the Bolivian Revolutionaries, 1941–1946." *Hispanic American Historical Review* (February 1972): 26–54.

Blum, John Morton. *From the Morgenthau Diaries: Years of War 1941–1945.* Boston: Houghton Mifflin, 1967.

————. *The Price of Vision: The Diary of Henry A. Wallace 1942–1946.* Boston: Houghton Mifflin, 1973.

Bohlen, Charles E. *Witness to History, 1929–1969.* New York: Norton, 1973.

Braden, Spruille, *América y el mundo.* Lima: Ed. "C.E.U.C.," 1960.

————. *Diplomats and Demagogues: The Memoirs of Spruille Braden.* New Rochelle, N.Y.: Arlington House, 1971.

————, and Ellis O. Briggs. *Our Inter-American Policy.* Department of State Publication 2456. Inter-American Series 28. Washington, D.C.: GPO, 1946.

Briggs, Ellis O. *Anatomy of Diplomacy: The Origin and Execution of American Foreign Policy.* New York: McKay, 1968.

————. *Farewell to Foggy Bottom: The Recollections of a Career Diplomat.* New York: McKay, 1964.

Bruce, James. *Those Perplexing Argentines.* New York: Longmans, 1953.

Bullitt, William C. *For the President: Personal and Secret.* Boston: Houghton Mifflin, 1972.

Byrnes, James F. *All in One Lifetime.* New York: Harper's, 1958.

Cabot, John Moors. *First Line of Defense: Forty Years' Experiences of a Career Diplomat.* Washington, D.C.: School of Foreign Service, Georgetown University, 1979.

————. *Toward Our Common American Destiny.* Freeport, N.Y.: Books for Libraries Press, 1955.

Campbell, Thomas M., and George C. Herring, eds. *The Diaries of Edward R. Stettinius, Jr.* New York: New Viewpoints, 1975.

Castañeda, Jorge. *Mexico and the United Nations.* New York: Manhattan Publishing, 1948.

————. "Nonintervention: The First Step toward Coexistence." In *Interven-tion in Latin America*, edited by C. Neale Ronning, pp. 167–175. New York: Knopf, 1970.

Cater, Douglas. *Power in Washington*. New York: Random House, 1964.

Cehelsky, Marta. "Guatemala's Frustrated Revolution: The 'Liberation' of 1954." Master's thesis, Columbia University, 1965[?].

Chardkoff, Richard Bruce. "Communist Toehold in the Americas: A His-tory of Official United States Involvement in the Guatemalan Crisis 1954." Ph.D. dissertation, Florida State University, 1967.

Child, John. *Unequal Alliance: The Inter-American Military System 1938–1978*. Boulder, Colo.: Westview Press, 1980.

Colby, William E., with Peter Forbath. *Honorable Men*. New York: Simon & Schuster, 1978.

Collier, Peter, and David Horowitz. *The Rockefellers*. New York: Holt, Rine-hart & Winston, 1976.

Conil Paz, Alberto, and Gustavo Ferrari. *Argentina's Foreign Policy 1930–1962*. Translated by John J. Kennedy. Notre Dame, Ind.: University of Notre Dame Press, 1966.

Conn, Stetson, and Byron Fairchild. *The Framework of Hemisphere De-fense*. Washington, D.C.: Office of the Chief of Military History, Depart-ment of the Army, 1960.

Connell-Smith, Gordon. *The United States and Latin America: An Histori-cal Analysis of Inter-American Relations*. London: Heinemann, 1974.

Cook, Blanche Wiesen. *The Declassified Eisenhower: A Divided Legacy*. Garden City, N.Y.: Doubleday, 1981.

Copeland, Miles. *The Game of Nations: The Amorality of Power Politics*. New York: Simon & Schuster, 1969.

Corson, William R. *The Armies of Ignorance: The Rise of the American In-telligence Empire*. New York: Dial Press, James Wade, 1977.

Coutinho, Lourival. *O General Góes Depoe*. Rio de Janeiro: Coelho Branco, 1955.

Crassweller, Robert. *Trujillo: The Life and Times of a Caribbean Dictator*. New York: Macmillan, 1966.

Cuevas Cancino, Francisco. *Roosevelt y la buena vecindad*. Mexico City: Fondo de Cultura Económica, 1954.

Dallek, Robert. *Franklin D. Roosevelt and American Foreign Policy 1932–1945*. New York: Oxford University Press, 1979.

Dinerstein, Herbert S. *The Making of a Missile Crisis, October 1962*. Bal-timore, Md.: Johns Hopkins University Press, 1976.

Dozer, Donald M. *Are We Good Neighbors?* New York: Johnson Reprint Corp., 1972.

Dreier, John C. *The Organization of American States and the Hemisphere Crisis*. New York: Harper & Row, 1962.

————. "The Special Nature of Western Hemisphere Experience with Inter-national Organization." In *International Organization in the Western Hemisphere*, edited by Robert W. Gregg, pp. 9–46. Syracuse, N.Y.: Syra-cuse University Press, 1968.

———. "Taking Stock of Inter-American Relations." *DSB* (30 April 1951): 688–693.

Duggan, Laurence. *The Americas: The Search for Hemisphere Security.* Foreword by Herschel Brickell. New York: Holt, 1949.

———. "Political and Economic Solidarity of the Americas." *Vital Speeches,* (1 December 1940): 524–528.

Dulles, Allen Welsh. *The Craft of Intelligence.* New York: Harper & Row, 1963.

Dulles, John W. F. *Vargas of Brazil: A Political Biography.* Austin: University of Texas Press, 1967.

Eder, George Jackson. *Inflation and Development in Latin America: A Case Study of Inflation and Stabilization in Bolivia.* Ann Arbor: Graduate School of Business Administration, University of Michigan, 1968.

Eisenhower, Dwight D. *The White House Years: Mandate for Change 1953–1956.* Garden City, N.Y.: Doubleday, 1963.

Eisenhower, Milton S. *The Wine Is Bitter: The United States and Latin America.* Garden City, N.Y.: Doubleday, 1963.

Fairbank, John King. *Chinabound: A Fifty-Year Memoir.* New York: Harper, 1982.

Ferguson, Yale H., ed. *Contemporary Inter-American Relations: A Reader in Theory and Issues.* Englewood Cliffs, N.J.: Prentice-Hall, 1972.

Francis, Michael J. *The Limits of Hegemony: United States Relations with Argentina and Chile during World War II.* Notre Dame, Ind.: University of Notre Dame Press, 1977.

Franck, Thomas M., and Edward Weisband. *Word Politics: Verbal Strategy among the Superpowers.* New York: Oxford University Press, 1971.

Fuentes, Carlos. "Farewell Monroe Doctrine." *Harper's* (August 1981): 29–35.

Gardner, Lloyd. "The Dulles Years, 1953–1959." In *From Colony to Empire,* edited by William Appleman Williams, pp. 386–429. New York: Wiley, 1972.

Geiger, Theodore. *Communism Versus Progress in Guatemala.* Planning Pamphlets no 85. Washington, D.C.: National Planning Assn., 1953.

Gellman, Irwin F. *Good Neighbor Diplomacy: United States Policies in Latin America, 1933–1945.* Baltimore, Md.: Johns Hopkins University Press, 1979.

Gerassi, John. *The Great Fear: The Reconquest of Latin America by Latin Americans.* New York: Macmillan, 1963.

Gervasi, Frank Henry. *The Real Rockefeller.* New York: Atheneum, 1964.

Gott, Richard. *Rural Guerrillas in Latin America.* Rev. ed. Harmondsworth: Penguin, 1973.

                  "The Cold War Comes to Latin America." In *Politics and Poli-
                  Administration,* edited by Barton J. Bernstein, pp. 149–
                  drangle Books, 1970.
                  nment of Latin America: A History of the Myths and
                  ood Neighbor Policy.* Chicago: Quadrangle Books, 1971.
                  ing in State.* Garden City, N.Y.: Doubleday, 1952.

Gurtov, Melvin. *The United States against the Third World: Antinationalism and Intervention*. New York: Praeger, 1974.

Hanson, Simon G. "The End of the Good Neighbor Policy." *Inter-American Economic Affairs* (Autumn 1953): 3–49.

Harkness, Richard, and Gladys Harkness. "The Mysterious Doings of CIA." *Saturday Evening Post* (30 October, 6 and 13 November, 1954).

Hilton, Stanley E. *Brazil and the Great Powers, 1930–1939: The Politics of Trade Rivalry*. Latin American Monographs, no. 38. Austin: University of Texas Press, 1975.

————. "Brazilian Diplomacy and the Washington–Rio de Janeiro 'Axis' during the World War II Era." *Hispanic American Historical Review* (May 1979): 201–231.

Hoffmann, Stanley, ed. *Contemporary Theory in International Relations*. Englewood Cliffs, N.J.: Prentice-Hall, 1960.

————. "Restraints and Choices in American Foreign Policy." *Daedalus* (Fall 1962): 668–704.

Hooker, Nancy Harvison, ed. *The Moffat Papers: Selections from the Diplomatic Journals of Jay Pierrepont Moffat 1919–1943*. Cambridge, Mass.: Harvard University Press, 1956.

Hoopes, Townsend. *The Devil and John Foster Dulles*. Boston: Little, Brown, 1973.

Hull, Cordell. *The Memoirs of Cordell Hull*. 2 vols. New York: Macmillan, 1948.

Hunt, E. Howard. *Give Us This Day*. New York: Arlington House, 1973.

————. *Under-Cover: Memoirs of an American Secret Agent*. New York: Putnam's, 1974.

Immerman, Richard H. *The CIA in Guatemala: The Foreign Policy of Intervention*. Austin: University of Texas Press, 1982.

————. "Guatemala as Cold War History." *Political Science Quarterly* (Winter 1980–81): 629–653.

Israel, Fred L., ed. *The War Diary of Breckenridge Long: Selections from the Years 1939–1944*. Lincoln: University of Nebraska Press, 1966.

Jonas, Susanne L. *Test Case for the Hemisphere: United States Strategy in Guatemala, 1950–1974*. Berkeley, Cal., 1974.

Jones, Joseph M. *The Fifteen Weeks: (February 21–June 5, 1947)*. N.Y.: Viking, 1955.

Kelly, Sir David. *The Ruling Few or the Human Background to Diplomacy*. London: Hollis & Carter, 1952.

Kennan, George F. *Memoirs, 1925–1950*. Boston: Little, Brown, 1967.

Kirchwey, Freda. "Guatemala Guinea Pig." *Nation* (10 July 1954): 21–23.

Kolko, Gabriel. *The Politics of War: The World and United States Foreign Policy, 1943–1945*. New York: Random House, 1968.

Little, Richard. *Intervention: External Involvement in Civil Wars*. London: Martin Robertson, 1975.

Loewenheim, Francis L.; Harold D. Langley; and Manfred Jonas, eds. *Roosevelt and Churchill: Their Secret Wartime Correspondence*. New York: Saturday Review Press, 1975.

Lowenthal, Abraham F. "'Liberal,' 'Radical' and 'Bureaucratic' Perspectives on U.S. Latin American Policy: The Alliance for Progress in Retrospect." In *Latin America and the United States: The Changing Political Realities*, edited by Julio Cotler and Richard R. Fagen, pp. 212–235. Stanford, Cal.: Stanford University Press, 1974.

———, and Albert Fishlow. *Latin America's Emergence*. Pamphlet no. 243. New York: Foreign Policy Assn., 1979.

McCann, Frank D., Jr. *The Brazilian-American Alliance, 1937–1945*. Princeton, N.J.: Princeton University Press, 1973.

McCann, Thomas P. *An American Company: The Tragedy of United Fruit*. Edited by Henry Scammell. New York: Crown, 1976.

Marchetti, Victor, and John D. Marks. *The CIA and the Cult of Intelligence*. New York: Knopf, 1974.

Marroquín Rojas, Clemente. *La derrota de una batalla: (Réplica al libro "La batalla de Guatemala" del ex-Canciller Guillermo Toriello)*. Guatemala City, 1955[?].

Martin, John Bartlow. *Overtaken by Events: The Dominican Crisis—from the Fall of Trujillo to the Civil War*. New York: Doubleday, 1966.

———. *U.S. Policy in the Caribbean*. Foreword by M. J. Rossant. A Twentieth-Century Fund Essay. Boulder, Colo.: Westview Press, 1978.

Martz, John D. *Communist Infiltration in Guatemala*. New York: Vantage, 1956.

———, and Lars Schoultz, eds. *Latin America, the United States, and the Inter-American System*. Boulder, Colo.: Westview Press, 1980.

Massing, Hede. *This Deception*. New York: Duell, Sloane & Pearce, 1951.

Matthews, Herbert. *A World in Revolution*. New York: Scribner's, 1971.

Miller, Edward G., Jr. "The Conduct of Hemispheric Relations." Speech, 19 January 1952. *DSB* (11 February 1952): 208–210.

———. "Nonintervention and Collective Responsibility in the Americas." *DSB* (15 May 1950): 768–770.

Morgenthau, Hans J. "The Mainsprings of American Foreign Policy: The National Interest vs. Moral Abstractions." *American Political Science Review* (December 1950): 833–854.

———. *Politics among Nations: The Struggle for Power and Peace*. 5th ed. New York: Knopf, 1973.

Morris, George. *CIA and American Labor: The Subversion of the AFL-CIO's Foreign Policy*. New York: International Publishers, 1967.

Morris, Joe Alex. *Nelson Rockefeller*. New York: Harper's, 1960.

Murphy, Robert D. *Diplomat among Warriors*. New York: Doubleday, 1964.

Olden, Herman. *U.S. over Latin America*. New York: International Publishers, 1955.

Peterson, Harold F. *Argentina and the United States, 1810–1960*. New York: University Publishers, 1964.

Peurifoy, John E. "Meeting the Communist Challenge in the Western Hemisphere." *DSB* (6 September 1954): 333–336.

Phillips, David Atlee. *The Night-watch*. New York: Atheneum, 1977.

Phillips, William. *Ventures in Diplomacy*. Boston: Beacon Press, 1952.

Potash, Robert A. *The Army and Politics in Argentina, 1928–1945: Perón to Frondizi.* Stanford, Cal.: Stanford University Press, 1969.

Powers, Thomas. *The Man Who Kept the Secrets: Richard Helms and the CIA.* New York: Knopf, 1979.

Pratt, Julius W. *Cordell Hull, 1933–1944.* 2 vols. The American Secretaries of State and Their Diplomacy series, edited by Robert H. Ferrell and Samuel Flagg Bemis. New York: Cooper Square Publishers, 1964.

Prieto, Indalecio. *Comment et pourquoi je suis sorti du ministère de la défense nationale: Les intrigues des russes en Espagne.* Paris: Imp. Nouvelle, 1939.

Prouty, Leroy Fletcher. *The Secret Team.* Englewood Cliffs, N.J.: Prentice-Hall, 1973.

Ransom, Harry Howe. *Central Intelligence and National Security.* Cambridge, Mass.: Harvard University Press, 1958.

———. *The Intelligence Establishment.* Cambridge, Mass.: Harvard University Press, 1970.

Rennie, Ysabel F. *The Argentine Republic.* New York: Macmillan, 1945.

Ronning, C. Neale, ed. *Intervention in Latin America.* New York: Knopf, 1970.

Roosevelt, Kermit. *Countercoup: The Struggle for the Control of Iran.* New York: McGraw-Hill, 1979.

Rositzke, Harry August. *The CIA's Secret Operations.* New York: Reader's Digest Press, 1977.

Salisbury, Harrison E. *Without Fear or Favor: The* New York Times *and its Times.* New York: Times Books, 1980.

Samponaro, Frank N. "The Committee for Political Defense and Hemispheric Security." *Social Science Journal* (1979): 29–42.

Schlesinger, Arthur M., Jr. "Good Fences Make Good Neighbors." *Fortune* (August 1946): 130–135.

———. *A Thousand Days: John F. Kennedy in the White House.* Cambridge, Mass.: Houghton Mifflin, 1965.

Schlesinger, Stephen. "How Dulles Worked the Coup d'Etat." *Nation* (28 October 1978): 439–444.

———, and Stephen Kinzer. *Bitter Fruit: The Untold Story of the American Coup in Guatemala.* Garden City, N.Y.: Doubleday, 1982.

Schneider, Ronald M. *Communism in Guatemala, 1944–1954.* New York: Praeger, 1959.

Schorr, Daniel. *Clearing the Air.* Boston: Houghton Mifflin, 1977.

Skidmore, Thomas E. *Politics in Brazil, 1930–1964.* New York: Oxford University Press, 1967.

Slater, Jerome. "The Decline of the OAS." *International Journal* (Summer 1969): 497–506.

———. *The OAS and United States Foreign Policy.* Columbus: Ohio State University Press, 1967.

Smith, Joseph B. *Portrait of a Cold Warrior.* New York: Putnam's, 1981.

Smith, Oscar Edmund, Jr. *Yankee Diplomacy: U.S. Intervention in Argentina.* Dallas, Tex.: Southern Methodist University Press, 1953.

Smith, Thomas Bell. *The Essential CIA*. Privately printed, 1975.

Smith, Walter Bedell. *My Three Years in Moscow*. Philadelphia: Lippincott, 1950.

Snepp, Frank. *Decent Interval*. New York: Random House, 1977.

Stern, Laurence. *The Wrong Horse: The Politics of Intervention and the Failure of American Diplomacy*. New York: Times Books, 1977.

Stockwell, John. *In Search of Enemies: A CIA Story*. London: Andre Deutsch, 1978.

Stoessinger, John G. *Crusaders and Pragmatists: Movers of Modern American Foreign Policy*. New York: Norton, 1979.

Strong, Sir Kenneth. *Men of Intelligence*. London: Cassell, 1970.

Taylor, Maxwell D. *Swords and Plowshares*. New York: Norton, 1972.

Tillema, Herbert K. *Appeal to Force: American Military Intervention in the Era of Containment*. New York: Crowell, 1973.

Tinnin, David B., and Dag Christensen. *The Hit Team*. Boston: Little, Brown, 1976.

Toriello Garrido, Guillermo. *La batalla de Guatemala*. Mexico City: Cuadernos Americanos, 1955.

U.S. Congress. House. Select Committee on Communist Aggression. Subcommittee on Latin America. *Hearings on Guatemala*. 83rd Congress, 2d sess., 8 October 1954. 9th Interim Report.

———. Senate. Committee on Foreign Relations. *Hearing on Nomination of Dean G. Acheson to be Secretary of State*. 81st Congress, 1st sess., 13 January 1949.

———. ———. Committee on the Judiciary. *Hearings on the Communist Threat to the U.S. through the Caribbean*. 87th Congress, 1st sess., 27 July 1961.

U.S. Department of State. *A Case History of Communist Penetration: Guatemala*. Publication 6465. Washington, D.C.: GPO, 1957.

———. *Intervention of International Communism in Guatemala*. Publication 5556. Washington, D.C.: GPO, 1954.

———. *Tenth Interamerican Conference*. Publication 5693. Washington, D.C.: GPO, 1955.

Vandenberg, Arthur H., Jr., ed. with the collaboration of Joe Alex Morris. *The Private Papers of Senator Vandenberg*. Boston: Houghton Mifflin, 1952.

Wagner, Robert Harrison. *United States Policy toward Latin America: A Study in Domestic and International Politics*. Stanford, Cal.: Stanford University Press, 1970.

Welles, Sumner. *"Good Neighbor" Policy in the Caribbean*. Address, Charlottesville, Va., 2 July 1935. Washington, D.C.: GPO, 1935.

———. *Inter-American Relations*. Address, Washington, 10 December 1934. Washington, D.C.: GPO, 1935.

———. "Intervention and Interventions." *Foreign Affairs* (October 1947): 116–133.

———. *On the Need for a Spirit of Tolerance in Inter-American Relation-*

ships. Address, Washington, 6 December 1937. Washington, D.C. GPO, 1937.

————. *Seven Decisions That Shaped History*. New York: Harper's, 1951.

————. *Where Are We Heading?* New York: Harper's, 1946.

Westerfield, H. Bradford. *The Instruments of America's Foreign Policy*. New York: Crowell, 1963.

Whitaker, Arthur P. *The Western Hemisphere Idea*. Ithaca, N.Y.: Cornell University Press, 1954.

Wicker, Tom, et al. "C.I.A.: Maker of Policy or Tool?" *New York Times* (25–29 April 1966).

Williams, Edward J. *The Political Themes of Inter-American Relations*. Belmont, Cal.: Duxbury Press, 1971.

Wise, David. *The American Police State: The Government against the People*. New York: Random House, 1976.

————. *The Politics of Lying: Government Deception, Secrecy and Power*. New York: Random House, 1973.

————, and Thomas B. Ross. *The Invisible Government*. New York: Random House, 1964.

Wood, Bryce. *The Making of the Good Neighbor Policy*. New York: Columbia University Press, 1961.

————. "Self-Plagiarism and Foreign Policy." *Latin American Research Review* (Summer, 1968): 184–191.

Woods, Randall Bennett. *The Roosevelt Foreign-Policy Establishment and the "Good Neighbor": The United States and Argentina, 1941–1945*. Lawrence, Kan.: Regents' Press, 1979.

Woodward, Sir Llewellyn. *British Foreign Policy in the Second World War*. London: H.M.S.O., 1962.

Yergin, Daniel. *Shattered Peace: The Origins of the Cold War and the National Security State*. Boston: Houghton Mifflin, 1977.

Index